P9-DUK-123

DATE DUE

NO 15 '05			
~~AP 6 '06~~			
AP 27 '06			
MY 18 '06			

DEMCO 38-296

Italy

WORLD BIBLIOGRAPHICAL SERIES

General Editors:
Robert G. Neville (Executive Editor)
John J. Horton

Robert A. Myers   Hans H. Wellisch
Ian Wallace   Ralph Lee Woodward, Jr.

John J. Horton is Deputy Librarian of the University of Bradford and currently Chairman of its Academic Board of Studies in Social Sciences. He has maintained a longstanding interest in the discipline of area studies and its associated bibliographical problems, with special reference to European Studies. In particular he has published in the field of Icelandic and of Yugoslav studies, including the two relevant volumes in the World Bibliographical Series.

Robert A. Myers is Associate Professor of Anthropology in the Division of Social Sciences and Director of Study Abroad Programs at Alfred University, Alfred, New York. He has studied post-colonial island nations of the Caribbean and has spent two years in Nigeria on a Fulbright Lectureship. His interests include international public health, historical anthropology and developing societies. In addition to *Amerindians of the Lesser Antilles: a bibliography* (1981), *A Resource Guide to Dominica, 1493-1986* (1987) and numerous articles, he has compiled the World Bibliographical Series volumes on *Dominica* (1987), *Nigeria* (1989) and *Ghana* (1991).

Ian Wallace is Professor of German at the University of Bath. A graduate of Oxford in French and German, he also studied in Tübingen, Heidelberg and Lausanne before taking teaching posts at universities in the USA, Scotland and England. He specializes in contemporary German affairs, especially literature and culture, on which he has published numerous articles and books. In 1979 he founded the journal *GDR Monitor*, which he continues to edit under its new title *German Monitor*.

Hans H. Wellisch is Professor emeritus at the College of Library and Information Services, University of Maryland. He was President of the American Society of Indexers and was a member of the International Federation for Documentation. He is the author of numerous articles and several books on indexing and abstracting, and has published *The Conversion of Scripts and Indexing and Abstracting: an International Bibliography*, and *Indexing from A to Z*. He also contributes frequently to *Journal of the American Society for Information Science*, *The Indexer* and other professional journals.

Ralph Lee Woodward, Jr. is Professor of History at Tulane University, New Orleans. He is the author of *Central America, a Nation Divided*, 2nd ed. (1985), as well as several monographs and more than seventy scholarly articles on modern Latin America. He has also compiled volumes in the World Bibliographical Series on *Belize* (1980), *El Salvador* (1988), *Guatemala* (Rev. Ed.) (1992) and *Nicaragua* (Rev. Ed.) (1994). Dr. Woodward edited the Central American section of the *Research Guide to Central America and the Caribbean* (1985) and is currently associate editor of Scribner's *Encyclopedia of Latin American History*.

R

VOLUME 30

Italy

Lucio Sponza and Diego Zancani

Compilers

CLIO PRESS

OXFORD, ENGLAND · SANTA BARBARA, CALIFORNIA
DENVER, COLORADO

Riverside Community College
Library
4800 Magnolia Avenue
Riverside, California 92506

NOV   '96

© Copyright 1995 by ABC-CLIO Ltd.

DG417. Z99 S66 1995
Sponza, Lucio.
Italy

on may be reproduced, stored in any
by any means, electronic, mechanical,
ermission in writing of the publishers.

in Publication Data

aphical Series;

Zancani, Diego
s

016.945

ISBN 0–903450–44–5

ABC-CLIO Ltd.,
Old Clarendon Ironworks,
35A Great Clarendon Street,
Oxford OX2 6AT, England.

ABC-CLIO Inc.,
130 Cremona Drive,
Santa Barbara,
CA 93116, USA.

Designed by Bernard Crossland.
Typeset by Columns Design and Production Services Ltd., Reading, England.
Printed and bound in Great Britain by Bookcraft (Bath) Ltd., Midsomer Norton.

THE WORLD BIBLIOGRAPHICAL SERIES

This series, which is principally designed for the English speaker, will eventually cover every country (and many of the world's principal regions), each in a separate volume comprising annotated entries on works dealing with its history, geography, economy and politics; and with its people, their culture, customs, religion and social organization. Attention will also be paid to current living conditions – housing, education, newspapers, clothing, etc. – that are all too often ignored in standard bibliographies; and to those particular aspects relevant to individual countries. Each volume seeks to achieve, by use of careful selectivity and critical assessment of the literature, an expression of the country and an appreciation of its nature and national aspirations, to guide the reader towards an understanding of its importance. The keynote of the series is to provide, in a uniform format, an interpretation of each country that will express its culture, its place in the world, and the qualities and background that make it unique. The views expressed in individual volumes, however, are not necessarily those of the publisher.

VOLUMES IN THE SERIES

Contents

Contents

Contents

Introduction

Italy has experienced a rich, if chequered, history: from the the rise and decline of the Roman Empire to the establishment of the Papacy and the Roman Catholic Church; from the inception of the universal values of the Renaissance to Christopher Columbus and the discovery of America (named, of course, after the Florentine Amerigo Vespucci); from the cultural nationalism and political activism of the 19th century (the Risorgimento) to the emergence of the totalitarian philosophy of Fascism and the brutal regime of Mussolini in the 20th century. Indeed, it is virtually impossible to understand the history of Western civilization without appreciating the significance of the remarkable developments which have taken place in the Italian peninsula. The architectural and other physical accomplishments, as well as the intellectual achievements of Italians, have been of incalculable importance and have extended over a period of almost two millennia. As was recently pointed out by *The Economist* ('Survey on Italy', 26 June 1993): 'if most Europeans . . . measure their national history by centuries, then surely the Italians should measure theirs by the millennium'.

Over the centuries Italy has also been characterized by a number of important and dramatic contrasts. In the present century alone, for example, one thinks of the formidable power and influence of the Roman Catholic Church on the one hand and, on the other, the mirror-like role of the Italian Communist Party, the most powerful Communist Party in the Western world and a true cultural and political phenomenon. At the same time the country has also experienced: the co-existence and interdependence of economic dynamism and political paralysis; the apparently permanent conflict between national (and even European) aspirations and local loyalties; and the development, in the face of archaic forms of lawlessness, of a highly advanced constitutional and juridical framework which contrasts sharply with a low, almost non-existent, level of civic awareness.

Over the years, however, the overall impact of these contrasts and contradictions has been limited and some would even argue that Italians have actually thrived on them.

The roots of some aspects of Italian socio-economic and political life can be traced back as far as Roman times and the political problems and scandals of the early 1990s are a case in point. When the true levels of government corruption, which even involved former Prime Ministers, were exposed, much of the political system which was established after the Second World War was damaged. At the time of writing, a new election is about to be called. This follows the short-lived experience of the centre-right government led by Silvio Berlusconi, the tycoon-turned-politician whose indelible smile and monopolistic control over commercial television secured him an extraordinary success at the 1994 election. At this stage it is impossible to judge what will be the outcome of these new elections and whether the apparent turmoil we are witnessing at present is the prelude to a real phase of rapid change. Some suggest that it will be the beginning of a Second Republic, whilst others argue that this has in fact already emerged, at the 1994 election.

It is this mixture of innovation and tradition, complexity and uncertainty that epitomizes Italian history and contemporary society. Indeed, the very origin of the term 'Italy' is problematic in itself. It is commonly accepted that the name dates back to the 5th century BC, and also that it originated in the toe of the peninsula, but here scholarly agreement ends. Some argue that the word derives from the name Italo, a mythical king who ruled over the wine-making people (Enotri) in Calabria, whilst others claim that 'Italia' was a district in the same province where cattle-raising was the dominant activity. Only by the middle of the 1st century AD was the name extended to designate the whole peninsula, which was by then under complete Roman control. This meant that 'Italia' indicated both a geographical and a political entity. The former remains to the present day; the latter, however, was subject to the vicissitudes of the Roman Empire and its collapse brought about fragmentation and conflict.

The economic future of the area after the collapse of the Roman Empire was largely determined by its geography. Situated in an advantageous position in the heart of the Mediterranean, the peninsula was also part of Europe and this led to opportunities for local autonomy and development. Rich and powerful city-states, such as Florence, Genoa, Milan and Venice, emerged as independent and jealous political formations, and thus for a long time prevented the re-establishment of Italy as a political entity. This development did not, of course, take place until 1871 (the Risorgimento).

During the last fifty years an economic revival has taken place in Italy. These post-Second World War developments have, to the amazement of many, seen Italy transformed from a relatively backward rural society into one of the wealthiest countries in the world; a truism which is formally recognized by Italy's membership of the G7 'club' of industrial powers. Nonetheless, the late entry of Italy into the league of large-scale industrial countries exacerbated the social and cultural imbalances among the various parts of the peninsula and some areas, particularly in the south of the country, continue to be economically and culturally disadvantaged. Moreover, the relatively recent establishment of Italy as a nation-state leaves its inhabitants still questioning whether they are really unified in their sentiments and aspirations. The dual existence of 'Italy' as a political entity and 'the Italians' as a people with many common features, but also very differing characteristics (such as regional dialects) is a phenomenon which is reflected in many of the works in this bibliography.

The bibliography

In this work we have included a wide range of publications that will either interest scholars and informed readers, or appeal to the more general reader whose objective is to discover more about the country. With this in mind, we have included an extensive selection of books on subjects such as 'Travel guides' and 'Food and drink' as well as more scholarly works. In fact, in terms of an appreciation of the variety of Italian life, traditions and patterns of change, a great deal can be gained from books which fall into the more 'popular' categories. In the section on food and drink, for example, the books which have been included are intended to convey the flavour of Italian cuisine but they also help us to understand that the concept of 'Italianess' is really quite elusive. Indeed, Italian cuisine is not what is normally experienced abroad and the Italians themselves perceive it as being more variegated and regionally based.

As with all the volumes in the *World Bibliographical Series*, the present bibliography is principally designed for the English-speaker and it therefore consists of mainly English-language publications, each with a substantial annotation. Inevitably, this means that the bibliography as a whole reflects the interests and attitudes of the anglophone world towards Italy and Italian affairs. Notwithstanding this, very few aspects of Italy's history and contemporary affairs have been neglected by foreign scholars, who have always been attracted by the country's art treasures, beautiful landscapes and intellectual achievements. In addition, both American and British writers (the two principal English-language nationalities who have contributed to Italian studies) are keen observers of historical, social and political developments in Italy and come second only to the French in their interest in literary, ideological and philosophical discourse and to the Germans in their coverage of the visual arts, music and linguistics. Because of the international significance of the English language, important works written in Italian and other languages have been translated into English; some have also been written in English by non-native speakers and published in their own countries.

With regard to the range of works included in this bibliography, we felt it was also important to include a variety of more specialized books in order to demonstrate the narrow but interesting areas that scholars, especially non-Italian, have chosen to cover. In the field of politics in the late 1970s and early 1980s, for example, much attention was devoted to the political and social crisis which engulfed the country, and the fear that a Communist government was likely to be elected at a time when the country was afflicted by terrorism and violence. It was clearly necessary to illustrate this crucial period in Italy's recent history and a wide selection of relevant books on this subject have therefore been included. The situation in the field of the arts is similar and several lesser-known painters have been included alongside those who are more famous. Our objective has been not to reinforce stereotypes about Italy and the Italians but simply to recognize their importance. Certain topics, therefore, are inevitably more extensively explored than others and may reflect a degree of attention which would not necessarily be true of other countries.

It should be noted that many of the references to major works in Italian which have not been translated into English, as well as other publications which, for reasons of space, we have not been able to include in this bibliography, can be found in the bibliographies of some of the books we have annotated. This would include, for example, the lengthy series on Italian history and literature produced over many years by leading Italian publishers, such as Einaudi's *Letteratura italiana* and *Storia d'Italia*, with its sequels of *Annali* and *Regioni* and the most recent multi-volume history of post-war Italy. On the other hand, in the section on dictionaries, for example, it was considered necessary to include a larger than usual number of works in Italian. These are supplemented by an adequate number of bilingual dictionaries as well as scientific and technical ones. We chose not to include translations in the literature section since even a small sample of translations of major modern novelists (such as Calvino, Fenoglio, Gadda, Moravia, Pavese, Sciascia and Vittorini), while ignoring contemporary writers (such as Bufalino, Busi, Bonaviri, Consolo, Sanvitale, Tabucchi and Vassalli), would have lengthened the bibliography inordinately. The same judgement was generally applied to anthologies, although some on poetry and prose have been included. Some classic material has been included, even if printed many years ago, but in general we have adopted the notional cut-off date of 1975. It should be noted, however, that this policy has not been applied to bibliographies which are still in print and widely used.

It is an inescapable fact that bibliographies are never complete, and selective bibliographies can never satisfy everyone. As we sent our bibliography to the printers we realized that it had taken a long time to compile and although we had made a conscious effort to put ourselves in the shoes of the user, we recognized that inevitably some omissions would become apparent. Notwithstanding this, a large number of books containing substantial bibliographies have been included and these do provide additional references. It is to be hoped that readers, whatever their interests, will find this volume a valuable research tool and that they will discover entries which stimulate their interest in Italian studies.

Acknowledgements

We would like to thank all those who have given us help, advice and expertise, in particular: Hélène Bellofatto; Roberto L. Bruni; Adolfo Di Luca; Barbara Garvin; Giulio C. Lepschy; Giuseppe Melecci; David Mendel; Valentina Olivastri; Lino Pertile; Michael Talbot; the staff of the British Library; the staff of the Templeman Library, University of Kent at Canterbury; and especially Stephen Holland and Margaret Smyth; Piero Bellettini, of the Biblioteca Comunale dell'Archiginnasio in Bologna; and Fabio, Leo and Sandro Zancani for their valuable suggestions and practical help. Last but not least, we are grateful to Dr Robert Neville for patiently awaiting the submission of the manuscript and to Ms Sarah Leatherbarrow for her editorial expertise.

Chronology

1600-1500 BC	Middle Bronze Age (Apennine) civilization.
1000 BC	Last stage of Late Bronze Age. Regional differentiation begins. Early settlements on the site of Rome.
900 BC	Iron Age civilization. Settlements in Apulia, northern and central Italy.
753 BC	Traditional date for the founding of Rome.
720 BC	Sybaris is founded by the Greeks in the extreme south of the peninsula. This part of Italy became known as 'Magna Graecia'.
715 BC	According to tradition the first king of Rome, Numa Pompilius, is installed.
650 BC	The Etruscans, well established in north and central Italy, seek to infiltrate into the Campania district, but the Romans bar their way to a certain extent.
c. 615 BC	The Etruscans at Rome.
c. 600 BC	Possible first incursion of Celts into northern Italy.
520 BC	Tarquinius Superbus makes Rome undisputed head of the Latin League.
510 BC	Tarquinius Superbus is banished from Rome. Rome becomes a republic.
477 BC	Romans defeated by the Etruscans in a battle on the Cremera river.
473 BC	Development of inland Etruscan cities. They flourish in the Po valley and the Adriatic region (Bologna, Marzabotto and Spina).
454 BC	Roman plebeians force the Patricians to begin a reform and a codification of the law.
410 BC	Celts (Gauls) migrate south across the Alps.
390 BC	A tribe of Celts, under Brennus, defeats the Romans. Rome is besieged and largely sacked.

350 BC	The Gauls who threaten Rome once again are decisively beaten.
340 BC	The Romans defeat the Latin League.
283 BC	Rome, after defeating allied Etruscans and Gauls, is the undisputed master of northern and central Italy.
282-275 BC	Pyrrhus, the king of Epirus called to help Tarentum (mod. Ital. Taranto) against the Romans, is finally defeated. End of Greek influence in southern Italy.
264-241; 218-201 BC	First and Second Punic wars secure Rome's control of the Mediterranean.
222 BC	Mediolanum (Milan), a Celtic city, is taken by the Romans.
218 BC	Hannibal sets out from Cartagena, in North Africa, to march round the Mediterranean coast to invade Italy. He reaches the Po valley in the autumn and defeats the Romans near Piacenza.
202 BC	Scipio (Africanus) finally defeats Hannibal at the battle of Zama near Carthage.
90-89 BC	Italian populations threaten Rome in the Social War. The Roman Senate agrees to their demands for Roman citizenship.
72-71 BC	Spartacus's slave war.
60-51 BC	Julius Caesar conquers Gaul and visits Britain.
49-42 BC	Provision for granting of Roman citizenship to northern Italian populations.
49 BC	Caesar crosses the little river Rubicon to return to Roman soil. The fight with Pompey means civil war.
46 BC	Caesar defeats Pompey's supporters, returns to Rome and after a four-day triumph he is made Dictator and Consul for ten years. He introduces the Julian Calendar.
44 BC (March)	Sixty senators led by Cassius and Marcus Brutus conspire against Julius Caesar and he is assassinated. His grand-nephew Octavian (born in 63 BC) claims succession.
27 BC	Octavian becomes Augustus. The building of temples theatres, public baths etc. contributes to the splendour of Rome. Virgil begins his *Aeneid*.
17 BC	The Secular Games are celebrated in Rome, on Augustus's orders, to salute the beginning of a new and prosperous age.
13 BC	Building of the Altar of Peace is begun on the Campus Martius in Rome.

14 AD	Augustus dies and Tiberius succeeds him.
37	Tiberius is succeeded by Caius Caesar called 'Caligula' (Little Boots), a nickname given him as a child by soldiers.
41	Caligula is murdered. Claudius is made emperor.
41-54	Rule of Emperor Claudius.
43	The Romans invade Britain.
64	A great fire breaks out in Rome. Nero is suspected of having started it but he blames the Christians and many are tortured and killed.
79 (August)	Vesuvius's eruption covers Pompeii and Herculaneum in lava and ashes.
117-138	Rule of Emperor Hadrian.
222-235	Emperor Alexander Severus fails to check Vandals and Longobards (Lombards).
276-282	Emperor Probus defeats Vandals, Alamanni, Franks and Burgundians.
285	Partition of the Empire into Western and Eastern Empires under Emperor Diocletian.
313	Under Emperor Constantine the Great Milan Edict is issued, recognizing Christianity as a legal religion.
361-363	Rule of Emperor Julian.
383-407	Roman legions evacuate Britain.
395	Definite partition of Eastern and Western Empires.
410	Alaric and the Visigoths sack Rome.
452	Attila and his Huns invade Italy.
455	The Vandals sack Rome.
476	Fall of the Roman Empire. The last emperor, Romulus Augustulus is deposed by the general of the West Roman Army Odoacer.
489-526	Theoderic, king of the Ostrogoths, governs Italy.
529	Abbey of Montecassino founded by St. Benedict of Nurcia.
568	The Longobards (Lombards), coming from the plains near the Danube, cross the Alps into North-east Italy with their king, Alboin.
572	Alboin takes Pavia, which becomes the capital of the Lombard kingdom.
652; 667	Islamic fleets plunder Sicilian and Italian coasts.
712-744	Liutprand, king of the Lombards, prepares law code for Lombards and Romans.
756-774	Desiderius, King of the Lombards.

771	Desiderius moves on Rome to build support there against the Franks led by Charlemagne.
773-774	Charlemagne takes Pavia, deposes Desiderius and makes himself king of the Lombards.
800 (25 December)	Coronation of Charlemagne as emperor in Rome.
827	Moslems land on Sicily in holy war for the conquest of the island.
830	Palermo and western Sicily under the Moslems.
846	Arabs pillage Rome.
888-924	Berengar of Friuli, King of Italy.
967 (25 December)	Otto II crowned emperor in Rome.
981-983	Otto II's wars against Saracens in southern Italy.
996 (May)	Otto III crowned emperor in Rome.
1001	Romans rebel against Emperor and Pope.
1016	Pisa and Genoa rid Sardinia of Moslem pirates. Norman knights arrive in southern Italy.
1037	Conrad II, emperor of the Salian House, promulgates a law on fiefs, protecting the rights of lower vassals.
1038-47	Conrad II confirms Aversa and later Apulia and Calabria as fiefs of the Normans.
1058	First known communal charter. Convention between the inhabitants of Nonantola, near Modena, and their abbot.
1069-1106	Emperor Henry IV. Controversy over nomination (investiture) of bishops.
1072	Normans conquer Palermo and by 1091 their occupation of Sicily is completed.
1076	Pope Gregory VII excommunicates Henry IV.
1077	Henry obtains absolution at Canossa in northern Italy but continues to invest bishops.
c. 1080	Irnerius teaches the *Digest* at Bologna.
1128-30	Conrad, King of Italy.
1152-90	Emperor Frederic I Barbarossa (Red beard).
1154-55	Italian expedition of Frederic I. Privilege to University of Bologna.
1158	Punishment of Milan during Frederic's second Italian expedition.
	Diet of Roncaglia (northern Italy) confirms regalian rights to emperor and consulate to cities.
1162	Frederic destroys Milan.
1167-68	Lombard League rebuilds Milan and founds Alessandria.

1176	Victory of Lombard League over Frederic at Legnano.
[1181]-1226	Saint Francis of Assisi.
1183	Peace of Constance confirms the autonomy of cities and their possession of regalian rights.
1211-50	Emperor Frederic II.
1224	Frederic founds the University of Naples.
1265-1321	Dante Alighieri.
1266/76-1337	Giotto.
1277	The Visconti family, with Archbishop Otto, begin 'Signoria' over Milan.
1303-74	Francesco Petrarca (Petrarch).
1307-78	Residence of the popes at Avignon in Southern France.
1313-75	Giovanni Boccaccio.
1347-48	The 'black death' plague hits most Italian and European cities.
1378	Florence, ruled by a merchant oligarchy, acquires Arezzo.
	Rising of the Ciompi, textile workers in Florence.
1378-1402	Gian Galeazzo Visconti rules over Milan. His expansionist policy was to threaten Florence.
1401-21	Lorenzo Ghiberti's bronze reliefs, north portal of baptistery of Florence.
1406	Florence conquers Pisa.
1411-20	Venice occupies Friuli.
1412-47	Filippo Maria Visconti Duke of Milan.
1414-35	Joanna II Queen of Naples. The Houses of Anjou and Aragon fight for succession.
1430-32	David of Donatello.
1431-1506	Andrea Mantegna.
1434-64	Cosimo de' Medici 'the Elder' governs Florence, which is still, formally, a republic.
1444-52	Palazzo Medici-Ricciardi built in Florence.
1444-82	Federico da Montefeltro Duke of Urbino.
1444-1514	Bramante.
1447-55	Pope Nicholas V, the first humanist pope. He supports scholars and Latin studies in Rome.
1452	Borso D'Este, Marquis of Ferrara, is created Duke of Modena and Reggio by Emperor Frederic III.
1452-1519	Leonardo Da Vinci.
1453	Mohammed II conquers Constantinople.
1454	Peace of Lodi, near Milan, between Francesco Sforza, Duke of Milan since 1450, and Venice.
1455	*Italian League* is formed to maintain peace in Italy.

1458-64	Pope Pius II, Enea Silvio Piccolomini, a well-known humanist, builds the town of Pienza.
1468-79	War of Venice against the Turks.
1469-92	Lorenzo de' Medici 'the Magnificent' governs Florence.
1471	Ercole d'Este is created Duke of Ferrara by the Pope, Paul II.
1473-81	Building of the Sistine Chapel in the Vatican by Pope Sixtus IV.
1475-1564	Michelangelo.
1476	Galeazzo Maria Sforza, Duke of Milan, is murdered in December while attending Mass.
[1477]-1576	Titian (Tiziano Vecellio).
1478	Lorenzo de' Medici is wounded in an attack by the Pazzi family and his brother is killed.
1478-1510	Giorgione.
1483-1520	Raphael from Urbino.
1492-1503	Pope Alexander VI (Borgia).
1494	Death of King Ferrante of Naples. Claims of the French are disregarded by the pope who confirms succession of Ferrante's son, Alfonso.
1494	King Charles VIII of France invades Italy with the support of Ludovico il Moro of Milan.
1499-1502	Cesare Borgia, son of Alexander VI, conquers Romagna with the help of the French.
1500	The treaty of Granada partitions southern Italy between France and Spain.
1513-21	Pope Leo X, the son of Lorenzo the Medici 'the Magnificent'.
1516	Ludovico Ariosto publishes his poem *L'Orlando furioso*.
1519-56	Emperor Charles V.
1521	Condemnation of Luther. Pope Leo sides with the emperor.
1523-34	Pope Clement VII, cousin of Leo X.
1527	Sack of Rome by imperial troops. The Florentines expel the Medici and establish a republic.
1530	After the coronation of Charles V in Bologna, imperial troops reinstate the Medici in Florence. Alessandro de' Medici becomes hereditary duke.
1534-49	Pope Paul III, of the Farnese family.
1534-41	Michelangelo paints the Last Judgment in the Sistine Chapel.

1537	Alessandro de' Medici is murdered and succeeded by Cosimo as Duke of Tuscany.
1542	Founding of the Papal Inquisition.
1545-47	First assembly of the Council of Trent.
1546	Philip II of Spain is invested with the state of Milan by his father Charles V.
1547	Pier Luigi Farnese, Duke of Parma and Piacenza and son of Pope Paul III, is murdered in Piacenza.
1551-52	Second assembly of the Council of Trent.
1554	Philip II of Spain is given Naples and Sicily by Charles V.
1559	The treaty of Cateau-Cambrésis confirms Milan, Naples and Sicily to the Spanish Hapsburgs.
1563	Final Assembly of the Council of Trent.
1546-64	Michelangelo builds the dome of St. Peter's church in Rome.
1570	Andrea Palladio publishes his *Four books on architecture.*
1571	Battle of Lepanto in the Greek sea: the Venetian and papal fleets destroy the Turkish fleet.
1575	Torquato Tasso publishes his poem *Gerusalemme liberata.*
1600	Giordano Bruno is burnt as a heretic in Rome.
1603	The Accademia dei Lincei for the study of science and letters is founded in Rome by Prince Federico Cesi.
1613	Academy publishes Galileo's work on sun-spots.
1630-32	Plague epidemic affects all Italian cities.
1632	Galileo publishes his *Dialogo sopra i due massimi sistemi del mondo tolemaico e copernicano* (A Dialogue upon the two maximum world systems, of Ptolomaeus and Copernicus). The book was seized by the Inquisition and Galileo condemned in 1633.
1647	Popular uprising in Naples led by Masaniello (Tommaso Aniello) against tax exploitation.
1657-63	Gianlorenzo Bernini builds the colonnade in front of St. Peter's church in Rome.
1668-1744	Giambattista Vico, philosopher.
1672-1750	Ludovico Antonio Muratori, historian and librarian of the Duke of Modena.
1713	Treaty of Utrecht: Spanish possessions in Italy ceded to Austria and the Duchy of Savoy becomes kingdom.
1714	Elisabetta Farnese, from Parma, marries Philip V of Spain.

1734-35	Don Carlos, son of Philip V and Elisabetta, conquers Naples and Sicily.
1738	In the treaty of Vienna Don Carlos is made King of Naples and Sicily. The duchy of Parma and Piacenza passes to Austria and Tuscany to Duke Francis of Lorraine, husband of Maria Theresa, daughter of Emperor Charles VI.
1748	Peace of Aachen. Maria Theresa is recognized as Empress. Milanese territory as far as Lake Maggiore passes to the House of Savoy. Parma and Piacenza with Guastalla goes to Don Felipe, son of Elisabetta Farnese and brother to Don Carlos who is confirmed in Naples and Sicily.
1764	Publication of Cesare Beccaria's *Dei delitti e delle pene* (On crimes and punishments): argues for the abandonment of death penalty and torture.
1768	Corsica ceded to France by Genoa.
1796	General Napoleon Bonaparte fights against Austria and wins in Lombardy, and against Piedmont.
1796-97	Declaration of the Repubblica Cispadana and its incorporation in the Cisalpine Republic.
1797 (May)	Dissolution of the Serenissima Republic in Venice and French occupation of the city.
1797 (October)	Treaty of Campoformio. Napoleon receives Milan and Modena, Austria receives Venice and its inland territories up to the Adige river.
1802	Transformation of the Cisalpine Republic into the Italian Republic with Napoleon as its president.
1804-14	Napoleon is made emperor of the French.
1805	Venetia passes to the kingdom of Italy.
1809	The papal state is terminated and its territory annexed to France.
1813-1901	Giuseppe Verdi.
1814	Napoleon abdicates. The previous ruling families return to their territories. Maria Luigia, daughter of Emperor Francis, is in Parma.
1820-21	Revolutions in Naples and in Piedmont.
1827	Alessandro Manzoni publishes the first edition of his historical novel *I promessi sposi*.
1831-34	First attempts at insurrection in northern Italy, organized by Mazzini's 'Young Italy'.
1831-49	Charles Albert, King of Sardinia, under pressure to grant a more liberal constitution (promulgated in March 1848 and known as *Statuto albertino*).

1831	Failure of a revolution led by Ciro Menotti in Modena and failure of uprisings in Parma, Reggio and Bologna.
1846-78	Pope Pius IX raises the hopes of the intellectuals who were working for the unification of Italy, only to later withdraw his support.
1848	Constitutions are granted in Tuscany, in Piedmont and in the Papal State.
	The 'five-day uprising' (*Cinque giornate*) in Milan against the Austrians after a revolution in Vienna of 12 March.
1848-49	Daniele Manin declares the Republic of Venice.
	Piedmontese army attacks Austria but is defeated.
1849-78	Victor Emmanuel II of Savoy is King of Sardinia and King of Italy from 1861.
1852-59	Camillo Cavour is prime minister of the kingdom of Sardinia and of Italy from 1861.
1855	Sardinian intervention in Crimean War against Russia.
1859	Piedmont and France at war with Austria; Piedmont annexes Lombardy and the Duchies.
1860-61	Garibaldi and his 'Mille' (a thousand red shirts) conquer Sicily and the kingdom of Naples for the kingdom of Italy. Piedmont annexes Marches, Umbria and Abruzzi (Abruzzo and Molise).
1861	Victor Emmanuel of Savoy is proclaimed King of Italy (March). Death of Cavour (June).
1866	Italy and Prussia at war against Austria; acquisition of Venetia.
1870	Italian troops occupy Rome. The pope considers himself a prisoner.
1874	Pius IX forbids Catholics to participate in elections.
1876	Fall of the Right in government; accession of the Left.
1878-1900	Umberto (Humbert) I of Savoy becomes king of Italy.
1882	Franchise of men over the age of twenty-one who can read and write and pay twenty lire taxes.
	Triple Alliance between Austria, Germany and Italy.
1888	Tariff war with France.
1892	Socialist Party founded at Genoa Congress.
1896	Ethiopian War; Italians defeated at Adowa.
1899	Foundation of FIAT in Turin (*Fabbrica Italiana Automobili Torino* [Italian Car Factory, Turin]).
1900-46	Emmanuel III.
1911-12	Libyan War with Turkey. Libya, the Dodecanese islands and Rhodes are given to Italy.

1912	Near-universal male suffrage introduced.
1914 (August)	Italy, at the beginning of the First World War, declares its neutrality.
1915-18	Italy takes the side of the Allies in the First World War.
1917	The Austrian Army defeats the Italians on the Isonzo front at Caporetto.
1918	Victory of Italy and the Allies in Vittorio Veneto and armistice with Austria.
1919	Italian Popular (Catholic) Party founded. Start of the Fascist movement. D'Annunzio seizes Fiume (Rijeka).
1922 (October)	Mussolini's black shirts march on Rome. King Victor Emmanuel III makes Mussolini premier.
1924	Mussolini obtains a strong majority for his government in manipulated elections.
	The socialist MP Giacomo Matteotti is murdered by Fascists. The anti-fascist opposition leaves Parliament in the so-called Aventine secession.
1925 (January)	Threatening speech of Mussolini in the Chamber of Deputies.
1926	Fascist Labour Charter. 'Exceptional Decrees' on public security; dissolution of anti-fascist parties: dictatorship is completed.
1929	Agreement of Italy with the Pope (Lateran Pacts). The Vatican State is created.
1934	Conference of Italy, France and Britain at Stresa (Lake Maggiore). Mussolini and Hitler meet in Venice.
1935-36	Conquest of Ethiopia.
1938	Mussolini tolerates *Anschluss* (annexation) of Austria to Germany. Racial laws are promulgated.
1939	Mussolini occupies Albania (April) and concludes Pact of Steel with Hitler's Germany (May). Beginning of Second World War (September). Italy is a non-belligerent country.
1940	Italy declares war on France and Britain (10 June) and launches an unsuccessful attack on Greece.
1943	Allied landing in Sicily (10 July). Mussolini is dismissed by Victor Emmanuel III; Marshal Badoglio appointed as Prime Minister (25 July).
	Italian Armistice with Allies (8 September). Italy declares war on Germany. The Fascists found the *Repubblica Sociale Italiana* in the north with the support of Germany (October).
1944 (June)	Rome is liberated by Allied troops.

1945 (April) German capitulation in Italy. Mussolini captured by partisans and executed (28 April).

1946 Election of the Constituent Assembly. Referendum result against monarchy.

1947 Constitution of the Italian Republic. In force from January, 1948.

1948-52 Reconstruction with Marshall Plan aid.

1948 (April) The Christian Democrats obtain a narrow but secure majority in parliamentary elections.

1948-55 Luigi Einaudi first President of the Republic.

1949 Italy's entry into NATO.

1950 Founding of *Cassa per il Mezzogiorno* (Southern Italy Aid Fund).

1951 Italy's entry into the European Coal and Steel Community.

1955-62 Giovanni Gronchi, President of the Republic.

1957 (March) Treaties of Rome create the basis for the European Economic Community.

1962 First centre-left government, with the participation of the Socialist party from 1963.

1962-64 Antonio Segni, President of the Republic.

1964-71 Giuseppe Saragat, President of the Republic.

1968-69 Student agitation and workers strikes of *autunno caldo* (hot autumn).

1969 (December) A bomb in a Milan bank kills sixteen people. The so-called 'strategy of tension' and terrorism has started.

1970 Autonomous regional administrations and regional councils are created as envisaged by the constitution.

1971-78 Giovanni Leone, President of the Republic.

1973 The secretary of the Italian Communist Party proposes the possibility of co-operation with the Christian Democrats, the so-called *compromesso storico* (historic compromise).

1974 (May) A referendum called to repeal a divorce law produces 59.3 per cent in favour of divorce.

1976-78 Communist Party support Andreotti's government.

1977 Osimo Treaty: Italy and Yugoslavia ratify agreement ending Second World War border dispute.

1978 The President of the Christian Democrats, and former prime minister Aldo Moro is kidnapped by the Red Brigades and then murdered.

1978-85 Sandro Pertini, the first socialist president of the Italian Republic.

1980 (August)   A bomb at Bologna railway station kills eighty-five people.

1981   Attempt on the life of Pope John Paul II in St. Peter's Square (May). Giovanni Spadolini, a historian and a member of the Republican Party, is made prime minister. First non-Christian Democrat premier since 1945 (June).

1982   Calvi, the chairman of the Banco Ambrosiano, is found hanged under Blackfriars Bridge in London (June). General Alberto Dalla Chiesa, prefect of Palermo, his wife and his chauffeur are murdered by the mafia in Palermo (September).

1983   Members of the Red Brigades, including the murderer of Aldo Moro, are condemned to life imprisonment (January). Bettino Craxi becomes the first socialist prime minister of Italy (August).

1985-92   Francesco Cossiga, President of the Republic.

1986   Government crisis. Craxi resigns, but returns as prime minister in August.

1987   Parliamentary elections show gains for both Christian Democrats and Socialist Party (June). In Sicily 338 mafia suspects are condemned for murder, drug trafficking and extortion (December).

1989 (July)   Giulio Andreotti, aged seventy-one, forms the government (his sixth one) with five parties.

1990   At the first conference of the Lombard League its leader proposes the division of Italy into three republics.

1991   The Communist party congress votes in favour of changing the name of the party to *Partito Democratico della Sinistra* (PDS) (Democratic Party of the Left) (February).

Giulio Andreotti forms his seventh government (April).

1992   Investigations by judges like Antonio Di Pietro, in Milan, uncover a widespread network of corruption and bribes involving top businessmen and senior politicians. National elections: losses of Christian Democrats, and ex-Communists; gains of the *Lega Nord* (Northern League) (April).

Judges Falcone (May) and Borsellino (July) killed by the mafia in separate car-bomb explosions. Oscar Luigi Scalfaro elected President of the Republic (May). Monetary crisis and devaluation of the lira (September).

1993   New laws for local and national elections: mayors elected directly by voters; replacement of proportional system for Parliamentary election with mixed system.

Partial local election successes of left-wing alliances. Berlusconi decides to enter the political arena with a conservative new party (*Forza Italia*).

1994 Christian Democratic Party renamed Popular Party: right-wing group secedes. Parliamentary election (March) won by centre-right coalition led by Berlusconi (*Forza Italia*, *Lega Nord* and the neo-fascist *Alleanza Nazionale*). Coalition collapses (December) after withdrawal of *Lega Nord*. Judge Di Pietro resigns from judiciary.

1995 Interim government led by Lamberto Dini to pass urgent financial reforms and to prepare for new national election.

Further split of Popular Party in view of regional election, when centre-right lost ground to heterogeneous centre-left (April).

The Country and Its People

General

1 **Italian first! From A to Z.**
Arturo Barone.   Folkestone, England: Paul Norbury Publications, 1989.
248p. bibliog.
A practical, useful and often amusing compendium which discusses the impact that
Italy and its history, culture and people have had on the making of the western world.
The author's intention is 'to project a totally different picture of the Italians from that
which normally springs to mind'. The work is divided into two parts: the first ('The
facts') consists of a small encyclopaedia of famous Italians in the fields of
architecture, the arts, clothes, communication, economics, the law, folklore, food and
drink, lifestyle, politics, sport, travel and the sciences; and the second part ('The
debate') provides a discussion of the Italian influence on Britain, a historical profile
of the Italians and considerations of the causes of their successes and failures.

2 **The Italians.**
Luigi Barzini, Jr.   London: Hamish Hamilton, 1964. 352p.
The *New York Times* stated that 'No one who loves Italy and the Italians should miss
this book'. It is dazzlingly wide-ranging, covering such topics as 'the importance of
spectacle', 'Mussolini or the limitations of showmanship', 'the power of the family'
and 'Sicily and the Mafia'. It is snappy and entertaining, but not a serious analysis
and although it is informative about the complex Italian character (or characters), it is
also misleading, in that it reinforces the stereotyping of Italians. Furthermore, the
manners and morals depicted here have become less relevant during the past thirty
years of rapid and dramatic change in Italy. Nevertheless, it is of use for a broad
overview. Many subsequent editions have been published in both Great Britain and
the United States.

3   **The Italians: how they live and work.**
Andrew Bryant.   New York: Holt, Rinehart & Winston, 1976. 2nd ed.
164p. 2 maps.

Italy has changed so much in the last twenty years that even the new edition of this book only partially reflects the characteristics of today's Italians. However, social habits and ways of life do not change as quickly as the economic and political landscapes, and with this proviso the present book is still useful. It is divided into seven main chapters, which deal, respectively, with: the geographical and historical background; the political system; housing, eating and drinking and social services; work (the largest chapter, with a survey of economic activities and occupations); education; transport; and leisure. A couple of pages at the end provide 'hints for visitors' which may still be relevant today.

4   **Italian dynasties: the great families of Italy from the Renaissance to the present day.**
Edward Burman.   Wellingborough, England: Equation, 1989. 192p.
bibliog.

There are eight great families considered here, although the subtitle is a little misleading because most of the coverage for each family is limited to the golden era of the Renaissance itself and the period immediately prior to it. Their subsequent history is only summarily discussed in the final lines of each chapter. The dynasties covered are those of Visconti (Milan), Este (Ferrara), Colonna (Rome), Sforza (Milan), Malatesta (Rimini), Gonzaga (Mantua), Medici (Florence) and Farnese (Parma). Each chapter is divided into sections according to the prominent members of the various dynasties and the gallery is preceded by a historical introduction and accompanied by numerous pictures and illustrations. This is followed by a list of further readings and a short guide to places to visit.

5   **Italy today: social picture and trends, 1984- .**
Censis.   Rome: Franco Angeli, 1985- . annual.

These annual publications provide very useful summaries of the yearly voluminous reports on social conditions in Italy, which Censis (Centro Studi Investimenti Sociali) has been producing since 1967. The first volume in English appeared in 1985 (128p.); the subsequent issues grew larger and reached 300 pages by the early 1990s. They cover a wealth of information and contain statistics, comments, interpretations and forecasts on the main trends discernible in Italian society. Using the same structure as the original reports, the summaries begin with general remarks on the year concerned, followed by a section on underlying phenomena and trends. A larger part is devoted to analyses of such social arenas as education, the labour market, health care and social security, public administration, and the media. An appendix concludes the books, normally supplying statistical tables and an overall assessment of the social conditions and trends.

6   **The Times guide to the people of Europe.**
Edited by Felipe Fernández-Arnesto.   London: Times Books, 1994.
416p. bibliog.

This book deals extensively with Italy. Not only are Central and Southern Italians treated separately, but there are specific entries on the Piedmontese, Sicilians, and

Sardinians, with reference to the history, customs, popular beliefs, language and food of these groups of Italians. The information provided is succinct and can be used as a sound introduction to a fundamental characteristic of Italy: regional variety.

7 **Stato dell'Italia.** (The state of Italy.)
   Edited by Paul Ginsborg.   Milan: Il Saggiatore-Bruno Mondadori, 1994. 704p.

Over one hundred experts have contributed to this excellent survey of contemporary Italy. Concise and readable entries provide suggestions for further reading. The first part establishes the physical and historical context, and includes regional profiles. The contents are then arranged under headings such as: society (social structures, women, family, health, religion, and the mafia); economy (industrial system, North-South divide, and employment); the State (main institutions, public administration, justice, welfare, and education); and culture (journalism, mass media, arts, science, technology, and sport). The final part looks into foreign policy and current affairs, with an interesting collection of views on the momentous outcome of the 1994 election. In particular, the editor writes a perceptive comment on the defeat of the 'Progressists' by the right-wing coalition led by Berlusconi. Statistical tables and graphs illustrate this comprehensive panorama on the changing face of Italian society.

8 **Italia ventesimo secolo: la politica, le guerre, i rivolgimenti sociali, le scienze, la tecnologia, le arti, gli spettacoli, lo sport, la moda, il costume.** (Italy in the 20th century: politics, wars, social upheavals, science, technology, arts, performing arts, sport, fashion, costume.)
   Edited by Carlo Graffigna.   Milan: Selezione del Reader's Digest, 1980. 707p.

Because of its clear layout and good use of illustrations and diagrams this book could be of use even to readers with a limited knowledge of Italian. It provides the sort of clear information on recent social and political history, on the arts, sport, and fashion which is normally found in larger encyclopaedias.

9 **Italy.**
   Muriel Grindrod.   London: Benn, 1968. 244p. 5 maps.

A highly informative book on the development of the Italian State and society in the twenty-five years that followed the end of the Second World War. The historical background is outlined in the first part, with some emphasis on the fascist era, while five chapters of the second part provide a chronological survey of post-war Italy, from the drafting of the Republican Constitution to the centre-left coalition government. The following chapters focus on such issues as: post-1945 foreign policy; economic development (with a stress on industry, agriculture and foreign trade); the southern problem (the case of Sicily is highlighted); the social question; and education. A statement in the concluding section is also valid for the subsequent history (after 1968) of contemporary Italy: 'Politics have failed to keep pace with the drive and vitality, the adaptability to modern needs, shown by Italians in other departments of life, and particularly in the economic sphere'.

10 **Italian labyrinth: Italy in the 1980s.**
   John Haycraft. Harmondsworth, England: Penguin, 1987. (First
   published by Secker & Warburg, 1985.) 314p. 2 maps. bibliog.

Haycraft has written this highly readable portrait of contemporary Italy, with the aim of illustrating the many contradictions and paradoxes of Italian society. Explanations are also offered, but do not enter into any great depth. The book is the outcome of extensive travel throughout Italy, a country that the author has known 'for almost half a century', and innumerable interviews and meetings with all sorts of people, from the then President of the Republic (Sandro Pertini) to the obscure secretary of a trade union in Potenza, in the far south. Chapters deal with such diverse topics as the country's economy, institutions, the family, the Church, and the arts. This is a kaleidoscopic account of Italy and the Italians in which the dominant theme is the omnipresence and apparent omnipotence of the family. Another recurrent note is the vitality of Italians and their inexhaustible desire to express their views of each other.

11 **Rome: the sweet tempestuous life.**
   Paul Hofmann. London: Harvill Press, 1983. 245p.

This is an anecdotal chronicle of life in Rome as directly experienced by the author between the late 1970s and early 1980s. There are frequent excursions into the political, social and cultural recent past of the Eternal City. The lively style and perceptive observations compensate for the fragmentary structure of the book, which deals with such topics as the State's connection with the Vatican, terrorism and the kidnapping lore, life around cafés and *trattorie*, prostitution, the murky world of politics and football, pious institutions, bureaucratic labyrinths, the cult of the siesta, and the press corps.

12 **Italy: a country shaped by man.**
   Turin: Fondazione Giovanni Agnelli, [1983]. [146p.].

This is the catalogue of a Giovanni Agnelli Foundation travelling exhibition which toured the United States but equally it can stand on its own. The purpose of the exhibition was 'to provide the average American with a key to understanding Italian history as well as to interpreting Italy and Italians as they pursue their everyday life'. The contents are divided into three parts, each introduced by an essay, and the original text in Italian is attached. M. Pacini wrote the first essay, which provides the title to the book, and in it he introduces a variety of man-made landscapes with the reproduction of old maps and photographs of buildings, and town and countryside views. G. Chiaramonte's essay accompanies a selection of old and contemporary photographs by well-known studios and artists while the last essay, by G. Briganti, discusses examples of anonymous works of art and is intended to approach the Italian artistic heritage from an unconventional point of view.

13 **Italy.**
   Russell King. London: Harper & Row, 1987. 222p. 7 maps. bibliog.

A compact and readable book which broadens the contours of the author's previous study, *The industrial geography of Italy*. This work consists of six chapters, of which the first three deal with the political, social and economic development of Italy since its establishment as a united country in the mid-19th century, but with more emphasis on the post-1945 period. The most interesting feature is the stress placed on the regionally differentiated patterns of industry, which appropriately is taken up again and expanded upon in the second half of the book. Here the topics covered are: urbanization and related issues; transformation of agriculture and rural life; and regionalism and peripheral development, geared to small and dynamic firms. King does not ignore the dark side of this type of development, based on 'sweated labour and tax evasion', and often hailed as the panacea to the impasse of sustained economic growth.

14 A place in Italy.
Simon Mawer. London: Sinclair-Stevenson, 1992. 240p.

Mawer has produced a lively and entertaining account of his first two years of settlement in Italy, with his wife and his son who was born there. Having failed to find accommodation in Rome, they had to settle in a nearby village called Avea and the Italian way of life there is closely observed with sympathy and wit. The narrative is often made vivid by dialogues and the use of Italian phrases (sometimes colourful swearing) and there are interesting comments on festivities, social customs and eating and drinking habits. Also included are references to political institutions and to the relationship between citizens and the authorities. The legalistic rigidity of the bureaucracy is sometimes used to the citizens' advantage: it seems that women wishing to sunbathe topless at sea-resorts, succeeded in their quest because of the rigid application of legislation on equal rights.

15 Your home in Italy.
Flavia Maxwell. London: Longman, 1989. 143p. 1 map.

Published in association with Allied Dunbar Financial Services Ltd., this is intended as a helpful and easy guide to the 'joys and pitfalls of building or owning property' in Italy, whether as permanent expatriates there, or as holiday residents. A wealth of information is broken down into many chapters, each containing general and specific sections. The topics range from a survey of 'where to buy' (outlined region by region) to the actual process of purchasing and building, and coping with banks, the tax system, settling in, and with the Italian laws on succession. There is also a chapter with sensible advice on utilities, running costs and maintenance, insurance, and crime. On this, Maxwell points out that 'for all its reputation Italy is not the criminal sink of iniquity it is said to be'; however, it is suggested that all anti-burglary precautions should be taken. There is also a glossary.

16 Living in Italy: the essential guide for property purchasers and residents.
Yves Menzies. London: Robert Hale, 1991. 4th ed. 224p. 3 maps.

Although perhaps not strictly essential to everybody, this guide, which was first published in 1987, is useful even to ordinary visitors to Italy, because of its detailed information on virtually all aspects of living in Italy. Menzies offers constant evaluation of favourable and unfavourable features and some paradoxes of Italian society are indicated in the first introductory chapter. A general survey of the country's history and main characteristics is supplied in the next three chapters, whilst the following chapters touch upon: communications; law and order; family law; property transactions; the 'condominium'; cars and driving; boating; banking; insurance; health and pensions; taxation; gardening; food, wine and shopping (the longest chapter); education; utilities; restoring property; and building your own house. There are also appendices which supply advice on practical matters, such as writing a cheque. Italian words are sometimes misspelt.

17 **Italy: the fatal gift.**
William Murray.   New York: Dodd, Mead & Co., 1982. 256p.

The title derives from Lord Byron's exclamation: 'Italia! O Italia! Thou who hast / The fatal gift of beauty'. The contents are a collection of exuberant pieces, the outcome of many and extended visits to Italy and they are divided into two parts: those written between 1947 and 1952, when Murray was a music student and part-time journalist (mostly) in Rome; and those which have been written since 1962, mostly as reportages for *The New Yorker*. The latter collection is more varied and covers Milan, Naples and Tuscany, as well as Rome. Past and current events are skilfully mixed, in a continuous effort to observe and interpret the lives of Italians, who are listed by Murray in the following order: 'terrorists, policemen, actors, politicians, bureaucrats, opera singers, peasants, businessmen, journalists, artists, grifters, criminals, students, priests, and every single law-abiding citizen'. This is a real and charming gallery of assorted characters.

18 **The last Italian: portrait of a people.**
William Murray, introduction by Jan Morris.   London: Grafton Books, 1991. 254p. 1 map.

In a sense, this is a sequel to Murray's first book on his Italian connection and experience, *Italy: the fatal gift* (q.v.). As in the previous volume, some of the material included here first appeared in American magazines. It is a collection of articles about various events and topics, and a highly readable mirror of the multi-faceted Italian character. In the words of Jan Morris, 'this is a work not about the appearances or even the reputation of Italy, but about the straight contemporary truth of it [. . . Murray] has an eye for the corrupt and the absurd, as well as for the splendid'. There are five parts, arranged around rather loose themes: 'Romans from Rome'; 'Legacies' (including memories of the battle for Cassino); 'Neapolitan connections'; 'Entrepreneurs'; and 'Emigrants', including a section with the title given to the book, referring to 'the end of an era' for Italian-Americans in San Francisco.

19 **Italia, Italia.**
Peter Nichols.   London; Basingstoke, England: Macmillan, 1973.
346p. 2 maps.

This is a kaleidoscopic account of the customs and manners of Italians, by a writer who knew them well, as for many years he was the Italian correspondent for the London *Times*. The public and private dimensions of Italian life are examined in this work, with clarity and sympathy. It is presented in a readable style and is full of interesting and perceptive anecdotes, ranging from male and female relationships, politics, parties and politicians, industry and the State, family and friends, and regional differences. Systematic references to Italy's remote and recent past are made, in order to stress the continuity and change within post-war society. With regard to the diversity of people, Nichols points out that 'there is no such thing as an Italian - there are only Tuscans, Lombards, Piedmontese, Sicilians, Venetians, Emilians, Sardinians, Neapolitans and so on, all as unlike each other as men from opposite ends of the earth'.

20 **Italian neighbours: an Englishman in Verona.**
Tim Parks. London: Heinemann, 1992. 330p.

In the afterword to this excellent book, written by an expatriate novelist, it is stated that 'rather than a travel book [. . .] I should call this an arrival book. For by the end, this small square handkerchief of Italy I live in has become home for me. Hopefully, for just a moment, the reader will have been able to feel at home here too'. The 'square handkerchief' is Montecchio, near Verona, but the perceptive observations contained in the nearly forty chapters offer insights into the life and manners of Italians in general. It is a gallery of fascinating cameos inspired by circumstances, events and recurrences. They are given Italian titles, and range from *Afa* (hot, humid air), *Una bustarella* (a little envelope, a bribe), *I morti* (the dead), *Viva, viva, Natale arriva* . . . (at Christmas), to what needs no translation: *Mamma*.

21 **Live and work in Italy.**
Victoria Pybus, Rachael Robinson. Oxford: Vacation Work, 1992.
168p. 1 map. bibliog.

In this comprehensive, matter-of-fact survey of Italian institutions, regulations and practices, useful information can be found by those who are looking for employment opportunities, planning to start a business, or living and retiring in Italy. The book is in two parts: 'Living in Italy', which has chapters on residence and entry regulations, property purchase and rental, daily life and retiring; and 'Working in Italy' which contains chapters on starting and running a business, and employment. Some personal case-histories of British expatriates are included in the appendix. The text is interspersed with lists of useful addresses, a directory of major employers, and actual advertisements on behalf of property dealers and English schools. There are also misspellings of Italian words and other small inaccuracies.

22 **Gods over Italy.**
Edgar Reynolds. Rickmansworth, England: Chiltern Press, 1985.
216p.

Reynolds describes his book as 'a personal travelogue, extracts from the diaries of a long-time traveller in Italy'. Descriptions of places are interwoven with historical and cultural references, and, above all, with witty and sympathetic comments on whatever and whomever is observed. The result is a collection of independent pieces of various lengths and on different topics, but all full of insights. Several are focused on Rome, but southern Italy is also frequently discussed, notably Sicily and the ancient parts of Magna Graecia. Venice, Bologna and Naples are also visited, while other sections deal with such general subjects as food and rain (rather than drinks). In the author's words, it is a gallery of pictures 'more in the spirit of Italian *capriccio* rather than anything approaching Roman *gravitas*'.

23 **The new Italians.**
Charles Richards. London: Michael Joseph, 1994. 284p. 2 maps.
bibliog.

The author has kept to the subject of what was originally to be entitled 'An idiosyncratic portrait of Italy and the Italians'. Having lived in Italy as the correspondent for the newspaper *The Independent*, Richards knows the country and the people well. In the early 1990s, he 'found Italy in a state of flux, with great uncertainty about where the revolution that was throwing out a fifty-year-old political system would lead'. His is an optimistic conclusion, however, because Italians are considered to be resourceful enough to come through their predicament. The book is enjoyable and informative and it ranges from the political and economic scenery to regionalism and cuisine, the role of the family and the Church, the mafia and general criminality, immigration and Bossi's League. A glossary completes the book.

24   Italian country living.
Catherine Sabino, photographs by Guy Bouchet, design by Paul Hardy. London: Thames & Hudson, 1988. 276p.

Beautifully illustrated, this travellers' book reveals that 'Italy's most abundant riches lie in her varied countryside'. Italy without Florence, Rome and Venice sounds a blasphemous proposition, but the stunning photographs of the countryside, mountain scenery, minor seaside resorts and lake districts, almost succeed in making the reader (or rather, the viewer) oblivious to the great cities. The photographs of luxurious house interiors which are also included in the book give the false impression that when you step out of Italian cities you enter a wonderland, where life is full of physical, moral and, not least, economic wealth. A traveller's guide at the end provides information on the four practical aspects upon which the volume concentrates: hotels, restaurants, excursions and shopping.

25   How to find out about Italy.
F. S. Stych.   Oxford: Pergamon Press, 1970. 320p. bibliog.

Although now over twenty years old, this is still a useful book. Its aim is to indicate to the general reader a wide range of sources of information on virtually all aspects of Italy's life and culture. They are all drawn from printed sources found in libraries, archives, societies and similar institutions. Eleven chapters cover the following topics: bibliography, libraries and archives; encyclopaedias, periodicals and newspapers; philosophy and religion; the social sciences; language and linguistics; the natural sciences; applied science and technology; the fine arts, entertainment, and sport; literature; geography; archaeology, biography, and history.

26   Getting it right in Italy: a manual for the 1990s.
William Ward.   London: Bloomsbury, 1990. 391p. bibliog.

Comprehensive and easy to consult, the various topics in this work are treated in short, sharp-focused entries and a parallel, integrating text with background information, laid out in separate columns. The eight broad parts cover: society (with sections on the family, childhood and youth, sexuality, friendship and social relations); the country (city outlines, the environment, regionalism, racism and xenophobia); the State (historical factors, parliament and the Constitution, foreign policy, and defence); politics (the government, the parties, and political characteristics); the system (asocial behaviour, crime, the police, bureaucracy, and justice); the economy (the role of government, the big business dynasties, financial services, and the social dimension); leisure, the arts and the media (consumerism, free time, the arts, and the media); and body, mind and spirit (eating and drinking, medicine, sport, education, mental health, religion, death and superstition).

27 **Who's who in Italy: 1994 edition.**
Edited by Giancarlo Colombo. Bresso, Milan: Who's Who in Italy
S.r.l., under licence from Who's Who AG, Zurich, 1994. 2 vols. 1 map.
The publication of *Who's who in Italy* by Sutter's International Red Series publishing
group was resumed in 1977 and extensively revised ten years later. This is an updated
version of the 1988 edition and consists of concise biographical and institutional
entries in the fields of politics, science, business, the arts and entertainment. In
addition to a survey of Italian history, economic development and political life, this
edition also includes some useful notes on the recent changes in the banking system
(by G. C. Cantoni). Commenting on the political turmoil of the early 1990s (at the
end of the historical overview), it is pointed out that 'the year 1992 marked the
beginning of the institutional upheaval that may be termed the passage from the First
to the Second Republic'.

28 **Italians.**
David Willey, photographs by Fulvio Roiter. London: British
Broadcasting Corporation, 1984. 160p. 1 map.
This book is the result of a series of documentary films by BBC Television. Each
episode centres on one of the ten individuals who were selected from all over the
peninsula to talk about themselves, and around those original characters there are
references to many more. Their individual background is broadened so as to allow an
appreciation of the social and cultural context. The protagonists include a Calabrian
farmer, a successful business woman from Milan, a shop-floor steward at Alfa-
Romeo, the communist mayor of a small village in Basilicata, a semi-retired Tuscan
restorer, a lively *bagnino* (beach-master) from Rimini, a nun living in Umbria, and an
international model-turned-actress. There are graphs and many coloured pictures
taken by a leading Italian photographer.

Photographic surveys

29 **A day in the life of Italy: photographed by 100 of the world's
leading photojournalists on one day, April 27, 1990.**
San Francisco, California: Collins, 1990. 224p. 1 map.
This is a large-format, hardback book which includes a large selection of photographs
taken on the one day indicated in the subtitle, throughout Italy. This interesting
project results in a visual festival of Italian life in virtually all its facets: work;
leisure; family; city and country life; by day and by night. Some photographs are
stunningly beautiful for their composition and setting; others capture aspects of
everyday actions, without concession to the form. There are images of widely
different ways of life, such as a shepherd asleep in the Umbrian mountains, compared
to a group of fashion models caught in a Milan studio; there are also photographs
which focus on the atmospheric colours of the early or late hours of the day. A full
list of the photographers is supplied at the end of the work, together with a map of

Italy showing the places of assignments. Each photograph is accompanied by an informative caption.

30   **Italy: one hundred years of photography.**
Texts by Cesare Colombo, Susan Sontag.   Florence: Fratelli Alinari, 1988. 190p.

A selection of photographs from the famous collection of the Alinari brothers, arranged for an exhibition in the United States and Canada. The first plate, taken in 1884, shows the interior of a large conservatory; and the last photograph, taken in 1984 by a meteorological satellite and processed by a computer, embraces the Italian peninsula and most of Europe. The anthology is arranged in six sections, each with an introduction by Colombo, and in them, aspects of changing social life are connected with the evolution of photography. The sections are characterized by chronological order and thematic unity: turn of the century; pre-First World War transformation; inter-war years (including a beautiful picture by Cartier-Bresson); the Second World War (with two notable items by Robert Capa); reconstruction and economic revival; and the age of 'mass rituals'. Captions are highly laconic and a biographical catalogue is included.

31   **The Italian townscape.**
Ivor De Wolfe, sketches and plans drawn by Kenneth Browne, photographs [mostly] by Ivy De Wolfe.   London: The Architectural Press, 1963. 280p.

The more than 400 photographs gathered here, and the elegant narrative which links them, are now part of history, since the book was written and the photographs taken at the height of the Italian 'economic miracle'. In the introductory chapter the author welcomed the 'racing up' of the standard of living there, but also warned that it would throw 'the door open to commercial exploitation posing as free enterprise, posing as progress, posing as the thing that excuses any enormity in the developers' handbook of crime'. A revised edition does not exist, perhaps because it would have been too painful to monitor the full consequences of rapid growth and exponential tourist expansion. The contents are arranged around the following themes: the new art; the street; the town; the Italian tradition; objects; earth; air; fire; and water.

32   **Images of Italy.**
Anne Garrould, introduced by John Julius Norwich.   London: Pyramid Books, 1990. 144p.

A collection of images of Italy's monuments, sights and people, this volume starts with pictures of the Colosseum and other ancient Roman buildings, moves down to Paestum, Pompeii and Herculaneum (with asides into Amalfi and Abruzzo), and further down to Sicily. From there, the camera travels north, with images of the big lakes and the Alps in winter and spring; and Milan's Duomo and Galleria. Featured next are the hilly landscapes of Emilia and Tuscany, where the camera visits Siena and its Palio, followed by Urbino and Assisi. Spoleto is paid a little attention, before other Tuscan cities are explored, concentrating on Pisa and Florence in particular. A new turn to the north leads to Verona, which is portrayed almost as an introduction to the final and larger section devoted to Venice. In many cases the selection offers well-known and obvious images. All photographs are accompanied by informative captions.

33 **Tuscany from the air.**
Giuseppe Grazzini, photographs by Guido Alberto Rossi. London:
Thames & Hudson, 1991. 192p. 1 map. bibliog.

Sumptuously illustrated, this square-shaped book presents an overview of the history of the Tuscan landscape and society, after which the wealth of beautiful photographs is divided into six sections: the three old capitals (Florence, Siena and Pisa); the other main cities; the hills; the mountains; the coast; and the islands. Each section is introduced by a short essay and each picture is accompanied by an informative caption.

34 **Italia mia.**
Gina Lollobrigida. Maidenhead, England: McGraw-Hill, [1975].
[158p.]

The famous actress had to disguise herself while she travelled up and down the Italian peninsula taking photographs of her fellow-countrymen. In disguise she took some 20,000 pictures, out of which she chose the 191 included in this collection, most of which are in black-and-white. It is an assorted collection aimed at representing 'an Italy of real people, of humble artisans, of habitual devotion, of simple pleasures, of family feelings, tourist landscapes, of monuments so famous that now they have become almost invisible', as Alberto Moravia writes in the introduction. Captions consist of vague references to the illustrations, thus emphasizing the impressionistic and idiosyncratic nature of this selection. Children, in their natural or studied postures, are the subject of an interesting series of images.

35 **Italy: a photographic journey.**
Text by Rupert Matthews, photographs by Colour Library Books,
Telegraph Library. New York: Crescent Books, 1991. 128p.

In this large-size volume is contained a selection of fairly standard pictorial views of Italian landscapes and monuments, in which people are either absent or marginal by-standers. The photographs are accompanied by informative captions on historical background, and physical and cultural features. Some comments on the character of Italians and a review of their history, diversity and cultural achievements are offered in the text written by Matthews. This is a concise introduction to the country, mainly focused on the artistic treasures contained in the most famous cities.

36 **Italy from the air.**
Folco Quilici. London: Weidenfeld & Nicolson, 1987. 160p. 3 maps.

All twenty Italian regions are represented in this square-format collection of beautiful views of Italian cities, towns, villages, mountains, valleys, coasts and islands, captured by a famous aerial photographer. Some pictures are predictable, such as Venice's Grand Canal and Pompeii, but most of them consist of unusual or particular views, chosen with sensitivity to shapes, colours, proportions and contrasts. The photographs were taken from a helicopter hovering near the ground and at a relatively slow speed. Quilici's book is divided into three sections, corresponding to the north, the centre and the south of the peninsula and each section is preceded by a brief introduction to the physical characteristics of the land and cities included. Informative captions accompany every photograph.

Geography

General

37   **Italy: a geographical introduction.**
Jacques Béthémont, Jean Pelletier, translated from the French by E.
Kofman, edited by Russell King.   London: Longman, 1983. 220p.
18 maps. bibliog.

The first part of this work provides a survey of the physical, social and economic features of Italy, with the emphasis clearly on regional constraints, especially on the North/South divide. The second part consists of an analysis of the four main areas into which the peninsula is traditionally divided: the north; the centre; the mainland south; and the islands. In the conclusion no definite answer is given to the fundamental question of whether the socio-economic duality of Italy is likely to be reduced, maintained, or even deepened in the process of development that somehow involves the whole country. Strangely, a book which often refers to the twenty semi-autonomous regions does not contain maps of them and on the whole, cartographic illustrations are rather scarce and qualitatively poor. As a comprehensive geographical book, however, it is valuable, if only because very few are available in English on Italian geography.

38   **Italy.**
J. P. Cole.   London: Chatto & Windus, 1964. 271p. 57 maps and
diagrams. bibliog.

Inevitably all information on human geography needs a thorough appraisal after thirty years, especially because economic growth and social changes have deeply marked the three decades that have passed in Italy since publication of this book. However, the work does also deal with the physical features of the country and for this reason it is still relevant. Furthermore, this is a model study of regional geography, commencing with chapters on the physical, historical and political background as well as on population and settlement. The focus then moves from the main economic sectors (transport, agriculture and industry) to the regions of Italy, with detailed sections on the north, the centre and the south. A chapter is also devoted to the islands. There are many figures and tables; further quantitative information is supplied by the appendix.

39 **Western Mediterranean Europe: a historical geography of Italy, Spain and southern France since the neolithic.**
Catherine Delano Smith.   London; New York; Toronto; Sydney; San Francisco: Academic Press, 1979. 453p. bibliog. 32 maps.

A fine example of interdisciplinary work. The basic aim is to observe the landscape and pattern of life at all social levels in three major Mediterranean and European countries, across a wide historical perspective. Changes are noted, but it is also pointed out that they are often changes of form and not substance. Part one deals with 'People', ranging from the peasant farmers to the landowners and urban dwellers, and part two covers 'Land and land use', paying attention to the physical aspects of the landscape, crops and animals. In part three, two important changes in the environment are studied: the erosion on the hills and the siltation along the coast (Apulia and Sardinia are specific cases considered here). References to Italy are frequent, and particularly interesting are the pages on transhumance. There are many fine pictures and illustrations.

40 **A geography of Italy.**
D. S. Walker.   London: Methuen, 1967. 2nd ed. 296p. 53 maps and diagrams. bibliog.

Most of this book concerns the physical characteristics of the Italian peninsula, and therefore still remains quite relevant today. Its comprehensive and detailed contents are divided into four parts, with the first consisting of a wide-ranging survey of the relationship between geography and history. The second part deals with the climate, vegetation, orography, soils, seas and rivers. Part three, the main section of the book, is a thorough inspection of the natural features of the different geographical and administrative regions of the country, with some observations on human geography. The final part discusses economic geography and does need a substantial revision. As it is, however, this part offers a useful picture of post-war Italy, focusing on the profound transformation induced by the 'economic miracle' of the 1950s and early 1960s. There are many tables and a fine set of plates showing the great variety of landscapes and human settlements.

Special features

41 **Gardens of the Italian villas.**
Marella Agnelli, in collaboration with Luca Pietromarchi, Robert Emmett Bright, Federico Forquet.   London: Weidenfeld & Nicolson, 1987. 221p. 1 map. bibliog.

Six sections divide this visual feast, in chronological order and historical context. 'Reflections of an ideal world' refers to 15th-century gardens, of which Villa Medici, near Florence, is an example. 'Art, artifice and nature' introduces the first half of the

16th century, when gardens became a true art form (for instance, Villa Imperiale, near Pesaro). 'Drama and delight' were the imprint of the 17th century, when theatrical enchantment was planned on a grand scale (the Borromean Islands, Lake Maggiore, belong here). 'Geometry and grace' followed, at the end of the same century, under French influence (Villa Belgioioso, near Milan, is an example). 'The romantic spirit' was slow to appear in 18th-century Italy, and in this era the Villa Tritone, near Naples can be classed, among others. The final period is 'Modern inspirations' in which gardens are arranged in a more intimate and personal way, such as Agnelli's Villa Frescot, near Turin.

42 Italy: the hilltowns.
James Bentley, photography by Joe Cornish. London: George Philip, 1990. 208p. 1 map.

This lavishly illustrated, large-format book is an exploration of Italian hilltowns and the surrounding countryside, mostly in central Italy. As the author points out in his introduction, 'Italy's hilltowns sum up all that is most enticing about the country: its history, art, architecture and natural beauty [. . .] Moulded by millennia of wars, invasions, religious passion, enormous wealth, monarchical ambitions and the mundane concerns of the humble, these hilltowns offer a microcosm of western civilization scarcely found elsewhere'. The material is arranged in loose chronological order and divided into five parts: 'Greeks, Romans and Etruscans'; 'The might and grace of Romanesque'; 'The flowering of the Middle Ages'; 'From fortress to palace'; and 'Pilgrims and shrines'. The text is rich in historical references and the beautiful photographs range from glorious landscapes to exquisite details and warm views of domesticity.

43 Italian hilltowns.
Norman F. Carver Jr. Kalamazoo, Michigan: Documan Press, 1979. Reprinted, 1983. 192p. 1 map. bibliog.

The work of an architect and photographer, this is an attractive and informative visual document of small Italian hilltowns. The integration of architecture, man and landscape is vividly explored by means of both the camera (in black-and-white photographs) and the commentary. Virtually all the regions of Italy are visited, although the majority of the 175 photographs illustrate the life and environment of hilltowns in Tuscany, Umbria, Latium and Apulia. A map of Italy at the end of the book indicates the sixty-six locations concerned. Each photograph is accompanied by a concise, perceptive caption and there are two brief narrative sections on the differences between northern and southern Italian hilltowns, which neatly express their contents in their titles: 'The immutable north' and 'The inconstant south'.

44 Discovering the hill towns of Italy.
Paul Duncan, photographs by John Ferro Sims. London: Pavilion, 1990. 192p. 1 map.

The particular value of this book lies in the fact that the informative text is accompanied by beautiful colour pictures of breath-taking scenery, such as the view of Vitorchiano, a town built on volcanic soil, in Latium, and endearing details, such as the advertisements for wine and cake on a wall in Pescocostanza, Abruzzo. The places visited in the pictures are 'a mixture of lesser known hill towns as well as some of the old favourites'. Local festivals and rituals are described, and unusual regional events mentioned, in order to enhance the variety of local character and colour. Most Italian regions are included in the coverage and the journey starts, unusually, in the south (Sicily). Even more unorthodox is Duncan's recommendation to visit Basilicata 'above every other region'. Such preferential treatment of the south is justified 'as a way of illuminating the lesser known regions'.

45 The Italian lakes.
Aubrey Feist.   London; Sydney: B. T. Batsford, 1975. 207p. 1 map.

This is neither a guide nor a geography book; in the words of the author, 'it is simply a record of journeys spaced over a good many years, together with such observations and scraps of local lore as I have noted on the spot or found stored in my memory'. The less spectacular, but not unimportant lakes of central Italy are omitted from the coverage but specific sections are devoted to the Alpine lakes of northern Italy (Maggiore; Como; Garda) and the three small lakes of Lugano, Iseo and Orta. A final chapter departs from the lakes themselves and offers some thoughts on the three most famous cities within easy each and worth visiting: Milan; Bergamo; and Verona. The book is illustrated with several photographs and a map including all the relevant lakes.

46 Lombardy: the Italian lakes.
John Flower, photography by Charlie Waite.   London: George Philip, 1990. 216p. 6 maps.

The great physical and cultural variety of Lombardy is the underlying theme of this work, which Flower's elegant and informative writing and Waite's attractive photographs render a feast for both the mind and the eyes. Although the authors mainly focus on the Alpine lakes, the first chapter is devoted to Milan, which in Flower's words is 'Italy's brashest and most modern city'. Chapter two explores the flat lands and their cities. The three remaining chapters examine Lombardy's lakes and their districts in a fascinating journey from east to west: 'Lakes of Garda and Iseo'; 'Lake Como and the Valtellina'; and 'Lake Maggiore and the western reaches'. One particular merit of the book is the inclusion of little-known, enchanting places off the beaten track, without neglecting the tourist highspots.

47 The Dolomites of Italy: a travel guide.
James Goldsmith, Anne Goldsmith, with Giovanni Rizzardi, Gernot Mussner, Paolo Pompanin.   London: A & C Black; Edison, New Jersey: Hunter, 1989. 277p. 57 maps. bibliog.

This comprehensive guide is full of fine pictures, elegant drawings and accurate maps. Nearly thirty areas have been walked and hiked across, and readers are provided with a wide range of information, from historical references (particularly interesting are those concerning the Austro-Italian fighting there, during the First World War) to social, economic and geographical features. The book is divided into four main parts. The first deals with general characteristics of the Dolomites (geology, climate, flora and fauna) while the second part considers the summer activities of the area and the third looks into the winter sports. The last section offers information on itineraries, hotels and *pensioni*, and also contains a glossary. The text is interspersed with self-contained items with concise information for quick reference. There are general map-diagrams, maps for summer excursions and winter skiing maps.

48   The islands of Italy: Sicily, Sardinia and the Aeolian islands.
      Barbara Grizzuti Harrison, with photographs by Sheila Nardulli.   New
      York: Ticknor & Fields, 1991. 152p. 1 map.

A large-size book full of beautiful photographs with vague captions, which are not
always related to the narrative, this is a 'stream-of-consciousness' tale of the places
visited by an American writer with southern Italian origins. There are frequent
isolated quotations from such writers as Giuseppe Tomasi di Lampedusa, Giambattista
Vico, Italo Calvino and Leonardo Sciascia. Sicily is explored much more widely than
Sardinia and the Aeolian islands.

49   A world by itself: tradition and change in the Venetian lagoon.
      Shirley Guiton, illustrations by John Lawrence.   London: Hamish
      Hamilton, 1977. 202p. 1 map.

Two thirds of this book are devoted to one of the islands in the Venetian lagoon:
Burano, famous for its lace-making, colourful little houses, and a living community
with a strong sense of being different and unique. This character results from the
sufficient remoteness of the island from Venice, and its relatively large size. Murano,
a bigger, but much closer island to the head-city, is excluded from this affectionate
study of local traditions and ways of living. The other islands included here are
Torcello, 'a fading paradise' only visited now because of its great and ancient church,
and a luxurious restaurant; Santa Cristina, an abandoned tiny island, once occupied by
a convent; and San Francesco del Deserto, described as a real 'oasis of peace on
earth', with cypresses, a little church and a small community of friars. The narrative
is interspersed with historical references, anecdotes and fine drawings.

50   Italian waters pilot: a yachtsman's guide to the west and south
      coasts of Italy with the islands of Sardinia, Sicily and Malta.
      Rod Heikell.   St. Ives, England: Imray Laurie Norie & Wilson, 1991.
      3rd ed. 371p. maps.

As the subtitle indicates, this is primarily intended as a guide to people who are
wealthy enough to possess a yacht, although the author warns that 'impecunious and
not excessively rich yachties will find that they must plan their itineraries more
carefully than in the past to avoid marinas that are the most expensive in the
Mediterranean'. An introduction provides information on navigation and equipment,
Italian regulations, marine life, food, weather forecasts and other useful topics. The
bulk of the volume is then divided into eight chapters: 'The Ligurian coast'; 'Tuscan
coast and islands'; 'Tyrrhenian sea'; 'Sardinia'; 'Sicily'; 'Ionian sea'; 'South Adriatic
sea'; and 'Malta'. In each chapter, technical details (radiobeacons, major light,
mooring facilities) are provided for many ports and harbours and there are
innumerable maps and pictures, some of which appear in colour. The appendix
includes the list of relevant admiralty charts.

51   Villas of the Veneto.
      Peter Lauritzen, photographs by Reinhart Wolf, foreword by Sir Harold
      Acton.   London: Pavilion, 1988. 200p. 1 map. bibliog.

In his authoritative introduction, Lauritzen points out that the Italian villa reached a
peak of perfection with Andrea Palladio's work in the Veneto in the 16th century.
This large-format book is basically a gallery of splendid photographs illustrating the

setting, external features, architectural structures, gardens and interiors of thirty such palaces. The first villa visited is the famous Villa Foscari (*La Malcontenta*), the nearest to Venice, and the last is Villa Badoer, in the province of Rovigo. Each photograph is accompanied by an informative caption and a more comprehensive outline of the history and main features of the villas is supplied at the end of the book. In a rare reference to modern history we learn that Villa Pisani, near Padua, 'became a stage for one of the dramas of recent European history: it was the setting for Mussolini and Hitler's first meeting on 12 July 1934'.

52　**Italian gardens.**
Georgina Masson, with an introduction by Geoffrey Jellicoe.
Woodbridge, England: Antique Collectors' Club, 1987. Rev. ed. 300p. bibliog.

Lavishly illustrated, this large-size book, which was first published in 1961, maps a journey through Italian gardens, both in time and space. Renaissance, mannerism, baroque, and neoclassicism are the phases which characterize the evolution of the gardens and the changing concept they represent of society's relation to environment. The journey begins with the gardens of ancient Rome, and the presentation consists of a well-informed text and a selection of plates. This pattern is repeated in all subsequent chapters, which cover mediaeval and early humanist gardens, Tuscan gardens, Roman Renaissance gardens, gardens of the Marches and Venetia, and the gardens of northern Italy. A postscript on southern Italian gardens and a section on the flowers grown in Italian gardens (with their Latin and English names) conclude the book.

53　**Italian gardens: a visitor's guide.**
Alex Ramsay, Helena Attlee, edited by David Joyce.　London:
Robertson McCarta, 1989. 191p. 1 map. bibliog.

This is a practical, well-illustrated guide to nearly sixty of the best-known Italian gardens, mostly in northern and central Italy. A concise history and description of each is accompanied by such information as their precise location, facilities, opening times and how to apply for access (to private gardens). The material is arranged in regional order, with Piedmont the first region involved (with four gardens); it is followed by Lombardy (four), Liguria (four), Venetia (ten, with some of the famous villas on the river Brenta), Tuscany (nineteen), Emilia-Romagna and the Marches (four), Latium (eleven), and finally Campania (the only southern region present, with four gardens). A chronological table, biographical information on the artists concerned and a glossary complete the book.

Maps and atlases

54　**AA Baedeker's Italy.**
Germany: Mairs Geographischer Verlag, 1990-92.

A folding two-sided map in the scale of 1:750,000. It includes simplified maps of Rome, Milan, Venice, Florence and Naples. Some useful telephone numbers are also provided: police; road patrol; and some embassies (but not that of the British Embassy).

55 AA big road atlas: Italy.
Basingstoke, England: Automobile Association; Novara, Italy: Istituto Geografico de Agostini, 1995.

A large-sized road map, with a four miles to one inch scale. There are several outlines of town plans, route-planning maps and an indication of places of interest. A distance chart is included.

56 Italy.
Vienna: Freytag & Berndt, 1991-92.

A two-sided, folding, large road map in the scale of 1:650,000. Names of places are in Italian and sometimes also in German and the legend is in four languages (German, English, French and Italian).

57 Italy: Euro-road atlas.
Berlin: GeoCenter International, 1992-93. 256p.

This is a multilingual atlas and shows: motorways and trunk roads; motorway sectional maps; urban transit route maps (1:100,000); map sections in the scales of 1:800,000 and 1:300,000; and ferry lines. There are also several town plans and a useful administrative area map.

58 Italy.
Bern: Hallwag AG, [n.d.].

This is a road map in the scale of 1:100,000, with additional local maps (in various scales) of a number of towns and their surrounding areas. These include: Turin; Milan; Genoa; Venice (and Padua); Bologna; Florence; Rome; Naples; Messina (and the homonymous straights); and Palermo. It contains a sliding card providing inter-city distances in kilometres.

59 Italy.
Bern: Kümmerly & Frey, 1993.

A double road map in the scale of 1:500,000. As is customary, the two halves correspond to the northern and southern halves of the peninsula. Place names are in Italian but explanations are given in four languages: Italian; French; German; and English.

60 Philip's Italy.
London: Philip's, 1993.

This new edition of a detailed road map of Italy provides an indication of car ferries, beaches, national parks, historic buildings and natural landmarks. It is in the scale of 1:1,000,000, or sixteen miles to one inch. The legend is in French, German and Italian, as well as in English.

The Italians: how they live and work.
See item no. 3.

How to find out about Italy.
See item no. 25.

The industrial geography of Italy.
See item no. 728.

Tourism and Travel Guides

61 Berlitz: discover Italy.
Jack Altman, Jason Best. Oxford: Berlitz Publishing, 1993. 352p. maps.

An easy to use, complete and concise guide to the peninsula. The introductory section containing 'facts and figures' precedes an informative chapter on the country and its history, and on 'leisure routes and themes'. The actual guide is then divided so as to provide individual sections on the main Italian regions from the traveller's point of view: Central Italy; Tuscany, Umbria and the Marches; The North-East; The North-West; The South; and The Islands. Interspersed throughout the book are interesting profiles on such topics as Italian architecture and painting, the Etruscans' legacy and Italian cinema. The guide is fully illustrated and contains maps and town plans.

62 Baedeker's Italy.
Basingstoke, England: Automobile Association, 1991. 624p. 9 maps.

This is one of the new and revised editions of the famous Baedeker guides. These editions are characterized by their conciseness and practicality, as the main places of interest (cities, regions, lakes or particular districts) are listed in alphabetical order. This constitutes the largest section of the book and is appropriately called 'Sights from A to Z'. A survey of Italian history, art and culture, together with some basic facts and figures on the country, introduces the guide, and a section on 'practical information' (also organized 'from A to Z') concludes it. The latter ranges from travel to currency, emergencies, food and drink, hotels, restaurants, shopping and tipping. The guide contains many colour photographs, maps and drawings. There is also a large attached map of Italy.

63 Let's go Italy: 1995.
Edited by Howie Axelrod. London: Macmillan, 1995. 638p. maps.

This is also known as 'The budget guide to Italy', and the economic element is prominent throughout the book. This objective alone requires that editions are frequently revised and updated, and the publishers assure that this is done on a yearly basis. The contents include the expected set of general information, followed by the travel guide itself. This begins in central Italy, with Rome and its surrounding region, moves into Abruzzo and Molise, and proceeds to the Marches, Umbria and Tuscany. The main regions and districts of northern Italy are then visited. Finally, jumping across the peninsula and beyond, southern Italy, Sicily, Sardinia and Tunisia are explored. A useful glossary is included, along with maps and town plans.

64   Insight guide: Italy.

Edited by Katherine Barrett, Dorothy Stannard.   Singapore: APA Publications, 1994. 2nd ed. 371p. 14 maps.

A handsomely illustrated and popular guide, which maintains the traditional aims of the series; that of providing the traveller with a solid background of history, good writing and detailed reporting on 'destinations, warts and all'. The text is divided into three main parts: History; People and culture; and Places. A general and informative section (Travel tips) concludes the guide.

65   Italy: the rough guide.

Ros Belford, Martin Dunford, Celia Woolfrey.   London: Rough Guides, 1995. 2nd ed. 981p. maps.

First published in 1990, this is the fourth reprint of the second edition, which appeared as recently as 1993. Such success with the public may justify the publishers' claim that this is 'the most complete handbook to one of Europe's most diverse countries, getting behind the ordinary sights with an honest and contemporary approach'. The customary structure of travel guides is employed, beginning with basic facts and general information. Then follows the actual guide to the country, also in the traditional presentation of all its regions, from the north to the south, including Sicily and Sardinia. Relevant town plans are provided. The last section is entitled 'Contexts' and includes such topics as a historical profile, and an introduction to Italy's arts and architecture, cinema, music, literature, language and such social phenomena as 'mafia, 'ndrangheta and camorra'.

66   Blue Guide: southern Italy: from Rome to Calabria.

Paul Blanchard, atlas, maps and plans by John Flower.   London: Ernest Benn; New York: W. W. Norton, 1982. 4th ed. 358p. 1 atlas. 17 maps.

Similar to the companion volume on northern Italy (q.v.), this is a valuable, compact guide and an excellent companion for travellers. Carefully planned routes are offered throughout the volume. A historical summary by Stuart Rossiter precedes a study of art in southern Italy by Paul Williamson, followed by a glossary of art terms. There are also contributions on the geological features of the area, and on its British and American visitors. A section full of practical information introduces the reader to the main body of the book, which is divided into four parts: Latium (excluding Rome) and Campania (including Naples); the Basilicata and Calabria: Abruzzo and Molise; and Apulia. The volume contains a sixteen-page atlas, many plans, and some illustrations.

67 **The companion guide to Florence.**
Eve Borsook. London: Collins, 1979. 400p. 11 maps. bibliog.

First published in 1966, the originality of this book lies in the combination in each
chapter of a section describing the chief monuments and sights, with essays on
aspects of their history and cultural importance. There are eight such chapters, which
cover: Piazza della Signoria; Piazza del Duomo; the Bargello and Santa Croce
neighbourhood; from Santa Maria Novella to Ognissanti; the Arno; the Centre; 'Of
the Medici and the world of ideas'; and the Oltrarno. A final descriptive section
considers the Florentine countryside. Many illustrations and church plans are
included in the volume and there is also practical information on hotels, pensions,
places to eat, libraries, pharmacies and shopping.

68 **Fodor's Italy: 95.**
Edited by J. R. Carroll, K. Moehlmann, A. Stern. New York; Toronto;
London; Sydney; Auckland: Fodor's Travel Publications, 1994. 583p.
maps.

This is the most recent edition – at the time of compiling the present bibliography –
of a classic guide. It is comprehensive, concise and well structured, providing
information and advice on virtually anything worth 'doing and seeing' in Italy, such
as landscapes and arts, towns and villages and cuisine. The first part provides
suggestions on departing for Italy, arriving and staying there and leaving. A short
chronology is included and two essays on 'Italian art through the ages' (by S.
Brownlee) and 'The wines of Italy' (by H. Eyres). These are followed by the main
body of the guide, with chapters on the various principal cities and regions of the
country.

69 **Cadogan guides: Italy.**
Dana Facaros, Michael Pauls. London: Cadogan Books, 1994. 2nd ed.
1,116p. maps. bibliog.

A guide 'for independent travellers on all budgets' is how the publishers introduce
this voluminous work. It covers the traditional itineraries of any similar book on Italy,
as well as delving into the treasures and charms of lesser-known districts of the
peninsula, including their cooking and drinking habits. Practical information is
arranged in alphabetical order at the outset. Brief sections on Italian history, art and
culture introduce the reader-traveller to a journey throughout most of the regions in
the mainland (Sicily and Sardinia are excluded).

70 **Italy: the versatile guide.**
Leslie Gardiner, Adrian Gardiner. London: Duncan Petersen, 1994.
320p. maps.

In this flexible guide, which contains attractive illustrations, entries are arranged
alphabetically by region, providing an easy-reference tool. General information,
including a brief history of Italy, is supplied at first. Then the three broad divisions of
Italy (north, central and south) are effectively introduced, with hints at the arts, food
and wine of each area. Special attention is devoted to Rome, Florence, Venice, Sicily
and Sardinia.

71 **Italy: a travel survival kit.**
Helen Gillman, John Gillman. Hawthorn, Australia: Lonely Planet
Publications, 1993. 682p. maps.

A thorough guide covering all the traditional natural and man-made sights worth visiting in Italy, and consequently a highly concise – although voluminous – book. Facts about the country are first provided, including outlines of Italian history, geography, flora and fauna, politics and economics, art and culture, religion, language, and the mafia. Detailed and useful information is then offered, on such topics as travelling, accommodation and eating out. Rome is considered in particular detail, before the authors deal with northern, central and southern Italy, Sicily and Sardinia, in separate sections. A glossary and town plans are included.

72 **South Italy: a traveller's guide.**
Paul Holberton. London: John Murray, 1992. 237p. 1 map. bibliog.

The contents of this volume are less comprehensive than the title suggests, as only three regions of southern Italy are explored in two itineraries: Apulia ('The heel'); and Basilicata and Calabria (both strangely considered as 'The toe'). These are relatively little-known regions, with several features in common, but also very different from one another. In particular, Apulia has a much more interesting mediaeval history. Indeed, history and its testimony through monuments and works of art is constantly emphasized by Holberton. For the first itinerary he sets off from Benevento (in Campania) and roughly follows the old Appian Trajan Way through Apulia. The second itinerary starts at Eboli (also in Campania), crosses the mountainous parts of Basilicata and proceeds through Calabrian towns and villages. There are black-and-white plates, church ground plans, and genealogical maps of the relevant ruling dynasties.

73 **The companion guide to Venice.**
Hugh Honour. London: Collins, 1990. 3rd rev. ed. 304p. 15 maps.
bibliog.

This is an updated version of what has become a classic book, originally written in 1965 'for the visitor to Venice rather than for the armchair traveller'. The first four chapters are mainly concerned with the history of the *Serenissima* and its institutions, while the following eight chapters trace the development of the visual arts in Venice. The remaining eight chapters consider various aspects of the city's arts and life. Five appendices offer information on places of interest which are not mentioned in the text, hotels, restaurants, books about Venice, and shops. Returning to Venice for the present revised edition of the book, Honour was relieved to note that there had not been many changes, and that what had changed had been for the better, at least as far as works of preservation (rather than innovation) were concerned. The volume contains illustrations and plans of churches and palaces.

74 **Tuscany.**
Jonathan Keates, photography by Charlie Waite. London: George
Philip, 1988. 216p. 7 maps.

This is a gem among travel books. It is an intelligent, informative and beautifully-photographed journey of discovery from northern to southern Tuscany, through some of the most famous sites in the world, such as Florence and Siena, and some lesser known areas, such as Maremma. The history, culture and art of this multifaceted and variegated region is viewed with a sensitive understanding of its complexity. Having dealt with Florence in the introduction, the six chapters of the book are devoted, respectively, to: Lucca and the Garfagnana; Pisa, Elba and the northern Maremma; Siena and the Chianti; The Maremma and southern Tuscany; Prato, Pistoia and the north-east; and Arezzo and the south-east.

75 The Doge's palace in Venice.

Michela Knezevich.   Milan: Electa, 1994. 86p. bibliog. (Electa Art Guides).

This is one of the latest art guides in the series which includes Mantua, San Gimignano, the villas of Palladio, and numerous museums and monuments. After a historical introduction which briefly considers the history of Venice as well as that of the Doge's palace, the guide takes the reader through the palace, with the use of detailed ground plans, accurate information and crisp illustrations. A select and up-to-date bibliography completes the volume.

76 Exploring rural Italy.

Michael Leech.   London: Christopher Helm, 1988. 168p. 47 maps.

In this guide readers are taken off the beaten track of travellers' Italy and invited to explore countryside routes in all parts of the peninsula. For this purpose Leech has divided the country into twelve areas: Piedmont and the lakes (but mainly Lombardy); the Italian riviera; the Veneto (but also including Friuli-Venezia Giulia, and Trentino Alto-Adige); Emilia Romagna and the Marches; Umbria; Tuscany; Abruzzo; Latium; Campania and Molise; Apulia; Calabria and Basilicata; and the Islands (Sardinia and Sicily). For each of these areas several routes are devised, 'chosen for their scenic value and their cultural and historical associations'. Practical advice and information is provided on roads, maps, accommodation and food but the final recommendation is to learn a few Italian words beforehand, and to take a dictionary and a phrase book, even if 'in this country of flamboyant gestures, you can communicate a lot with your hands and your body'.

77 Venice and its lagoon: historical, artistic guide.

Giulio Lorenzetti, presented by Nereo Vianello, translated by John Guthrie.   Trieste, Italy: Lint, 1982. 1,025p. 14 itinerary-maps.

The original impression of this classic work, in Italian, dates back to 1926. Only after fifty years was it reprinted and it has remained a standard guide ever since, combining erudition with information. The three initial chapters introduce the history and cultural heritage of Venice. The main body of the book then consists of a detailed description of twelve itineraries: from St. Mark's Square to the Grand Canal (an itinerary on its own). The section on the lagoon and its islands follows and precedes a useful set of indexes of artists, places and buildings, art and history collections, chief burial and commemorative monuments, and illustrations. Equally useful information is provided on all practical aspects of tourism in Venice. All photographs are reproduced as they appeared in the first 1926 edition. There are also plans of palaces and churches.

78 **Blue guide: Florence.**

Alta Macadam, atlas, maps and plans by John Flower. London: Ernest Benn; New York: W. W. Norton, 1982. 232p. 15 maps. 1 atlas.

Marco Chiarini, the director at the time of publication of the Pitti Gallery, introduces this guide with a comprehensive essay on the Florentine Renaissance. A brief historical sketch of Florence follows, including the Medici family tree. Sections on practical information (hotels, restaurants, transport, amusements, churches, museums and collections) precede the central body of the book, which is divided into two parts: Florence (taking the lion's share) and its environs. Altogether, twenty-eight itineraries are recommended, starting with the Baptistery and the Duomo, at the heart of the city, and ending at Poggio a Caiano, some twenty kilometres outside Florence. The guide is hugely informative and clearly written. It is interspersed with black-and-white illustrations, plans of churches, museums and galleries, maps and a sixteen-page atlas at the end of the volume covering the plan of routes suggested in the text, the city of Florence (and in particular its centre), Fiesole and the Florence environs.

79 **Blue Guide: northern Italy: from the Alps to Rome.**

Alta Macadam, atlas, maps and plans by John Flower. London: Ernest Benn; New York: W. W. Norton, 1991. 9th ed. 784p. 1 atlas. 4 maps.

This is the most comprehensive guide to the upper half of the Italian peninsula and in the best tradition of the Blue Guides, it is full of valuable information on history, art and architecture. The first edition appeared in 1924 and has been continuously revised ever since. An introductory chapter on art in northern Italy (by A. Martindale) is followed by a glossary and a section on practical information. The main body of the book is then divided into six parts: Piedmont and Liguria (including Val d'Aosta); the lakes and Lombardy; Venetia; Emilia (including Romagna); Tuscany and northern Latium; and the Marches and Umbria. Many town plans are included, as well as ground plans for some of the important buildings in Florence, Mantua and Venice. A sixteen-page atlas of northern Italy is added at the end of the volume.

80 **Sicily.**

Alta Macadam, atlas, maps and plans by John Flower. London: A & C Black, Blue Guide, 1993. 4th ed. 319p. 34 maps and plans. 1 atlas.

This new edition has been rearranged to provide simpler and shorter itineraries. What has been retained, however, is the usual wealth of detail about hotels, restaurants and local transport, together with information about landscapes, towns and cities and their works of art. Helen M. Hills provides an introductory chapter on Sicily's art and architecture and this is followed by a short glossary. There is then a systematic description of thirty routes, commencing with a major section on Palermo and its environs (with an emphasis on Monreale), travelling through the other main provinces and ending in the Aeolian islands. Many black-and-white photographs and illustrations enhance this indispensable guide to Sicily which is both concise and comprehensive in its coverage.

81 **Tuscany.**
   Alta Macadam, maps and plans by John Flower.   London: A & C
   Black, Blue Guide, 1993. 445p. 16 maps.

This is possibly the most comprehensive guidebook in English to this most famous region of Italy. John Law provides a concise historical introduction and this is followed by a section containing practical information, ranging from driving and public transport, eating and accommodation, and a useful glossary of terms mainly on visual arts and architecture. The main body of this excellent guide is structured into thirty itineraries, both within cities and through the towns and countryside. Florence and her environs is featured first, followed by the northern mountains of the Mugello and then – almost literally step by step – the rest of this region glorified by art and nature, including less well-known but equally precious off-the-beaten-track places. There are many illustrations and ground plans, as well as town maps and one of the whole region.

82 **Umbria.**
   Alta Macadam, maps and plans by John Flower.   London: A & C
   Black, Blue Guide, 1993. 189p. 12 maps and plans.

A more recent addition to the valuable series of Blue Guides on Italian regions, this book begins with an historical introduction to Umbria, by John Law. A section on practical information and a glossary follow. The main part of the book explores twelve routes, beginning in and around Perugia, the regional capital city. The reader is guided through Assisi, Lake Trasimene, the Upper Tiber valley, Gubbio, Todi, Orvieto, Spoleto and Foligno. One aim of the guide is to provide information on smaller and lesser-known places, as well as on the usual famous cities and towns. This is an admirable objective in a region that offers so many works of art which are not as well known as those in neighbouring Tuscany, but which are set in equally beautiful surroundings. Black-and-white photographs are included in the text, mainly of buildings, townscapes and sculptures.

83 **Venice.**
   Alta Macadam, atlas, maps and plans by John Flower.   London: A & C
   Black, Blue Guide, 1994. 5th ed. 224p. 14 maps and plans, 1 atlas.

As is customary with these valuable Blue Guides, the contents are divided into three main parts. Two excellent sections in part one deal with Venetian art and architecture (by P. Rylands), and provide an historical survey of the city. The second part consists of detailed information about hotels, restaurants, transport, churches, theatres and museums, while the final and main part provides twenty itineraries around Venice's quarters, the islands of its lagoon, and a journey into the mainland up the Brenta Canal. Particularly interesting are the annotations on buildings and works of art restored during the years between the publication of the previous edition (1988) and the present version. Black-and-white photographs and other illustrations accompany the itineraries.

84 **The companion guide to Rome.**
Georgina Masson.   London: Collins, 1980. 6th ed. 541p. 27 maps.
bibliog.

This classic guide was revised to take into account the changes which had taken place since its first publication in 1965. Since it is highly recommended that the historical centre of the city be explored by walking, a warning is added here: 'Keep a sharp eye on your pocket-book or handbag – or better still don't carry a handbag at all', although Masson hastens to add: 'Do not let these warnings deter you from the joys of seeing Rome'. Indeed, the author succeeds in transferring her own love for the Eternal City to the reader, through the well-written comments on the itineraries offered, which include both the great sights (the Colosseum, the Forum, the Vatican Palace, to name only few) and Rome's humble squares and streets. Masson provides a wealth of historical information, often including fascinating anecdotes.

85 **Michelin Italy.**
Watford, England: Michelin, 1992. 313p. maps.

An eminently practical tourist guide, this publication consists of three parts. The first provides a historical outline (with the emphasis on Rome and the Papacy) and brief profiles on art, literature, cinema and today's Italy. The second and largest part is devoted to 'Sights'. These are arranged in alphabetical order, from 'Abruzzi massif' to 'Trapani'. One to three stars are awarded to such places of interest (one: interesting; two: worth a detour; and three: worth a journey). The final part contains general information on how to travel, principal festivals, admission times and charges to museums, galleries and parks.

86 **The which? guide to Italy.**
Ingrid Morgan.   London: Which? Books; Hodder & Stoughton, 1992.
2nd ed. 560p.

Published on behalf of the Consumers' Association, this is one of the best of the innumerable travel guides to Italy. It contains a wealth of relevant information, which is well arranged in nicely introduced sections. The main chapters deal with the northern lakes and mountains, Venice, Florence, Rome, Naples, Sicily and Sardinia, while other cities and regions are concisely explored. Drawings illustrate the guide, which also contains two glossaries, one on art and architecture, and the other on food.

87 **A traveller in southern Italy.**
H. V. Morton.   London: Methuen, 1983. 420p. 1 map. bibliog.

First published in 1969, this is a highly readable and enjoyable traveller's guide to the five regions of mainland southern Italy: Abruzzo and Molise (considered as one region); Apulia; Basilicata; Campania; and Calabria. Molise and Basilicata are treated only briefly, however; the bulk of the book covers Apulia and Campania, of which the Norman castles and cathedrals of the former are much in evidence, as is Naples with its legends. There are many references to relics of remote and classic times, when this part of the peninsula was an important component of Magna Graecia. Folklore traditions are described through direct participation, and aptly explored with emphasis on popular piety and pagan survival rituals.

88 **The Italian lakes.**
Richard Sale.   Marlborough, England: The Crowood Press, 1993.
144p. 1 map.

Thirty recommended walks around the Italian alpine lakes are described in this
volume and illustrated with photographs and drawings. They are divided into four
groups, according to their location: Lakes Maggiore and Orta; Lakes Lugano and
Como; from Lake Como to Lake Garda; and Lake Garda. A wide-ranging
introduction provides a historical background of the alpine region and information on
such practical issues as accommodation, transport, clothing and equipment.

89 **Off the beaten track: Italy.**
Richard Sale, Phil Whitney, Nancy Woodyatt.   Ashbourne, England:
Moorland; Old Saybrook, Connecticut: Globe Pequot Press, 1994. 2nd
ed. 333p. maps.

As the title indicates, this guide concentrates on places beyond the artistic wealth of
Rome and Florence, and the Italy of the traditional tourist routes. On the other hand,
the recommended itineraries do follow the customary sequence, starting in the north-
east (Val d'Aosta and Piedmont), and travelling down to central and southern Italy.
Some little-known areas are left out, as is Sardinia, whereas Sicily is included.

Italian first! From A to Z.
See item no. 1.

A traveller's history of Italy.
See item no. 129.

Travellers' Accounts and Companions

90 **Florence: a travellers' companion.**
Selected and introduced by Harold Acton, Edward Chaney. London: Constable, 1986. 333p. bibliog. 1 map.

This is an anthology of extracts from writings on buildings, monuments, various works of art and sites in Florence. They range from the 14th-century writer Giovanni Villani (on the Baptistry and the Ponte alle Grazie, for instance), to Lord Byron (on the church of Santa Croce); from Richard Lassels (on the Palazzo Pitti, among other things), to Michel de Montaigne (on the Palazzo Vecchio). Two shorter sections include similar extracts on the approaches to Florence (for example, part of a letter by Dylan Thomas on the hills around Scandicci) and on the topic 'life, customs and morals' (with a selection of diverse writers such as Boccaccio, Charles Dickens and the French historian Fernand Braudel).

91 **The golden honeycomb.**
Vincent Cronin. London; Toronto; Sydney; New York: Granada, 1985. 267p. 1 map.

First published in 1954 and regarded as a travel book classic, this is a well-written and perceptive work on Sicily. The central theme is the island's varied cultural past and its fascinating landscapes and affection and erudition are the ingredients in Cronin's description of Sicilian cities and towns, temples and valleys. Most of the chapters are dedicated to specific locations, such as Erice, Taormina, Etna, Syracuse, Enna, Noto and Palermo. There is little detail on contemporary life, which is why the book has not aged too much; but in the new introduction one reads that, for all the author's fascination with Sicilian history, he found it difficult to 'hit it off with the Sicilians'. The latter sentiment must have prevailed, in the end, since Cronin also admits that he never revisited the island after his sojourn in 1951. The illustrations reflect this idiosyncrasy.

92 **South Italy.**
Dana Facaros, Michael Pauls, illustrated by Pauline Pears. London: Cadogan Books; Chester, Connecticut: The Globe Pequot Press, 1990. 396p. 17 maps. bibliog.

This compact guide to the lower half of the Italian peninsula (Sicily and Sardinia are not included) is divided into eight parts. The first two deal, respectively, with general information – from travelling to shopping and even buying a house – and a survey of history and art. Part three is devoted to Rome, and the remaining sections concern the seven regions involved, in the following order: Latium; Campania; Calabria and the Basilicata; Abruzzo and Molise; and Apulia. At the end of the volume there is a glossary on architectural, artistic and historical terms. A chronology table and a list of useful Italian words (with emphasis on Italian menus) is also provided.

93 **Italy: a grand tour for the modern traveller.**
Charles FitzRoy. London: Macmillan, 1991. 313p. 1 map. bibliog.

Richard Lassels, a Roman Catholic priest, made several journeys to Italy between 1637 and 1663, acting as a tutor to various noblemen. FitzRoy follows Lassels's main route. In between chapters which deal with regions and wide areas, there are sections focusing on the four main cities of the tour: Florence; Rome; Naples; and Venice. A high degree of selectivity is therefore applied, with a declared emphasis on 'the places which seem to represent the abundance of culture in Italy'. This is systematically accompanied by observations on Italian art history, as noted and described by past travellers. Characteristic shops and restaurants – of today's Italy – are also mentioned with some details. The book is written in a lively style and interspersed with pleasant light drawings of monuments, urban scenes and landscapes. The author adds perceptive comments on the diversity of Italian culture.

94 **Italian journeys.**
Jonathan Keates. London: Picador, 1992. 312p.

Here is a book which is difficult to put down once you have started reading it. It is a captivating collection of thoughtful observations inspired by places and people up and down the Italian peninsula. True to the author's intention, 'this book makes travellers in Italy think, look and listen somewhat more carefully'. In some chapters Keates wanders from place to place in his relentless search for historical and cultural connections, with continuous references to his own experience. In other instances, the narrative is more focused on certain cities or regions such as Venice and Umbria. From single episodes the author sometimes raises his prose to instructive generalizations, such as 'English attitudes towards Italy show a remarkably sturdy refusal to accept the almost total reversal of socio-economic realities which has taken place during the half-century since Mussolini's overthrow'. The work was first published by Heinemann in 1991.

95 **Florence: a literary companion.**
Francis King. London: John Murray, 1991. 242p. 1 map. bibliog.

King offers a vivid picture of Florence through a wide-ranging selection of passages by famous writers who have visited the city and described its buildings and places, as well as their own sentiments and the attitudes of the Florentines. The first part is devoted to such visitors as Montaigne, Lassels, Milton, Evelyn and Addison, in earlier centuries, to Aldous Huxley, Harold Acton, Bernard Berenson, Sinclair Lewis and Violet Trefusis, in the 20th century. The second, larger part of the work discusses places of interest in Florence and its environs. The most quoted writers are Arnold Bennett, the Brownings, Lord Byron, Dickens, George Eliot, the Hawthornes, Henry James, John Ruskin and Stendhal. Black-and-white illustrations of places, monuments and writers are included.

96 Venice: a literary companion.
Ian Littlewood: John Murray, 1991. 260p. 8 maps.

This guide-book takes the visitor on a tour of the streets, squares and bridges of Venice, through the eyes of previous writers who have put down on paper their impressions and observations of the city. Familiar churches, palaces and canals are considered only in passing, since Littlewood and the literary witnesses he quotes are more interested in the elusive aspects of Venice and its inhabitants. The chapters are arranged in the form of five walks through the quarters of the city and one short cruise to neighbouring islands. The more frequently quoted authors are: William Beckford, Robert Browning, Lord Byron, Giacomo Casanova, Thomas Coryate, Théofile Gautier, W. D. Howells, Henry James, Frederick Rolfe, John Ruskin, George Sand and Percy B. Shelley. The work contains black-and-white illustrations.

97 Venice.
Jan Morris.   London; Boston, Massachusetts: Faber & Faber, 1993.
3rd rev. ed. 320p. 2 maps.

First published in 1960 under the name of James Morris, this is arguably the best descriptive book in English on Venice. It is an absorbing travellers' account in which historical and cultural references and perceptive observations are blended in a most vivid narrative style. Between a brief historical and geographical introduction and conclusive, general reflections on the allure of Venice, the main body of the book consists of three parts. The first examines the variety and character of the people who inhabit this amazing city, with some emphasis on pageantry, devotion and minorities. The second part is dedicated to Venice itself: her monuments; canals; celebrated 'stones' and 'bestiary'; social organization; wealth of oriental adornments; and other curiosities. The last part explores the setting of the lagoon and the surrounding islands and it is here that the 'half melancholic' nature of Venice – in Morris's view – is more forcefully noticeable. There is a concise chronology of Venice's history.

98 Venice: a travellers' companion.
Selected and introduced by John Julius Norwich.   London: Constable, 1990. 427p. 1 map. bibliog.

This is an illustrated collection of over 200 literary accounts of Venice and the Venetians, preceded by a historical introduction. The oldest piece is from a letter by the praetorian prefect of King Theodoric the Ostrogoth,˙AD 523, and among the most recent entries are excerpts from Jan Morris's celebrated *Venice* (q.v.). The majority of documents, however, belong to the last couple of centuries. The material is divided into two parts and arranged in topical sections. The first part covers the city itself: its early centuries and first impressions; the Doge's palace; St Mark's Basilica and square; the Rialto, palaces and hotels; the Riva; the Arsenal; the Ghetto; the Grand Canal, minor canals and gondolas; the lagoon; and the islands. The second part deals with life and social customs in the city, reflecting in particular: music; courtesans;

eating and drinking; and ceremonies. Poems dedicated to Venice, by Wordsworth and Byron conclude this literary journey.

99   The bandit on the billiard table: a journey through Sardinia.

Alan Ross.   London: Collins, 1989. 3rd ed. 207p. 1 map.

One of the rare travel books to be written on Sardinia, this is an account of a summer's journey and a memorable evocation of the island, its people and history. The author recalls the famous people who have visited it or lived there, and vividly describes Garibaldi's life on the tiny island of Caprera (just off the northern coast of Sardinia), and the visits of Admiral Nelson and Napoleon. There is also a sympathetic account of the customs and festivals of the people in the interior, the art of Romanesque churches, and a history of the island's colonizers from the Carthaginians, Romans, Vandals, Moors, and Aragonese, to the Savoy monarchy.

100   Naples: a travellers' companion.

Selected and introduced by Desmond Seward.   London: Constable, 1984. 315p. bibliog.

This is a guide to the Naples that was once a royal capital, which employs a wide selection of excerpts from classic and lesser-known writings. These range from mediaeval chronicles to a lament of 1863 for the demise of the Kingdom of the Two Sicilies. The first main section is dedicated to various monuments and districts of Naples, and contains pieces by writers such as Jacob Burkhardt, Pietro Giannone, Wolfgang Goethe, Lady Morgan and Sacheverell Sitwell. The second section covers the area surrounding Naples, with extracts, among others, from John Evelyn (on the Vesuvius) and Henry Swinburne (on Portici). The final section depicts the life, customs and morals of the city, and includes pieces by Augustus Hare (on the 'king of thieves') and L. Collison-Morley (on the *camorra* in the Bourbon period). A list of Neapolitan sovereigns and a chronology complete the book, which is further enhanced by fine illustrations.

101   Florence: city of the lily.

Christopher Stace, illustrated by Philip O'Reilly.   London: J. M. Dent & Sons, 1989. 303p. 3 maps.

The author confesses that '[he] went for a month's holiday [to Florence], and began the search of a lifetime'. Sometimes along the road he decided to put his thoughts down on paper, and the result is a passionate, fascinating exploration of Florence through a continuous intimate dialogue with himself – in near-diary form – as confronted with works of art, historical references, beautiful buildings, churches and museums, river banks and other enchanting sites. Observations on people in the streets (and their suggestive relations to paintings) are interspersed, together with descriptions of menus appreciated in various restaurants of the 'city of flowers'.

102   America's Rome: vol. 2: Catholic and contemporary Rome.

William L. Vance.   New Haven, Connecticut; London: Yale University Press, 1989. 498p. 2 maps. bibliog.

This is a book as much about America as it is about Rome; the first volume, which dealt with classical Rome, was the same. Modern Rome is explored here through the eyes of American writers, painters and sculptors, although the impossibility of reducing such varied experiences to an 'American' view of Rome is emphasized. Dividing the text into two parts, Vance first examines the representations of Rome as the centre of Catholicism, and then considers 'Victorian Americans and Baroque Rome', which is particularly interesting. The focus moves to contemporary Rome, with a robust section on the period between 1830 and 1945 (including pages on the last days of Papal Rome; and Rome of the House of Savoy: Mussolini's balcony), and a final section on the post-war years, including extensive references to works of fiction, poems and paintings. There are few illustrations, but those that are included are attractive, with the reproduction in colour of significant paintings.

103 **Rome: a literary companion.**

John Varriano.   London: John Murray, 1991. 278p. 10 maps. bibliog.

The work starts with an introduction on the 'lure of Rome', its massive literary legacy and some of its problems (for instance, the reader is told that 'Casanova was sexually assaulted by a policeman in 1761'). Informative descriptions and well-chosen quotations are included in the ten chapters which constitute the book, each of them representing a recommended walk. The first itinerary, from Piazza Venezia to the Capitoline Hill and the Imperial Forums, includes excerpts from such divers writers as the Marquis de Sade, Henry James, Dickens and Byron. The last walk is from the Tiber, past the Castel Sant'Angelo, to the Vatican, with quotations from Frances Trollope, Benvenuto Cellini, Mark Twain, John Updike, Oscar Wilde, Thomas Mann, Thomas Hardy, and several others. All the main sites are included in the walks, and some less obvious places are also explored, such as the Ghetto and the Protestant Cemetery.

Flora and Fauna

104 **A field guide to reptiles and amphibians of Britain and Europe.**
E. N. Arnold, J. A. Burton, illustrations by D. W. Ovenden. London:
Collins, 1980. 272p. maps. bibliog.

The introduction to this work deals with the biology of reptiles and amphibians and
their relationship to man. One section of the introduction is devoted to snake bites and
their treatment. The book deals, in specific sections, with salamanders and newts,
frogs and toads, tortoises, terrapins and sea turtles, lizards and amphisbaeanians
(worm lizards) and snakes. A chapter is devoted to the identification of amphibian
eggs and amphibian larvae. Each species or variety is treated succinctly in the text
which provides information on the areas where they can be found and their habitats,
colour, measurements, feeding and other distinctive features. A glossary and a
bibliography with reference to individual countries are provided. For Italy reference
is made to: L. Capocaccia, *Anfibi e rettili* (Amphibians and reptiles), Milan:
Mondadori, 1968; and S. Bruno, 'Anfibi e rettili di Sicilia' (Amphibians and reptiles
of Sicily), in *Atti dell'Accademia Gioenia di scienze naturali in Catania* (Proceedings
of the Accademia Gioenia of natural science in Catania), 1970, 7th ed., p. 1-144. Distribution maps and an index of Latin and English names complete the volume.

105 **Mediterranean wild flowers.**
Marjorie Blamey, Christopher Grey-Wilson. London: HarperCollins,
1993. 560p. maps.

A valuable guide which claims to be the first to describe and illustrate all the wild
flowers of the islands and all coastal regions of the Mediterranean from sea-level up
to 1,000 metres. The introduction outlines the book structure, the main habitats and
climates and this is followed by the texts which describe over 2,500 species and
varieties. The colour paintings of over 1,500 flowers were produced especially for this
book by Marjorie Blamey. A full index completes the volume.

106   **Serpenti d'Italia.** (Italian snakes.)
       Silvio Bruno.   Florence: Giunti, 1984. 188p. maps. bibliog.

This is a clear guide to the habitat, life and feeding habits of Italian snakes, and a useful book for their recognition. It is illustrated with both clear drawings and colour photographs and numerous tables are provided which show the distribution of reptiles. Also included are some maps of Italy which indicate the location of various snakes, from the harmless grass snake to the most poisonous viper. In the section on adders, clear information is provided about different types of poisons and antidotes.

107   **Animali e sentieri.** (Animals and footpaths.)
       Stefano Camanni, Luca Rossi, Gianni Valente.   Turin: Edizioni CDA, 1991. 236p. bibliog.

Essentially, this is a practical guide to the itineraries and the recognition of animals in Italian mountains, especially in the Alps, but also in Sardinia (where one can find the *muflone*, a rare type of mountain goat) and in some of the Italian natural parks. Both mammals and birds are described and well illustrated in colour and reasonable details are provided on habitats and other relevant areas.

108   **Butterflies and day-flying moths of Britain and Europe.**
       Michael Chinery.   London: Collins, 1989. 316p. (Collins New Generation Guide).

Chinery has included extensive information on all of the 360 European butterflies and 260 day-flying moths. This covers their: identification; characteristics; habitats; flight times; food plants; times of appearance of the egg; larva and pupa; as well as their range and status. The book is illustrated with over 1,500 colour paintings of every identified stage in the life-cycle of the butterfly or moth.

109   **Insects of Britain and Western Europe.**
       Michael Chinery.   London: Collins, 1986. Reprinted, 1993. 319p. (Collins Pocket Guides).

A general introduction begins this guidebook, followed by a key to identification, with drawings and a full description of insects, arranged scientifically from silverfish to beetles and 'covering all orders found in Europe' (listed on p. 11). It is noted that insects like Mantis, cicadas, crickets and certain types of flies and butterflies are more widespread in Italy than in Britain. The book contains over 2,300 illustrations.

110   **Ornitologia italiana.** (Italian ornithology.)
       Ettore Arrigoni Degli Oddi.   Milan: Hoepli, 1929. 1,046p. bibliog.

At the beginning of this volume there is an extensive bibliography of over 120 pages. As well as mainland Italy, the book also covers territories such as Corsica, Malta and Nizza, which are obviously important for many bird species. After a general introduction to the structure, life and migration of birds, the second part is devoted to a detailed description of orders and families of Italian birds. Descriptions are frequently accompanied by drawings and by notes on habits, types of song, nesting and food. All entries are consecutively numbered. At the end of the book there are detailed indexes which precede an appendix of thirty-five colour plates.

111   **I pesci d'acqua dolce in Italia: morfologia, distribuzione, pesca.**
(Fresh-water fish in Italy: morphology, distribution and fishing.)
Roberto De Vitalis, Gian Domenico Bocchi.   Florence: Editoriale
Olimpia, 1987. 100p.

A starting point for the study of fresh-water fish and a guide to the recognition of
numerous species. After an introduction and a historical section containing some
information on fossil fish, there is a key to identification. Each colour table represents
three types of the illustrated fish at three different stages of development. The tables
are neat and the explanation of habitat and other features is clear and well written.
The Latin and Italian names of fish are provided, both in the text and in the index.

112   **Enciclopedia agraria italiana.** (Italian agricultural encyclopaedia.)
Federazione Italiana dei Consorzi Agrari.   Rome: Ramo Editoriale
degli Agricoltori, 1952-85. 12 vols. + index.

Because of the many different areas covered by 'agriculture' an encyclopaedia of this
nature includes detailed information on plants, fruit and animals. This includes, of
course, their use as food, as in the case of *abbacchio*, which is a regional term used in
the area of Rome to indicate a 20-25 days' old lamb, and which otherwise indicates
roast lamb. Plants, agricultural technology, history, chemical substances used in
agriculture, insects, pests and the use of water resources; this and much more emerge
from just one volume.

113   **Fiori delle Alpi.** (Flowers of the Alps.)
Luigi Fenaroli.   Florence: Giunti, 1986. 158p. maps. bibliog.

This work forms part of a series by the same author, a specialist on Italian botany.
The book is relatively slim, but highly informative on the origin and genesis of wild
flowers found in the Italian Alps, an area which is still particularly rich in pastures
and grassland. Some maps of northern Italy show the distribution of specific species.
It is a well-illustrated and reliable guidebook.

114   **Guida pratica ai fiori spontanei in Italia.** (A practical guidebook to
Italian wild flowers.)
Italian edition by Carlo Ferrari.   [Rome]: Selezione del Reader's
Digest, 1993. 447p.

This is a very detailed volume, lavishly illustrated and with a scientific description
and classification of wild flowers in Italy. It is one of the most comprehensive and
reliable guidebooks on the subject and aids in the recognition, classification and
distribution of a large variety of flowers, including ones growing in different climates,
such as the Alps or the shores of Italian islands.

115   **The Alpine flowers of Britain and Europe.**
Christopher Grey-Wilson.   London: Collins, 1979. Reprinted, 1992.
384p. 3 maps. bibliog.

The introduction is accompanied by maps showing the areas where Alpine plants
grow, which apart from Scotland and Wales, The Pyrenees and the Alps, include
mountain zones of the central Apennines in Italy. This is a comprehensive and
authoritative guide to the recognition and the classification of mountain flora.

Different types of flowers are schematically illustrated at the beginning of the book with bright colour drawings. Each page of text is illustrated on the facing page with detailed drawings.

116 **Where to watch birds in Italy.**
Lega Italiana Protezione Uccelli, co-ordinated by Marco Gustin, Barbara Lombatti, Marco Lambertini, translated by Barbara Lombatti with additional help from Ugo Faralli. London: Christopher Helm, 1994. 224p. maps. bibliog.

The LIPU is the Italian League for the Protection of Birds and it must be one of the very few such organizations to have a branch in the United Kingdom. This book is the guide for those who are interested in birdwatching in Italy: it lists 103 major sites and 61 sub-sites contained within them. The book opens with a general introduction on birdwatching in Italy and clear instructions on how to use the map with numbered sites. The actual sites are then described under the administrative region they are in, from Val d'Aosta to Calabria, Sardinia and Sicily. In each section information about the habitat, species, access, calendar and useful contacts are provided. An index to species and by site number (as indicated in the map of Italy at the beginning of the volume) completes the book which is illustrated only with black-and-white drawings.

117 **Mammals of Britain and Europe.**
David Macdonald, Priscilla Barrett. London: HarperCollins, 1993. 312p. maps.

This book claims to be the first 'to describe authoritatively all the species of mammals found in Europe and the seas around it'. The texts provide information on each species, such as: the colour; form; habitat; measurements; breeding; and behaviour. Bats are dealt with in a specific table. The book is illustrated with 64 colour plates and over 600 individual paintings of the animals, their tracks, nests, and feeding. In the description of mammal orders information about distribution is provided in small maps. It is therefore relatively easy to identify areas in Italy which host specific mammals (like the pine martens).

118 **Birds of Britain and Europe.**
Roger Tory Peterson, Guy Mountfort, P. A. D. Hollom. London: Collins, 1993. 5th ed. 261p. 366 maps.

This is a comprehensive guide for ornithologists, and has a very full and accurate text, completely rewritten for this edition. There are numerous maps in the appendix which show the distribution of some bird species. The maps allow the reader to identify the birds and areas in Italy where they can be found.

119 **Mushrooms and other fungi of Great Britain and Europe.**
Roger Phillips. London: Pan Books, 1983 (reprint). 287p. bibliog.

This is an excellent book on the subject, with a general introduction to the appearance and structure of fungi, and detailed information on their colour, stem, spores, gills or pores, indicative measurements, habitat and season. A clear indication of poisonous or edible fungi is also provided. There are approximately 900 colour photographs, mostly taken by the author, to illustrate specimens at different angles and sometimes at different stages of development. There are only a few mushrooms which exist solely in Italy and continental Europe, such as Caesar's mushroom, the *Amanita caesarea* which looks like an egg when closed or half-open, and which is commonly known as *ovolo* (little egg) in Italy.

120   **Flora d'Italia.** (Italian Flora.)
      Sandro Pignatti.   Bologna: Edagricole, 1982. 3 vols. maps. bibliog.
A fundamental descriptive book, this includes all the more developed plants (vascular plants) of Italy. It is aimed not only at specialists but at a variety of readers and was compiled over a long period and completed in twenty-five years. The three volumes include 5,599 items. Each entry provides detailed information about the morphology, habitat and ecology of the plant, frequently furnishing very interesting information about the history of a specific plant. For example, the now ubiquitous *Robinia pseudoacacia* was imported from America to France by Robin, the King's gardener, in 1601, and by 1662 it was being cultivated in the botanic gardens at Padua. Each entry is accompanied by detailed drawings, frequently of the stem, leaves and fruit or seed of the plant, and by small maps of Italy showing the distribution of the variety described. The volumes are completed by detailed indexes providing Latin and Italian names of all plants. The progressive numbering of entries was carried out with a view to a potential computerized usage of this Flora which supersedes all previous ones.

121   **Guida alla natura della Sardegna: flora, fauna, itinerari segreti.**
      (A guide to Sardinian nature: flora, fauna, secret itineraries.)
      Fulco Pratesi, Franco Tassi.   Milan: Mondadori, 1984. 3rd ed. 320p.
      maps.
In the 18th century a Jesuit scientist declared that 'in Italy one cannot find what exists in Sardinia and vice-versa'. The peculiar character of the island is underlined in this guidebook which was written with the collaboration of the World Wildlife Fund. Therefore, the rarity of certain animals (such as those inhabiting marine caves) and the peculiarity of Sardinian geology are underlined. Each region of Sardinia is then described and the plants and animals typical of that region are illustrated with drawings and colour photographs. The guidebook begins in north-western Sardinia, than deals with the east and the south. In an appendix there is a discussion of the major threats affecting natural resources in Sardinia, such as industry, hunting and poaching, urbanization and tourism. A list of the animals which have disappeared or are at present in danger of becoming extinct (like the Mediterranean seal) is provided at the end of the book.

122   **I funghi italiani.** (Italian mushrooms.)
      Nando Togni.   Modena: A. P. S., 1989. 370p. bibliog.
Mushroom collecting can be a difficult activity in Italy since many woods are either private property or are covered by local bye-laws which require the would-be collector to have a special identity card and to have paid a fee. There are many books on mushrooms and in this one Togni offers a general introduction to larger fungi, followed by a good description of species and suggestions for the cooking of edible ones. Unfortunately the illustrations are provided by sketches and drawings in the text, although colour tables are included in an appendix.

123   **La Flora.** (Italian Flora.)
Touring Club Italiano.   Milan: Touring Club Italiano, 1958. 272p.
maps. bibliog.

The second volume in a series entitled 'Conosci l'Italia' (Know Italy) by the Italian Touring Club. After a general introduction on botany and plant structure, the book deals with trees, bushes and flowers of Italy, organized in a geographical manner, according to region. A short section on fungi and mushrooms is also provided. The text was written by numerous specialists, and it provides a reliable introduction to the subject. The book is illustrated with 195 maps and drawings, 199 black-and-white photographs and 260 in colour.

124   **La Fauna.** (Italian Fauna.)
Touring Club Italiano.   Milan: Touring Club Italiano, 1959. 272p.
maps. bibliog.

This is the third volume in a series entitled 'Conosci l'Italia' (Know Italy), published by the Italian Touring Club, which included one volume each on the physical aspects of the country, its flora and its fauna. After an introduction on animal classification, this volume deals with: the fauna of the Alps (found both on land and in water); the terrestrial fauna of mountains and plains including birds; animals in a human environment, such as insects found in cultivated soil, parasites, and animals found in houses; underground animals; the fauna of marine shores; and marine animals, including the now rare monk seal *Monachus monachus*. Two final chapters are devoted to the origins of the Italian fauna (palaeofauna) and the measures taken for the protection of rare species in Italy. This authoritative but readable book is written by specialists (mentioned in the preface by the Touring Club Chairman) and is illustrated with 361 maps and drawings, 237 black-and-white photographs, and 252 in colour.

125   **Flora italica.** (Italian flora.)
Pietro Zangheri.   Padua: Cedam, 1976. 2 vols. bibliog.

The aim of this work is to facilitate the identification of Italian plants, especially those which are native to the country. It uses technical terms but these are properly explained in the introductory section in a special glossary. Individual plants are described under each family in the first volume which includes a detailed index of Latin and Italian names of plants. The second volume includes 210 tables with drawings of leaves, flowers, fruit and stem, made by the author.

Italian waters pilot.
See item no. 50.

History

General

126   Dictionary of modern Italian history.
Edited by Frank J. Coppa.   Westport, Connecticut; London:
Greenwood Press, 1985. 497p.

As the editor states in the preface, 'this volume surveys in alphabetical order the chief
events, personalities, institutions, systems, and problems of Italy from the eighteenth
century to the present'. As a general aid to the reader, the dictionary contains an
introduction outlining the five periods considered (the 18th century, 1800-61, 1861-
1922, 1922-45, and 1945-84) and five appendices: a chronology of important events;
the list of prime ministers of Piedmont and Italy; the presidents of the Italian republic;
the kings of Piedmont (from Emmanuel Philibert) and Italy; and the Popes (18th
century to the present). This is a useful volume for quick reference and altogether
contains 754 entries, most of them corresponding to personalities throughout history.
This is an invaluable source of information, despite the bias in favour of Italo-
Americans, or US-based Italians.

127   A concise history of Italy.
Christopher Duggan.   Cambridge, England; New York; Melbourne:
Cambridge University Press, 1994. 320p. 6 maps. bibliog.

This is a fine introduction to today's Italy from an historical point of view. It is a
readable survey of the country and contains a well-organized wealth of details,
through which runs a stimulating thread: the Italian search for a national identity. An
original first chapter provides the key-note to this approach, by examining 'the
geographical determinants of disunity'. The next two chapters offer a succinct
account of what happened from the fall of the Roman Empire to the time of the
French Revolution. The last two centuries are considered in a much more detailed
manner in six chapters, from the formation of a united Italy to the present
predicament of the Italian Republic. On this topic, Duggan concludes with pessimism,

'it was far from clear in 1993 upon what basis the pieces could be put together again'. The book is enriched by a range of illustrations and statistical tables.

128 **Italy: a short history.**
Harry Hearder.   Cambridge, England; New York; Port Chester, Melbourne; Sydney: Cambridge University Press, 1990. 285p. 7 maps. bibliog.

A valuable synthesis of Italian history, from prehistoric times to the late 1980s, Hearder describes this work as an 'heir' to his (and Daniel Waley's) old *Short history of Italy*. The nine readable chapters are arranged in strict chronological order and are clearly indicative of their topics: Italy in the classical world; the early Middle Ages; the high Middle Ages; the Renaissance; the political and cultural eclipse (covering, perhaps too abruptly, the 16th and 17th centuries); the *Risorgimento* (1790-1861); from unification to fascism (1861-1922); fascism (1922-45); and Italy since World War II (1945-89). The events of the early 1990s have tested Hearder's final sentence, compressing his positive view of Italian and European history: 'it is unlikely that [Italy] will fail to contribute greatly to a Europe which may well be on the threshold of a brilliant new era'.

129 **A travellers' history of Italy.**
Valerio Lintner.   Aldlestrop, England: The Windrush Press, 1989. 278p. 5 maps. bibliog.

Intended for holiday-makers and travellers who wish to know more about the country they are visiting, the main body of this comprehensive text offers a historical survey of the Italian peninsula from the ancient times to the fascist era and post-war Italy. Lintner provides a lucid and readable account, accompanied by numerous illustrations and maps. In the coverage of contemporary Italy the author focuses on the economic advance, but also emphasizes the persistent shortcomings. In particular, he refers to the huge budget deficit, the regional imbalances, the mafia, and the old paradoxes and problems of the political system. Appendices include: lists of Roman emperors, popes, emperors, Neapolitan kings and Venetian doges of the Renaissance; artists; heads of State, popes and prime ministers of united Italy; a chronology of major events; election results (1946-87); and a glossary of the main cities and places of interest cited in the text.

130 **The Italian world: history, art and the genius of a people.**
Edited by John Julius Norwich.   London: Thames & Hudson, 1983. 268p. 4 maps.

This is a lavishly-illustrated account of the journey through history, from the pre-Roman Italian peninsula to the present, with texts by leading historians. The editor provides an overview of the Italian cultural achievement in his introduction. The titles of the following six chapters indicate the period to which they refer and its connotation: Rome and the Empire: prehistory to AD 500 (K. Christ); The medieval centuries: 500-1350 (B. Ward-Perkins); Humanism and Renaissance: 1350-1527 (J. R. Hale); Disaster and recovery: 1527-1750 (E. Cochrane); The age of romanti-cism: 1750-1860 (F. Haskell); and Modern Italy (F. Andreucci). This is both an enjoyable survey and an effective introductory guide to more specific interests on Italian culture. A balance is struck between the social and economic characteristics, and the cultural achievement in each section, with the exception of the last chapter, in which the focus is on political and social development.

131 **History of the Italian people.**
Giuliano Procacci, translated by Anthony Paul. Harmondsworth, England: Penguin, 1986. 478p.

First published in Italian in 1968, this concise book has appeared in English in various editions since 1970. In his introduction Procacci writes that, on the one hand, Italy's long and varied history 'has contributed to the formation and development of modern European civilization', but on the other hand, he also points out that as a result of all the political upheavals and reverses, Italians have acquired patience and endurance – some may add cynicism. From this dual perspective Procacci unfolds, in a superb synthesis, one thousand years of Italian history, commencing with the self-governing cities of the 11th century, through to the Renaissance ('Greatness and decadence'), the Age of Reform, Romanticism and the *Risorgimento*, the 'difficult take-off' at the turn of the century, fascism, and finally to 'post-war hopes and frustrations'. This is an invaluable introduction to Italian history.

132 **Italy in the last fifteen hundred years: a concise history.**
Reinhold Schumann. Lanham, Maryland; New York; London: University Press of America, 1992. 2nd ed. 397p. 7 maps. bibliog.

This is an impressive historical synthesis, packed with events and always accompanied by perceptive comments. Part one surveys over six centuries, from the end of the Roman Empire to the age of the Communes and Crusades. Part two reaches into the high Renaissance, in the middle of the 16th century and part three explores the centuries of decline, with an emphasis on the 18th century, from the enlightenment to Italy under Napoleon. Part four considers the last two centuries, from the *Risorgimento* to fascism and post-war democracy. At the end of each part a chapter is devoted to relevant achievements in the arts, political thought and economic development. An epilogue discusses the last twenty years, from terrorism to the transformation of the Communist Party into the Democratic Party of the Left. There is a useful chronology and the genealogies of some famous families are included in their appropriate sections.

Ancient

133 **Archaeology and Italian society: prehistoric, Roman and Medieval studies.**
Edited by Graeme Barker, Richard Hodges. British Archaeological Reports, International Series, no. 102. Papers in Italian Archaeology, 1981. 342p.

This is a collection of papers presented at a seminar on Italian archaeology held in February 1980 at Sheffield University. The volume contains twenty-seven different reports divided into three main sections: Artefact analysis: social and economic reconstruction; Site and settlement interpretation; and Regional and landscape studies. Some papers deal specifically with trade (such as L. H. Barfield, 'Patterns of North Italian trade 5000-2000 BC', H. Blake, 'Pottery exported from Northwest Italy between 1450 and 1830: Savona, Albisola, Genoa, Pisa and Montelupo'). Papers in sections two and three are mostly on Rome, central and southern Italy. Numerous drawings complement the volume.

134 **Landscape and society: prehistoric central Italy.**
Graeme Barker. London; New York; Toronto; Sydney; San
Francisco: Academic Press, 1981. 281p. 20 maps. bibliog.
The stability of central Italy for such a long period is at the heart of the author's preoccupations; he says in the preface: 'at the least this book is a reasonably comprehensive collection of facts and figures about prehistoric societies in central Italy'. After an introduction to the changes in landscape in early Italy and a review of the neolithic settlements in central Italy (5000-3000 BC), this book deals with neolithic settlements (3000-2000 BC), with the problem of immigration from the eastern Mediterranean, and goes on to discuss the bronze age (2000-1000 BC). Part two covers 'Approaches to prehistoric life' and technology and subsistence. The book is illustrated with sketches of many stone, metal and pottery artefacts, and with numerous clear maps and tables.

135 **Who was who in the Roman world, 753 B.C.-A.D. 476.**
Edited by Diana Bowder. Oxford: Phaidon Press, 1980. 257p. 6 maps.
bibliog.
Famous and not so famous names make up this illustrated encyclopaedia of Romans and people connected with them. The first person to appear is Ablabius, 'Praetorian prefect, A.D. 329-37', and the last is Zenobia, 'Queen of Palmyra, circa A.D. 266-73'. The longest entries are those on Augustus, 'Octavian, 63 B.C.-A.D. 14' and Caesar, 'Gaius Julius, 100-44 B.C.', with two and a half columns each. The shortest entry, with only three lines, is devoted to Amandus, 'Gallic usurper, circa A.D. 286'. Virtually anyone who was somebody falls between these two extremes. Each entry, however small, is completed with references to sources. Useful graphs on the main dynasties are provided at the end of the volume.

136 **Ancient Italy before the Romans.**
A. C. Brown. Oxford: Ashmolean Museum, 1980. 86p. maps. bibliog.
(by D. Ridgway).
This booklet admirably illustrates the findings of ancient Italy from around 3000 BC to 30 BC. It is clearly written, informative, up to date and reliable. Based mainly on archaeological material existing in the Ashmolean Museum, Oxford, it also contains precise references to Italian discoveries.

137 **The houses of Roman Italy, 100 B.C.-A.D. 250: ritual, space, and decoration.**
John R. Clarke. Berkeley, California; Oxford: University of
California Press, 1991. 411p. 3 maps. bibliog.
One objective of this book is to put Roman interior decoration back into context. This involves a detailed description of mosaic floors, painted walls and ceilings,

emphasizing the role of such an ensemble in the overall plan of the house. Another aim is 'to document, through descriptions, photographs, and drawings, wall paintings and mosaics that future generations will probably never see', because of the destructive results of excavations, let alone natural disasters, such as the 1980 earthquake. After two general chapters which cover the whole period, the book is divided into sections in roughly chronological order. The book contains many illustrations and a glossary.

138 **The Roman empire: economy, society and culture.**
Peter Garnsey, Richard Saller.   London: Duckworth, 1987. 231p.
1 map. bibliog.

Garnsey and Saller have divided the book into four parts. The first focuses on the importance of the Mediterranean as the basis for the Roman Empire, which was built with a small amount of bureaucracy and concerned with the essentials: 'the maintenance of law and order, and the collection of taxes'. Part two, which covers the economy (chapter three 'An underdeveloped economy'), land use and management, discusses the needs of the city of Rome, whose approximately one million residents at the time of Augustus, are described in terms of consumers and suppliers. Part three deals with the organization of society and the family and part four with religion and culture. After the extensive bibliography a list of Roman emperors is provided.

139 **The history of the decline and fall of the Roman Empire.**
Edward Gibbon, with an introduction by Hugh Trevor-Roper.
London: Everyman's Library, 1993. 6 vols. maps.

Described at one time as a bridge that carried the reader from the ancient to the modern world, this is a new edition of the well-known (if not well-read) historical and literary masterpiece. The first volume appeared in 1776, the next two volumes in 1781, and the last three in 1788. The enlightened spirit of that age pervades this work throughout and civic ethos and free institutions are shown to be the preconditions to material and spiritual progress. This monumental study can be divided into two parts. The first deals with the fluctuations and developments of the Roman Empire, from AD 180 to its dissolution (in the West) in 476. The second half portrays in broad strokes the following one thousand years, up until the collapse of the eastern branch of the old empire. A masterly epilogue examines mediaeval Rome and the dawn of the Renaissance. Equally memorable, in the first volume, are the two chapters on the rise of Christianity. Here, in his sagacious and elegant prose, Gibbon wrote that 'the Christians, in the course of their intestine dissensions, have inflicted far greater severities on each other than they had experienced from the zeal of the infidels'.

140 **Cities of Vesuvius: Pompeii and Herculaneum.**
Michael Grant.   London: Weidenfeld & Nicolson, 1971. 240p. maps.
bibliog.

A popular history and description of the towns destroyed by Vesuvius. The narrative begins with an examination of the people, and the way they were found after excavation, frozen in their daily activities and in an attempt to escape from vulcanic ash and fumes. It then deals with public and private buildings, paintings, mosaics and furniture, farms and trade, public and sexual life.

141 **Crossroads of the Mediterranean: papers delivered at the international conference held at Brown University 1981.**
Edited by T. Hackens, Nancy D. Holloway, R. Ross Holloway.
Providence, Rhode Island: Brown University; Louvain-la-Neuve, Belgium: Université Catholique de Louvain, 1983. 372p. maps.

The volume contains a number of scholarly papers, some of which are extremely lengthy, such as 'Central and southern Italy in the late bronze age' (p. 55-122). The contents of the volume are as follows: S. S. Lukesh, 'Italy and the Apennine cultures'; A. M. Bietti Sestieri, 'Central and southern Italy in the late bronze age'; J. P. Morel, 'Greek colonization in Italy and the West (problems of evidence and interpretation)'; J. de la Genière, 'Contributions to a typology of ancient settlements in southern Italy (9th to 4th centuries BC)'; P. G. Guzzo, 'Lucanian, Brettians and Italiote Greeks in the fourth and third centuries BC'; M. S. Balmuth, 'Advances in Sardinian archaeology'; E. Nielsen, 'Some observations on early Etruria'; R. Ross Holloway, 'Recent research in prehistoric Sicily'; I. and M. Edlund, 'Sacred and secular: evidence of rural shrines and industry among Greeks and Etruscans'; H. Fracchia, 'Two mythological scenes from Western Lucania'; M. Gualtieri, 'Two Lucanian burials from Roccagloriosa with appendix'; E. Nielsen, 'Speculations on an ivory workshop in the orientalizing period'; P. G. Warden, 'The *colline metallifere*: prolegomena to the study of mineral exploitation in central Italy'; and B. Giletti, 'Ion microprobe analysis of glazes from Megara Hyblea'.

142 **The economy and society of Pompeii.**
William Jongman.   Amsterdam: J. C. Gieben, 1988. 415p. maps.
bibliog.

The city of Pompeii, with 8,000-12,000 inhabitants, represents Roman urbanism at its most impressive. It is therefore chosen here for an in-depth study of its economy, population, production, agriculture and urban manufacturing, such as textiles, as well as of its society and politics. Jongman considers general problems concerning the use of sources and of methodology in a thorough introduction on 'questions and rules'. The book also contains numerous diagrams and black-and-white illustrations, as well as one detachable map.

143 **The anthropology of the Lombards.**
István Kiszely.   B.A.R. International Series (6,I), 1979. 2 vols. in one (translated from the Hungarian). 622p. bibliog.

In the first few pages of this book there is a summary of what is known of the Lombards from the Elbe to Pannonia to Italy. Some of them, according to the author, are still living near Macugnaga in the Mount Rosa area of the Italian Alps and in the Lessini mountains. The rest of the book is devoted to a detailed and specialized study of Lombard graves across Europe and a tabulation of skeletal measurements and data concerning also the average life expectancy of such populations, many members of which died in a violent manner as shown by the fractured skulls. The book concludes with an extensive bibliography.

144   **The first style in Pompeii: painting and architecture.**
Anne Laidlaw.   Rome: Giorgio Bretschneider, 1985. 358p. bibliog.

A record of approximately 400 examples of first style (the style of Pompeian decoration that imitates masonry, usually painted in various colours) mural decoration in Pompeii 'based on a study of 180 buildings that have, or once had, such decorations'.

145   **The mute stones speak: the story of archaeology in Italy.**
Paul MacKendrick.   New York; London: W. W. Norton, 1983.
2nd ed. 491p. maps. bibliog.

A well-informed account of Italian archaeological discoveries, especially concerned with Rome and southern Italy. Although the first two chapters discuss prehistoric Italy and the Etruscans, all the remainder revolve around Rome. The chapter titles convey the idea of the 'high popular' style of the book: Early Rome and Latium; Roman colonies in Italy; Nabobs as builders: Sulla, Pompey, Caesar; Augustus: buildings as propaganda; Hypocrite, madman, fool and knave [Tiberius, Caligula, Claudius, Nero]; The victims of Vesuvius; Flavian Rome; Trajan: port, forum, market, baths and column; An emperor-architect: Hadrian; Antonines through Constantine (AD 138-337); and Caesar and Christ. The bibliography is extensive.

146   **Corruption and the decline of Rome.**
Ramsay MacMullen.   New Haven, Connecticut; London: Yale
University Press, 1988. 319p. 1 map. bibliog.

The author does not believe in the notion of a monolithic Roman empire, and pays due attention to regional variations in economic, social and cultural activities. He notes that in some cases, in eastern towns for example, prosperity continued until well into the 4th century AD, and 'decline' is therefore a relative notion. Evidence is gathered and frequently illustrated in statistical diagrams from the number of shipwrecks, type and quantity of amphoras, and similar data. Three appendices deal with 'fourth-century barbarians in the emperor's service', 'Leaders' in the army and bureaucracy, and 'soldiers in cities'. In the latter appendix quotations are collected in order to show that a large number of soldiers were stationed in cities especially after 300 AD.

147   **The Roman port and fishery of Cosa, a center of ancient trade.**
Anna Marguerite McCann, et al.   Princeton, New Jersey: Princeton
University Press, 1987. 353p. maps. bibliog.

A serious and meticulous contribution to the history of ancient harbours. The Roman port of Cosa (Portus Cosanus) was located 138 kilometres north-west of Rome on the Thyrrhenian coast of ancient Etruria, and a Latin colony and port was established there in 280 BC. This book contains a thorough collection of historical and archaeological evidence of the port and of its importance and is illustrated with numerous drawings.

148 **Studies in nuragic archaeology: village excavations at nuraghe Urpes and nuraghe Toscono in west-central Sardinia.**
Edited by Joseph W. Michels, Gary S. Webster. B.A.R. International series, no. 373, 1987. 169p. maps.

This is a detailed description of excavations carried out by the Pennsylvania State University research team since 1982 in two Nuragic villages in Sardinia. It represents a substantial contribution to our knowledge and understanding of the somewhat mysterious stone buildings in the shape of truncated cones which are scattered all over Sardinia. Clear drawings accompany the text.

149 **A history of earliest Italy.**
Massimo Pallottino, translated by Martin Ryle, Kate Soper. London: Routledge, 1991. 206p. 11 maps. bibliog.

This is a major work of synthesis which combines a comprehensive description of events with a critical assessment of the significance of the Italian peninsula and its peoples in the Mediterranean world, during the first millennium BC. One of the main arguments of the book is that regional identities which still characterize Italy had their foundations in pre-Roman times. There are five sections: parts one and two consider the methodological approach and the birth of historical Italy. Part three deals with the period between the 8th and the 5th century BC, which includes the Greek colonization and Etruscan expansion. Part four covers the 5th and 4th centuries BC, and concentrates on the development of Italic peoples while part five explores the Roman unification and the issue of Italic continuity. There is a useful chronology table and several plates.

150 **Roman Italy.**
Timothy W. Potter. London: British Museum Publications, 1987. 240p. 3 maps. bibliog.

This is a highly readable survey of Roman Italy, written by an archaeologist and historian, and with an emphasis on the social rather than the political dimension. It is a successful combination of accessibility and scholarship, which, arranged broadly in chronological order, pays attention to a number of important topics. Two introductory chapters on the land and the pre-Roman populations in the peninsula are followed by a consideration of the rise of Rome, before the author examines: 'cities and urbanisation'; 'villas, farms and the countryside'; 'roads, aqueducts and canals'; 'the balance of trade'; and 'gods and their temples'. Finally, two chapters deal with later Roman Italy, the rise of Christianity and the aftermath of Roman civilization. There are many illustrations and a gazetteer of sites to visit throughout the peninsula.

151 **Italy before Rome.**
John Reich. Oxford; Lausanne, Switzerland: Elsevier-Phaidon, 1979. 151p. 7 maps. bibliog.

The volume opens with a chronological table from approximately 900 to 273 BC which provides a clear introduction to archaeological findings in the whole of Italy. Numerous illustrations from Etruscan and other tombs, from wall paintings and from collections of jewels and other items enliven the text. The book concludes with a glossary which provides an explanation of technical terms and of mythological references.

152 Pompeii: an architectural history.

Lawrence Richardson, Jr. London; Baltimore, Maryland: Johns Hopkins University Press, 1988. 445p. 1 map. bibliog.

An authoritative study of the development of architecture in Pompeii. After a preliminary section which deals with the city plan, its fortifications, and its water and sewer systems, part two deals with the tufa period, between 200-80 BC. The third part covers the early Roman Colony, between 80-30 BC, part four discusses the Julio-Claudian buildings of 30 BC-62 AD, and part five considers the period from the earthquake to the eruption in AD 62-79. Each part is organized in a similar fashion and covers: the public buildings; the houses; the villas; and the tombs. The volume concludes with three appendices on the stones and building techniques of Pompeii, with ground plans covering the excavations of Pompeii up until 1969. A glossary and an index are also included.

153 The land of the Etruscans from prehistory to the Middle Ages.

Edited by Salvatore Settis. London: Frederick Muller, 1985. 96p. maps.

This excellent introduction to the area of Italy which roughly corresponds to modern Tuscany, part of Umbria and Latium, contains scholarly and yet straightforward texts. Part of the book is devoted to individual towns and cities, such as Arezzo, Chiusi, Florence, Orvieto, and many more. It provides an account of their archaeological and historical interest, and insets devoted to 'implements, language, religion, agriculture, metallurgy, ceramics and trade'. The book is well illustrated.

154 The Roman world.

Edited by John Wacher. London: Routledge, 1990. 2nd ed. 2 vols. maps. bibliog.

A number of specialists have contributed to this vast enterprise in an attempt to provide the latest information and interpretations concerning the many different aspects of Roman civilization. They begin with an outline of Celtic Europe and progress to the formation of the Roman army, the frontiers, and the cities and villages of the empire. Of particular interest is chapter thirteen, 'Urbanization in Italy and the western empire' which is also illustrated with numerous maps and photographs. Volume two considers rural life, the economy, society, religion and burial, with a chapter on the rise of Christianity and one on burial customs in Rome and the provinces.

Mediaeval

155 Emperor to emperor: Italy before the Renaissance.

Edward Burman. London: Constable, 1991. 288p. 13 maps. bibliog.

This is a selective study of mediaeval Italy which combines scholarship with readability. Part one is entitled 'Benedictine Italy and its enemies, 529-1100' and deals with various invasions and influences, focusing on Lombard Pavia,

Montecassino, Muslim Palermo, Byzantine Bari and Norman Cefalù. Part two covers the following century until the death of Emperor Frederick II in 1250 and is concerned with the new forces which paved the way for the economic achievement of Italy in later centuries. There are also chapters devoted to the maritime republic of Genoa, the rise of the northern *comune* of Cremona, the new religious fervour, and the Emperor Frederick II and his octagonal 'Castel del Monte' in Apulia. A short 'Epilogue, 1250-1300' concludes the work with fascinating observations on the link between mediaeval Italy and the origins of the Renaissance. Drawings, illustrations and a chronology are also included.

156 **Before the Normans: southern Italy in the ninth and tenth centuries.**
Barbara M. Kreutz. Philadelphia: University of Pennsylvania Press, 1991. 228p. 3 maps. bibliog.

The fragmentation of southern Italy in the 9th and 10th centuries was not obliterated by the subsequent intervention of the Normans. As Kreutz notes, 'the modern *regioni* of southern Italy largely replicate the pre-Norman segmentations [. . .] But in addition, and most interesting, within these *regioni* once Lombard, many of today's administrative subdivisions closely correspond to the old Lombard gastaldates'. Such continuity is the result of the tight local control exercised by Lombard rulers, which constitutes the dominant theme of this study. After an introductory chapter which places the study in its historical context, three chapters are devoted to major issues during the 9th century: the first Arab impact; the Carolingian crusade; and the resulting new political configuration. The larger part of the book covers developments in the 10th century, focusing first on Amalfi and Salerno, and then on Campania as a whole. An epilogue provides a projection into the 11th century and beyond.

157 **Italy in the age of Dante and Petrarch, 1216-1380.**
John Larner. London; New York: Longman, 1980. 278p. 4 maps.

An introductory chapter discusses the idea of Italy in the 13th and 14th centuries. The effective starting point is the failure of Frederick II to unite Italy under his crown, and the consequent disintegration of any wider political unity. The narrative then focuses on various aspects of social, economic and cultural life, such as: the family; the nobility; political conflict and party-leaders; the countryside; merchants and workers; food, war, and government; and religious life. The final section returns to a more general narrative and a discussion of the difficult decades between 1340 and 1380; war, famine, and plague occurred at that time, profoundly affecting the population. Nevertheless, the new elite culture of Humanism was triumphing and technological development was not halted. The invention which Larner singles out as a symbol of those decades is the mechanical clock.

158 **Patricians and Popolani.**
Dennis Romano. Baltimore, Maryland; London: The Johns Hopkins University Press, 1987. 220p. bibliog.

Romano deals with the period at the end of the 14th century, and treats themes such as: family structure and marriage ties; the world of work; parochial clergy; neighbourhoods; and patronage. This is a sound social history of Early Renaissance Venice based on first-hand material.

159   **The Italian city-republics.**
       Daniel Waley.   London; New York: Longman, 1988. 3rd ed. 212p.
       2 maps. bibliog.

Originally written as a textbook for school and college students of Italian history and
literature, this volume has become an established work of scholarship, accessible to
general readers for the clarity of the exposition and the stimulating arguments. Waley
deals with the republican city-states in northern and central Italy, between the late
11th and the early 14th century. His book conveys a true picture of the social and
political environment of the independent city-republics, in which 'proximity gave the
population a fundamental and wide community of interest'. A new chapter is added to
this edition, surveying the relevant historiography. Another new feature is the
chronological gazetteer of the major cities and towns. There are also many
illustrations.

Renaissance and modern

160   **The civilization of the Renaissance in Italy.**
       Jacob Burkhardt, translated by S. G. C. Middlemore, with a new
       introduction by Peter Burke and notes by Peter Murray.
       Harmondsworth, England: Penguin, 1990. 389p.

This classic study of the Italian Renaissance first appeared in Germany in 1860 and has
seen many translations and reprints since then. Middlemore's translation is in itself a
classic, as it was produced in 1878, based on the second edition of the book (1869).
This recent edition is commendable for the lucid and stimulating introduction by Peter
Burke, which contains suggestions for further reading. Burke argues that Burkhardt's
work 'has been an inspiration to later cultural historians, despite their rejection of
some of his conclusions'. The book is divided into six parts: 'The State as a work of
art'; 'The development of the individual'; 'The revival of antiquity'; 'The discovery of
the world and of man'; 'Society and festivals'; and 'Morality and religion'.

161   **Life in Italy at the time of the Medici.**
       John Cage.   London: B. T. Batsford; New York: G. P. Putnam's
       Sons, 1968. 207p. 1 map. bibliog.

A highly informative, illustrated survey of the life and manners of Italians during the
15th and 16th centuries, the era of the Renaissance. Political diversity within the
peninsula was reflected in the different systems of money, weights and measures, as
well as in social habits and languages, although Tuscan Italian had come to
predominate among the upper classes. The thirteen chapters of the book concentrate
on such topics as: the aristocracy; the merchants and landowners; the artisans and
artists; the town labourer; the peasant; the Church; education; music and the theatre;
spectacles; sport, games and war; and the role of women. The final section deals with
the establishment of social norms – one of the less tangible but more permanent
products of the Renaissance, which was to set its stamp on the whole of Western
society.

162 **Italy in the age of reason, 1685-1789.**
Dino Carpanetto, Giuseppe Ricuperati, translated by Caroline Higgitt.
London; New York: Longman, 1987. 358p. 2 maps. bibliog.
Part of the Longman History of Italy series edited by Denys Hay, this book is probably the best survey of 18th-century Italy available in English. It is written in a traditional fashion and pays more attention to institutions, state policies and elites, although it does also contain useful information on population, class structure and social change. The emphasis is on the changes and development of intellectual life in all the regional states which made up Italy. The work is divided into six parts dealing, respectively, with: demography, economy, classes and institutions (Carpanetto); political ideas in the first half of the century (Ricuperati); reform policies in that first half (Carpanetto); the transition from the reforms to the crisis of the 'ancien regime' (Carpanetto); the political and economic debates during the Enlightenment (Ricuperati); and the historical debate and the Italian Enlightenment (Ricuperati).

163 **Italy: 1530-1630.**
Eric Cochrane, edited by Julius Kirshner.   London; New York:
Longman, 1988. 313p. 1 map.
The manuscript of this book was almost completed when Cochrane died. Therefore, a projected final chapter and a postscript taking the story up to 1690, were never written. The book begins with the Sack of Rome in 1527, and ends with the trial and condemnation of Galileo in 1633. An enormous scholarly work is contained in the intervening chapters, which places an emphasis on Mannerism, the Tridentine reform of the Catholic Church, the cultural achievement and consolidation of the first decade of the 17th century, and the subsequent destabilization. This is a cultural history of Baroque Italy. The achievements of high Renaissance, and the bold experiments of their Mannerist and early Baroque successors represent the central themes of Cochrane's synthesis. A series of paintings and other works of art are included, together with a map of Italy and an appendix containing tables of succession for the main Italian States.

164 **The cheese and the worms: the cosmos of a sixteenth-century miller.**
Carlo Ginzburg, translated by John Tedeschi, Anne Tedeschi.
Harmondsworth, England: Penguin Books, 1992. 177p.
Originally published in Italian in 1976, this work quickly became a classic, with various editions published in English. It is the story of a trial in late 16th-century Italy of a self-taught, intellectually vivacious miller (Menocchio) who was accused of heresy. His rich imagination combined with a sense of social injustice to produce a subversive and eccentric cosmology. Court records are set in the historical context, and the relationship between high and official learning, popular religion and peasant culture is brilliantly explored. As Ginzburg wrote in his preface to the English edition, the book 'is intended to be a story as well as a piece of historical writing. Thus, it is addressed to the general reader as well as to the specialist'.

165   **The Italian Renaissance in its historical background.**
Denys Hay.   Cambridge, England: Cambridge University Press, 1977.
2nd ed. Reprinted, 1994. 228p. 1 map. bibliog.

This excellent introduction to the Renaissance was first published in 1961. The
current (1994) version is a reprint of the second (1977) edition. The work had its
origin in a series of lectures given at the Queen's University of Belfast, and this has
contributed to the lively and unaffected style in which it is written. Another merit is
the broad historical approach of the study in which a critical evaluation of attitudes
and ideas is combined with a sober assessment of artistic and scientific achievements.
In the revised edition, of which this is the most recent reprint, the scope of the last
chapter was widened, so as to offer more insights into the influence of Renaissance in
England. The early chapter on 'The problems of Italian history' is also of value to
those interested in contemporary Italy. The text contains illustrations, mainly of
works of art.

166   **Italy in the age of the Renaissance, 1380-1530.**
Denys Hay, John Law.   London; New York: Longman, 1989. 372p.
7 maps.

This book deals with a much studied period of Italian history. However, the
precedence here is given to events in the south, the islands and the countryside, thus
redressing the traditional over-emphasis on the urban reality of the peninsula,
especially on Florence and Venice. A historiographical survey and an interesting
section on the images of Italy at that time (seen through both Italian and foreign eyes)
constitute the introductory first part. Part two deals with the central political issue of
the relationship between society, the State and the Church (five chapters), whereas
part three considers the regional histories of the southern, the papal, and the northern
States (four chapters). A shorter final part, in two chapters, surveys learning, the arts
and music. A list of the Popes, from Gregory XI (1370-78) to Clement VII (1523-24)
is included as an appendix, together with genealogical tables of the dynasties ruling
Naples, Sicily, Savoy, Milan and Florence.

167   **Law, family and women: toward a legal anthropology of
Renaissance Italy.**
Thomas Kuehn.   Chicago; London: The University of Chicago Press,
1991. 415p. bibliog.

The result of intensive research, this impressive scholarly work is based on legal
sources of Florentine history and consists of ten self-contained but related essays
divided into three parts and centred on the three topics indicated by the title. The
opening essay on 'Law and arbitration in Renaissance Florence' is particularly
interesting. A recurrent theme in the essays which form the second part (on the
family) is the question of legitimacy and illegitimacy, and in the final part, which
concerns women, an absorbing essay addresses 'some ambiguities of female
inheritance ideology'. As the author points out, in Renaissance Italy 'the law was
implicated throughout society [. . .] Awareness of legal rules and the operation of
legal mechanisms were present on a regular (that is, daily) basis'.

168 **Domestic strategies: work and family in France and Italy, 1600-1800.**
Edited by Stuart Woolf. Cambridge, England; New York; Port Chester, New York; Melbourne; Sydney: Cambridge University Press; Paris: Editions de la Maison des Sciences de l'Homme, 1991. 207p. bibliog.

Four out of the five essays collected here concern Italy. In the first, O. Raggio writes about the social relations and control of resources in an area of transit (eastern Liguria) in the 16th and 17th centuries; trade, whether legal or illegal, created extensive networks of co-operation and dependence, cutting across the social classes. C. Poni analyses the rules and practices of three guilds in Bologna which were linked together by the trading of skins (butchers, tanners and shoemakers); their transactions suggest the existence of an extraordinary modern structure. The Turin tailors' guild is studied by S. Cerutti, who examines group and trade strategies and shows how 'a guild could aggregate different social groups and thus change its own distinctive characteristics'. Turin is also involved in the last essay, by S. Cavallo, who deals with the conceptions of poverty and poor-relief in the second half of the 18th century.

19th century

169 **The Risorgimento and the unification of Italy.**
Derek Beales. London; New York: Longman, 1981. 2nd ed. 176p. 6 maps.

First published in 1971 and mainly aimed at sixth-formers and university students, this is a book which any reader interested in the *Risorgimento* would appreciate for its cogent argument and lucid exposition. The work is divided into two parts. The first consists of concise sections on the various phases of the *Risorgimento*, from the beginning of the second half of the 18th century to the advent of unification in 1861. The second part presents a wide selection of documents arranged in chronological order, such as: papers from Vincenzo Cuoco's history of the 1799 Neapolitan revolution; Mazzini's instructions to the members of 'Young Italy' (1831); diplomatic despatches from Rome (in 1848) and Turin (in 1849); and a letter from Cavour on Garibaldi's expedition to Sicily.

170 **The origins of the Italian wars of independence.**
Frank J. Coppa. London; New York: Longman, 1992. 188p. 2 maps. bibliog.

The Italian wars of independence consisted of a series of major or minor conflicts between 1848 and 1849, 1859 and 1860, and in 1866. Coppa considers the incorporation of Rome (1870) as the 'fourth war', in this readable and scholarly study of the relevant events and developments occurring both in the peninsula and in the European context. Interesting and original research for this book was done in the Vatican archives. At the end, Coppa suggests that the unresolved issues with Austria-Hungary for the control of Trent and Trieste 'eventually propell[ed] Italian entry into the First World War, which some have dubbed Italy's fifth and final war of liberation'. A useful glossary is included.

171 **Conflict and control: law and order in nineteenth-century Italy.**
John A. Davis.   Basingstoke, England; London: Macmillan, 1988.
398p. 4 maps.

This is an original and penetrating study of social history. The issue of 'law and order', both before and after the unification of Italy, is analysed in the various contexts of legislation, politics, civil society, and economic development. There are two parts: the first deals with the 'Old Order' and covers roughly the first sixty years of the century; the second examines 'the making of the New Order' after 1860, and includes two important chapters on crime and the southern problem (with an emphasis on the mafia and the camorra). By the 1890s, the Italian liberal system had been struck by a crisis, when it failed to adjust to the emergence of mass politics and drifted towards nationalism and imperialism. Thus the notion of 'an enemy within' and the fear of political and social subversion became the new justification for maintaining a repressive system of law and order.

172 **Society and politics in the age of the Risorgimento: essays in honour of Denis Mack Smith.**
Edited by John A. Davis, Paul Ginsborg.   Cambridge, England; New York; Port Chester, New York; Melbourne; Sydney: Cambridge University Press, 1991. 279p. 3 maps.

Aspects of 19th-century Italian social history and politics are dealt with here against a comparative European background. Such variety can best be conveyed by indicating the subjects and their authors: The crisis of *ancien régime* in southern Italy (J. A. Davis); war and society in Napoleonic Italy (F. Della Peruta); the debate on poverty in Italy and Europe during the Restoration (S. Woolf); politics and lawlessness in early nineteenth century Sicily (G. Fiume); marriage and family early in the century (M. Barbagli); banditry in the Po Valley in mid-century (P. Ginsborg); labouring women in northern and central Italy (S. Ortaggi Cammarosano); Garibaldi in England (D. Beales); and the middle classes in Liberal Italy (A. Lyttelton). An essay by Mack Smith himself, on Francesco De Sanctis, completes the collection. The book includes a bibliography of Mack Smith's writings on 19th-century Italy.

173 **Daniele Manin and the Venetian revolution of 1848-49.**
Paul Ginsborg.   Cambridge, England; London; New York; Melbourne: Cambridge University Press, 1979. 417p. 3 maps. bibliog.

Unlike G. M. Trevelyan's classic work with roughly the same title, published in 1923, this is a study based on an impressive range of primary and secondary sources. More importantly, Ginsborg sets the Venetian revolution and Manin's role in their historical context in an exemplary manner for clarity of the narrative and incisiveness of the insights. The book consists of ten chapters: the first two provide the historical background to Venetian society and to the 1848 revolution. This is then analysed in a month-by-month order of events. The concluding chapter offers an overall assessment of that portentous year, and Ginsborg suggests that the ultimate failure of the Venetian republican revolution, based on an effective alliance between the liberal bourgeoisie and the popular classes, 'cast its long shadow over the life of the new nation State'.

174   **The unification of Italy.**
John Gooch.   London: Routledge, 1989. 42p. 1 map.
First published by Methuen in 1986, and part of the Lancaster Pamphlets series of historical topics, this concise and clear study deals with the political process which resulted in the unification of Italy. Mainly intended for students in secondary education, it will also be useful to history undergraduates, to students of Italy, and to those interested in that area of history. The narrative sequence of events is accompanied by comments which build up into a coherent argument, for example, that the *Risorgimento* was not driven by a general plan, but was rather a haphazard process at the end of which the political change did not involve any social revolution. The various and contending forces that struggled to achieve the aim of unification are surveyed and their role assessed. A map and a time chart of main events from 1807 to 1870 precede the text and a list of suggested further readings is added at the end.

175   **Economics and liberalism in the Risorgimento: a study of nationalism in Lombardy, 1814-1848.**
Kent R. Greenfield.   Baltimore, Maryland: The Johns Hopkins University Press, 1965. Rev. ed. 303p.
First published in 1934, this book appeared in Italy in 1940, translated by Gino Luzzatto (a prominent economic historian who had lost his academic post after the introduction of anti-Semitic legislation). The story of the struggle for freedom against despotism, which is the underlying theme in Greenfield's study, was welcomed by liberal Italian historians. This new edition contains an introductory essay by another leading Italian historian of the same school of thought, Rosario Romeo, and this ensured that the Italian version became, again, a major source for historical and contemporary debate in the mid-1960s. The book consists of two parts: the first on 'Economics', the second on 'Thought and action'. Both are based on rigorous and documented scholarly research. The second part, in particular, includes an exhaustive assessment of nationalist journalism in Lombardy and several references to the central figure of Carlo Cattaneo.

176   **Italy in the age of the Risorgimento, 1790-1870.**
Harry Hearder.   London; New York: Longman, 1983. 325p. 4 maps. bibliog.
Part of the Longman History of Italy series, in this book the author skilfully revisits the 'age of the *Risorgimento*' striking a balance between the recognition of the achievement of Italian nationalism, on the one hand, and the investigation of less glamorous issues upon which recent historical research has made important inroads, on the other. The underlying general history of the *Risorgimento* is here weaved through the stories of the various States of the peninsula before unification. There are four parts: an introductory discussion on the conflicting interpretations of the period; a survey of the various regions of Italy; the description and assessment of the actual making of the nation-state; and an examination of culture in 19th-century Italy. Useful bibliographical notes are included at the end of each chapter.

177 **Risorgimento: the making of Italy, 1815-1870.**
Edgar Holt. London; Basingstoke, England: Macmillan, 1970. 320p.
7 maps. bibliog.

This is a well-written survey of the *Risorgimento*, based on extensive knowledge of
secondary sources, in both Italian and English – from the classical works in English
by Bolton King and G. M. Trevelyan to the more recent scholarship led by Denis
Mack Smith. The object of the book is simply 'to provide a reasonably concise
answer to the question, "What was *Risorgimento* and what happened in it?"'. The
answer unfolds in several short chapters, each of which is divided into clearly defined
sections. Chapters on the life and actions of the leading protagonists are woven into
the rigid chronological order of the narrative. These character-centred chapters refer
to Mazzini, Pius IX, Cavour and Garibaldi, but not to Victor Emmanuel, let alone
Charles Albert.

178 **Liberty and order: the theory and practice of Italian public
security policy, 1848 to the crisis of the 1890s.**
Richard B. Jensen. New York; London: Garland, 1991. 331p. bibliog.

This study concentrates on the Italian social and political crisis of the 1890s; the
subtitle is therefore somewhat misleading. The preceding half-century is considered
only as the background to the social upheaval which first erupted in Sicily, spread to
other parts of Italy where anarchist propaganda was effective, and culminated with
bread riots in Milan at the turn of the century. The common response of the
authorities was martial law and repression and the patterns of such a response
constitute the central theme of Jensen's work. In contrast with the conventional
historical view of the period, the author argues that the 1890s cannot simply be
categorized as a reactionary decade. He demonstrates that those years only make
sense when the progressive forces at play are also considered in their struggle – and
eventual triumph – against the reactionaries. A documentary appendix includes
extracts from public security legislation (in Italian).

179 **A history of Italian unity: being a political history of Italy from
1814 to 1871.**
Bolton King. New York: Russell & Russell, 1967. 2 vols. 4 maps.
bibliog.

This is a reprint of a 1924 revised edition of the classic which first appeared in 1899
(published by J. Nisbet & Co., London). Until that time Italy had attracted the
attention of art, rather than political historians in the English-speaking world, and
King was the initiator of a tradition which was to be continued by G. M. Trevelyan
and Denis Mack Smith. This is an accurate and sympathetic account of the 'Italian
revolution'; that is the process which began with the fall of Napoleon and ended with
the unification of Italy (1861) and the proclamation of Rome as the capital of the
kingdom (1871). 'Sanity and liberalism' were what King most admired in that
successful story, and even in the brief critical post-script added to the 1924 edition,
under the shadow of fascism, he stated that Italy was likely to 'be swept back in
another great popular movement into the ways of freedom and progress, from which
alone her salvation can come'.

180   **The democratic movement in Italy, 1830-1876.**
      Clara M. Lovett.   Cambridge, Massachusetts; London: Harvard
      University Press, 1982. 285p. bibliog.

The subjects of this important study are the thinkers, propagandists and agitators who advocated social change (as well as political unification, secularization and constitutional government) during the *Risorgimento*. Obvious figures such as Mazzini and Garibaldi are prominent, but lesser-known characters are also considered: some 150 men altogether. Strangely, for a female scholar, the absence of women is not commented upon. Three introductory chapters consider the many aspects of the 'Italian revolution', and the chronology of events, which constitutes the main text, is interspersed with topical discussions of relevant developments. For instance, a chapter is devoted to the 'experiments in democratic leadership' between 1848 and 1849. The epilogue surveys the career of surviving democrats by the last quarter of the century. Lovett argues that the leadership failure was due to external, social, economic and political factors and that, despite this, the democrats did make a lasting impact on the development of modern Italy.

181   **Cavour and Garibaldi: 1860: a study of political conflict.**
      Denis Mack Smith.   Cambridge, England: Cambridge University
      Press, 1985. 485p. 1 map.

First published in 1954, this is the book that established the author's reputation as an authority on Italian modern history. By concentrating on that single, portentous year of 1860, a deeper understanding of the historical process which led to the unification of Italy was possible, in the light of the conflict between moderatism and ràdicalism, as personified by Cavour and Garibaldi, respectively. It was considered a masterly revisionist approach which debunked the pseudo-patriotic mythology which had transformed those two protagonists into harmonious icons, and was so deeply rooted among Italian historians. In addition, the book had a formidable impact in Italy. For this alone, apart from its elegant narrative and robust scholarship, this is a classic study on the making of Italy in particular, and of European history in general.

182   **The making of Italy: 1796-1866.**
      Denis Mack Smith.   London: Macmillan, 1988. New ed. 428p. 4 maps.
      bibliog.

Twenty years after its first appearance this fine collection of extracts from primary and secondary (but rare) sources was reissued with a short new preface by the author. Documents are drawn from an impressive variety of sources: books and journals; archives and diaries; and correspondence and reports. They are set in their proper historical context by concise introductions throughout the book. The material is divided into twenty-four topics, arranged in chronological order, from 'The Napoleonic period, 1796-1815' to 'Rome' (referring to the city's annexation to the Kingdom of Italy in 1870). War, diplomacy and the protagonists of the *Risorgimento* are in evidence, but social and cultural problems also emerge in various chapters, especially in connection with the southern regions. This is the best English-language account of the *Risorgimento* using documents.

183   **Victor Emmanuel, Cavour and the Risorgimento.**
Denis Mack Smith.   London: Oxford University Press, 1971. 381p.
5 maps.

Although this is organized as a collection of essays, rather than a systematic study, the division into self-contained chapters does not obscure the coherent design of this scintillating work on the *Risorgimento*, which focuses on two protagonists and their relationship: King Victor Emmanuel II and Prime Minister Camillo Benso, Count of Cavour. The areas of discussion vary and this contributes to the interest of the book: from constitutional history to diplomatic relations, to economic, social and military issues. Some chapters have become classic cameos of Italian history; for instance, 'The peasants' revolt in Sicily, 1860', and 'Cavour and the problem of regionalism'. In the words of the author, 'the intention has been to choose a number of controversial episodes and problems which seem crucial to any general interpretation of the *Risorgimento*, and then to see how they look in the light of the documentation which is now available'.

184   **Italian anarchism, 1864-1892.**
Nunzio Pernicone.   Princeton, New Jersey: Princeton University
Press, 1993. 326p. bibliog.

This is an exhaustive study of the ascendancy, transformation and decline of Italian anarchism, from the arrival of Bakunin in Italy (1864) to the establishment of the Italian Socialist Party, which excluded the anarchists (1892). The basic text is divided into three parts, as follows: part one considers the role played by Bakunin and the rise of the International Workingmen's Association in Italy (1864-72); and part two examines the relationship between the Italian Anarchist Federation and the International, within the context of insurrections and repression (1872-80). The last decade is thoroughly analysed in part three, which opens with the defection of Andrea Costa to the socialist camp, emphasizes the tireless attempts by Malatesta to invigorate the movement, and ends with the anarchists' isolation. Their ultimate failure, Pernicone argues, is that they 'underestimated the power of the liberal state just as they overestimated the revolutionary capabilities of the Italian masses'.

185   **The Risorgimento: state, society and national unification.**
Lucy Riall.   London; New York: Routledge, 1994. 101p. 3 maps.
bibliog.

Based on extensive research, this is a fine work of synthesis, which makes an important and complex period of Italian history accessible to students, teachers and general readers. Unlike most books on the same subject, which are organized in a chronological order, Riall adopts a broad thematic approach. She first considers the years between 1815 and 1860 in the context of the wider history of the country, and studies the *Risorgimento* in relation to social and economic development, and the slow making of a national culture. In the final brief chapter on the 'post-*Risorgimento*', the author writes that 'the experiences of Liberal Italy, its failure to develop as a full parliamentary democracy and, thus, its eventual collapse into fascism, could be traced back to the process of national unification and to the struggles of the *Risorgimento*'.

186   **The Risorgimento: thought and action.**
Luigi Salvatorelli, translated by Mario Domandi.   New York;
Evanston, Illinois; London: Harper Torchbooks, 1970. 202p.

As Charles Delzell writes in the introduction, this classic study of the making of Italy
is a 'minor masterpiece of distillation'. In it Salvatorelli argues that much of the
thought and action of the *Risorgimento* was still relevant in post-fascist Italy. After
outlining the historical problem of actually defining the period, the author examines
its background through an assessment of the politics and culture of the 18th century,
the 'first revolutionary crisis' during the Napoleonic years, and the developments in
the 1820s and 1830s. An entire chapter is then devoted to 1848, that key year of the
'national revolution'. The following long section explores the issues of Cavour's
Piedmont, the process of unification, the role of Garibaldi and the 'Roman question'.
A short final chapter surveys the emergence of nationalism and fascism in the light of
the post-*Risorgimento* crisis.

187   **The unification of Italy, 1815-1870.**
Andrina Stiles.   London: Hodder & Stoughton, 1989. 98p. 2 maps.
bibliog.

First published in 1986 in the 'Access to A-Level History' series by the same
publishers (now renamed 'Access to History'), this is a concise and readable
introduction to the unification of Italy. It will be of particular use to students and also
interesting to the general reader. The five chapters focus on the unfolding of events
and on the personalities involved: 'Italy 1815-52'; 'Piedmont, Cavour and Italy';
'Garibaldi and Italy'; 'Napoleon III and Italy'; and 'The Kingdom of Italy'. At the
end of each chapter there is a 'Study Guides' section which includes a relevant chart
of the main topics.

188   **Politics and class in Milan, 1881-1901.**
Louise A. Tilly.   New York; Oxford: Oxford University Press, 1992.
355p. 2 maps.

Tilly provides a thorough investigation of the structural changes and political
struggles that shaped working class formation in Milan, with frequent references to
the broader Italian canvas. The work is an important study of Italian society at the end
of the 19th century and consists of three distinct but interrelated parts. First, there is a
detailed account of economic change, population growth, occupational structure,
migration, conditions of life and work, and workers' institutions. This is followed by
case studies on strike patterns, some specific industries and women workers. Finally,
three chapters are devoted to a chronological study of working class political
formation: the creation and repression of a Workers' Party (1875-86); the making and
repression of a Socialist Party (1886-94); and the Socialist Party and the crisis of
1898. Several graphs and tables are included.

189   **Garibaldi [Trilogy].**
George M. Trevelyan.   London: Longmans, Green & Co., 1912.
3 vols. maps. bibliog.

This is the best-produced set of the famous 'Garibaldi Trilogy' which was written by
the Grand Old Man of English History, as Trevelyan was regarded by the reading
public. The three volumes first appeared separately, in 1907 (*Garibaldi's defence of*

the Roman Republic), 1909 (*Garibaldi and the thousand*), and 1911 (*Garibaldi and the making of Italy*). Whereas the first volume can stand on its own, as it deals with the self-contained events of 1848-49, the last two should be considered as two interdependent parts since they examine Garibaldi's expedition to Sicily and subsequent march on Naples, which unfolded in the spring and summer of 1860. In his autobiography Trevelyan explained that he chose to write on Garibaldi because 'his life seemed to [him] the most poetic of all true stories'. It was partly because of this romantic inspiration that the contradictions and conflicts between the moderate and radical forces were underestimated. Nevertheless, this classic work remains admirable for its scholarly endeavour, passionate thrust and elegant prose. Documentary appendices were added to each volume.

190   **A history of Italy, 1700-1860: the social constraints of political change.**
Stuart Woolf.   London: Methuen, 1979. 519p. 1 map. bibliog.

This book is a substantial and extended revision of what originally appeared as part of the massive and innovative *Storia d'Italia*, published by Einaudi (Turin). The importance of this work lies in the prominence given to the social and economic structures and changes, as well as in the coverage of the more traditional political development which resulted in the unification of Italy. The interaction between events in the peninsula and the wider European context is also a constant feature of the book, which consists of five parts: 'The re-emergence of Italy, 1700-60'; 'Enlightenment and despotism, 1760-90'; 'Revolution and moderation, 1789–1814'; 'The search for independence, 1815-47'; and 'The cost of independence, 1848-61'. An epilogue strikes a judicious balance between achievements and failures and there is also a useful glossary.

19th and 20th centuries

191   **Italy since 1800: a nation in the balance?**
Roger Absalom.   London; New York: Longman, 1995. 325p. 3 maps. bibliog.

The underlying suggestion of this absorbing account is that Italy is one of modern history's fascinating paradoxes. In less than one hundred years (with several wars in between) it changed from being a predominantly backward agrarian country into one of the world's leading industrial powers. Yet, Italian society has always been marked by cultural rifts, ideological conflict and all-round contradictions. The author effectively puts it thus: 'Over the last two centuries the Italian "nation" has been "remade" politically at least five times, and perhaps is about to be refashioned yet again. But, in another sense, little really seems to have changed during this period: deeply ingrained habits of mind and patterns of behaviour centred upon the single-minded pursuit of the interests of the individual, the family and the "clan", still dominate Italian "civil society" '. The book is richly illustrated.

192   **The troubled origins of the Italian catholic labour movement:
1878-1914.**
Sándor Agócs.   Detroit: Wayne State University Press, 1988. 251p.
bibliog.

The development of the early Catholic labour movement in Italy is discussed in this
study with particular attention paid to such topics as the Church's social philosophy,
the Catholic corporative doctrine, the alliance between wealth and the altar, and the
political and social reality of industrial workers and landless peasants. It is a well-
written synthesis of specialist works. The thomistic revival under Leo XIII is briefly
considered in the first chapter. Particularly interesting sections are those on: the
conception of the right to property as sanctioned by natural law; the rejection of the
principle of equality; the continuous attention (and condemnation) of class conflict;
and the relationship between Catholics and socialists. Agócs argues that the 'socialist
menace' brought about an alliance between the Church and the bourgeoisie, which
'eventually became one of the defining characteristics of the papacy of Pius X'
(1903-14).

193   **Sesto San Giovanni: workers, culture and politics in an Italian
town, 1880-1922.**
Donald Howard Bell.   New Brunswick, New Jersey; London: Rutgers
University Press, 1986. 295p. 2 maps.

The formation and development of the Italian industrial working class is studied here
through a detailed investigation of Sesto San Giovanni, the major factory suburb of
Milan. During the period considered, Sesto's economy was transformed and
traditional peasant agriculture, silk production and artisan manufacturing gave way to
heavy industry. Bell shows how cultural traditions and institutions played an
important role in the shaping of the Italian working class and its political orientation.
It is noted, in particular, how the workers' movement effectively challenged the
Catholic-dominated forces in local elections before the First World War. The
activities of the Socialist Party during the war years are examined, as are the struggles
and divisions of the left on the eve of the fascist seizure of power. An overview of the
subsequent social and political history of Sesto is provided in the concluding chapter.

194   **Italy, the least of the great powers: Italian foreign policy before
the First World War.**
Richard J. B. Bosworth.   London; New York; Melbourne; Sydney:
Cambridge University Press, 1979. 537p. 5 maps. bibliog.

This is an outstanding contribution to the inexhaustible debate on the relationship
between liberal Italy and fascist Italy. Bosworth's thorough research shows that as far
as foreign policy was concerned, a line of continuity characterized pre-1922 and
Mussolini's Italy. Chapter one contains an incisive survey of 'Society and politics in
Liberal Italy' and chapter two investigates the 'New political pressure groups and
foreign policy', with special attention devoted to nationalist groups. Chapter three is
devoted to the background and career of the Foreign Minister, Di San Giuliano and
chapter four focuses on the bureaucrats of foreign policy. In the following seven
chapters the main argument slowly takes shape through a fascinating analysis of
Italy's adventure in Libya, her relationship with the Triple Alliance and the Triple
Entente, Italian policy towards Turkey and the country's position at the outbreak of
the First World War. Some documents are included in the appendix.

195 **Modern Italy: images and history of a national identity.**
Edited by Omar Calabrese, co-ordinated by Carlo Pirovano and
translated by Christopher H. Evans, Richard Sadleir. Milan: Electa,
1982-86. 5 vols. bibliog.

Italian historians and other scholars have contributed to this massive, illustrated
history of Italy, from unification to the 1980s. Calabrese and Pirovano were assisted
by A. Abruzzese, C. Bertelli, U. Eco, V. Gregotti, M. Tafuri and N. Tranfaglia. Each
volume contains essays on the political, social and economic development of the
country and also includes chapters on the arts, the organization of culture and mass
communication. These are elegant accounts, accompanied by extended notes and
bibliographical references. The first four volumes cover Italy's history in a
chronological order, and their subtitles indicate their contents: From unification to the
new century; From expansion to the Second World War; War, post-war,
reconstruction, take-off; and The difficult democracy. The final volume (Visions of
the country: 1860-1980) contains essays on general themes and includes a detailed
chronology of events, and economic and cultural achievements.

196 **Modern Italy, 1871-1982.**
Martin Clark. London; New York: Longman, 1984. 444p. bibliog.
3 maps.

This is the absorbingly written tale of a society which appears to combine the most
radical changes with the most obstinate continuities. An introductory chapter
considers the 'themes and problems' throughout the century which are investigated in
the book, and provides a useful historiographical survey. The following seventeen
chapters are further divided into four chronologically coherent parts: 1871-1887
(three chapters); 1887-1914 (four chapters); 1914-1943 (six chapters); and 1943-1982
(four chapters). The emphasis on the third period is justified by the adopted focus on
State-society relationship as the central theme of the book. Between 1914 and 1943
the elites which made up 'high politics' (the government, the crown, the army, the
police, the judiciary, and the civil service) became completely divorced from 'low
politics' (local and parliamentary political activities). Clark's main thesis throughout
the book is that such separation was in fact a juxtaposition and a permanent feature of
a much broader history of Italian society.

197 **A history of modern Italy: documents, readings, and commentary.**
Shepard B. Clough, Salvatore Saladino. New York; London:
Columbia University Press, 1968. 657p. 4 maps. bibliog.

An anthology of over 100 excerpts from books and documents on the history of Italy
from the beginning of the 19th century to the 1960s. The material is divided into
seven chronological parts and arranged in chapters. Commentary is provided
throughout. Among the most famous documents, which are partially or fully
reproduced, are: the law on the Papal guarantees, 1871; The Pact of London, 1915;
Mussolini's first speech in parliament, 1921; Matteotti's speech of May, 1924, which
cost him his life; Mussolini's speech of January 3, 1925, marking the beginning of the
fascist regime; the Treaty and Concordat between Italy and the Holy See, 1929; the
anti-Semitic legislation, 1938; an account of the last, momentous meeting of the
fascist Grand Council of 24-25 July, 1943; the Republican Constitution; and passages
from speeches by Moro, Togliatti and Nenni on the entry of the left into the political
arena, 1962-63.

198   **Studies in modern Italian history: from the Risorgimento to the republic: Festschrift for A. William Salomone.**
Edited by Frank J. Coppa.   New York; Berne; Frankfurt, Germany: Peter Lang. 1986. 299p.

This is a collection of useful and interesting essays by various authors, in four parts. The first deals with the *Risorgimento* (that is, the period of the struggle for independence from the Austrian Empire in the 19th century), focusing also on its origins, the issues of the Catholic Church and the developing socialist movement. The second part covers the so-called *Giolittian* era (from Prime Minister Giolitti) of liberal government in the early 20th century, as well as colonialism and the 'southern question'. The third part concentrates on the social upheaval which followed the First World War, placing the emphasis on the left-wing revolutionary movement and the rise of fascism; it also deals with the development of terrorism in modern Italy. The fourth and final part examines Italy's foreign relations from the 1880s to the 1980s.

199   **Gramsci and Italy's passive revolution.**
Edited by John A. Davis.   London: Croom Helm; New York: Barnes & Noble Books, 1979. 278p.

This is a collection of essays on the political, social and economic aspects of Italy's modern history. Gramsci's concept of 'passive revolution' is central to his writings, indicating the persistent domination by the bourgeoisie of apparent social changes. This is the implicit theme of the various contributions, as the editor explains in his stimulating introduction; he also writes a chapter on the origins of the 'southern problem'. The other authors and their topics are: P. Ginsborg, 'Gramsci and the era of the bourgeois revolution in Italy'; A. Lyttelton, 'Landlords, peasants and the limits of liberalism'; F. M. Snowden, 'From sharecropper to proletarian: the background to fascism in rural Tuscany, 1880-1920'; A. A. Kelikian, 'From liberalism to corporatism: the province of Brescia during the First World War'; and P. Corner, 'Fascist agrarian policy and the Italian economy in the inter-war years'.

200   **Italian culture in the industrial era, 1880-1980: cultural industries, politics and the public.**
David Forgacs.   Manchester, England; New York: Manchester University Press, 1990. 231p. bibliog.

Forgacs deals here with three of the modern cultural industries – publishing, cinema and broadcasting – and with their impact on society in the century after 1880. During that time Italy's predominantly rural society was gradually transformed into a leading industrial nation. In this work the emphasis is placed on the mediating role of cultural industries, and on their connections with political power (the author acknowledges his debt to Gramsci's concept of hegemony). The work broadly follows a chronological order, accounting for the changes in the cultural industries and their relations with the political system. The radical alternative to the dominating media (that is, the left and the Communist Party) is then discussed. This is followed by a review of some of the main theoretical themes on the relationship between international capitalism and technological innovation in communications.

201 **The fall of the House of Savoy.**
Robert Katz. London: Allen & Unwin, 1972. 439p. 7 maps. bibliog.

The Savoy dynasty, which could claim at one time to be the oldest ruling house in Europe, has commonly been regarded as insignificant in its contribution to history. Katz agrees with this judgement but also thinks that it ought to have been taken more seriously, if only for the circumstances of its longevity. After a brief introductory section on the 'the family album' up to 1878 (the year in which Victor Emmanuel II died), Katz devotes substantial sections to Humbert I and Queen Margherita (1878-1900), and Victor Emmanuel III ('the little king'). He splits the latter's long reign into two parts: from his enthronement after his father was murdered (1900) to 1922, when he invited Mussolini to become prime minister; and from that momentous decision to his resignation in the vain hope of saving the dynasty (1946). Appendices include the genealogical table of the House of Savoy.

202 **Italian foreign policy, 1870-1940.**
C. J. Lowe, F. Marzari. London; Boston, Massachusetts: Routledge & Kegan Paul, 1975. 476p. bibliog.

This work provides a comprehensive survey of Italian foreign policy from the completion of the country's unification (with the annexation of Rome) to Italy's entry into the Second World War. The authors also give adequate emphasis to the main recurrent themes which informed the country's foreign policy throughout the period. The elements of continuity are traced, demonstrating that the fascist foreign policy was basically no different from the strategy pursued by Crispi and Sonnino at the turn of the century. The contents are divided into two parts, each subdivided into chapters focusing on major issues. Part one covers the period from 1870 to the immediate aftermath of the First World War; and part two deals with Mussolini's foreign policy. At the end of the volume there is a selection of relevant documents, including private and archive papers, items from correspondence and diaries, and extracts from treaties and agreements.

203 **Italy: a modern history.**
Denis Mack Smith. Ann Arbor, Michigan: The University of Michigan Press, 1969. Rev. ed. 542p. 2 maps. bibliog.

This history of modern Italy first appeared in 1959 and soon became the classic work which no scholar and reader of Italian history and contemporary society could ignore. Mack Smith's book is an outstanding achievement of scholarship and lively writing: it is a comprehensive work based on vast and meticulous research, and providing acute judgements throughout. This new edition includes a perceptive treatment of Italy's post-war development, which places an emphasis on the 'economic miracle' and the shift to the left during the 1960s. The thirteen chapters are arranged in strict chronological order and cover specific ranges of years, with three exceptions: the first two chapters explore Italy's conditions before and at the time of political unification (1861); and a chapter on fascism investigates the theory and practice of the regime. An appendix includes Italy's prime ministers and heads of State, and the Popes.

204 **Italy and its monarchy.**
Denis Mack Smith. New Haven, Connecticut; London: Yale
University Press, 1989. 402p.

Mack Smith is the first historian to explore the political development of modern Italy
focusing on the role played by its monarchs. From the country's unification in 1861 to
the demise of the monarchy in 1946, Italy had four kings: Victor Emmanuel II
(1861-78); Humbert I (1878-1900); Victor Emmanuel III (1900-46); and Humbert II
(only for a few weeks, in 1946). The influence they exercised at crucial moments in
the country's history is stressed by the author with his customary lively style, balance
and solid scholarship. The first two chapters are dedicated to the first two kings whilst
the following three chapters cover the long reign of Victor Emmanuel III. The verdict
on Italy's monarchs is sober and severe: apart from their personal shortcomings, their
systematic abuse of power resulted in continuous obstruction of effective
parliamentary government and the abetting of fascism. Their portraits are included.

205 **The crisis of the Italian parliamentary system, 1860-1915.**
Armand Patrucco. New York; London: Garland, 1992. 318p. bibliog.

The central theme of this book is the undermining of the Italian parliamentary system
by systematic criticism and the eventual rejection of representative democracy, to the
extent that the roots of fascism can be traced well before the post-First World War
crisis. After two introductory chapters on the historiography and the sources of anti-
parliamentary criticism and thought in Italy, Patrucco addresses the changing patterns
of such attitudes, following a chronological order. The chapters are: The federalist
critique, 1861-76; The decline of political parties, 1876-82; Gaetano Mosca and the
new criticism, 1882-90; The crisis of the parliamentary regime, 1890-1900; and The
Giolittian period, 1900-14. Two further chapters then focus on Vilfredo Pareto's
impact on anti-parliamentary thought. The author concludes by emphasizing the
connection between such subversive intellectual positions and the rise of fascism.

206 **Italy: liberalism and fascism, 1870-1945.**
Mark Robson. London: Hodder & Stoughton, 1992. 154p. 3 maps.
bibliog.

Part of the publishers' 'Access to History' series, this book appears from the title to
be the sequel to the work by Andrina Stiles (q.v.). In fact, Robson concentrates on the
rise, consolidation and development of fascism. Students of modern Italy and general
readers will appreciate this accessible and concise account of Mussolini's regime,
which is accompanied by useful charts, a chronological table and a glossary. An
introductory chapter connects the unification of Italy and the subsequent processes
with fascism. The second chapter considers liberal Italy (1870-1915), and the
following five chapters focus, respectively, on the rise of fascism, the making of a
dictatorship, Mussolini's political system, economy and society, foreign policy and
the Second World War. A final, brief chapter surveys continuity and change in post-
war Italy.

207 **Italy from liberalism to fascism.**
Christopher Seton-Watson. London: Methuen, 1967. 772p. 8 maps.
bibliog.

From the moment of its appearance this book has ranked among the most important
studies of modern Italian history, focusing on the crucial transition 'from liberalism to

fascism'. Despite the enormous production of studies on the same period since its publication, this ponderous volume has lost nothing of its compelling qualities. These lie in: the great attention devoted to the interaction between Italy's domestic and foreign policies; the presentation of large and small political events (the main thrust of the book) against the background of economic development and social change; and the unfailing balance of judgement. After a prologue covering the formation of Italy (1859-70), four parts deal, respectively, with the periods of consolidation (1870-87), stresses and strains (1887-1901), expansion (1901-14), and crisis (1914-25). A list of cabinet and leading ministers for the whole period completes the volume.

208   **Modern Italy: a topical history since 1861.**
       Edited by Edward R. Tannenbaum, Emiliana P. Noether.   New York:
       New York University Press, 1974. 395p. 1 map.

Although dated, especially by historiographical standards, this collection of essays by leading scholars (mostly American) can still be read with interest and profit. The history of Italy since unification is arranged by topics in chronological order and an outline of the country's history from 1861 to the early 1970s is provided by the introduction. Each of the following fifteen chapters is a self-contained essay. These fall into three sections: politics and ideology (with contributions by A. W. Salomone, S. Saladino, R. Sarti, E. A. Carrillo, and N. Kogan); intellectual, religious and cultural developments (E. R. Tannenbaum, R. Grew, E. P. Noether, and R. Romeo); and foreign policy and diplomacy (W. C. Askew and R. Albrecht-Carré). A closing commentary by A. Aquarone focuses on some general themes.

20th century

Special studies

209   **Italy and the approach of the First World War.**
       Richard J. B. Bosworth.   Basingstoke, England; London: Macmillan,
       1983. 174p. bibliog.

The triple purpose of this work is outlined by the author in his preface. Firstly, he aims to provide a survey of what modern scholarship says about Italy's part in the causation of the First World War and, secondly, to persuade historians in Anglo-Saxon universities that the relatively ignored period of Italian history before fascism is worth less cursory treatment. The third objective is to suggest that Italian historians may benefit from the insights of an outsider who can 'offer some knowledge of the wider context in which Italy was and is placed abroad, and some understanding of the international structure to which Italy has contributed'. Italy's foreign policy decisions, such as the war on Turkey (1911-12) for the conquest of Libya, and the entry into the First World War (1915) 'brought drastic damage to the always fragile social and economic base of the Liberal system'. Bosworth's conclusion transcends those dramatic years and suggests that 'within the complex structures of world capitalism, for Italy, from 1860 to 1945, social crisis came from war, and war from foreign policy'.

210 **Antonio Gramsci and the revolution that failed.**
Martin Clark. New Haven, Connecticut; London: Yale University Press, 1977. 255p. bibliog.

At the end of the First World War Italy became a laboratory of intense political struggle and ideological debate. The war effort had stimulated economic growth in northern regions and workers were experimenting with direct forms of industrial democracy. The fascist movement, the first mass Catholic Party and the Communist Party were all launched at that time. Clark provides a fascinating account of the historical background to this period from the point of view of the Turin labour movement facing the rise of fascism. The figure of Antonio Gramsci is necessarily at the centre of the analysis, so that the book oscillates between biography and political theory, within the setting of a dramatic moment in Italian history. The legacy of Gramsci's factory councils is vividly discussed and it is shown to have become an important element in the philosophy of the Italian Communist Party after the Second World War.

211 **Italian intervention in the Spanish civil war.**
John F. Coverdale. Princeton, New Jersey: Princeton University Press, 1975. 456p. 11 maps. bibliog.

In what is the most comprehensive and balanced study of Mussolini's intervention in Spain, Coverdale provides a mine of perceptive observations on the nature of fascist foreign policy. The book is divided into three parts, corresponding to three distinct phases of the intervention. In the first part Coverdale describes the background to the limited involvement up to Italy's recognition of Franco, in November 1936. Secondly, he considers the period from that time to the battle of Guadalajara (March 1937), during which Italian aid increased enormously and Mussolini tried to influence both the military and the political conduct of Franco's war. The final and longer phase lasted until the end of the war. Coverdale concludes that Italy's contribution to the Nationalist victory was important, if only because, without it, the German commitment would have been marginal. There are maps relating to military operations and appendices containing statistical information.

212 **The crisis of liberal Italy: monetary and financial policy, 1914-1922.**
Douglas J. Forsyth. Cambridge, England: Cambridge University Press, 1993. 370p. bibliog.

After an introductory chapter on the political economy of Giolittian Italy (1901-14), this major study surveys and assesses the problems that crippled the Italian economy during the First World War, and then focuses on the post-war crisis which opened the way to fascism. Forsyth's central argument is that the eventual collapse of liberal Italy can be illuminated through a critical analysis of the monetary and financial policies pursued by the Italian governments. These policies, the author maintains, provide 'a particularly useful prism through which to view political conflict'. Four problems are scrutinized: the large budget deficits and the failure to reform the tax system; the vulnerability of banks; the persistent tension between the authorities and the leading commercial banks; and the crisis of the balance of payments and the growing financial dependence, first on Britain and later on the United States. Many tables and figures are contained in the appendix.

213 **The Pope and the Duce: the international impact of the Lateran Agreements.**
Peter C. Kent. Basingstoke, England; London: Macmillan, 1981. 248p. bibliog.

This is a study of the effect of the 1929 Lateran Agreements on Italian foreign policy, and of the impact of Church-State relations on the development of such a policy between 1929 and 1935. After an introductory chapter on Mussolini and Pius XI, Kent analyses the areas of co-operation and conflict between the Church and State before 1929. He then addresses the issue of the changing perspectives in 1929, concentrating on the clash over Catholic action (1931-32) and exploring the wider context of European political development, in order to conclude with some general comments on the impact of Italian foreign policy. 'What is initially striking about the relations between the Italian fascist government and the Papacy under Pius XI – the author writes – is the extent to which they were in agreement on the basic international problems of the inter-war period', although they 'had not reached these conclusions in the same way'.

214 **Ice crash.**
Alexander McKee. London: Souvenir Press, 1979. 326p. 2 maps. bibliog.

This is a detailed and vivid account of the airship flight over the North Pole, which ended in tragedy and polemic. The leader of the expedition was Umberto Nobile, an aeronautical engineer and explorer, who designed the airship *Norge* with which he had successfully flown over the North Pole two years earlier with Roald Amundsen. Part one of the book tells the story of this early flight. Nobile also designed the airship *Italia* which was to crash in 1928 and the story of its fatal flight is told in part two. Part three, which more or less constitutes the second half of the volume, deals with the difficult operations of searching for and rescuing the survivors. Among the people who lost their lives in the rescue mission was Amundsen. Nobile was blamed for the airship's loss and was also accused of improper conduct although McKee considers the accusation to be ill-founded. There are several photographs included in the text.

215 **From elite to mass politics: Italian socialism in the Giolittian era, 1900-1914.**
James Edward Miller. Kent, Ohio; London: The Kent State University Press, 1990. 265p. bibliog.

Miller argues that one of the main reasons for the failure of the Italian Socialist Party (PSI) to transform Italian society during the Giolittian years was their narrow social base. The maintenance of a structure which was only 'representative of a small portion of Italian industrial and agrarian workers', and which virtually excluded southern peasants, seriously undermined the PSI political options. The narrative focuses on the years between 1908 and 1914, when the 'revolutionary' wing of the party replaced the reformists at the helm, and modified the PSI organization and strategy. Ultimately, however, the left proved that it lacked effective strategic alternatives to the politics of parliamentary reform. A short epilogue outlines the story from 1915 to 1922, when the 'revolutionary' Mussolini became the prime minister, as the fascist Duce.

216 **The emergence of political Catholicism in Italy: Partito Popolare, 1919-1926.**
John N. Molony.   London: Croom Helm, 1977. 225p. bibliog.

The short-lived history of the first Italian political party inspired by social Catholicism, and established by a priest (Don Luigi Sturzo), is told here in an informative and sympathetic manner, based on secondary sources. Since the story of the *Partito Popolare* (PP) was to a large extent the life-story of Sturzo during the post-First World War years, his presence is very pervasive. Attention is paid to the alliance of the fascist government and the Vatican to bring about the destruction of the PP, and the main aim of the book is indeed an attempt to understand what happened. The political aims of the Vatican, Molony argues, clashed with Sturzo's democratic vision. They were: the return to a political and economic *status quo*, against the fear of growing socialism; and finding a solution to the Roman Question. Both objectives would have been thwarted by supporting Sturzo's Party.

217 **Italian labor in protest, 1904-1914: political general strikes to protest *eccidi*.**
Melinda Murtaugh.   New York; London: Garland, 1991. 342p. bibliog.

Eccidi, Murtaugh explains at the onset of this work, 'is the plural of the Italian for *eccidio*, which means "slaughter" or "massacre" [. . . and it] was the most apt characterization of the working-class casualties that resulted from violent confrontation between workers and Public Security'. In other words, the book discusses class war in Italy in the decade preceding the First World War. The use of the State's strong arm against organized labour had a long history. Indeed, the first chapter deals with this violent background, before attention is directed to the 1904 general strike with a description and analysis of the events, the reaction and consequences. The subsequent 'class battles' throughout the peninsula are then studied in detail. Finally, an extended chapter is focused on the 'red week' of June 1914, which is regarded as 'the most serious domestic crisis that the Kingdom of Italy had undergone since unification'.

218 **The Vatican and Italian fascism, 1929-32: a study in conflict.**
John Pollard.   Cambridge, England; London; New York; Melbourne; Sydney: Cambridge University Press, 1985. 241p. bibliog.

This scholarly work addresses both the events leading up to the signature of the 1929 Lateran Pacts and the relationship between the Vatican and the Italian government in the following three years. The new balance of power between the two parties had an uncertain start but the eventual compromise solution ensured several years of harmony. After introducing the two protagonists (the Church and the fascist government), the author outlines the background to the 'conciliation' and the reactions it provoked, paying particular attention to the diplomatic dimension. The subsequent events, the 'creeping crisis' of 1929-30, and the major crisis of 1931, are then carefully analysed. Pollard's conclusion is that the *modus vivendi* adopted by the Pope and the Duce was based on their mutual opportunism. Appendices include the full text of the Lateran Pacts.

219 **Violence and great estates in the south of Italy: Apulia, 1900-1922.**
Frank M. Snowden. Cambridge, England; London; New York;
Melbourne; Sydney: Cambridge University Press, 1986. 245p. 1 map.

Unlike the rest of southern Italy at the turn of the century, where peasants failed to organize effective political opposition to the power of landlords, Apulian agricultural labourers 'exhibited a fierce determination to make their own history', as Snowden writes. The aim of this work is to explain the characteristics of Apulian agricultural life, describing in detail the economic organization of the latifundia and the repressive social system of exploitation of the landless labourers. This provided a fertile ground for revolutionary syndicalism before the First World War. Post-war agitation and occupation of lands provoked a violent reaction by the landlords and marked a period of gestation of Apulian fascism.

220 **Industrial imperialism in Italy: 1908-1915.**
Richard A. Webster. Berkeley, California; London: University of
California Press, 1975. 392p.

In the few years which preceded the First World War, 'Italy's essential dilemmas as a nation-state came to light, provoking a series of crises and wars that did not really end until the mid-1950s', when the country showed remarkable economic progress and became a founding member of the European Economic Community. This is the main thesis of Webster's important book, which is centred on Italy's imperialism in the early 20th century. At the root of that phenomenon, the author argues, was the industrial-financial imbalance, which the ruling class tried to redress by expanding political and economic influence abroad (the Libyan war was the apotheosis of this policy). The work consists of two parts: firstly, an examination of the economic foundations; followed by an analysis of the politics of Italian imperialism on the eve of the Great War.

The First World War

221 **Domestic factors in Italian intervention in the First World War.**
Simon Mark Jones. New York; London: Garland, 1986. bibliog.

The Italian nationalist movement and its industrial allies, Jones argues, regarded war 'as a great opportunity to sweep away the supposedly socialistic Giolitti and establish Italian politics firmly on a new course, both internally and in a more expansionist foreign policy'. Yet, he also points out that no clear-cut distinction can be made between nationalism and liberalism, since the campaign for war joined virtually all non-socialist newspapers and periodicals on the eve of Italy's entry into war. The study first examines the decline of Giolittian Italy and the roots of Italian imperialism. A survey of the relationship between Italy and the Balkans is then followed by an analysis of the crisis of neutrality, and of the political and economic mobilization for war. The numerous quotations included in the text are in their original language – most in Italian, some in French.

222   **In the shadow of the sword: Italy's neutrality and entrance into the Great War, 1914-1915.**
William A. Renzi.   New York; Berne, Switzerland; Frankfurt, Germany; Paris: Peter Lang, 1987. 359p. 1 map. bibliog.
The historical background to the Sarajevo crisis, which precipitated the First World War, is outlined in the early chapters of this work, with particular attention paid to the relationship between Italy and her allies (Germany and Austria-Hungary). The main body of the book is devoted to a meticulous account and analysis of Italy's diplomacy during the months of neutrality. The battle of the Marne and the Russian advance into Galicia were the determinant factors in the Italian government's eventual decision to enter the war on the side of the Entente, but the hesitations reflected the complexity of Italy's position, with a propaganda effort being made by both the Entente and the German-Austrian camps. In this connection, Renzi examines the launching of Mussolini's pro-intervention newspaper, *Il Popolo d'Italia*. The negotiations with the Entente and the Pact of London are then considered.

223   **Italy and the Great War: politics and culture, 1870-1915.**
John A. Thayer.   Madison, Wisconsin; Milwaukee, Wisconsin: The University of Wisconsin Press, 1964. 463p.
The near-half century between the completion of Italy's unification with the annexation of Rome (1870) and the country's entry into the First World War (1915) is analysed in detail by Thayer, in as far as politics and culture are concerned. The main thesis is that the relentless dissatisfaction, particularly among Italian intellectuals, during that period helps to explain the conflict between 'neutralists' and 'intervention-ists', the crisis of May 1915, and the eventual decision by the government and king to declare war on Austria-Hungary. The argument is well structured in twelve chapters, commencing with a discussion on the concept of *Risorgimento* after the occupation of Rome, and concluding with 'the war as cultural crisis'. It can be argued, however, that eschewing the socio-economic dimension leaves a lot that has not been explored.

Fascism

224   **Mussolini and fascist Italy.**
Martin Blinkhorn.   London; New York: Routledge, 1990. 47p. 2 maps. bibliog.
This concise and informed account of Italian fascism was first published in 1984 by Methuen. Attention is paid to the roots of fascism through an effective look at Italian history from the unification (1861) to the country's entry into the First World War (1915). The war itself and the following years are then examined. Brief but considered sections are devoted to the road to dictatorship after the March on Rome, Mussolini's domestic and foreign policy, his imperial ambitions, and eventual decline and fall. A concluding section on the various interpretations of Italian fascism offers a stimulating opportunity for furthering an interest in the subject. A comprehensive time chart introduces the booklet and a suggested list of further reading is included at the end.

225   **Fascist Italy and the disarmament question, 1928-1934.**
       Joseph A. Bongiorno.   New York; London: Garland, 1991. 209p.
       bibliog.

Within the context of the extensive League of Nations negotiations on disarmament
between 1919 and 1940, the Italian fascist government followed a policy which, in
the relatively short period covered by this book, ranged from total hostility to outright
support. At the root of such extremely diverse positions were the changing
circumstances which Italy had to face *vis-à-vis* its attempt to establish a consistent
foreign policy. Bongiorno argues that this policy changed from Mussolini's hard-line
approach to Grandi's more moderate stance. An introductory chapter outlines Italian
diplomacy from 1922 to 1928, when the Kellogg-Briand pact was signed. The
following chapters analyse the subsequent six years of varied and difficult
negotiations, until their eventual failure in 1934, when 'Mussolini announced plans
for increases in armament and military expenditures'.

226   **The faces of fraternalism: Nazi Germany, fascist Italy and
       imperial Japan.**
       Paul Brooker.   Oxford: Clarendon Press, 1991. 397p. bibliog.

The opening chapters of this volume outline the social origins of the three
'fraternalist' regimes, in order to provide a historical background to their comparative
study. It is argued that such social origins differed significantly in each of the three
cases, and that the adoption of a 'fraternalist' social policy had therefore more to do
with those countries' social, political and military concerns. Although each chapter
contains cross references to the three types of 'fraternalism', four chapters focus on
Italy. Chapter two looks into the origins of Italian fascism; chapter nine deals with the
'sacerdotal' character of the fascist system; chapter ten addresses the issue of the
regime's policies towards the Roman Catholic Church and the youth; and chapter
eleven covers the indoctrination through various forms of social organizations. Some
theoretical questions are raised in the appendix.

227   **Historical dictionary of fascist Italy.**
       Edited by Philip V. Cannistraro.   Westport, Connecticut; London:
       Greenwood Press, 1982. 658p. 6 maps.

Fifty-six scholars have contributed to this impressive volume; most of them are
American, with a few British and Italian experts. The purpose of the dictionary is
twofold: firstly, 'to provide students with basic information, definitions, and
descriptions'; and secondly, 'to provide scholars with a fundamental research tool
containing detailed factual data not easily obtained elsewhere'. It is the most
comprehensive reference source on Italian fascist history, combining the character of
a biographical dictionary (containing nearly 450 names) with a general encyclopaedia
of inter-war Italy (with entries on State and Fascist Party organizations, policies and
generally relevant events). There are some infelicitous imbalances, however. For
instance, only four women are allotted an entry of their own and all of these are
somehow connected with Mussolini: Balabanoff; Petacci; Sarfatti; and, of course,
Donna Rachele. In addition, there are fine sections on architecture, literature and
music, but none on science. Ten appendices offer further details.

228   **Agrarian elites and Italian fascism: the province of Bologna, 1901-1926.**
Anthony L. Cardoza.   Princeton, New Jersey: Princeton University Press, 1982. 477p. 11 maps. bibliog.

This is not simply a local history book on the origins of fascism. In addition, it is a study of the patterns of landownership, agricultural enterprise, and labour relations in the countryside, which gave rise to a new agrarian leadership and strategy, especially in the Po Valley, before the First World War. This is investigated in the important province of Bologna, where 'the situation reflected the larger stresses and strains of rapid but uneven industrialization and political democratization on the Italian peninsula'. In the post-war crisis the agrarian leadership there (as well as in other parts of Italy) was on the defence and re-established its dominance through the violent anti-socialist crusade by fascism. The continuities between pre-war and post-war development in elite politics, the agricultural economy and labour relations are emphasized with the conclusion that fascism was the instrument for sharper confrontation.

229   **Fascism in Ferrara: 1919-1925.**
Paul Corner.   London: Oxford University Press, 1975. 300p. 1 map. bibliog.

This case study of the origins, emergence and early development of fascism in Ferrara does not address a marginal historical phenomenon. Corner persuasively argues that 'it was Ferrara that formed the spearhead of the extremely rapid expansion of agrarian fascism which – at the beginning of 1921 – effectively rescued the town-based fascism from political extinction'. It was no coincidence that one of the most prominent of fascist leaders, Italo Balbo, had his political base in Ferrara. The result of extensive research, this study first considers the local political tension that existed during the Great War and its immediate aftermath, when the socialists won a portentous electoral victory. The attitudes of the middle-class, the beginning of reaction and the eventual triumph of fascism are investigated through a study of personalities. The socio-economic structure of the province, in which old forms of farming and modern techniques coexisted, is also taken into account.

230   **Mussolini.**
Renzo De Felice.   Turin: Einaudi, 1965- .

A colossal study of the *Duce* in which his biography is interwoven (some would say confused) with the history of fascism and, indeed, the history of Italy throughout the first half of the 20th century. This is a work of immense scholarship and influence and the result of compulsive and thorough research in public and private archives, both in Italy and abroad. The still unfinished story consists of four parts and, to date, seven volumes, each with some 800 pages on average. These are: *Il rivoluzionario, 1883-1920*; *Il fascista* (two volumes: *1921-25* and *1925-29*); *Il Duce* (two volumes: *1929-36* and *1936-40*); and *L'alleato* (Hitler's ally – two volumes covering the years *1940-43*). Two more volumes are expected to conclude the series on the final years of Mussolini's life: 1943-45. Some would argue that when De Felice began his study he took a more balanced approach and that subsequently he has shown growing empathy for his character-subject. However, shifting perspectives are to some extent inevitable when more than thirty years are spent on a study. All volumes are enriched by the inclusion of important documents in their appendices, although their practical value would have been further enhanced if analytical indexes, instead of the meagre lists of cited peoples' names, were included.

231   Fascism: an informal introduction to its theory and practice.
Renzo De Felice, an interview with Michael A. Ledeen.   New Brunswick, New York: Transaction Books, 1976. 128p.

The original text of this interview appeared in Italian in 1975, and became a source of heated debate and a best-seller. The reason for such controversial success was De Felice's suggestion that fascism as a 'movement' had to be distinguished from fascism as a 'regime'. If the latter was an authoritarian, fractured system, the former (upon which De Felice insisted in the interview) was 'that part of fascism that has a certain vitality'. The controversy was not the result of prejudiced Italian historians who antagonized De Felice, as Ledeen mischievously suggests. In fact, it was Denis Mack Smith (no less an authority on Mussolini than De Felice) who labelled De Felice's view as 'a monument to the Duce'. Such poignancy aside, the interview began by exploring the theoretical background of De Felice's mammoth work on Mussolini and fascism. Several issues are discussed here.

232   Interpretations of fascism.
Renzo De Felice, translated by Brenda Huff Everett.   Cambridge, Massachusetts; London: Harvard University Press, 1977. 248p.

De Felice divides his narrative into two parts. Part one looks at fascism as a European phenomenon, surveying the literature on the subject, which ranges from the view of fascism as 'Europe's moral disease' to that which classifies it as a manifestation of totalitarianism. Part two is focused on the 'Italian interpretations of Italian fascism'. This is particularly interesting for readers who are unable to consult the vast, relevant body of literature written in Italian. De Felice begins with an outline of the history of fascism and a discussion on the problem of its origins. Four interpretative phases are suggested: prior to the assassination of Matteotti (1924); during the fascist regime; the post-liberation debate; and more recent cultural and historical discussions. De Felice concludes by offering his views on the relationship between fascism and capitalism. Charles Delzell provides a useful introduction and a bibliography of Renzo De Felice's works.

233   The Nationalist Association and the rise of fascism in Italy.
Alexander J. De Grand.   Lincoln, Nebraska; London: University of Nebraska Press, 1978. 238p. bibliog.

This book is the main contribution in English to the study of the nationalist origins of fascism. De Grand argues that 'Italian nationalism, as elaborated between 1903 and 1923 [when it merged with the Fascist Party], was one of the crucial ingredients in the mix which eventually became fascism and that its influence steered fascism in the direction of traditional conservative authoritarianism'. Thus the potential radicalism in Mussolini's movement was contained and Italian fascism was rendered quite different from German Nazism. The longest chapter is devoted to the First World War: it was during the last year of the war, in fact, that Mussolini's position on foreign policy drew closer to that of the nationalists.

234 **Italian fascism: its origins and development.**
Alexander J. De Grand. Lincoln, Nebraska; London: University of
Nebraska Press, 1982. 174p. 1 map. bibliog.
This is a lively, readable account of Italian fascism, set in its historical context.
'Italy's fascist regime – De Grand argues – was essentially a conservative response to
a crisis within Italian capitalism and to a break down of the liberal parliamentary
system that had developed in the nineteenth century'. The first part considers the
historical background. The two following, less condensed parts of the work discuss
'The Fascist regime in ascendancy, 1922-35', and 'The downward spiral, 1935-45'.
Within the chronological arrangement of the chapters, the emphasis shifts whenever
necessary from the domestic political scene to economic issues, from the regime's
foreign policy to the 'political culture' of fascism. In his conclusion, the author
reintroduces the distinction, common to other historians, between the 'fascist
movement' and the 'fascist regime'. A useful bibliographical essay is added at the
end of the book.

235 **The culture of consent: mass organization of leisure in fascist
Italy.**
Victoria De Grazia. Cambridge, England; London; New York;
Melbourne; Sydney: Cambridge University Press, 1981. 310p. bibliog.
This is a major investigation into the social history of fascist Italy. How fascism
organized leisure-time activities is the focus of the book, which expands on the
broader implications of such policies. The wider European canvas is also taken into
account. The basic leisure-time organization investigated by De Grazia is the *Opera
Nazionale Dopolavoro* (National After-work [Leisure] Organization). The first two
chapters provide a general introduction and outline the history of *Dopolavoro*, while
the impact of the organization on various economic sectors and social classes is
assessed in the following three chapters. Specific habits and pastimes are
subsequently examined. Finally, there is an analysis of the fascist organization of
leisure as an element of mass culture. The conclusion stresses that 'the ideological
consensus engendered by [these] diversionary pastimes [...] was bound to be
superficial and, in the end, fragile'.

236 **Mussolini's enemies: the Italian anti-fascist resistance.**
Charles F. Delzell. Princeton, New Jersey: Princeton University
Press, 1961. 620p. bibliog.
A relatively old book, this is still the only comprehensive account in English of the
Italian opposition to fascism. It is divided into two parts. The first part deals with the
'clandestine opposition', whose beginning arguably dates from 1924 (in the aftermath
of the murder of Matteotti) to 1943 (when Italy surrendered to the Allies). There is a
survey of the anti-fascist forces up until 1934, when the communists signed a 'unity
of action' pact with the socialists. The period of the 'popular front' (1934-39) and the
early war years are then explored. The second part covers in detail the armed
resistance from September 1943 to April 1945. The attention is directed to the
complex relations within the armed groups, between them and the Allies, as well as
between them and the Italian monarchist government. The final chapter surveys the
legacy of the resistance and outlines the subsequent Italian political development.

237 **Fascism and the mafia.**
Christopher Duggan. New Haven, Connecticut; London: Yale
University Press, 1989. 322p. 1 map. bibliog.

As the author states at the beginning of the work, 'this is a study, not of an organization, but of an idea'. The central thesis is, in fact, that mafia is a 'way of life' and an 'attitude of mind', rather than a secret society. The first part of the book discusses the development of that 'idea' after Sicily became part of the Italian State in 1860. The second, much larger part, is an investigation of the anti-mafia crusade launched by the fascist government between 1925 and 1929, when it is pointed out that the oversimplified view of the mafia as a criminal organization was exploited for political purposes. A brief epilogue deals with Sicily in the 1930s and during the Second World War. One of the main sources for this intense study were the private papers of Cesare Mori, the prefect of Palermo and the executor of fascist policies, who was suddenly forced to retire.

238 **Rethinking Italian fascism: capitalism, populism and culture.**
Edited by David Forgacs. London: Lawrence & Wishart, 1986. 209p.

This is an excellent collection of essays in which the editor himself provides a contribution on fascism as seen from the left. P. Corner considers it in relation to its precedence of liberalism, and highlights the failure of the latter 'to institutionalize political conflict'. T. Abse presents a case-study on the rise of fascism in Leghorn, where class struggle was sharp, while J. Steinberg considers the case of Calabria, where Mussolini's movement failed to make any serious impact. L. Caldwell argues that progressive welfare coexisted with anti-feminism and G. Nowell-Smith and L. Pertile demonstrate that cinema and literature, respectively, were relatively autonomous from the regime. Finally, L. Passerini deals with the oral memory of fascism, and R. Kedward draws the conclusion by pointing out that the revisionist approach to Italian fascism should help to better understand authoritarian liberal regimes. A chronology of fascism and a glossary are included.

239 **The Italian fascist party in power: a study of totalitarian rule.**
Dante L. Germino. Minneapolis, Minnesota: University of
Minnesota Press, 1959. 181p. bibliog.

Many important works on Italian fascism have been written since the appearance of this book, but as the first scholarly study of the role of the fascist party, it can still be read with interest. Germino concentrates on the period which began in January 1925, when Mussolini cowed parliamentary opposition, and ended with the outbreak of the Second World War. The book commences with a discussion of the forging of the party as 'a new tool for a new despotism' before investigating its role in maintaining Mussolini's regime and its flexible structure. Other topics are: the party leaders and followers; the policies implemented to achieve the regimentation of youth; the internecine struggles; and the party's alliance with the bureaucracy, the army and the police. The final chapter examines the control of the mass media.

240 **Young Mussolini and the intellectual origins of fascism.**
A. James Gregor. Berkeley, California; London: University of
California Press, 1979. 271p. bibliog.

The author traces the complex intellectual formation of young Mussolini, from anti-nationalist and anti-monarchist socialism to national syndicalism. He puts forward an interesting and provocative argument, claiming that the young Mussolini's heretical Marxism prefigured the revolutionary Marxism which was to characterize the modern world. Less controversial, perhaps, is the concluding statement that 'the First World War had reshaped Mussolini's revolutionary socialism into the first mass-mobilizing, developmental nationalism of the twentieth century'. This is also the embryo of the subsequent major work by Gregor, *Italian fascism and developmental dictatorship* (q.v.).

241 **Italian fascism and developmental dictatorship.**
A. James Gregor.   Princeton, New Jersey: Princeton University Press, 1979. 427p. bibliog.

A study of fascism as an ideological and political system, seen as one of the two 'mass mobilizing, developmental regimes that have become so prominent in the twentieth century' (the second one being, of course, the Soviet system). This is a revisionist work, similar to that carried out in Italy by Renzo De Felice and built around the concept of development. The modernizing and industrializing intentions of Mussolini's regime, Gregor maintains, have been neglected by most historians, who could not distance themselves from their aprioristic conviction that fascism was reactionary. The central argument is that the fascist belief system stemmed from the ideas of the syndicalists, who advocated 'a new nationalism that would animate proletarian nations in their struggle against the dominant plutocracies'. The importance of such fascist ideologues as Angelo Olivetti, Sergio Panunzio and Alfredo Rocco is stressed.

242 **Town and country under fascism: the transformation of Brescia, 1915-1926.**
Alice A. Kelikian.   Oxford: Clarendon Press, 1986. 228p. 2 maps. bibliog.

This is a 'microhistorical study' of a key manufacturing province in the heart of northern Italy, in the dramatic ten years between Italy's entry into the First World War and the consolidation of Mussolini's regime. By 1915 Brescia's economy was notably changing from farming to manufacturing, while the centre of gravity of the province was shifting from a rural to an urban environment. The war effort accelerated the pace of transformation, but the district remained socially heterogeneous, with a strong presence of Roman Catholic organizations. The focus of this well-researched and vividly-written book is on the relationship between economic development and the rapid fortunes of fascism in the early 1920s. Brescia saw neither the emergence of a sophisticated workers' movement, nor (consequently) a rabid reaction from the industrial and business circles, but the social conflicts in Italy as a whole loomed large.

243 **Mussolini unleashed, 1939-1941: politics and strategy in fascist Italy's last war.**
MacGregor Knox.   Cambridge, England; London; New York; Melbourne; Sydney: Cambridge University Press, 1982. 385p. bibliog.

A common view of the fascist foreign policy after 1935 is that it was a reflection of Mussolini's opportunism in the light of increasing German preponderance. In this detailed study of Italy's entry into the war Knox argues instead that Mussolini's policies and strategy had been consistent in their aim to dominate the Mediterranean, building on the inherited colonial conquest, and – in so doing – maintaining a compressed social order at home. The book concentrates on the uneasy decision by the Duce not to enter the war at its onset, his subsequent growing impatience, and the fatal step of joining Germany in arms in June, 1940. This is followed by an analysis of the disastrous attempt to invade Greece and the end of Italy's ambitions as a great power. The book is based on vast research and has made considerable use of the diary of Ciano, Mussolini's son-in-law and acknowledged successor. This is discussed in a brief appendix, which includes statistical tables.

244 **Believe, obey, fight: political socialization of youth in fascist Italy, 1922-1943.**
     Tracy H. Koon.   Chapel Hill, North Carolina; London: University of North Carolina Press, 1985. 343p. bibliog.

Three main components constitute this interesting study of fascist socialization: a survey and evaluation of the themes used for youth-oriented propaganda; a detailed description of the apparatus of socialization; and an assessment of the results of the youth programme. The process of political indoctrination of the young, Koon points out, can be divided into four chronological stages: firstly, the period ending with the Matteotti crisis (1924), during which period fascism struggled to become a regime; secondly, the years up to the early 1930s, when the first generation of 'socialized' youth emerged; thirdly, the subsequent years, when efforts were made to control a deviant tendency shown by politically-involved youth; and finally, the 'Starace era', still in the 1930s and culminating in the outbreak of the Second World War, when distinct forms of rejection of, or active opposition to the system became apparent.

245 **Fascism: a reader's guide: analyses, interpretations, bibliography.**
     Edited by Walter Laqueur.   London: Wildwood House, 1976. 478p. bibliog.

This is intended both as a critical review of studies on fascism twenty-five years after the end of the war, and as a survey of the issues which were (and to some extent still are) subjects of controversial debate. It is one of the earliest and most comprehensive attempts at offering an interdisciplinary approach to the study of fascism, with contributions by historians, political scientists, economists and sociologists. J. J. Linz provides an original introduction to a comparative study of fascism in a sociological and historical perspective and A. Lyttelton contributes with an excellent essay on Italian fascism. There are various pieces of German Nazism and forms of fascism in eastern and western Europe, and Latin America. The last sections include chapters on fascist ideology and economy, and on the interpretations of fascism.

246 **The seizure of power: fascism in Italy, 1919-1929.**
     Adrian Lyttelton.   London: Weidenfeld & Nicolson, 1987. 556p. 1 map. bibliog.

This superb study of Italian fascism was first published in 1973. It provides a factual and analytical account of its rise, development, seizure of power, and transformation into a system of 'unilateral totalitarianism'. The complicated interaction between the Italian State and the fascist party is examined in detail and with insight. Within a broadly chronological structure, the narrative often focuses on major issues, such as the relationship between Mussolini and his allies; the role of employers and the fate of trade unions; the origins of the Corporate State; and the fascist economy, ideology, culture and propaganda. An afterword written for the present edition surveys the recent research and debates on fascism. Considering the contemporary radical right, Lyttelton observes that 'if fascism survives as a political and ideological force, the fascist epoch has nonetheless closed and is not likely to recur'.

247 Mussolini's Roman Empire.
Denis Mack Smith. London; New York: Longman, 1976. 322p. 1 map. bibliog.

In this book Denis Mack Smith deals with Mussolini's foreign policy and the changing relationship of fascist Italy with the rest of the world. It is an authoritative study of Mussolini's diplomacy, colonial policies and bellicose postures. Mack Smith cogently argues that Mussolini 'deliberately steered his fascist movement into imperialism and into a succession of wars that left Italy prostrate'. The explanation of the dictator's war aims is masterfully conducted through a strict chronological order, from the fascist seizure of power in 1922 to 'the logical conclusion of fascism', that is its final collapse and utter defeat. As in all works by Mack Smith, scholarship of the highest quality is accompanied by a vigorous, scintillating narrative.

248 Italian fascism, 1919-1945.
Philip Morgan. Basingstoke, England; London: Macmillan, 1995. 209p. 1 map. bibliog.

A concise and readable study of Italian fascism, mainly based on a wide and sensible selection of secondary sources but also on the author's own research. It is divided into three parts. Part one (1919-29) includes a survey of pre-First World War Italy and of the political crisis of 1919-21 which opened the way to Mussolini's success. The two phases of 1922-25 (between 'normalisation' and 'revolution') and 1925-29 (the construction of the 'totalitarian state') are then examined, with more attention paid to the latter. Part two is devoted to the years of the 'great depression' (1929-34), and to those of the building of the empire (1935-36). Part three also distinguishes two sub-periods: the years of the 'fascistisation' of the country and its alliance with Germany (1936-40); and the war years up to the fall of Mussolini in 1943. The climatic story of the 'Italian Social Republic' (1943-45) is briefly examined in the epilogue.

249 International fascism: new thoughts and new approaches.
Edited by George L. Mosse. London; Beverley Hills, California: Sage Publications, 1979. 386p.

Mosse's introductory essay outlines a general theory of fascism, basing it on nationalistic mystique and the attempt to find a 'third way' between communism and capitalism. Hugh Seton-Watson's concluding essay, on the other hand, emphasizes that 'all fascist movements combine, in varying proportions, a reactionary ideology and a modern mass organization'. In between those two contributions, the contents of the book are divided into four parts, one of which is dedicated to Italian fascism. This consists of four essays: A. Lyttelton, 'Fascism in Italy: the second wave' (that is, the relaunch of the fascist drive after the assassination of Matteotti in 1924); P. Melograni, 'The cult of the Duce in Mussolini's Italy'; D. Settembrini, 'Mussolini and the legacy of revolutionary socialism'; and M. A. Ledeen, 'Renzo De Felice and the controversy over Italian fascism'.

250 **Fascism in popular memory: the cultural experience of the Turin working class.**
Luisa Passerini, translated by Robert Lumley, Julia Bloomfield.
Cambridge, England; London; New York; Melbourne; Sydney:
Cambridge University Press; Paris: Editions de la Maison des Sciences de l'Homme, 1987. 244p.

Passerini's research is a complex and important exercise in oral history. Over sixty men and women were interviewed; born between 1884 and 1922, most of them were in the prime of their lives at the height of the fascist era. They represent a cross-section of the working class of Turin, the Italian city with the highest degree of industrialization. The book is composed of three parts. Part one investigates the cultural identity of the interviewees through their autobiography and self-representation. Part two moves from the analysis of cultural identities to the conceptions of the world and of the self; it is here that people tell their story *vis-à-vis* fascism, indulging in the cherished memory of acts of small subversion such as jokes, songs, graffiti and obscenities. Part three considers the small-scale, everyday events as they were remembered by the subjects. An appendix with data on the interviews is included.

251 **The syndicalist tradition and Italian fascism.**
David D. Roberts. Manchester: Manchester University Press, 1979.
410p. bibliog.

This is the only systematic study of the relationship between Italian syndicalism and fascism. Syndicalism, as a militant trade-union movement, was deeply entrenched in the principle of class struggle; it was therefore generally thought that its legacy to the fascist conception of class harmony under corporatism had been muted. Roberts disagrees. His argument is unfolded through an analysis of the origins of Italian nationalism and syndicalism, and their development during the First World War and the post-war years until the rise of fascism and Mussolini's seizure of power. The continual action by syndicalists of publicizing their proposals for radical changes during the fascist regime is assessed, and the final chapter draws some general conclusions on Italian fascism in European history.

252 **Fascism and the industrial leadership in Italy, 1919-1940: a study in the expansion of private power under fascism.**
Roland Sarti. Berkeley, California; London: University of California Press, 1971. 154p. bibliog.

Sarti argues that Italian industrialists under fascism maintained their independence and exercised powerful political leverage. In fact, by the end of the Second World War, the industrialist leadership was more entrenched in the social and economic system than they had ever been before. An introductory section examines the relationship between fascism and industrialists before the March on Rome. The second part of the book considers the development of that relationship into an alliance (not without difficulties) in the early years of Mussolini's government. Part three is entitled 'The rewards of partnership' and focuses on, among other topics, the regimentation of labour, the emergence of the corporative State and the pursuit of autarky. A shorter fourth section considers the rise of public enterprise and the industrialists' reaction to the increase of political pressure after 1935.

253   **The fascist revolution in Tuscany, 1919-1922.**
      Frank M. Snowden.   Cambridge, England; London; New York;
      Melbourne; Sydney: Cambridge University Press, 1989. 295p. 1 map.
      bibliog.

The title should actually read 'The fascist counter-revolution', since that was the true role played by fascism, and this is also the main argument of Snowden's study. Tuscany is a unique case in that the chief components of fascist support, both industrial and agrarian, were concentrated there in their most powerful forms. The book, in three parts, analyses the reasons for this support and how far it related to national patterns. The first part deals with agrarian fascism, tracing its origin in the crisis of the traditional *mezzadria* system of land tenure, in the last decade of the 19th century. The second part looks into industrial and urban Tuscany, and part three explores the relations between the 'black shirts' and State officials.

254   **The birth of fascist ideology: from cultural rebellion to political
      revolution.**
      Zeev Sternhell, with Mario Sznajder, Maia Asheri, translated from the
      French by David Maisel.   Princeton, New Jersey: Princeton
      University Press, 1994. 338p. bibliog.

This book is based on two assumptions: the first is that 'fascism, before it became a political force, was a cultural phenomenon', and the second is that 'in the development of fascism, its conceptual framework played a role of special importance'. The main thesis emerging from these assumptions is that Italian fascism possessed a coherent ideology with deep roots in the crisis of European civilization at the turn of the century; a revolt against the values of the Enlightenment. The argument is sustained through a detailed study of Georges Sorel's thought and legacy, with the focus on revolutionary syndicalism in Italy and its off-shoot, described as 'the socialist-national synthesis'. The last section of the book discusses Mussolini's path 'from the critique of Marxism to national socialism and fascism'. The same theme of a transition from a basic cultural rebellion into a political revolution is reiterated in the epilogue.

255   **Fascism in Italy: society and culture, 1922-1945.**
      Edward R. Tannenbaum.   London: Allen Lane, 1973. 411p.

Tannenbaum describes and explains various aspects of the daily life and cultural developments of Italians under fascism, rather than studying the politics of the regime, as is more common. Out of necessity continuous references are made to the historical setting and to specific events, but the contents are not arranged in chronological order. The focus moves, from chapter to chapter, to such topics as the life of the fascist party, 'socialization and conformity', education, Catholicism, popular culture and propaganda, literary and artistic trends, and intellectual and cultural life. Regrettably, sport is neglected. Concluding the chapter on 'economy and labour', Tannenbaum writes that 'neither Balbo's transatlantic flights nor the creation of the African Empire could compensate Italy's working masses for their basic poverty and insecurity'. There are several illustrations.

256 **State control in fascist Italy: culture and conformity, 1925-43.**
Doug Thompson. Manchester, England; New York: Manchester
University Press, 1991. 174p. bibliog.

An engaging synthesis, drawing from a wide range of secondary sources, and focusing on the means of political and social control employed by the fascist regime. The book consists of five parts. Firstly, the establishment of the dictatorship through legislation is considered, referring to the years 1925-29. Secondly, the concomitant suppression of residual opposition is explored, together with the emergence of new forms of anti-fascism. Thirdly, the function of some important institutions which contributed to the legitimization of the system is examined (in particular, the Catholic Church). Thompson then concentrates on the instruments of propaganda and persuasion: from education to youth organization, the arts and the media. The final chapter discusses the collapse of 'consensus', mainly as a result of military disasters during the Second World War. The thrust of the argument is constructed around Gramsci's concept of bourgeois hegemony.

257 **The nature of fascism.**
Edited by Stuart J. Woolf. London: Weidenfeld & Nicolson, 1968. 261p.

This collection of essays represents a stimulating introduction to fascism (both in its general and in its Italian version) for the wide range of perspectives it offers and for the conciseness of its contributions. The contents are divided into four parts. The first discusses fascism and the polity, and includes essays on: fascism as a political system (N. Kogan); fascism and modernization (A. F. K. Organski); and the political 'instrumentality' of fascism (J. Sole-Tura). The second part explores the relation between fascism and society, and contains two essays on fascism and class (G. Germani and S. L. Andreski). Part three deals with fascism and the economy, and includes a theoretical piece (by the editor), an essay on the Italian case (S. Lombardini), and one on Nazi Germany (T. W. Mason). The final part concentrates on the relationship between fascism and the intellectuals and consists of a general contribution (G. L. Mosse), and one on Italian fascism (P. Vita-Finzi).

Foreign relations

258 **Test case: Italy, Ethiopia, and the League of Nations.**
George W. Baer. Stanford, California: Stanford University, Hoover
Institution Press, 1976. 376p. 1 map. bibliog.

This is an exploration of foreign policies and international security, focused on the 'test case' of the provisions implemented by the League of Nations after Mussolini's act of aggression against Ethiopia. Ultimately Mussolini triumphed on three fronts, gaining: military conquest of Ethiopia; diplomatic defeat of the League on the issue of sanctions; and enthusiastic support in Italy. The signs of indecision, weakness and confusion, especially on the part of Britain and France, were misread by Mussolini, and represented the first step towards his alliance with Hitler and – ultimately – towards the Second World War. Twelve chapters analyse all the aspects of the 'test case' and its wide background, stressing the 'double policies' of Britain and France, America's neutrality, the Mediterranean theatre and the German military occupation of the Rhineland. The dramatic few months between the autumn of 1935 and the spring of 1936 are examined in exemplary fashion.

259   **Russia and Italy against Hitler: the Bolshevik-Fascist rapprochement of the 1930s.**
Joseph Calvitt Clarke III.   New York; Westport, Connecticut; London: Greenwood Press, 1991. 218p. bibliog.

The author argues that ideological and political differences between the Soviet Union and fascist Italy did not inhibit the rapprochement in 1933-34, nor was it intended on either side to alienate Berlin after Hitler's assumption of power. Part one of the book provides the backdrop to the rapprochement, from early relations between the two countries to Mussolini's proposed four-power pact early in 1933. Part two examines in greater detail the road towards the Italian-Soviet Pact of Friendship, Neutrality, and Non-aggression, of September 1933. Finally, an epilogue outlines the subsequent difficulties and eventual collapse of that bilateral relationship, at the time of the Spanish civil war. Figures on Soviet-Italian trade are included.

260   **Italo-British relations in the eastern Mediterranean, 1919-1923: the view from Rome.**
Louis A. Cretella.   New York; London: Garland, 1991. 445p. 3 maps. bibliog.

Cretella discusses a relatively neglected area of Italian foreign policy in the wake of the First World War. He has carried out a comprehensive study of Italy's diplomacy which aimed at commercial and economic expansion in Asia Minor, after the defeat of Turkey and in the hope of joining France and Britain as major western powers in the eastern Mediterranean. A tripartite agreement (1920) appeared to meet Italy's expectations, but eventually Britain declined its support since the British financial interests were not keen to see Italy's ambitious programme achieved. As a result, 'the Eastern Question constituted [. . .] one of several issues that divided Italy from its former wartime allies from 1919 to 1923'. It also contributed to the dissatisfaction, shared by many Italians, with the post-war diplomatic position of their country in Europe – and this had no small part in the surge of nationalistic feelings and the rise of fascism.

261   **Trieste, 1941-1954: the ethnic, political and ideological struggle.**
Bodgan C. Novak.   Chicago; London: The University of Chicago Press, 1970. 526p. 4 maps. bibliog.

The subject of this rather outdated book has been recently revived, as a consequence of the break-up of Yugoslavia, and the entry of neo-fascists into Berlusconi's government (1994): they wasted no time in claiming the return to Italy of the lands ceded to her eastern neighbour at the end of the Second World War. The Italian-Yugoslav border dispute of 1941-54 is viewed here as a struggle of nationalisms (Italian, Slovenian and Croat) in an ethnically mixed territory. The broadest context of international politics provides the background to the study. Five years after the appearance of this book Italy and Yugoslavia signed a treaty which recognized the *status quo* and committed the Yugoslav government to providing compensation to the Italians who had lost their properties when fleeing Istria and Dalmatian territories. Berlusconi's government maintained that this commitment had not been observed.

262 **Italian support for Croatian separatism, 1927-1937.**
James J. Sadkovich. New York; London: Garland, 1987. 485p.
7 maps. bibliog.

This academic work addresses a little-known historical issue which has acquired poignancy in the light of the disintegration of Yugoslavia in the 1990s. The complicated Italo-Yugoslav relations are comprehensively investigated in eight very concentrated chapters. Until the late 1920s, Sadkovich argues, Mussolini's desire to establish Italy's dominance in the Balkans did not involve the manipulation of the Croatian dissatisfaction with the Serbs. Even when, later, the Italian government did support Ante Pavelić and the Ustaša (the fascist Croats), close contact was also maintained with other Croatian leaders and movements (notably the Peasant Party). The Italian support for Croatian separatism came to an end in 1937, when Mussolini 'sacrificed the Ustaša to obtain a pact with Belgrade'.

263 **The United States and fascist Italy, 1922-1940.**
David F. Schmitz. Chapel Hill, North Carolina; London: The
University of North Carolina Press, 1988. 273p. bibliog.

Schmitz examines the concerns and expectations of American political leaders in relation to Mussolini's Italy up until the country's entry into the Second World War. A particularly interesting thesis is that the early experience with fascist Italy influenced President Roosevelt's thoughts about European problems during the 1930s, and that one consequence of this was his policy of economic appeasement towards Hitler's Germany. In fact, the wider European context is consistently acknowledged by Schmitz, who concludes by drawing a general, contemporary lesson from his study: 'The history of relations with fascism in Italy raises serious questions for those who believe the United States can profit from supporting right-wing dictatorial regimes today'.

The Second World War

264 **A strange alliance: aspects of escape and survival in Italy, 1943-45.**
Roger Absalom. Florence: Leo S. Olschki, 1991. 343p. bibliog.

Nearly 50,000 Allied prisoners of war held in Italy escaped in September 1943, after the Italians surrendered and the Germans took over much of the peninsula. They were supported and helped by hundreds of thousands of Italian peasants although such willingness to aid the fugitives did not arise so much from anti-fascist sentiments, as from their 'understanding of the human predicament [. . . so that] those in trouble with authority were never regarded as aliens'. The outcome of a long and passionate research (also involving the discovery of important material in American archives), this book represents a fascinating contribution to Italian history, but also to social anthropology, in that the big question raised is 'when and how peasants make the transition to a world staged and managed by and for the non-peasant minority, and how they can abet or resist the pressures to do so'.

265   **The brutal friendship: Mussolini, Hitler, and the fall of Italian fascism.**
Frederick William Deakin.   Harmondsworth, England: Penguin Books, 1966. 575p. bibliog. (Part one of the original version published with the same title in 1962).

This is the first half of Deakin's classic work on the fall of Italian fascism. It is a meticulous study of the events leading to the meeting of the Grand Council of Fascism (24-25 July, 1943), which was instrumental in the removal of Mussolini. The starting point is the summer of 1942, when the fortunes of the Axis armies began to be reversed. The setting is outlined in the first chapters of the first part, which carries the story as far as the winter crisis (1942-43). The overall military scene and diplomatic front, in the shadow of Stalingrad, is explored in the second part, while the third part deals with the defeat in northern Africa and its immediate aftermath in Italy. The final part concentrates on the landing of the Allies in Sicily, the meeting of Mussolini and Hitler at Feltre, and the monarchist coup of July, 1943.

266   **The last days of Mussolini.**
Frederick William Deakin.   Harmondsworth, England: Penguin Books, 1966. 378p. bibliog. (Parts two and three of the original version published in 1962, as *The brutal friendship*).

This is the second half of Deakin's absorbing day-to-day story of the fall of Italian fascism. It consists of a large first section, resuming the narrative from the return of Mussolini and the setting up of his puppet Republic in the autumn of 1943, to the first months of 1945. The succinct second section covers the last weeks of the war in Italy and the literally 'last days of Mussolini'. This painstaking account of two-and-a-half years focusing on the collapse and disintegration of fascism concludes with the executions of the Duce, his mistress and the leading fascists who had stayed with him in his clumsy attempt to escape to Switzerland. There is also an appendix on the German authorities and the seizure of the Italian foreign archives (1943-44).

267   **The other Italy: Italian resistance in World War II.**
Maria De Blasio Wilhelm, drawings by Enzo Marino.   New York; London: W. W. Norton, 1988. 272p. 1 map. bibliog.

A readable account of the Italians' fight against fascism between 1943 and 1945. The first chapter outlines the origins of anti-fascism and provides a relevant chronological table (1936-43). A mainly thematic approach is then pursued in the following chapters, which deal with: the anti-German 'four days' of Naples; the mountain partisans in Piedmont; the songs of the Resistance; the partisans in the cities and in the countryside; women of the Resistance; the Jews in Italy; the Catholic 'loyal opposition'; the unification of the Resistance movement; and the final insurrections. Photographs and drawings illustrate the book.

268   **Italy 1943-1945.**
David W. Ellwood.   Leicester, England: Leicester University Press, 1985. 313p. 3 maps. bibliog.

This book is divided into three parts, dealing with 1943, 1944, and 1945, respectively. Within this simple chronological arrangement, Ellwood conducts a thorough investigation of the liberation of Italy, at two interdependent levels: 'the story of the

Italian Question in international politics after the surrender of September 1943'; and the story of the Allied presence in the Italian peninsula, with immense political and economic consequences. It is a well-written and balanced study, based on a wide range of primary and secondary sources. The role of the armed Resistance and its complex political implications are scrupulously evaluated as is the short-sightedness shown towards it by the Allies. At the end, 'stability and prosperity were offered – from outside – as the beacons of the future, but the delicate, self-regulating equilibrium required by the working of power in the West [. . .] was far from guaranteed'.

269   War in Italy: 1943-1945: a brutal story.
Richard Lamb.   London: John Murray, 1993. 335p. 5 maps. bibliog.

There are very few accounts of the Italian campaign which place the emphasis more on people than on military operations, and this is one of them. The narrative combines chronological order with a thematic approach. The focus moves from the fate of Italian Jews under the Nazis to a general assessment of the German atrocities against ordinary citizens as well as against the soldiers who would not surrender (as was the case in the Balkans and the Aegean). Other interesting topics covered are the organization of Mussolini's republican army; the relationship between the Italians and the Allied prisoners of war; the divisions and conflicts within the Resistance forces, and their relations with the British SOE (Special Operations Executive) and the American OSS (Office of Strategic Services). One important point made by Lamb is that, in his tragic role as a defeated figure under German control, Mussolini still tried to shield the civil population from unmitigated Nazi brutality.

270   Naples '44.
Norman Lewis.   London: Collins, 1978. 206p.

A fascinating chronicle, in the form of a diary, of the one year Lewis spent in Naples as an NCO in the Field Security Police (attached to the American 5th Army). The author draws from his own notes made at the time for filing official reports. In the tragic setting of devastated Naples and of its near-starving inhabitants, innumerable episodes are told, in which humour, warmth and pathos are skilfully blended. It is a true Rabelaisian story, a kaleidoscope tale of different human characters, each of them devising their own attempt at surviving; such as the unemployed lawyer who saved his energies by staying in bed most of the day, walking slowly and 'stopping to rest every few hundred yards in a church'. Not all characters inspire sympathy, however; for instance, the priest who visited the FS Police headquarters, 'with a pocketful of denunciation, [and] asked for a permit to be allowed to carry a pistol'.

271   War in Val d'Orcia: a diary.
Iris Origo.   London: Century Hutchinson, 1985. 239p. 1 map.

The first entry in the diary is 30 January 1943 and the last is 5 July 1944. It is an eye-witness, absorbing account of civilian life in southern Tuscany, during the last stage of the Italo-German alliance (when many Italian cities were heavily bombed), the Allies' landing in Sicily, the dismissal of Mussolini, the German invasion of the peninsula, the armistice, the transformation of the whole of Italy into a battlefield, the emergence of the Resistance, the withdrawal of the Germans from central Italy, and the arrival of the Allied troops. In his introduction to this new edition, Denis Mack Smith refers to the diary as 'a minor masterpiece'. Through Origo's perceptive observations on daily events a dramatic story unfolds of 'individual tragedy and suffering, but at the same time of great generosity, courage, and even heroism'. A historical setting is provided both by the introduction and the author's own preface. The book was first published in 1947 by Jonathan Cape.

272 **All or nothing: the Axis and the Holocaust, 1941-43.**
Jonathan Steinberg.   London; New York: Routledge, 1990. 320p. 3 maps. bibliog.

Many Jews in occupied territories were saved by the muted but effective action of resistance, enacted by the Italian military and civil authorities behind Mussolini's back. Steinberg's book is the first thorough study of the reasons why the Italians acted so differently from their allies and masters. It is a work which contributes enormously to the understanding of the Italian-German relationship and the story of Italian Jews under fascism. The book is based on a vast range of primary sources, and is divided into two sections: 'The events' and 'Explanations'. In the first section, the author examines all the evidence he could gather as to what happened to Jews in territories occupied by German and Italian forces: Croatia, Greece and Southern France. The second part consists of four fascinating essays on the cultural contrasts which may offer an explanation for the different attitude towards the Jews.

Post-Second World War

273 **Power in Europe? Great Britain, France, Italy and Germany in a postwar world, 1945-1950.**
Edited by Josef Becker, Franz Knipping.   Berlin; New York: Walter de Gruyter, 1986. 583p.

This volume contains essays on a wide range of interesting topics on the post-war years. B. Vigezzi writes on 'Italy: the end of a "great power" and the birth of a "democratic power" '. A. Varsori discusses 'De Gasperi, Nenni, Sforza and their role in post-war Italian foreign policy'. S. Galante looks into 'Italy's mass political parties in the years between the Great Alliance and the Cold War'. R. H. Rainero contributes with 'The Italian Communist Party and the Italian imperial problem'. There is also an essay by V. Zamagni on 'The reconstruction of Italian industry, 1946-1952'. E. Decleva concentrates on 'The Italian liberal-democratic press and the reality of the international situation (1945-1949)'. The two final contributions are by E. Di Nolfo ('The Shaping of Italian foreign policy during the formation of the East-West blocs') and E. Aga Rossi ('Italy at the outbreak of the Cold War').

274 **A history of contemporary Italy: society and politics: 1943-1988.**
Paul Ginsborg.   London: Penguin Books, 1990. 586p. bibliog. 1 map.

Compulsory reading for anybody interested in the history of post-war Italy, this large volume is elegantly written and widely documented. It combines a thorough analysis of the changes and continuities in Italian society, with admirable sensitivity when dealing with the human dimension of the story. Chapters are arranged in a strict chronological order, commencing with 'Italy at war', and ending with 'Italy in the 1980s', but appropriate emphasis is put on important issues, such as the agrarian reform of the 1950s and the 'economic miracle' of the 1950s and 1960s. Some major threads are followed throughout; for instance, the analysis of the role of the family takes into account the differences in various parts of Italy. A statistical appendix containing a wealth of tables and graphs completes this outstanding work.

275 **America and the reconstruction of Italy, 1945-1948.**
John L. Harper.   Cambridge, England; London; New York;
Melbourne; Sydney: Cambridge University Press, 1986. 213p. bibliog.

This is a scrupulous study of the early post-war years in Italy, concentrating on the American role in the reconstruction of the country's economic and political system. The large amount of detail included in the account does not impede the narrative flow. The first chapters prepare the ground for the subsequent analysis, with information on the historical, political and economic background. The advent of De Gasperi is emphasized, and the tensions within the coalition government he led (including the conservative Liberals and the Communists) are examined. The relief operation under the United Nations' agency UNRRA is considered, as well as the concurrent political crisis and deflationary measures on the economy. The concluding chapter touches upon the Marshall Plan and the following period, and Harper comments that 'America lacked the necessary intellectual and political resources to address Italy's historic problems of poverty, disunity, and vulnerability'.

276 **A political history of Italy: the post-war years.**
Norman Kogan.   New York: Praeger, 1983. 366p. bibliog.

This is the result of the amalgamation of two books published under similar titles in 1966 and 1981. Only minor adjustments were made to what is an authoritative description of the major political and economic events, from 1945 to the early 1980s. Intentionally, only passing attention is directed to cultural trends and social issues. Yet, Kogan's conclusion is that the real heroes of this story are not those who are household names, but ordinary people, who survived difficult tests throughout the post-war years (especially the critical 1970s) with remarkable resilience. A rigid chronological order is followed, with chapter titles clearly indicating their contents: from 'postwar settlement' to 'the difficulties of "centrism" ', 'the economic boom', and 'the evolution of the communists'. There is a useful glossary and a synoptic table of events (to October, 1980).

277 **The rebirth of Italy, 1943-50.**
Edited by Stuart J. Woolf.   London: Longman, 1972. 264p. bibliog.

The 'rebirth of Italy' between 1943 and 1950 can be considered from various angles: in terms of the transition from monarchy to republic, from fascism to democracy, from war to peace, and from economic havoc to a reconstruction which laid the foundations of the 'economic miracle'. These and other aspects are discussed here in the following contributions: the politics of the Italian Resistance (G. Quazza); Italy and the allied powers (G. Warner); the rebirth of the party system (F. Catalano); the south and national politics (P. A. Allum); the republican constitution (P. Vercellone); the role of the Catholic Church (G. Poggi); economic policy during the reconstruction (M. De Cecco); and a general assessment, by the editor. The book includes a chronology, tables with the election results (1946 and 1948), and the names of government ministers (excluding, of course, Mussolini's governments).

Economic history

278 **The European economy.**
Edited by Andrea Boltho.   Oxford: Oxford University Press, 1982.
668p. bibliog.

This is an important and rare work on the comparative economy of the main European
countries, consisting of three distinct but complementary parts. In particular, part
three offers monographs on various countries or areas. G. M. Rey outlines the phases
of economic growth in Italy after the Second World War following the traditional
pattern: the years of rapid growth (1951-63); the years of stabilization (1963-69); and
the years of crisis (1969-79). Rey highlights certain trends through the thirty-year
span, in particular the growth of the industrial sector at the expense of agriculture; he
also notes that, at the time of his writing, two negative features were prominent: a
record budget deficit and a record rate of inflation. References to the Italian economy
are frequent throughout the volume. There are many tables and graphs.

279 **From peasant to entrepreneur: the survival of the family economy
in Italy.**
Anna Cento Bull, Paul Corner.   Oxford; Providence, Rhode Island:
Berg, 1993. 174p. 1 map. bibliog.

The focus of this fine study is the area around Como (north of Milan) and its silk
industry during the course of the last 150 years, but its scope is broader. Como and
the silk industry are taken to exemplify 'certain aspects of a specifically Italian
process of industrialization', namely, the successful development and mushrooming
of small family-based firms which stem from a rural background. This important
conclusion on an 'Italian model' of economic development is persuasively argued in
the last section of the book. The preceding chapters provide a historical analysis of
the case study: from a survey of 19th-century peasant families and labour to the
agrarian crisis at the end of that century; the impact of the First World War and
fascism (contemporary to the decline of the silk industry); and the post-war changes.
It is, therefore, a study of transition from an agricultural to an industrial economy.

280 **The economic history of modern Italy.**
Shepard B. Clough.   New York; London: Columbia University Press,
1964. 458p. 1 map.

This is a classic study of Italy's economic progress from unification to the 'economic
miracle' of the late 1950s. It is an impressive and valuable work, despite the
subsequent development of more sophisticated theoretical approaches to economic
history. Two introductory chapters are followed by a fine synthesis on the foundation
for economic growth laid down between 1861 and 1914, with a focus on agriculture,
banking, commerce, population, emigration, and labour. Clough then considers the
Italian economy during the First World War and its aftermath, before the attention is
centred on fascism and its economic policies, the Second World War and its
immediate consequences, the economic reconstruction and development up to 1960.
A final chapter deals with the national income and the Welfare State. There are
various tables and more statistical data and graphs are included in the appendix.

281 **Merchants, monopolists and contractors: a study of economic activity and society in Bourbon Naples, 1815-1860.**
John A. Davis.   New York: Arno Press, 1981. 340p. bibliog.

First appearing as an Italian translation in 1979, this is the reproduction of a doctoral dissertation. It represents a thorough study of the response of the southern Italian mainland (Sicily is excluded) to the challenge of industrialization and focuses on the activities, organization and behaviour of 'merchants, monopolists and contractors' in the main branches of economic life. The work is divided into three parts. Part one examines the nature of commercial activities, emphasizing their relationship with the agricultural sector. In part two these activities are explored in greater detail and it is argued that 'the wealth and power of the leading interests relied on the creation of monopolistic preserves which were jealously guarded, making them hostile to attempts to favour expansion or change'. Part three deals with the consequences of these activities and the structure of political power exercised by the conservative commercial elites.

282 **Capitalism in the Risorgimento: joint-stock banking and economic development in the kingdom of Sardinia, 1843-1859.**
Paul M. Howell.   New York; London: Garland, 1992. 268p. 4 maps. bibliog.

A major contribution to the study of economic development in Piedmont during the two decades preceding the unification of Italy, a movement which was spearheaded by that regional kingdom. Two fundamental innovations were introduced, which characterized the economic development of early 19th-century Europe: the joint-stock bank and the railroad. Much of this book is devoted to them, and to their close relationship. In particular, emphasis is placed on the expansion of one bank (the *Cassa del Commercio e dell'Industria*, established in 1853) and the involvement of French capital in the construction of the Italian railroad and the Fréjus tunnel. In his conclusion, Howell pays tribute to Cavour's contribution to the achievements of Piedmont, but also adds that with the unification of the peninsula 'the strength of regional and particularist interest [. . .] undermined the cohesive policy and modern-looking coalition of State and capital that had characterised Cavourian Sardinia'.

283 **In search of stability: explorations in historical political economy.**
Charles S. Maier.   Cambridge, England: Cambridge University Press, 1987. 293p.

The essays contained in this book have also appeared in various journals and are divided here into two parts, which deal with: 'Ideology and economics from World War I to mid-century'; and 'Collective preferences and public outcomes'. There are several references to Italy; in particular, the most extended chapter deals with 'The economics of Fascism and Nazism'. It is based on a wide survey of the relevant literature and statistical sources (some tables are included), and discusses the main arguments on economic development under non-democratic conditions. The constant comparison between the Italian and the German case is very interesting. Maier maintains that 'the Italian economy probably underwent more qualitative change under fascism than did the German [. . .] Nevertheless, the fascists did not really succeed in pushing through structural changes outside the regions already on their way to development'.

284 **Pastoral economics in the Kingdom of Naples.**
John A. Marino. Baltimore, Maryland; London: The Johns Hopkins
University Press, 1988. 381p. 6 maps.

This is a study of the economic and social conditions of 16th- and 17th-century
southern Italy. Its scope is wider than the title suggests as it provides a variety of
implications for the culture of Italy as a whole, as well as a model of analysis for
Mediterranean agricultural and pastoral cultures in general. The work discusses the
structure of pastoral society in the Apulian plain, and the ways in which the Bourbon
State attempted to reconcile the conflicting interests of sheep farmers and graziers
with those employed in agriculture (including landowners' interests). There emerges a
complex system of sheep and land ownership, administration, commerce, taxation,
social stratification and culture, centred in the customs house of Foggia. A history of
transhumance and of the laws regulating the seasonal migration of shepherds from the
Middle Ages is provided, as well as the political implications for regulated
government.

285 **Land and economy in Baroque Italy: Valpolicella, 1630-1797.**
Peter Musgrave. Leicester, England; London: Leicester University
Press, 1992. 202p. 1 map. bibliog.

The 17th and 18th centuries, the Age of Baroque, marked economic stagnation and
decline in Italy, and the Republic of Venice was no exception, whether in its far-away
outposts or mainland territory. The district studied here is north of Verona, and is
almost solely known as a wine-growing area. Musgrave's study of its economic
history is a fascinating contribution to the understanding of economic decline in
general. This is achieved through vast research among primary sources, paying
special attention to the peculiar confederate structure of the lands under Venetian
rule. Important chapters are devoted to the system of agricultural production and land
ownership. In his conclusion the author stresses that, in explaining the worsening
economic conditions of the region, a major factor was 'the loss of the ability to
respond to crisis in any other way than to collapse'.

286 **The Italian war economy, 1940-1943: with particular reference to
Italian relations with Germany.**
Angela Raspin. New York; London: Garland, 1986. 462p. bibliog.

This study of Italy's war economy until the fall of Mussolini mainly resorts to
German literature on the subject and is therefore largely representative of a German
viewpoint. This is, firstly, because the German archives are the best source for the
reconstruction of the economic issues in those years, and secondly because Italy
heavily depended upon German economic support. The condition of the Italian
economy at the outbreak of the war and during the subsequent period of Italian 'non
belligerence' is outlined. The analysis of Italy's first two war years follows,
concentrating on the problems of the supply of strategic and raw materials, labour and
food, trade clearing with Germany and arms. Raspin finally argues that 'the real
Italian response to the failure of the system with which she entered the war was not to
change the system in order to make war more effectively, but to discard the system in
order to make peace'.

287 **Italy, 1920-1970.**
Sergio Ricossa, translated by Muriel Grindrod.   In: *Contemporary economies*, vol. 1.   Edited by Carlo M. Cipolla.   Hassocks, England: The Harvester Press, 1977, p. 266-322. bibliog.

At the beginning of the fifty-year period covered in the text Italy was a semi-developed country; but by the end of it, she was poised to become one of the leading industrialized countries. The transformation is charted here with systematic reference to statistical data. Italy's inter-war economic development was slow and the dual (North/South) character of the country's economy became more pronounced. After the Second World War, Italy's economic growth took off, and Ricossa provides a cogent analysis of the 'miracle' and its limitations. He concludes with observations on the changing conditions in the labour market, which was a major issue at the end of the 1960s.

288 **An economic history of liberal Italy, 1850-1918.**
Gianni Toniolo.   London: Routledge, 1990. 192p. bibliog.

This is a textbook on the origins of Italy's industrialization. It is divided into three parts: chapters one to four survey the statistical evidence of such macro-indicators as national product, demand, banking and finance, welfare, and productivity from the mid-19th century to the 1920s (thus crossing the upper time limit set in the title). Chapters five to eleven offer a chronological account of economic events, with an emphasis on the changes which took place during the first fifteen years of the 20th century (the 'Giolittian era'). The final chapter has a historiographical character, and deals with the interpretations of Italy's economic development in the period under consideration. The debate on this will continue, and suggestions that Italy's economic conditions were stagnant for most of the second half of the 19th century may have to be substantially revised when research now in progress is completed.

289 **The economic history of Italy, 1860-1990: recovery after decline.**
Vera Zamagni.   Oxford: Clarendon Press, 1993. 413p. 6 maps.

A broad interpretative and comparative account of the economic development of Italy since its unification is provided in the comprehensive introduction to this work. The main body of the book is then divided into three parts. Part one deals with the long period of economic take-off (1860-1913), focusing on agriculture and regional imbalances, the transition from craftsmanship to industrial production, the role of international trade and the banking system, state intervention, and the social and cultural background. Part two examines the period between the First World War and the rise of fascism, and the economic policies and conditions of industry and finance under Mussolini. Part three surveys and analyses the post-war boom, concentrating on the rebuilding of the economy, the 'economic miracle' and the subsequent crises and recovery. In her conclusion, Zamagni points out that 'the distinctive feature of the Italian case [...] is its limitless flexibility, typical of small businesses'. Many statistical tables are included.

Social history

290 Fate and honor, family and village: demographic and cultural changes in rural Italy since 1800.
Rudolph M. Bell.   Chicago; London: The University of Chicago Press, 1979. 270p. 1 map. bibliog.

Four rural towns in different parts of the Italian peninsula are examined by Bell: Albareto, in the Apennine valleys between Genoa and Parma; Castel San Giorgio, between Naples and Salerno; Rogliano, near Cosenza (in Calabria); and Nissoria, in central Sicily. This is a fascinating study which combines the insights of the anthropologist and the social historian. The essence of the Italian peasant's response to the challenge of life, Bell argues, is contained in four words: *fortuna* (fatalism), *onore, famiglia* and *campanilismo* (loyalty to the values of village life). The physical setting and the history of the four villages is outlined in the first two chapters, followed by chapters on the perception of time and space, the role of the family, working practices and emigration. There are several tables and figures. Interesting appendices contain further figures, definitions of social categories and lists of occupations.

291 The doge of Venice: the symbolism of state power in the Renaissance.
Åsa Boholm.   Gothenburg, Sweden: Institute for Advanced Studies in Social Anthropology (IASSA), 1990. 298p. bibliog.

The result of meticulous research carried out under the heading of 'the semantics of political processes', this work studies the rituals and forms associated with dogeship in Venice, within a broadly anthropological framework. It is illustrated with twelve plates.

292 The historical anthropology of early modern Italy: essays on perception and communication.
Peter Burke.   Cambridge, England; London; New York; Melbourne; Sydney: Cambridge University Press, 1987. 281p. bibliog.

A collection of scholarly essays on different topics, mainly concerning 16th- and 17th-century Italy, these are studies of cultural history, which the author presents as a contribution to 'historical anthropology'. The book is divided into two parts: 'Modes of perception', and 'Modes of communication'. The former includes studies on the classification of people and the perception of religious forms; the latter contains essays on a wide range of topics, such as: 'insult and blasphemy'; 'conspicuous consumption'; 'the carnival of Venice'; and the Masaniello revolt in Naples (1647). The revolt is analysed in connection with a powerful symbol of people's identity: the Virgin of Mount Carmel. 'The tragedy of Masaniello – Burke writes – is that he was a sansculottes leader without aristocratic or bourgeois support'.

293 The magic harvest: food, folklore and society.
Piero Camporesi.   Cambridge, England: Polity Press, 1993. 253p.

This is a collection of essays inspired by Camporesi's interest in the history of popular mentality. It is centred on the social symbolism of food and its associated rituals, with examples taken mainly from the regions of Emilia-Romagna and Tuscany. Although originally written at different times and on various occasions, the essays are united by a clear thread: 'the dietary customs of modern Italy and the folklore and anthropology of food, from the pre-industrial period to our own day' The most comprehensive essay, entitled 'Bourgeois cooking in the nineteenth century', first appeared as an introduction to a new edition of the most celebrated manual of Italian cooking – Artusi's *La scienza in cucina* (1891). In another essay 'The age of the soya bean', Camporesi laments 'the casual mixing and overlapping of culinary languages [and the] provincialization of taste' now affecting the best of Italian cooking traditions. A glossary concludes the book.

294 **L'arte della cucina in Italia: libri di ricette e trattati sulla civiltà della tavola dal XIV al XIX secolo.** (The art of cookery in Italy: recipe books and treatises on table civilization from the 14th to the 19th century.)
Edited by Emilio Faccioli. Turin: Einaudi, 1987. 878p. bibliog.

After a general detailed and scholarly introduction to the history of gastronomy in Italy, the book collects the complete texts, or large excerpts from, over thirty recipe books, treatises, or descriptions concerning food, wine, and table customs. Excerpts range from the early 14th century by the Bolognese Pietro De' Crescenzi (in Latin with the Italian translation opposite), to a text on pâtisserie by a cook of the king of Piedmont. Each text is prefaced by a historical introduction and all rare gastronomic terms are annotated, but not, unfortunately, collected in a final glossary. For further works of bibliography, reference is made to standard works such as Katherine Golden Bitting, *Gastronomic bibliography* (San Francisco, 1939), André Simon, *Bibliotheca gastronomica* (London, 1953), and Lord Westbury, *Handlist of Italian cookery books* (Florence, 1963).

295 **Architettura contadina in Valtrompia.** (Peasant architecture in Valtrompia.)
A. Fappani, S. Fontana, et al. Milan: Silvana Editoriale, 1980. 142p.

This book will be of interest to anybody concerned with the architecture of Valtrompia, a remote part of northern Italy in the territory of Bergamo in Lombardy. In this area examples of 15th-century 'noble' architecture coexist with the buildings constructed by farmers for their own families. The study of peasant architecture is part of the larger study of folk culture in Italy and its interest lies in the adaptation to the immediate needs of subsistence farmers.

296 **Prostitution and the State in Italy, 1860-1915.**
Mary Gibson. New Brunswick, New Jersey; London: Rutgers University Press, 1986. 297p. bibliog.

The first piece of legislation to control prostitution in modern Italy was promulgated by Cavour in 1860, on the eve of the unification of the country. The stated motive of the Cavour Act was to prevent the feared spread of venereal disease among the Piedmontese soldiers who were about to become the new Italian army. However, Gibson explains that the real purpose was 'to preserve a practice desired by a great number of Italian men, yet at the same time extend the power of the central state over its female practitioners'. The registration of prostitutes was criticized by early feminists and democrats and although the system was slightly liberated towards the end of the century, it was only completely abolished in 1958. Gibson offers an account of the development of state policy and the regulation of prostitution in the first part of the book. The second part provides a social profile of prostitutes, and a study of police surveillance and medical examination.

297   **The Merton tradition and kinematics in late sixteenth and early seventeenth century Italy.**
Christopher Lewis. Padua: Antenore, 1980. 328p. bibliog.
This study, based on a PhD thesis at the Warburg Institute, University of London, investigates the scientific tradition stemming from Merton College, Oxford, to find that it was little studied during the period 1570-1620 when Galileo and other early 17th-century scholars were studying natural philosophy in Pisa, Padua, and the Jesuit Collegio Romano. Contrary to the accepted historical hypothesis, Lewis proves that 'knowledge of the Merton tradition was rather shaky' in Galileo's time, although Galileo seemed to use a Mertonian concept of velocity.

298   **The political economy of shopkeeping in Milan, 1886-1922.**
Jonathan Morris. Cambridge, England: Cambridge University Press, 1993. 312p. 1 map. bibliog.
In this major academic work Morris considers a much-neglected complex stratum of Italian society: the lower middle classes. It is highly readable, despite the frequent references to statistical tables, graphs and figures. The author's chief aim is to study the emergence of a small-trader movement in Milan after 1885. The establishment of a shopkeepers' federation was accompanied by the creation of a newspaper and a bank, linked to the movement. A variety of political stances culminated in a failed attempt to establish a collaboration with the left. From the early years of the new century the movement gradually shifted to the right, because of their opposition to State interference in their activity. The main argument of the book is on the former period, with a concise final chapter on the growing gap between the shopkeepers and local socialist administrators. There are interesting insights on the sense of identity of Milanese shopkeepers.

299   **Prophecy and people in Renaissance Italy.**
Ottavia Niccoli, translated from the Italian by Lydia G. Cochrane. Princeton, New Jersey: Princeton University Press, 1990. 208p.
Originally published in Italian (*Profeti e popolo nell'Italia del Rinascimento*) in 1987, this is a fundamental study of prophecies, monsters, divination and propaganda in broadsheets, apparitions and signs, apocalyptic preaching and related topics from the beginning of the 16th century until 1530. The book contains a wealth of critically-studied information, and is a source and a stimulus for further study on so-called 'popular' texts in the Renaissance. The book is well illustrated, and has an index, but, although there are extensive footnotes, there is no bibliography.

Colonialism

300 **Lion by the tail: the story of the Italian-Ethiopian war.**
Thomas M. Coffey. London: Hamish Hamilton, 1974. 369p. 1 map.
bibliog.

In a period of only six months Mussolini's colonial army had conquered Ethiopia. As a consequence, the Italian kingdom turned into an empire and Mussolini enjoyed the most glorious moment of his career. Yet it was the very seed of his eventual downfall, because it pushed him into Hitler's embrace. The wider historical context of the Italian-Ethiopian conflict is not explored, as the book provides a detailed chronicle of the war (December 1935-May 1936). Nevertheless, the exhaustive research upon which it is based, the highly-readable narrative style, and the balanced approach to the subject, make this book a valuable contribution to the knowledge of the last Italian thrust to build a colonial empire. Five years after victory, Ethiopia was lost. Coffey concludes by quoting large extracts from the impassioned speech delivered by Haile Selassie – the deposed real Emperor of Ethiopia – at the League of Nations.

301 **Italian colonialism in Somalia.**
Robert L. Hess. Chicago; London: The University of Chicago Press, 1966. 234p. 3 maps. bibliog.

The collapse of law and order and the widespread tribal fighting for supremacy in the early 1990s have focused world-wide public attention on Somalia and its past. This study still offers relevant insights for the understanding of the country's more recent plight, since the despotic ruler whose removal precipitated the crisis (Siad Barre) had maintained strong links with Italy. Hess first discusses the Italian settlement, at the turn of the century, along the southern Somalian coast. The narrative then divides into three topics: the making of the colony (1905-23); the northern protectorates (1889-1923); and the fascist era of imperial expansion (1923-41). The limited success of Italian colonialism in Somalia is underlined in the final chapter. Appendices contain statistical information and the reproduction of various agreements and conventions.

302 **Italian colonialism: a case study of Eritrea, 1869-1934: motive, praxis and result.**
Yemane Mesghenna. Lund, Sweden: Series Skrifter utgivna av Ekonomisk-historiska föreningen i Lund, vol. 58, 1988. 256p. 2 maps. bibliog.

Eritrea was the first Italian colony in Africa, its original small establishment dating back to 1869. This is a valuable doctoral dissertation which addresses three central questions: what caused Italy's policy of expansion?; how did Italian colonialism pursue its economic policies?; and did Italy gain economically from Eritrea? Two chapters tackle the first question with Mesghenna arguing that 'Italian imperialism was intoxicated by economic factors'. Five chapters then address the second question through a ponderous empirical investigation. The central figure here is the colonial governor Ferdinando Martini, whose 'doctrine' was to lay the foundation for economic exploitation. Finally, one chapter deals with the difficult evaluation of Italian colonialism in Eritrea. What seems to be certain is that Italy 'sat and twiddled its thumbs rather than stretching its arms into action'. Statistical tables and the list of colonial governors are included.

303   **Haile Selassie's war.**
Anthony Mockler.   Oxford: Oxford University Press, 1984. 454p.
10 maps. bibliog.

A major scholarly work on the war between Italy and Ethiopia (then called Abyssinia) in 1935-36, this is much more than just an account of a military campaign. Mockler's main concern is to investigate the Ethiopian people's life and culture at that tragic juncture of their country's history, their resistance to a superior military power, and their eventual freedom, regained with the help of the British army during the Second World War. The author makes use of an impressive number of written and oral sources from both sides. There is also a prologue on the defeat of the Italians at Adowa, in 1896, in their first attempt to invade Ethiopia. Part one briefly deals with the two countries before 1935, part two covers the 1935-36 war, and part three examines the collapse of the Italian empire in East Africa, in 1941. The author also includes: special notes on Ethiopia's history, geography and language; a glossary; and an analytical section on the sources.

304   **Italian colonialism in Eritrea, 1882-1941: policies, praxis and impact.**
Tekeste Negash.   Uppsala, Sweden: University of Uppsala, 1987.
217p. 4 maps. bibliog.

The aim of this study is twofold: on the one hand, it is an analysis of the political impact of Italian colonialism on Eritrean society. This is achieved through an assessment of the policies adopted by the Italian authorities on economic and educational matters. On the other hand, it is intended as a theoretical work on the ideology of colonialism. As part of the latter objective, there is an interesting discussion at the end on the Italian colonial impact on Eritrean national consciousness. Such consciousness did not arise, it is argued, because the colonialists' educational policy was 'intentionally constructed to prevent the emergence of a western educated elite'. However, this is regarded as a minor negative effect. More important was the impact on some demographic, economic and political developments, notably the considerable increase in the Tigrinyans as a percentage of the total population.

305   **Fourth shore: the Italian colonization of Libya.**
Claudio G. Segrè.   Chicago; London: The University of Chicago Press, 1974. 238p. bibliog.

Few works in English deal with Italian colonialism and Segrè's book is a valuable contribution on the subject. The first two chapters, which constitute part one of the study, concentrate on the origins of the colonization of Libya. The second, more extensive part investigates the policies pursued by successive governors (Volpi, De Bono, Badoglio, and Balbo) and examines three different perspectives of the colonization: those of the colonist families; the technical experts; and the Libyans themselves. The whole undertaking, the author concludes, had 'a baroque quality [. . .] brilliant but enormously expensive and ultimately empty [. . .] Despite all claims which were made for it, the colonization did little or nothing to help resolve Italy's pressing economic and social problems'. An authoritative bibliographical essay concludes the book.

Cities and regions

306   **Storia della Campania.** (A history of Campania.)
      Edited by Francesco Barbagallo.   Naples: Guida, 1978. 2 vols. 634p.
      bibliog. (Originally published in 30 instalments by the periodical *La
      Voce della Campania* between March 1976 and May 1977).

This is an attempt to write 'popular' history by a team of thirty-eight specialists. It is somewhat unusual in Italy to write the history not of a kingdom, or a duchy, but of a region, although Campania (originally the area around Capua and etymologically connected with it) has had an identity of its own throughout the centuries. Volume one, following a chapter by Giuseppe Galasso which discusses the historical justification of the notion of 'region' as applied to Campania, covers the period from ca 5000 BC to 1815. Volume two studies 1815 to 1975. This work adequately covers themes such as material culture, territory, and politics (by Percy Allum) and provides an extensive bibliography (p. 601-34).

307   **Politics and culture in Renaissance Naples.**
      Jerry H. Bentley.   Princeton, New Jersey: Princeton University Press,
      1987. 327p. 2 maps. bibliog.

Although this work reads well it does not shine for its originality, and very few primary sources are quoted in the footnotes. However, the book is useful for its discussion of the pattern of patronage in chapter two, though, given some macroscopic inaccuracies (such as the confusion between Francesco Sforza and Filippo Visconti on p. 59) it should perhaps be used with some caution.

308   **A medieval Italian commune: Siena under the Nine, 1287-1355.**
      William M. Bowsky.   Berkeley, California; London: University of
      California Press, 1988. 327p. maps. bibliog.

The 'Nine' referred to in the title were the members of the ruling oligarchy in Siena, whose influence on Sienese life was considerable, as commissioners of architectural and artistic works, and general organizers of society. Bowsky's work discusses their deeds and the history of Siena in the Middle Ages. The themes are treated topically rather than chronologically in seven chapters: Resources: natural and human; Urban magistracies; Legislation and justice; The commune uses force; Diplomacy and foreign relations; Rule of the merchants: the government and economics (of great interest to the organization of wealth in mediaeval Tuscany); and The civic ideal. An index is included.

309   **Florence in the forgotten centuries, 1527-1800: a history of**
      Florence and the Florentines in the age of the Grand Dukes.
      Eric Cochrane.   Chicago; London: The University of Chicago Press,
      1973. 593p. 2 maps. bibliog.

This is a marvellous, thought-provoking and entertaining book, in which Cochrane succeeds in sharing with the reader his erudition and his wit. It contains six parts, referring to specific decades and built around notable characters. The relevant decades and the corresponding protagonists are: the 1540s, Cosimo de' Medici, 'who turned a worn-out republic into a well-run monarchy'; the 1590s, Scipione Ammirato, a historian who claimed to have solved just about all the problems of his age; the 1630s, Galileo Galilei, who 'turned the universe inside out'; the 1680s, Lorenzo Malgalotti, who 'looked in vain for a vocation and finally settled down to sniffing perfumes'; the 1740s, Giovanni Lami, who 'discovered the past and tried to alter the future'; and the 1780s, Francesco Maria Gianni who 'spent 25 years building a model state only to see it torn down in a single morning'.

310 **Land and power in late medieval Ferrara: the rule of the Este, 1350-1450.**
Trevor Dean.   Cambridge, England: Cambridge University Press, 1988. 212p. maps. bibliog.

An impressive analysis of land management in Ferrara in which the relationship between feudal lords, their neighbours and central government is studied. The transformations which occurred in the use of fiefs is followed through, with the conclusion that 'feudalism in 1450 was certainly different from feudalism in 1250, but it was not decayed'. The book is also valuable for its up-to-date bibliography.

311 **A history of Sicily.**
Moses I. Finlay, Denis Mack Smith, Christopher Duggan.   London: Chatto & Windus, 1986. 246p. 3 maps. bibliog.

This is an abridged and revised version of the three-volume book with the same title, by Finlay and Mack Smith, which appeared in 1968. The chronological table at the end of the work demonstrates the wide range of influences, dominations and forms of government that Sicily experienced. The masters who followed the early Greek and Phoenician colonizers were: the Romans; the Byzantines; the Arabs; the Normans; the Germans; the French; the Spaniards; and eventually, the Italians. This extraordinary story is told by strict adherence to chronological order, but with emphasis on the periods in which important changes took place; for instance, when Sicily was annexed to the peninsula as part of the new Italian kingdom. In the last chapter the post-war years are covered, up until the early 1980s, when mafia criminal activities hit the headlines. There are fine illustrations.

312 **Chianti: the land, the people and the wine.**
Raymond Flower.   London: Croom Helm, 1978. 305p. 1 map. bibliog.

Flower's book is primarily an account of the history of the region which gave its name to the celebrated wine. Chianti is situated at the centre of Tuscany, which itself is at the centre of Italy, and its history reflects such centrality. For example, in the Middle Ages the area was the main stage for the portentous struggle between the German emperors and the popes. With the final domination of Florence over Siena, the history of Chianti became firmly linked to the fortunes of the Florentine rulers, until the 19th century, when the regional State gave way to the kingdom of Italy. All this is vividly chronicled by Flower. Appendices provide further information on various aspects of Chianti's history, and the wine. The text is enhanced by illustrations and a detailed map of *Chianti Classico* (the wine).

313 **Storia di Milano.** (A history of Milan.)
Milan: Fondazione Treccani degli Alfieri, 1953-66. 16 vols. indexes (1 vol.).

A monumental history in which each volume is dedicated to a different period of approximately 120 years, from Celtic and Roman times to the First World War. The works cover political and social history and all aspects of society and culture. Art, costume, and literature are all covered in extensive, scholarly, but readable chapters, written by leading specialists. An authoritative mine of reliable information on Milan and its territory.

314 **God and money: Florence and the Medici in the Renaissance.**
Richard Fremantle. Florence: Olschki, 1992. 61p. ('Pocket Library of "Studies" in Art', no. 26).

Fremantle has written a very clear and succinct (to the point of lacking nuances) account of the background to and the development of the artistic Renaissance in Florence which flourished under the immense patronage of Cosimo de' Medici (estimated at the equivalent of 150-250 million dollars) and later of his grandson Lorenzo. Comparisons with today's world are discretely made, with the conclusion that if the Renaissance was the product of tension between Church and Trade (God and Money) the tension which exists today between technology and ecology may produce our own Renaissance. The work contains neither a bibliography or footnotes, but it is illustrated with seventy black-and-white plates.

315 **Chioggia and the villages of the Venetian lagoon: studies in urban history.**
Richard J. Goy. Cambridge, England; London; New York; Melbourne; Sydney: Cambridge University Press, 1985. 349p. 27 maps. bibliog.

Goy provides a fascinating mosaic of urban and social histories, concentrating primarily on the important trade centre of Chioggia, and tracing its history from the high Middle Ages onwards. On this island settlements grew up along the major axis of a navigable waterway, with subsequent development along a series of parallel secondary axes. A similar layout can also be found in the other smaller communities of the lagoon examined here: Pellestrina and settlements in Lido, and the three main islands in the northern part of the lagoon (Burano, Mazzorbo and Torcello). Murano is also considered, together with some quarters of Venice itself. Fascinating, if fragmentary notes at the end of the book point out the development of harmonious relationships between the waterways and the *campi* (squares) and *calli* (narrow streets) in this backyard of Venice. There are many handsome illustrations and statistical appendices.

316 **Ferrara: the style of a Renaissance despotism.**
Werner L. Gundersheimer. Princeton, New Jersey: Princeton University Press, 1973. 313p.

Gundersheimer attempts to synthesize the achievements and the shortcomings of four rulers of Ferrara belonging to the Este family: Niccolò III (1393-1441); Leonello (1441-50); Borso (1450-71); and Hercules (1471-1505). He therefore covers the Renaissance period just preceding the reign of Alfonso during which poets such as

Ariosto flourished. This is a sensible discussion of policies and of social history in an important but relatively neglected area of Italian history. Reference is constantly made to the documents produced by scholars and humanists in Ferrara. The latter are divided into two categories: the nobleman who writes; and the professional man of letters or court poet. According to the author 'the social history of humanism in *Quattrocento* Ferrara must be interpreted as the gradual decline of the second type of humanist in the court, and the growing ascendancy of the first'. No bibliography is provided, but an index is included.

317 Rome: the biography of a city.
Christopher Hibbert.   London: Viking, 1985. 387p. 2 maps. bibliog.
As the author writes, 'this book is intended to be an introduction to the history of Rome and the social life of its people from the days of the Etruscan kings to those of Mussolini'. The historical outline is accompanied by many fine illustrations and the lively narrative style makes it attractive, as well as practical, to visitors of the 'eternal city'. The book is divided into three parts. Part one covers the many centuries from classical Rome to its sacking by Imperial (German) troops, in 1527. The second part surveys the next four-and-a-half centuries, with an emphasis on Baroque, the 'Settecento', the troubled 19th century, and 'Roma fascista'. A brief epilogue charts the subsequent years, with particular reference to the Church and Italian politics. The final part contains detailed notes on all the main buildings and works of art mentioned in the text.

318 Venice: the biography of a city.
Christopher Hibbert.   London: Grafton, 1988. 435p. 2 maps. bibliog.
A handsomely-illustrated book, intended for the general reader as an introduction to the history and social life of Venice, from the earliest memories to the 1960s. It is arranged in three parts, the first two following a chronological order. Part one deals with the city's historical and cultural development from 500 AD to the loss of independence (1797) and the following 'Napoleonic interlude' (1789-1814). Part two covers the period from the beginning of Austrian domination in 1814 to the disastrous flood of 1966. A chapter is dedicated to Ruskin's Venice (1849-71). A concise epilogue deals with the 1970s and 1980s, and refers (among other things) to the special legislation passed by the Italian government for the preservation of the city. Part three consists of a glossary, a 'note on the gondola', a list of Doges and, above all, notes on the buildings and works of art mentioned throughout the book.

319 Florence: the biography of a city.
Christopher Hibbert.   London: Penguin Books, 1994. First published by Viking, 1993. 398p. 3 maps. bibliog.
This is a lavishly illustrated and well-written history of Florence, which places much emphasis on the city's archaeology, art, architecture, literature and social life. Perceptive visitors can gain great insight if they explore Florence after having read this book. It is divided into twenty-seven sections beginning with 'The Roman City, 59 BC-AD 405', through several chapters on the Age of Renaissance and concluding with 'Flood and restoration, 1966-1992'. It also contains: useful and nicely illustrated notes on buildings and works of art; a table of principal events; and a plan of the Medici family, from 'Averardo detto Bicci (d.1363)' to the three children of Cosimo III, the last of whom (Anna Maria, wife of William, Elector Palatine) died in 1743.

320 **Siena: a city and its history.**
Judith Hook. London: Hamish Hamilton, 1979. 258p. bibliog.

A popular history and a very good introduction to Siena and its monuments, this monograph covers the city from mediaeval times to modern-day activities. Separate chapters include such topics as: Medieval Siena; the rule of the Nine; the Cathedral; the Campo, Siena's world-famous square; and art and society in Siena. Written in a very readable manner, the text is interspersed with erudite quotations and an index is included.

321 **Padua in the age of Dante.**
J. K. Hyde. Manchester, England: Manchester University Press; New York: Barnes & Noble, 1966. 349p. 3 maps. bibliog.

This is a social history of Padua in the Middle Ages. It deals with the relationship between the city and its surrounding region, the position of noblemen and magnates and their influence in an area where knights often came to constitute a class of substantial landowners. Judges, doctors of law and guildsmen are dealt with in an accurate and authoritative reconstruction which studies the expansion of the commune of Padua until the dawn of the Renaissance. This meticulous history is complemented by three appendices: the Paduan Guilds in 1287; the Statute of April 1378; and the matricula of the Paduan college of Doctors of Law. Genealogical tables and an index are also included.

322 **Humanistic historiography under the Sforzas: politics and propaganda in fifteenth-century Milan.**
Gary Ianziti. Oxford: Clarendon, 1988. 254p. bibliog.

A study of how the 'image' of the rulers of Milan, and in particular of the duke Francesco Sforza, was created and maintained in 15th-century Italy. There is evidence of the direct involvement of the duke's chancery and in particular of his secretary in inviting scholars and humanists to collect material and to write 'histories of the family' which then circulated to improve the image of Sforza, his ancestors and his activities.

323 **Venice: a maritime republic.**
Frederic C. Lane. Baltimore, Maryland; London: The Johns Hopkins University Press, 1973. 505p. 11 maps. bibliog.

This is a classic history of Venice as an independent city-state, written by an economic historian who carried out intensive studies of Venetian shipping. Consequently, maritime matters receive special attention, with Lane arguing persuasively that nautical affairs were at the centre of the city's expanding wealth, institutions and social structure. Other aspects of Venetian life are appropriately considered. The initial chapters deal with the origin, the early development of the city and its progressive conquest and organization as a sea power. Lane suggests that at the time of highest triumph the symptoms of disintegration had already begun to show: it was then that Venice 'turned westward' and started its expansion on the mainland. The slow decline of Venice's power was set in motion by the 'oceanic challenge' in the 16th century and sealed by Napoleon at the end of the 18th century. Many fine illustrations are included in the text.

324 **The Commune of Lucca under Pisan rule, 1342-1369.**
Christine E. Meek. Cambridge, Massachusetts: The Medieval
Academy of America, 1980. 127p.

One of the few books written in English on the subject of the domination of Pisa over
the neighbouring town of Lucca, this is of special interest to political historians.
However, the only bibliography is in the footnotes, and there is no index.

325 **The Venetian empire: a sea voyage.**
Jan Morris. Harmondsworth, England: Penguin Books, 1990. 200p.
3 maps. bibliog.

In the author's own words, this is 'a traveller's book, geographically arranged, but
space and time are jumbled in it', and in it Morris wanders 'at will from the
landscapes and sensations of our own day into events, suggestions and substances of
the past'. It is a very enjoyable story, beginning at the end of the 12th century and
concluding with the fall of the Venetian Republic, at the end of the 18th century. One
of the recurrent themes is the ambiguous relationship Venice had with Islam, since
she depended upon it, as well as competing with it. The turning point that marked the
beginning of the end of the Venetian empire, Morris argues, was in 1470, when the
Venetians lost Euboea to the Turks, an event compared with the fall of Singapore in
1941, which pointed to the doom of the British empire. A gazetteer and a chronology
conclude the book, which also contains reproductions of old pictures. The volume
was first published by Rainbird in 1980.

326 **A history of Venice.**
John Julius Norwich. Harmondsworth, England: Penguin Books,
1983. 673p. First published by Allen Lane in two volumes, 1977, 1981.

This is the standard English-language work on Venetian history and an absorbing
account of the one thousand years of Venice's history as an independent city-state,
from its emergence in the 8th century to its fall in 1797, when it was invaded by
Napoleon's armies. This fascinating story is told in a fluent narrative style, with
occasional references to major buildings and monuments. The first of four parts deals
with the city's origin, early development and growing fortunes, up until the Fourth
Crusade (1205). The second part covers the subsequent two centuries of 'imperial
expansion' while part three is devoted to the consolidation of Venice as a European
power, with its ultimate triumphs in the early 16th century. The last section surveys
the long decline which followed the victory of Lepanto (1571), down to the end of the
'Most Serene Republic'. The book includes black-and-white illustrations and a list of
the Doges (726-1797).

327 **Storia di Genova.** (History of Genoa.)
Teofilo Ossian De Negri. Milan: Martello, 1968. 846p. bibliog.

A well-documented history of Genoa which emphasizes the earlier and mediaeval
periods, with a special interest in the military, political and diplomatic aspects. There
are no footnotes and all references are contained in the bibliography. The book
contains both colour and black-and-white illustrations. It would be easier to consult if
it were provided with an analytical index.

328 **Rome, from its foundation to the present.**
Stewart Perowne, photographs by Edwin Smith.   London: Paul Elek,
1971. 248p.

A superbly-illustrated history of 'the Eternal City'. Perowne notes in his stimulating
introduction that unlike Jerusalem and Athens, the other two cities at the origin of
western civilization, 'Rome has never stopped; for more than two and a half millennia
Rome has lived. Again and again, it has seemed that Rome must die, but always
Rome has recovered, to radiate unsullied some new shaft of her prismatic glory'.
Such genuine enthusiasm and a robust erudition inform this volume. Rome's cultural
and artistic development is monitored up until the middle of the present century.
However, it is perhaps appropriate that the past dominates over the present, with
much emphasis placed on classical Rome, the Middle Ages, the Renaissance and the
Baroque.

329 **Rome in the Renaissance: the city and the myth: papers of the
thirteenth annual conference of the center for Medieval & early
Renaissance studies.**
Edited by Paul A. Ramsey.   New York: State University of New
York at Binghampton. 431p.

The book contains twenty-nine papers of interest to: town planners (J. S. Ackerman
'The planning of Renaissance Rome, 1450-1580'); art historians (C. Dempsey
'Mythic inventions in counter-Reformation painting'; H. Wohl, 'Martin V and the
revival of the arts in Rome'); cultural and literary historians (C. T. Davis, 'Rome and
Babylon in Dante'; J. B. Trapp, 'The poet laureate: Rome, "Renovatio" and
"Translatio imperii" '); as well as to drama specialists (J. L. Simmons, 'Shakespeare
and the antique Romans'; M. Cottino-Jones, 'Rome and the theatre in the
Renaissance'). Some city plans are provided in the volume.

330 **The Kingdom of Naples under Alfonso the Magnanimous: the
making of a modern state.**
Alan Ryder.   Oxford: Clarendon Press, 1976. 409p. maps. bibliog.

Alfonso V of Aragon (1396-1458) proclaimed himself king of Naples in 1435.
However, this was followed by seven years of civil war and it was only in 1442 that
his reign became secure. Ryder presents a model study of the king's interests in
literature and falconry among others, of his household and of the administration of the
kingdom. This is an authoritative source of information.

The Italians: how they live and work.
See item no. 3.

Italy.
See item no. 9.

Garibaldi.
See item no. 336.

Cavour.
See item no. 337.

Mussolini.
See item no. 338.

Mazzini.
See item no. 339.

Mussolini and the Jews.
See item no. 347.

Preachers of the Italian ghetto.
See item no. 348.

The Jews in Piedmont.
See item no. 349.

Benevolence and betrayal – five Italian Jewish families under fascism.
See item no. 353.

Men of respect: a social history of the Sicilian mafia.
See item no. 498.

How fascism ruled women: Italy, 1922-1945.
See item no. 531.

Neo-fascism in Europe.
See item no. 610.

The radical right: a world directory.
See item no. 612.

After Mussolini: Italian neo-fascism.
See item no. 613.

Italian fascisms: from Pareto to Gentile.
See item no. 619.

The architectural history of Venice.
See item no. 794.

Renaissance architecture in Venice 1450-1540.
See item no. 795.

Studies in Italian Renaissance architecture.
See item no. 796.

Pienza: the creation of a Renaissance city.
See item no. 797.

Venetian architecture of the early Renaissance.
See item no. 798.

Bologna.
See item no. 799.

Italy and the English Renaissance.
See item no. 808.

Strangers at home: Jews in the Italian literary imagination.
See item no. 844.

Fascism in film.
See item no. 864.

Struggles of the Italian film industry during fascism, 1930-1935.
See item no. 867.

Book production and letters in the Western European Renaissance.
See item no. 999.

The world of Aldus Manutius.
See item no. 1000.

Nicholas Jenson and the rise of Venetian publishing in Renaissance Europe.
See item no. 1001.

Modern Italian history: an annotated bibliography.
See item no. 1052.

Renaissance humanism 1300-1550.
See item no. 1062.

Iter italicum: a finding list of uncatalogued or incompletely catalogued humanistic manuscripts.
See item no. 1063.

Gender and sexuality in Renaissance and Baroque Italy.
See item no. 1074.

Biographies and
Memoirs

331 **Alcide De Gasperi: the long apprenticeship.**
Elisa A. Carrillo. Notre Dame, Indiana: University of Notre Dame
Press, 1965. 185p. bibliog.
This is the sole biography of the Christian Democrat prime minister who guided Italy
from 1945 to 1953, and died in 1954. The intended second volume, which was to deal
with those important years, was never written. Nevertheless, because of the eventful
and dramatic circumstances in which De Gasperi formed and put into practice his
political views, the story told here is of great interest. After an introduction on De
Gasperi's cultural formation, Carrillo deals with his participation in Austrian politics;
De Gasperi was born an Austrian citizen and eventually became a deputy of the
parliament in Vienna. She then moves on to his involvement in Italian politics; he
became the general secretary of the Catholic Popular Party in 1924. After the
dissolution of his party and a brief imprisonment, De Gasperi found employment at
the Vatican Library, and returned to political life and prominence after the fall of
fascism.

332 **Dizionario biografico degli italiani.** (Biographical dictionary of the
Italians.)
Rome: Istituto della Enciclopedia Italiana, 1960- . irreg.
In thirty-five years (1960 to 1993), forty-three volumes of this monumental and
unique work have appeared, fully covering only names beginning with A to D.
Readers will be interested to know the background to this important and frustrating
enterprise. As early as 1925 the necessity was recognized for a comprehensive
biographical dictionary of Italians, but the initiative was so ambitiously
comprehensive as to escalate to some 400 thousand personal cards in the subsequent
few years. Faced with an impossible task, a protracted debate ensued as to what
should be excluded, resulting in a compromise. In addition, the war and post-war
years virtually stopped both the actual proceedings and the wishful plans. When
scholars, under the guidance of the original editor (Fortunato Pintor), resumed their
labours, the target was set for the first volume to appear in time to celebrate the
centenary of Italy's political unification (1961); this aim was achieved when the

volume with names from Aaron to Albertucci appeared in 1960. In the same year Pintor died. Since then, volumes have been published regularly, but too slowly to satisfy the expectations of scholars and students.

333 Mattei: oil and power politics.
Paul H. Frankel. London: Faber & Faber, 1966. 190p.

Enrico Mattei was a successful entrepreneur and political manipulator. He was the decisive factor in the establishment of ENI (the State's energy and chemicals holding company), which he led until he died in 1962. Frankel dismisses the rumours that sabotage might have been behind the crash of Mattei's personal aircraft which caused his death. As a study of 'oil and power politics' and international intrigue, this is still one of the best sources on Mattei's background. A short first part sketches the origins of Italian (that is, Mattei's) resentment of world powers and international oil companies. The second part investigates Mattei's career, accounting for the intricacies of Italian politics and the forces at play in the international economic theatre. In the final section there are insights on what the 'Mattei experience' meant as far as the role of public enterprise was concerned.

334 Agnelli and the network of Italian power.
Alan Friedman. London: Mandarin Paperbacks. 2nd ed. 1989. 367p.

This is the story of the expansion and rise to a hitherto unparalleled position of economic and financial power by the Agnelli family and their car manufacturing company, Fiat. The author, an investigative journalist for the *Financial Times*, traces the background and life-style of the Agnellis over a period of nearly a century, and focuses on their dealings with the White House and the Pentagon, and with the governments of the former USSR and Libya, as well as their illegal sale of ballistic missile technology to third world countries. The book is overtly political and is intended to expose 'a ruthlessly managed and arrogant network of power which virtually amounts to a shadow Italian government'.

335 Anna Kuliscioff: from Russian populism to Italian socialism.
Claire LaVigna. New York; London: Garland, 1991. 245p. bibliog.

In the words of the author, this is an attempt 'to take the Russian-born partner of Filippo Turati out of the shadow of myth and to bring her under the light of historical analysis'. Besides being a well-researched biography of one of the people who inspired and contributed to the establishment of the Italian Socialist Party, this is a study of the history of that party from its origins to 1913, when the reformist faction to which Kuliscioff belonged was defeated by the 'revolutionary' elements, who included Mussolini. Only a few final pages are devoted to the thoughts and actions of the protagonist from 1913 to 1925, the year in which she died and in which Mussolini virtually completed the destruction of Italy's parliamentary system.

336 Garibaldi.
Denis Mack Smith. London: Hutchinson, 1957. 214p. 1 map.

The British scholars' long-established love for Garibaldi, which reached its apotheosis in Trevelyan's 'trilogy' (q.v.), was relaunched after the Second World War by Mack Smith. Compared with Trevelyan's epic work, this is an agile, concise profile of Garibaldi's life and the formidable series of events in which he eagerly took part as a leader. The author emphasizes Garibaldi's role as a 'professional liberator', which made him not only a great national hero, but also a 'great internationalist'. The story unfolds in a captivating narrative style, punctuated by insights as to the historical setting and also human nature.

337 Cavour.
Denis Mack Smith. London: Weidenfeld & Nicolson, 1985. 292p.
2 maps. bibliog.

This is a highly readable, authoritative and provocative biography of the mastermind of Italy's unification. In the work Cavour is presented as a Machiavellian pragmatist, who 'sometimes [. . .] made what by his own admission were serious mistakes of judgement and employed methods that he knew would be thought discreditable'. The first half of the book considers the relatively uneventful early life of Cavour and his political career as Prime Minister of the Kingdom of Sardinia, when he turned the region (Piedmont, in particular) into the most prominent and progressive state in Italy. The second half focuses on the last three years of his life, from the forging of the alliance with France, to the ultimate triumph against all odds. To add to the drama of events in 1859-60, Cavour suddenly died, in June 1861 (aged fifty), only a few months after the proclamation of the Kingdom of Italy.

338 Mussolini.
Denis Mack Smith. London; Glasgow; Toronto; Sydney; Auckland:
Paladin-Grafton Books, 1987. 495p. bibliog.

First published in 1981, this is an outstanding biography of the fascist leader. No less scholarship is condensed here than is involved in the multi-volume biography of the Duce by Renzo De Felice (q.v.), which is only available in Italian. A brilliant portrait is painted of the man and the politician, organized in a tight chronological order, from his youth to the end. The author makes it clear in the preface that 'this [unlike De Felice's] is a political biography of Benito Mussolini, not a history of fascist Italy, and still less a general history of the years between 1920 and 1945 when fascism became a dominant theme in European politics'. According to the author, the Duce's supreme ability, which explains both his successes ‚and failures, was 'as a propagandist whose public statements and private comments were often intended to conceal the truth as much as to reveal it'. Mack Smith's crisp, witty style makes this book fascinating as well as instructive reading.

339 Mazzini.
Denis Mack Smith. New Haven, Connecticut; London: Yale
University Press, 1994. 302p. 2 maps.

In a bibliographical note at the end of this book, it· is pointed out that 'As we approach the end of the twentieth century it is surprising to find that the best biography of Mazzini in any language is probably that written in English as long ago as 1902 by [. . .] Bolton King'. Future historians will refer to this authoritative study in analogous terms. It is well written and rich in perceptive considerations and Mazzini's thoughts and actions are examined with sympathy, but also with the necessary degree of dispassionate detachment. Particularly stimulating are the pages which analyse Mazzini's relationship with religion and socialism. The work is arranged in strict chronological order, but only the first of ten chapters deals with the protagonist's life before arriving in London as an exile in 1837. Some portraits of Mazzini and samples of his handwriting illustrate the book.

340   **A need to testify.**
    Iris Origo.   London: John Murray, 1984. 274p.
An essay on biography precedes the four main chapters which form the book. These
are dedicated to Lauro de Bosis, Ruth Draper, Gaetano Salvemini and Ignazio Silone,
all of whom were close friends of the author, linked to each other 'not only by their
unswerving devotion to a common cause – the defeat of fascism – but by the
conviction that their main purpose should be to bear witness to the reasons for this
faith'. It is arguable, however, to what extent the second element applies to the
famous American actress Ruth Draper, whose political orientation appears to have
been mainly a reflection of her love for Lauro de Bosis. The subtitles to the four
chapters indicate the dominant note of each portrait: for Lauro de Bosis it is 'Icarus';
for Draper, 'and her company of characters'; for Salvemini, 'the man who would not
conform'; and for Silone, 'a study of integrity'.

341   **Italo Balbo: a fascist life.**
    Claudio G. Segrè.   Berkeley, California; London: University of
    California Press, 1987. 466p. bibliog.
Balbo was the fascist hero *par excellence*: a decorated soldier in the First World War;
fascist *squadrista* around his town of Ferrara; one of the four commanders to lead the
'March on Rome'; an aviator and founder of the Italian air force; acclaimed Atlantic
aerial cruiser; governor of Libya; and commander of Italian forces in North Africa.
He was shot down there (presumably) by mistake by Italian anti-aircraft batteries, a
few weeks after Italy entered the Second World War. Segrè provides a readable and
scholarly biography of this glamorous and controversial figure who also enjoyed
international fame and became an emissary of Mussolini's Italy. Yet, as the author
points out, Balbo's fascism is difficult to define because 'he was a man of action more
than a thinker'.

Who's who in Italy: 1994 edition.
See item no. 27.

Memoirs of a fortunate Jew: an Italian story.
See item no. 350.

Pasolini: a biography.
See item no. 852.

Puccini: a critical biography.
See item no. 949.

Population

Demography

342   Four centuries of Italian demographic development.
Carlo M. Cipolla.   In: *Population in history: essays in historical
demography.*   Edited by D. V. Glass, D. E. C. Eversley.   London:
Edward Arnold, 1965, p. 570-87.

This concise essay, written thirty years ago, still offers a valuable outline of Italian
demographic development from the 16th century to the 1950s. It is estimated that ten
million people lived in the Italian peninsula in 1500; there were forty-eight million in
1950. Cipolla first provides some general information on the trends in birth and
mortality rates up until the 19th century; he then focuses on the 19th and 20th
centuries, noting that the annual rate of increase of the total population stepped up
after 1820. As from 1870, a new phase started, described by scholars as 'demographic
transition' and which entailed: a falling death rate; and a stable (relatively high) birth
rate until the end of the century, after which it took a downward turn. Although in the
1890s Italy entered the phase of industrial advance, the demographic pressure could
only be reduced by mass emigration. The final section of the essay notes the regional
variations within the peninsula.

343   Italy.
Lorenzo Del Panta.   In: *European demography and economic growth.*
Edited by W. R. Lee.   London: Croom Helm, 1979, p. 196-235.

The section on Italy begins with a brief look at the 18th century, when 'improvements
in sanitary conditions resulted in a progressive decline of infectious diseases'.
Demographic growth throughout the 19th century was sustained and by the end of the
century, three factors were interacting: mass emigration; a decline in birth rate; while
the mortality rate continued to fall. On balance, 'the natural growth rate tended to
increase continuously from 1880 to 1930, except for the decade marred by the First
World War'. In the general perspective, the twenty million people registered in 1821
became thirty million in 1881, forty in 1931, and fifty in 1961. There are stimulating

comments on the pro-natal propaganda during the fascist regime, such as that it 'contributed to the reinforcement of conservative elements in Italian society [. . .] and retarded the process of female emancipation'.

344   **A history of Italian fertility during the last two centuries.**
Massimo Livi-Bacci.   Princeton, New Jersey: Princeton University Press, 1977. 311p. bibliog.

The first chapter of the book deals with fertility from Napoleonic times to 1861, the year of Italy's political unification. Under apparent uniformity, 'small pockets of lower fertility are seen to be already well established'. The following six chapters cover in detail the regional development of fertility from 1861 to 1971, with the focus on its decline. It is noted that this pattern was common to other European countries during the same period, but that Italy's pace of decline was slower than that in western European countries and faster than that in other Mediterranean countries. Such a decline was influenced by territorial and class differences, as well as by social, economic and cultural changes in Italian society. An impressive battery of statistical tools are employed to determine the impact of the main factors on fertility differentials and trends in the various regions and provinces.

Minority groups

The Jews

345   **Prisoners of hope: the silver age of the Italian Jews, 1924-1974.**
Henry Stuart Hughes.   Cambridge, Massachusetts; London: Harvard University Press, 1983. 188p.

Hughes introduces his book with an interesting essay on the history of Italian Jews, 'the most ancient of minorities'. The following chapters focus on some well-known writers, often against the cultural background of their cities. Firstly, for example, Trieste and Rome are the setting for a presentation of Svevo and Moravia, respectively. The relationship between fascism and Italian Jewry is discussed before Hughes deals with Carlo and Primo Levi (the latter coined the expression 'prisoners of hope'). They were both from Turin, as was the next writer considered, Natalia Ginzburg. The author then turns to the city of Ferrara and Giorgio Bassani. The book concludes with reflections on 'the meanings of "survival" ', and it is argued that in their pursuit of self-definition the Italian Jews paradoxically became an integral part of the intellectual and unobservant Italian context.

346   **Gardens and ghettos: the art of Jewish life in Italy.**
Edited by Vivian B. Mann.   Berkeley, California; Oxford: University of California Press, 1989. 354p. bibliog.

This is the beautifully-illustrated catalogue of an exhibition held in New York. A foreword by Tullia Zevi and a preface by Primo Levi (which had been written for a similar exhibition) are followed by a stimulating opening essay by D. B. Rudermann. The other contributions are: 'The Jews in Italy from the *Risorgimento* to the Republic' (M. Toscano); 'The Arts of Jewish Italy' (V. B. Mann); 'Jewish art and culture in ancient Rome' (R. Brilliant); 'Hebrew illuminated manuscripts from Italy' (E. Cohen); 'Jewish ceremonial art in the era of the city states and the ghettos' (D. L. Bemporad); 'From *Risorgimento* to the Resistance: a century of Jewish artists in Italy' (E. Braun); and 'A millennium of Hebrew poetry in Italy' (A. Mandelbaum). The second half of the book is the catalogue proper, with illustrations ranging from early burial inscriptions to scrolls and synagogue interiors. Biographies of the artists, and a glossary, are included.

347 **Mussolini and the Jews: German-Italian relations and the Jewish question in Italy, 1922-1945.**
Meir Michaelis.   Oxford: Clarendon Press, published for the Institute of Jewish Affairs in London, 1978. 472p. bibliog.
At the outset of this book Michaelis indicates why the history of the Italian Jews is of special interest, despite the relatively small size of their community. It is pointed out that, 'firstly, its annals span well over twenty centuries and half a dozen successive civilizations. Secondly, the emancipation of Italian Jews was uniquely successful'. After surveying the historical background, this extensively researched study deals with the impact of German-Italian relations on the racial policy pursued by Mussolini. There are two parts to the work: from the march on Rome to the Spanish civil war (1922-1936); and from the Rome-Berlin Axis to the fall of fascism (1936-1945). Michaelis argues that the Mussolini-Hitler alliance fostered and moulded fascist anti-Semitic policy, 'despite the fundamental conflict of interest between the two countries and the divergence of views on Hitler's doctrine of nordic superiority'.

348 **Preachers of the Italian ghetto.**
Edited by David B. Rudermann.   Berkeley, California; Oxford: University of California Press, 1992. 168p.
Seven essays are included in this scholarly book, exploring a number of features of Jewish preaching in the ghettos of 16th- and early 17th-century Italy. Rudermann provides an introduction on the social and cultural context of Jewish life in the ghetto, and an essay on Azariah Figo's sermons. M. Saperstein writes on the general topic of Italian Jewish preaching. This is followed by M. Idel's study on Judith Moscato, a late Renaissance preacher. R. Bonfil deals with the case of Judah Del Bene, and discusses preaching as a method of mediation between elite and popular cultures. J. Weinberg contributes with an essay on the sermons of the Venetian Rabbi Leon Modena, whilst E. Horowitz concludes the collection with a piece on the emergence of the eulogy among Italian Jewry in the 16th century.

349 **The Jews in Piedmont.**
Edited by Renata Segre.   Jerusalem: Tel Aviv University, The Israel Academy of Sciences and Humanities, 1986-90. 3 vols.
This massive collection of records preserved in the archives of Piedmont provides the basic material for a history of the Jews in that part of Italy, from the Middle Ages to the end of the 18th century. In some instances the contents of the documents are condensed into a few lines, but there are also full texts in their original language (Latin or Italian), with a synthesis in English. Innumerable details of individuals,

families and their relationship with institutions and authorities (both civil and religious), emerge in a complex tapestry. Particularly interesting are the documents containing the census data on Jews living in a number of cities and towns, at various times. The third volume includes a useful and comprehensive index of names of people and institutions.

350 **Memoirs of a fortunate Jew: an Italian story.**
Dan Vittorio Segre. London; Glasgow; Toronto; Sydney; Auckland: Paladin, 1988. 2nd ed. 273p.

By resorting to his diaries 'written daily or intermittently since 1940', Segre reconstructs both the major and the mundane events of his life with wit and insight. He was brought up in fascist Italy, within a prosperous Jewish family from Piedmont who admired Mussolini. Ettore Ovazza, the best-known fascist Jew, was his cousin. Segre emigrated to Palestine, aged sixteen, on the eve of the outbreak of the Second World War and later joined the Palestinian regiment of the British army, with which he returned to Italy and was, indeed, fortunate to find his family alive. The first part of the book portrays a 'Jewish-fascist childhood' and is particularly interesting for the perceptive observations on that strange combination – which did not appear so strange to him until Mussolini adopted an anti-Semitic stance in 1938. Moods and atmospheres are skilfully recreated in an entertaining and moving narrative.

351 **History of the Jews in the Duchy of Mantua.**
Shlomo Simonsohn. Jerusalem: Kiryath Sepher, Tel Aviv University, 1977. 902p. 2 maps. bibliog.

The story of the Jewish settlement in Mantua dates back to Roman times, but it became more significant between the 14th and the 18th century. Many of the historical records have survived, and Simonsohn has made full use of them for the writing of this impressive tome. After an outline of the history of the Jews in Mantua and its surrounding territory, the contents are arranged topically and concentrate on the following: the status of the Jews in the State of Mantua; demographic trends (only a few pages); the Jewish economy; the community (including analyses of its institutions and relations with other communities); society, religion and education (with interesting insights into the living conditions in the ghetto); literature, science and art; and scholars and learned men (a true biographical gallery). A documentary appendix is also included.

352 **The Jews in the Duchy of Milan.**
Edited by Shlomo Simonsohn. Jerusalem: The Israel Academy of Sciences and Humanities, 1982-86. 4 vols.

The first three volumes of this massive work include over 4,700 documents referring to the Jews in the Duchy of Milan during the four centuries between 1387 and 1788. The result is a documentary history of individuals and their families. In many cases the entries consist of summaries in English of the contents, but several documents are reproduced in their original text, either in Latin (in the earlier period) or in Italian. The last volume contains records of notarial deeds not included in the previous volumes; they are arranged by locality and by notary. The fourth volume also contains the indexes to the complete work.

353 **Benevolence and betrayal: five Italian Jewish families under fascism.**
Alexander Stille. London: Vintage, 1993. 365p. bibliog.
The story of five very different families is skilfully told by weaving individual memories into the broader historical context, with perceptive observations on human nature in general. The first family are the wealthy Ovazzas: Ettore, the central character, is a dedicated fascist and a leader of Turin's Jewish community. He and his family were murdered by the Germans. Also from Turin are the anti-fascist Foas: one of them (Vittorio) spent years in a fascist jail, was a Resistance fighter, and became a top trade unionist and a Senator. The third family, the Di Verolis were modest shopkeepers in the Rome ghetto, who lost relatives in Auschwitz and in the Ardeatine caves massacre. Next is the adventurous tale of Massimo Teglio, the 'Genoese red pimpernel' who saved many lives, in collaboration with the Catholic Church. Finally, the moving relationship between a father and his son is told, through the vicissitudes of the Schönheits from Ferrara, who survived Buchenwald.

354 **The Jews in Umbria: 1245-1435.**
Ariel Toaff. Leiden, Netherlands; New York; Cologne, Germany: E. J. Brill, 1993. vol. 1. 460p. bibliog.
The complete work is intended to trace the history of the Jews in Umbria through all available documents, until their expulsion from the region in 1569, on the orders of Pope Pius V. The nearly 900 items of archival records indicated in this first volume supply a wealth of information, enabling the researcher to perceive the important economic role which the Jews played in Umbria, and their relationship with the civil and Catholic authorities. Their daily life can also be appreciated through the many relevant details contained in the surviving documents. Each document, whether its full contents are submitted in their original Latin text or not, is presented with concise descriptions. Toaff's introduction offers a fascinating synthesis of the history (and histories) of Jews in Umbria from the 13th to the 16th century. There is also a useful glossary.

355 **The Italians and the Holocaust: persecution, rescue and survival.**
Susan Zuccotti. London: Peter Halban, 1987. 334p.
This is a well-researched work in which the narrative of historical events is interwoven with personal testimonies. The first five chapters provide a historical background of Italian Jews, the introduction of racial laws (1938) and the first phase of the war (1940-43). The subsequent seven chapters deal in detail with the unfolding tragedy following Italy's surrender and the occupation of two-thirds of the country by the Germans: here the story of 'persecution, rescue and survival' begins. Zuccotti argues that several factors contributed to the survival of most Italian Jews: the lack of anti-Semitic traditions in modern Italy; the limited presence of Jews and the high degree of their assimilation; the contempt for the authorities, which made the Italians sceptical of any form of anti-Jewish propaganda; and the altruistic and courageous behaviour of many individuals who did not hesitate to protect innocent victims.

Others

356 **Le minoranze linguistiche: stato attuale e proposte di tutela.**
(Linguistic minorities: the present situation and proposals for their protection.)
Edited by Roberto Ajello. Pisa: Giardini, 1984. 65p. (Atti del Convegno della Società Italiana di Glottologia, [Pisa, 16-17 Dec. 1982]).

The book, which contains the proceedings of a conference on linguistic minorities, is made up of three contributions by G. B. Pellegrini, G. R. Cardona, and A. Pizzorusso. Pellegrini deals with the German 'majority' of Alto Adige or South Tyrol, with Slovene, Friulian and Ladin. It is an extremely careful analysis with reference to an abundant scientific bibliography and some warning against the general, non-scientific attitude of journalists and others motivated by practical, that is, political, reasons. Cardona considers the general problem of minority languages and cultural contact with reference to South America and Turkey, whilst Pizzorusso outlines the legislation from 1946 to 1981 which has dealt with the problem of the protection of minorities in Italy. This is the least theoretical of all three essays.

357 **Educational aspirations of ethnic minorities: Slovenes in Italy.**
L. F. Baric. In: *'Nation' and 'State' in Europe: anthropological perspectives.* Edited by R. D. Grillo. London; New York; Toronto; Sydney; San Francisco: Academic Press, 1980, p. 61-71.

This study concentrates on the Italian area where the Slovenes are relatively numerous: the province of Trieste. The importance of education for ethnic minorities is emphasized, as are the contrasting, even puzzling conditions of the Slovene-speaking minority in that province, in which further and higher education is largely rejected in order to preserve their identity. This is because those who do enter further and higher education, Baric argues, eventually drift away from their community.

358 **The salt of another's bread: immigration control and the social impact of immigration in Italy.**
Roger Blackstone. London: Home Office, 1989. 104p. bibliog.

Unfortunately it appears that the British Home Office published only a limited number of copies of this report written on behalf of the Western European Union. It is a thorough investigation on a subject for which there are no similar works in English. Originally intended as a comparative study between the Italian and the British approaches to immigration control and related social issues, it eventually became more limited in scope. It is, in fact, a descriptive survey of the situation in Italy, with only passing reference to the United Kingdom. A chapter is devoted to the 1986 law which introduced an amnesty for illegal immigrants who regularized their position. The full text of the law is included in the appendix. Other interesting chapters focus on the typology and social aspects of immigration and on two 'city profiles': Milan and Turin.

359 **Ethnics in a borderland: an inquiry into the nature of ethnicity and reduction of ethnic tensions in a one-time genocide area.**
Feliks Gross.   Westport, Connecticut; London: Greenwood Press, 1978. 196p. 1 map. bibliog.

This is a sociological study of ethnicity and ethnic tensions, based on the case of the Italian-Yugoslav (now Slovene-Croatian) area around Trieste and the peninsula of Istria. Two major topics are covered in the two distinct parts of the book. Firstly, the concept of nationality is explored, with an analysis of the various ethnic and subethnic types inhabiting the region. Secondly, Gross surveys the historical development and international relations from the mid-19th century to the late 1970s, emphasizing the recurrent ethnic and political conflicts and the reduction of tensions following the end of the Second World War. He draws attention to the interdependence between inter-ethnic relations in this area and the broader international context, arguing that the general improvement of world-wide relations strongly affected the relevant borderland. A useful glossary is provided.

360 **World directory of minorities.**
Edited by the Minority Rights Group.   Harlow, England: Longman, 1990. 427p.

There are eleven sections in this volume, corresponding to large geographical areas. A final section with appendices includes extracts from original documents, such as the United Nations Charter on Human Rights. There are several references to Italy, with the emphasis placed on the two major minority groups: the Friulans and the Sardinians, respectively one per cent and 2.7 per cent of the Italian population. Other important localized minorities mentioned are the south Tyroleans and the Ladins, which make up sixty-six per cent and four per cent of the Bolzano province (but only 0.5 per cent of the total Italian population between them). Slovenes, mainly around Trieste, represent 0.1 per cent of the national total. There are also smaller and scattered minorities of Greeks, Croatians and Albanians (adding up to 0.17 per cent of the total population) and a small presence of gipsies (mostly of Yugoslavian origin). Finally, a marginal reference is made to Italians in the former Yugoslavia.

361 **Italiani dimezzati: le minoranze etnico-linguistiche non protette.**
(Italians by half: unprotected ethno-linguistic minorities.)
Massimo Olmi.   Naples: Edizioni Dehoniane, 1986. 173p. bibliog.

Sympathetic towards the plea of ethno-linguistic minorities, Olmi provides an outline of their numbers, location, social and cultural status (such as, religious cult, media, or whether any periodical publications appear in a particular language). The book is divided into ten chapters; the first one attempts a definition of 'minority' and the others deal with Italo-Albanian, Sardinians and Catalans of Alghero, Greeks, Slav minorities, German-speaking communities not from Alto Adige (Cimbri etc.), Ladins from the Dolomites and Friuli, Occitans, Valdensians and Franco-Provençal gipsies.

362 **Ethnic conflict and modernization in the South Tyrol.**
Flavia Pristinger. In: *Nations without a state: ethnic minorities in western Europe.* Edited by Charles R. Foster. New York: Praeger, 1980, p. 153-88.
The first half of this lucid and informative essay charts the history of the tension and conflict between the German-speaking people of South Tyrol (annexed to Italy in 1919) and the Italian State. The process of industrialization and massive Italian immigration promoted by fascism stimulated an attitude of self-defence and resurgent nationalism. A degree of autonomy was granted after the Second World War, but dissatisfaction soon set in because of the failure of the politics of collaboration practised by the dominant (Catholic) People's Party of South Tyrol, SVP. Further autonomy was granted at the end of 1969. The second half of the essay focuses on the social structure and political system (with statistical data). Pristinger argues that the strengthened autonomy reduced ethnic conflict and brought about a 'heavy integration between the Party [SVP] and civil society', although new opposition parties appeared in the 1970s.

363 **Recent immigration politics in Italy: a short history.**
John W. P. Veugelers. *West European Politics*, vol. 17, no. 2 (April 1994), p. 33-49.
The author points out that the politics concerning recent immigration to Italy can be divided into four phases. There was no policy and little control up until 1986, when public opinion forced an extension of foreign workers' rights and an amnesty campaign to benefit illegal immigrants. Subsequently, renewed public pressure in 1989 coincided and interacted with Italy's alignment with the Schengen group within the European Union. Finally, a phase of low political salience followed the crisis precipitated by the sudden flow of Albanians in 1991. The relationship between the mobilization of public opinion and immigration policy-making activity is emphasized. It is also argued that since 1991 various factors (notably the virtual collapse of Italy's post-war political system) have rendered immigration unimportant as a political issue.

Overseas population

General

364 **Italian emigration in the post-unification period, 1861-1971.**
Luigi De Rosa. In: *European expansion and migration: essays on the intercontinental migration from Africa, Asia, and Europe.* Edited by P. C. Emmer, M. Morner. New York; Oxford: Berg, 1992, p. 157-78.
With the support of extensive statistical tables included in an appendix, this essay outlines the main characteristics of Italian emigration, from the year of the country's political unification to the years in which that movement came to a halt, at least in its

traditional features. After introducing the periodization of the phenomenon, De Rosa surveys the geographical origin and destination of the emigrants. The final section deals with their economic achievements and the role of the Italian State and banks to safeguard the emigrants' savings.

365 **Italian emigration before and after the Second World War.**
Susan Hill. In: *European insights: post-war politics, society, culture.*
Edited by Audrey M. Brassloff, Wolfgang Brassloff. Amsterdam;
New York; Oxford; Tokyo: Elsevier Science Publishers, 1991, p. 139-53.
bibliog.
Hill provides a survey of Italian mass emigration since 1880, by dividing the history of the country into three periods: from 1880 to 1915; the inter-war years; and the post-Second World War period. The emphasis falls on the last period, for which migration within Italy as well as emigration (mainly to European countries) is considered. Two interesting case studies complete the essay, one on internal migration and the other on Italians in Bury, Lancashire, in England (who are mainly from the provinces of Avellino and Caserta, in the region of Campania).

Italians in the United States

366 **Italian Americans in the '80s: a sociodemographic profile.**
Edited by Graziano Battistella. New York: Centre for Migration
Studies, Giovanni Agnelli Foundation, 1989. 208p.
A collection of six papers complemented by six extensive appendices. The book presents data on Italian Americans which was compiled by the United States Bureau of Census, specifically for the Centre for Emigration Studies. There are numerous tables and figures in both the essays and the appendices. The social and economic reality of twelve million Italian Americans is investigated in the following order: 'Italian immigrants to the United States: the last 20 years', by the editor; 'Demographic and cultural aspects of Italian Americans' by J. Velikonja; 'Italian Americans and education' by F. X. Femminella; 'Italian American family life' also by Femminella; 'Economic characteristics of Italian Americans' by Karl Bonutti; and 'Italian Americans in selected areas: a comparison' by the editor. A selected bibliography on the subject would have been useful.

367 **Three generations of Italian American women in Nassau County,**
1925-1981.
Mary Jane Capozzoli. New York; London: Garland, 1990. 295p.
bibliog.
Capozzoli analyses the changes in the lives of Italian and non-Italian American women in suburban Nassau County (New York), through questionnaires and oral histories. The traditional strong features of familism and male superiority entered into conflict with the forces of change, due to assimilation and generational stress. Yet, it is argued that 'although adherence to Italian patterns weakened over time, the changes were ones of degree rather than of kind', so that while Italian and non-Italian women shared equally in such experiences as work practice, educational career, religious upbringing and sexual morality, 'the Italian woman's overall pattern was

unique'. A brief history of Nassau County is provided at the outset; the characteristics of the peasant women from southern Italy are then outlined. The final chapters compare the experiences of the Italian American women with those of other Nassau women.

368   **From Italy to San Francisco: the immigrant experience.**
       Dino Cinel.   Stanford, California: Stanford University Press, 1982.
       348p. bibliog.

The book is organized in two parts. The first part covers the regional origins of the emigrants, with emphasis being placed on the main four provinces from which emigrants to San Francisco were drawn (Genoa, Lucca, Cosenza and Palermo). It also discusses return migration, and the significance of emigration for Italian society. The second part considers the changes the emigrants underwent in San Francisco, focusing on certain aspects of their lives in the context of a more general analysis of community organization and development. Return migration often failed because it aroused 'unrealistic expectations in the countries of emigration and among the emigrants themselves'. As for those who settled in San Francisco, they adjusted to the host society slowly and with little disruption, so that 'Italian settlements in San Francisco were essentially miniatures of settlements in Italy'. There is a fine bibliographical essay on the sources used, as well as a comprehensive general bibliography. There are also several tables and pictures.

369   **The national integration of Italian return migration, 1870-1929.**
       Dino Cinel.   Cambridge, England: Cambridge University Press, 1991.
       280p.

This book is intended to be something more than a study of emigration. Cinel argues that many Italians who emigrated to the United States at the time of the mass exodus, particularly from southern Italy, went back there after failing to re-settle upon their return to Italy. A condition of double frustration developed, towards Italy and the United States, which those emigrants' descendants still harbour (especially towards America). In fact, despite the generally notable achievement of their ancestors in the adopted country, many Italian-Americans blame American society for 'unabated discrimination' and for forcing upon them the 'demise of their nature and traditions'. It is noted that most emigrants intended to return to Italy, but for some of them the return was the result of failure to 'make it' in the United States. Chapter eight is particularly interesting in that it shows different patterns of emigration, return migration, and the use of remittances and savings in various regions of southern Italy.

370   **Workshop to office: two generations of Italian women in New
       York City, 1900-1950.**
       Miriam Cohen.   Ithaca, New York; London: Cornell University Press,
       1992. 237p. bibliog.

In this well-researched study Cohen argues that the story of the Italian immigration to the United States, and particularly that of women, was characterized neither by integration and modernization, nor by the persistent continuation of different ethnic ways of life. Cohen shows, instead, that change and continuity were deeply intertwined and, more importantly, that their balance depended on the Italians' perception as to which was the most suitable course to take in order to achieve the maximum well-being of the family as a whole. It is also noted, however, that women 'were unequal beneficiaries of family strategies'. The shifting patterns in the family roles, work lives and schooling is examined, especially with reference to the 'first generation' of Italian-American women. Interesting comparisons with immigrant Jewish women are made, showing that structural changes in the economy influenced the educational and occupational patterns of both men and women, whatever their ethnic origin.

371 **Militants and migrants: rural Sicilians become American workers.**
Donna Rae Gabaccia. New Brunswick, New Jersey; London: Rutgers University Press. 239p. 5 maps. bibliog.
This is an excellent study of the social and political conditions in western Sicily with special reference to the town of Sambuca (chiefly known for the liquor to which it has given its name) and to the steady emigration of its inhabitants to the United States between 1880 and 1939. The author focuses on the geographical spread and social conditions of migrants from this town to the United States, the only country to which they tended to emigrate. Family ties, crafts and professions, forms of social political affiliations and mutual aid societies are examined in particular. In her conclusion, Gabaccia outlines some broad connections between economic change in American industrial cities and in the European countryside, and argues that the immigrants' experience 'might productively be viewed from an international perspective, rather than from the viewpoint of the individual nation-state'.

372 **Old bread, new wine: a portrait of the Italian-Americans.**
Patrick J. Gallo. Chicago: Nelson-Hall, 1981. 356p. bibliog.
This is a lively work which borrows from history, sociology, anthropology and political science, as well as from personal encounters and experiences. A comprehensive bibliography is included for those readers interested to pursue their knowledge of the subject. The narrative is structured in a roughly chronological order, but the focus moves from one relevant aspect to another. For instance, one chapter is devoted to the cultural role of the family and another to the religious life amongst the Italian-Americans. The last chapter, entitled 'From Columbus to Watergate', quotes from Nixon's infamous secret tapes, in which he expressed uncomplimentary remarks about the Italians. As it happens, and Gallo points this out, some of the President's accusers, who were responsible for his downfall, were Italian-Americans. Readers well versed in the Italian language will note a high number of misprints in Italian names and words.

373 **The golden door: Italian and Jewish immigrant mobility in New York City, 1880-1915.**
Thomas Kessner. New York: Oxford University Press, 1977. 224p. bibliog.
Southern Italians and East European Jews were the two major immigrant groups to settle in New York between 1800 and the First World War. Kessner tests the received idea that the Irish took longer than other immigrant groups to work themselves out of poverty, that the Jews had the highest degree of social mobility, and that the Italians fell in between those two cases. The changes in the occupational patterns among Italian and Jewish immigrants are analysed and compared; their relative geographical and social mobility is also studied. Ultimately, Kessner confirms that the Jews fared better than the Italians, partly because they placed a greater emphasis on education

and partly because the Italians 'often preferred to keep their ties with the community and sacrificed newer neighbourhoods as a trade-off for the amenities of "Little Italy" '. Two statistical appendices provide a measure of the quantitative approach pursued by the author.

374 **Monte Carmelo: an Italian-American community in the Bronx.**
Anthony L. LaRuffa. New York; London; Paris; Montreux, Switzerland; Tokyo; Melbourne: Gordon & Breach, 1988. 160p. 1 map. bibliog.

The number of Italian-Americans living in the New York district of the Bronx, near the Roman Catholic church named after the Madonna of Mount Carmel, reached 30,000 at some point after the Second World War. Considering that they only extended over an area of approximately one hundred square blocks, they represented a notable community on their own. LaRuffa provides an introductory description of the historical background of these immigrants, outlining their demographic, social and cultural development. The study is articulated at three levels: firstly, the community as a whole is observed through individuals, places and events (such as unlawful occurrences); secondly, family profiles are offered; and thirdly, the structures and symbols of community life are analysed. The final chapter deals with such issues as ethnicity and assimilation, the spatial dimension of the Italian-American community, and the 'mafia image'. The mid-July procession in honour of the Madonna is noted as a 'mecca of Italian-American ethnicity'.

375 **The Italian immigrant in urban America, 1880-1920, as reported in the contemporary periodical press.**
Salvatore Mondello. New York: Arno Press, 1980. 264p. bibliog.

By monitoring the leading monthly and weekly publications the author is able to study the reaction to the immigration of Italians to the United States during the decades when immigration was at its peak. In general, Mondello argues, the periodical press did not welcome the Italians, particularly during the depression years (1880-97) and writers accused the newcomers of exacerbating industrial problems. During the expansion years, between 1897 and 1914, a less negative attitude was adopted, although even then Italians were regarded with mixed feelings. As Mondello writes, 'the negative stereotype of Italian criminality was given more attention in the periodical press than the positive image of Italians as an artistic people'. It is therefore argued that the Italian immigrants had to overcome widespread prejudice in urban America.

376 **From immigrants to ethnics: the Italian Americans.**
Humbert S. Nelli. Oxford; New York: Oxford University Press, 1983. 225p. bibliog.

A fine synthesis of the long and complex history of Italians in the United States. They were despised at first, to the point of denying that they belonged to the domineering white race; but through hard work they became a component of the American middle class. The book is divided into three parts: the first briefly provides the context of the Italian presence in the United States and surveys the poor economic conditions they left behind in Italy. Part two examines various aspects of the immigrants' experience, focusing on such issues as housing, jobs, community institutions, and the family. Part three shows how Italian-Americans began the search for a new self-identity, and 'after decades of denying their origins they are proudly, even defiantly, affirming their "Italianness" '. It can be argued then, that 'as a group, Italian-Americans have completed the transition from immigrants to ethnic rediscovery'.

377 **The 1891 New Orleans lynching and US-Italian relations: a look back.**
Edited by Marco Rimanelli, Sheryl Postman. New York; San Francisco; Berne, Switzerland; Frankfurt, Germany; Berlin; Vienna; Paris: Peter Lang, 1992. 425p.

Nine essays are collected here, which consider the lynching of eleven imprisoned Italians who had been accused of murder and were recognized as being innocent the day before their killing. That flash of violence was the result of simmering xenophobic anti-Italian tensions. Various contributions show that the lynching was not a spontaneous outbreak, but had been 'secretly engineered by Louisiana's establishment in a strategy to exterminate the mafia, expropriate the rich Italian tropical fruit trade with Central America, and especially, cajole the independent-minded Italians from joining the White Supremacist front, which disenfranchised Louisiana's Blacks in 1898'. The ensuing diplomatic crisis between Italy and the United States is also considered in some of the essays. The contributors are: C. J. Bradely; L. Casilli; F. X. Femminella; S. Postman; and G. and M. Rimanelli. An interesting appendix provides information about the sixty 'great Italian jazz musicians of New Orleans'.

378 **Family and community: Italian immigrants in Buffalo, 1880-1930.**
Virginia Yans-McLaughlin. Urbana, Illinois; Chicago; London: University of Illinois Press, 1982. 286p. 1 map. bibliog.

In this scholarly work the author makes a study of southern Italian family life in one industrial city of the United States, and in so doing offers interesting insights into urban, labour and family history. The Italians were the last large European group to enter Buffalo, and were consequently discriminated against 'by both the upper- and the working-class citizens'. Nevertheless, in the face of harsh conditions, the Italian families survived, adjusted and even prospered. The central argument of the book is that this achievement was made possible by the cohesion of the families and the continuous support they afforded to their members, whether of a practical, emotional or financial kind. Remaining outside the family would not have been a realistic or comfortable option for those immigrants. As the map clearly shows, the Italian families were clustered according to their regional origin: Calabria; Campania; Abruzzo; and Molise.

379 **Puberty to manhood in Italy and America.**
Harben Boutourline Young, Lucy Ran Ferguson. New York; London; Toronto; Sydney; San Francisco: Academic Press, 1981. 284p. bibliog.

Over three hundred adolescent males were interviewed in Italy and America and their answers and views constitute the foundations of this book. Apart from the common link of age and sex, they all shared their grandparents' broad regional origin: southern Italy. The interviewees are divided into three groups, according to where they grew up: Boston, Rome and Palermo. An outline of the different environments introduces the study of adolescent development and the 'outcomes in early maturity'. The conclusion emphasizes, on the one hand, how 'emigration to a more auspicious environment may make for more harmonious physical growth, affect patterns of health or disease, and influence ways of thought and behaviour'. On the other hand, it is noted that broad similarities remain mainly as a consequence of the strong role of the family (particularly the southern family) which manages to perpetuate itself despite the changed environmental circumstances. There are many tables and notes on statistical methodology.

Italians in the United Kingdom

380 **Without a bell tower: a study of the Italian immigrants in south west England.**
Bruno Bottignolo. Rome: Centro Studi Emigrazione, 1985. 215p.
1 map. bibliog.

This is a study by an anthropologist of two communities of Italian immigrants: those who settled in Bristol and those who were based in Swindon. It is the result of research conducted in the second half of the 1970s. After some general information on the Italian immigrants in south-west England, Bottignolo examines their living conditions and personal relations, and underlines how the latter represented 'the principal bond uniting the Italians'. He then pays attention to the immigrants' social and political organization and the institutions which support it. Various attempts to set up their own organizations were successful at first but later failed. 'The lack of willingness necessary to bring about a community venture such as an Italian centre – the author argues – stemmed from the fact that the Italian immigrants did not consider themselves to be in permanent residence there'.

381 **The Italian factor: the Italian community in Great Britain.**
Terri Colpi. Edinburgh; London: Mainstream, 1991. 300p. 6 maps.
bibliog.

Nearly two centuries of Italian immigration to Britain are surveyed here. The historical aspect of the book is mainly based on secondary sources, and extensive research and interviews were carried out in order to provide a picture of the contemporary presence of Italians and their descendants in today's Britain. This alternative approach is borne out by the structure of the book, which is divided into two parts. The first part outlines the history of the Italians in Britain from 1800 to the Second World War, and is organized in a strict chronological order. The second part deals with the post-war years and combines a thematic and chronological order. The rapid growth and development of the community in the 1950s and early 1960s is noted, with particular attention paid to the role of the family. The final chapter looks at the main institutions which provide a framework for social life to the Italians. Illustrations are provided.

382 **Italians forward: a visual history of the Italian community in Great Britain.**
Terri Colpi.   Edinburgh; London: Mainstream, 1991. 191p. 1 map.

A large-size companion to Colpi's narrative history of the Italians in Britain (q.v. *The Italian factor*), this volume reproduces about 250 photographs and covers the last one hundred years. Most chapters represent specific decades and are introduced by a historical profile of the changes taking place in the community. Each photograph is accompanied by an informative caption. The entire collection consists of six categories of pictures, woven into the chronological order: included are photographs of family groups, work sites, leisure activities, ceremonies, special circumstances and personalities. As Colpi explains in the introduction, the book is 'for two sets of readers': for the British-Italians themselves, to remind them of the occupations and ways of life of their ancestors; and for the public at large, who still know little about the Italians in Britain.

383 **Lime, lemon & sarsaparilla: the Italian community in south Wales, 1881-1945.**
Colin Hughes.   Bridgend, Wales: Seren Books, 1991. 142p. 2 maps. bibliog.

The author's emotional reminiscences as a child enchanted by an Italian shop in Cefn Fforest give way to an informed and readable history of the Italians in South Wales from the last decades of the 19th century up until the Second World War. The background of poverty in the Italian mountain villages is also considered, as is the historical setting of the Welsh valleys where the emigrants arrived. It is noted, in fact, that most Italians came from one particular village in the province of Parma (Bardi). They shared the difficulties of the 1920s and 1930s with the Welsh people, and were assimilated into the native community, because of their relatively small numbers, their dispersal throughout the population, and their occupation as small shopkeepers.

384 **Casalattico and the Italian community in Ireland.**
Brian Reynolds.   Dublin: University College Dublin, Foundation for Italian Studies, 1993. 191p. 5 maps. bibliog.

This is a highly original study in which historical and anthropological methodologies are effectively applied. The introductory chapter surveys the history of Italian emigration in general and is followed by a chapter on the Italians in Britain and Ireland. The three remaining sections consider the specific district of central Italy, Casalattico, between Rome and Naples, from which most emigrants to Ireland came. Reynolds first establishes the regional setting and then focuses on the patterns and impact of local emigration and return migration. Because of the individualistic attitude of the returned emigrants, he argues that the local authorities in Casalattico ought to take the initiative and inject enthusiasm for civic enterprises extending outside the narrow circle of the town's inhabitants. He suggests that failing this, Casalattico will become a ghetto with a culture which is neither Italian nor foreign. Tables, graphs, plans and photographs (taken by the author) are included in the text.

385 **Italian immigrants in nineteenth-century Britain: realities and images.**
Lucio Sponza. Leicester, England: Leicester University Press, 1988. 372p. 4 maps. bibliog.

This is an informative book on a subject which has received scant attention. The work is constructed around the contrast between the realities and the representation of Italian immigrants. The first part deals with the Italians themselves, their material conditions, numbers, social and regional background, and the changing patterns of their trades. There is also an original case study of the emigration from the Parma region. The second part discusses British perceptions of the Italians, relating to such incidents as the employment of children in vagrant activities, the 'organ grinding nuisance', the question of the insanitary conditions in the Italian quarter, 'political subversion', 'violence' and 'criminality'. The appendices contain statistical tables and a selection of verses on Italian organ-grinders; a section with plates on Italian street musicians is also included.

Italians elsewhere

386 **Migrants or mates: Italian life in Australia.**
Edited by Gianfranco Cresciani. Sydney: Knockmore, 1988. 286p.

The Italians are the largest non-English speaking community in Australia. By the end of the 1980s they numbered more than half a million, the majority of them still retaining their Italian citizenship, despite (or because of) the 'vicious attempts to demonize them and their country of origin'. Cresciani has gathered photographs, letters, newspaper articles, notices and reports which show diverse aspects of the Italians' presence in that continent. It is a very interesting documentary collection, especially because it focuses on the toil, experience and culture of the community. The material is arranged in chronological order and consists of over eighty entries. The first is a photograph of Raffaello Carboni, a gold-digger who arrived in Australia in 1852; the last is an article (from *The Age*) alleging scandal in the setting up of an association affiliated to the Italian Communist Party in 1975.

387 **Far la Mérica: making it in America: the Italian presence in Rio Grande do Sul.**
Luis A. De Boni, Rovilio Costa, translated by Gisélia Silva. Porto Alegre, Brazil: Riochell, 1991. 209p. 8 maps. bibliog.

In what is virtually the only book in English on the Italian emigration to Brazil, the text of the original Portuguese version is also produced. The work consists of brief historical profiles of people and chronicles of events which characterized the Italian presence in Rio Grande do Sul. The tenuous chronological order is marked by a topical arrangement of the content. This is mainly focused on such economic and social topics as: farming labour; landowners; industrial workers; co-operation; political initiatives; marriage; religion; home medicine; and leisure and games. The most attractive part, however, is the rich collection of old photographs of people, buildings and objects, appropriately produced in sepia colour.

388   **Such hardworking people: Italian immigrants in post-war Toronto.**
Franca Iacovetta.   Montreal; Kingston, Canada; London; Buffalo,
New York: McGill-Queen's University Press, 1992. 278p. 2 maps.
By the early 1960s the Italians had replaced the Jews as Toronto's main non-British
ethnic group, and Toronto had replaced Montreal as the Canadian city with the largest
number of Italians: from a population of some 18,000 Italian immigrants in 1941, the
residents now claim an Italian heritage of more than 400,000. There are four central
themes in this book. Firstly, Iacovetta discusses the complex transformation of former
peasants into industrial workers before moving on to the issue of gender, with a
separate treatment of the roles and perceptions of men and women belonging to the
immigrant community. Thirdly, the relationship between immigrants and their host
society is examined before addressing the question of immigrant militancy and the
involvement of Italians in construction workers' strikes. This is a scholarly, well-
written book centred on southern Italians who arrived in Toronto before 1965, but its
perceptive considerations make it a notable contribution to the studies on Italian
emigration.

389   **Arrangiarsi: the Italian immigration experience in Canada.**
Edited by Roberto Perin, Franco Sturino.   Montreal, Canada:
Guernica, 1989. 251p. 1 map.
The Italian emigrants to Canada, Perin argues in the introduction, had to *arrangiarsi*
('make do' or 'get by') to survive, in the absence of their government's and the host
country's support. They had to sharpen their quick-wit, forethought and
inventiveness, and so they created an art. While Sturino writes on the links in chain
migration, an essay by R. F. Harney (the pioneer of these studies on the Italians)
considers the lessons that can be learned from the Italo-Canadian past. There are also
contributions by: N. Serio, on the images of Canada in Italian writings; B. Ramirez,
on Italian labour in Montreal, 1880-1930; G. P. Scardellato, on the Italians in British
Columbia; L. Lacroix, on Italian artists in Quebec; P.-A. Linteau, on the linguistic
and political aspects of the Italian presence in Quebec; S. Iannucci, on contemporary
Italo-Canadian literature; and W. Boelhower, who provides a theoretical framework
for the analysis of Italo-Canadian poetry.

390   **The Italians in Australia.**
Nino Randazzo, Michael Cigler.   Melbourne: AE Press, 1987. 197p.
2 maps. bibliog.
Part of the Australian Ethnic Heritage Series, this book outlines a century-long
history of Italian settlement in Australia, through their struggles and achievements. It
is noted that by 1981 there were nearly 280,000 persons in Australia who were born
in Italy. After two introductory chapters on Australia's Italian heritage, the authors
survey the 19th-century emigration which took place in all parts of the country:
Queensland; New South Wales; Victoria; and the 'new frontiers' (Tasmania, South
and Western Australia). The second half of the book is concerned with the Italian
presence in the 20th century: the focus here is on the 'turbulent 1930s', the war years
(with interesting pages on the Italian prisoners of war), and the post-war years. The
authors emphasize the Italians' entrepreneurship and contribution to Australian
society.

391   **Italians in Toronto: development of a national identity, 1875-1935.**
John E. Zucchi.   Kingston, Canada; Montreal: McGill-Queen's
University Press, 1988. 255p. 5 maps. bibliog.

By the end of the period studied by Zucchi the Italians in Toronto constituted a
sizeable community, with over 15,000 of them living there. No less than 160,000
Italian-born people were recorded there in the 1980s. This work looks into the inner
dynamics of that community, commencing with the first settlers in the 1860s:
Ligurian fruit and vegetable dealers and Tuscan plaster statuette vendors. They were
joined by people from Basilicata, mostly street musicians and pedlars, who later
became bootblack workers. By the end of the century Italians from other regions had
arrived in Toronto, to be employed in building sites, the food retail trade and in
catering. Depending on the time of their arrival, their regional origin and occupation,
these immigrants clustered in a few areas of the city, making it more appropriate to
refer to them as 'little Italies'. The subsequent development of a 'national identity'
therefore remains relatively superficial.

Emigration in a South Italian town.
See item no. 478.

Urban life in Mediterranean Europe.
See item no. 481.

Italian-Americans and religion.
See item no. 1075.

Languages and Dialects

General

392   L'italiano nelle regioni: lingua nazionale e identità ragionali.
(Italian in the regions: national language and regional identity.)
Edited by Francesco Bruni.   Turin: UTET, 1992. 1,038p. bibliog.

Bruni considers the evolution of the Italian language and its position in present-day regions, as documented mainly in its written forms. The existence of regionalisms and the relationship between dialect and the standard language are also discussed in this volume. The regions dealt with are, in the order in which they appear in the volume: Piedmont and Val d'Aosta; Liguria; Lombardy; Canton Ticino; Trentino and Alto Adige; Venetia; Friuli-Venezia Giulia; Dalmatia and Istria; Emilia and Romagna; Tuscany; Umbria; the Marches; Umbria, Rome and Latium; Abruzzi and Molise; Campania; Puglia (Apulia); Basilicata; Calabria; Sicily; Malta; Sardinia and Corsica. A substantial appendix is devoted to the origin and the diffusion of books in Italy, both manuscript and printed. An extensive bibliography and detailed indexes of words and names quoted complete the volume.

393   L'italiano nelle regioni: testi e documenti. (Italian in the regions:
texts and documents.)
Edited by Francesco Bruni.   Turin: UTET, 1994. 937p. bibliog.

This is the second part of *L'italiano nelle regioni* and it follows the same layout as the first volume (q.v.). For each region significant texts are provided, sometimes with extensive linguistic commentaries, from the earliest vernacular documents to present-day newspapers or even wall graffiti. Letters, diaries, and other personal writings are also used to illustrate a particular type of regional Italian.

394   The major languages of Western Europe.
Edited by Bernard Comrie.   London: Routledge, 1990. 314p. bibliog.

Apart from its general interest, a good introduction to the Indo-European languages, and a chapter on Latin and the Italic languages, this book devotes one chapter (twelve) to Italian (pages 269-92). The profile of the language is written by Professor Nigel Vincent and after a concise introduction to the historical development of Italian as a language it deals with its phonology, morphology and syntax.

395 **Storia e teoria dell'interpunzione: atti del convegno internazionale di studi – Firenze 19-21 maggio 1988.** (History and theory of punctuation: proceedings of the international conference – Florence 19-21 May 1988.)
Edited by Emanuela Cresti, Nicoletta Maraschio, L. Toschi.   Rome: Bulzoni, Università degli Studi di Firenze, Dipartimento di Italianistica, 1992. 569p. bibliog.

Although this may appear too specialized to be mentioned here, its inclusion is justified by the recent interest in the long-neglected area of punctuation. This is an important book which is relevant not only for the essays it contains on the use of punctuation in mediaeval manuscripts and in early printing, especially in the 16th century, but also for its relationship to intonation and other phenomena belonging to spoken Italian. The final essay is devoted to a comparison between the different punctuation systems of German, French and Italian. A few essays are accompanied by tables and illustrations from original texts, especially manuscripts. Unlike other collections of conference papers this is completed by a name index.

396 **Profilo dei dialetti italiani: Toscana.** (Profile of Italian dialects: Tuscany.)
Luciano Giannelli, edited by Manlio Cortelazzo.   Pisa: Pacini, 1976. 128p. 1 map. bibliog.

This volume dedicated to the dialects of Tuscany is just one example of the series of monographs on Italian dialects by region under the general editorship of Manlio Cortelazzo. Each volume includes an introduction to the dialects under consideration and a detailed description of their phonology, morphosyntax and lexis. All dialect examples are provided in a phonetic script (although not in the International Phonetic Alphabet) and each volume is completed by a dialect map and a 45rpm record containing the conversations recorded by natives of the region. These are transcribed in the text with commentary.

397 **The romance languages.**
Edited by Martin Harris, Nigel Vincent.   London: Routledge. 1990. 500p. 11 maps. bibliog.

This volume which provides an up-to-date picture of languages such as French, Spanish, Portuguese and Rumanian, as well as Latin, contains more than one chapter of interest to Italy. Chapter eight, written by Nigel Vincent, discusses Italian; chapter nine, written by Michael Jones, is devoted to Sardinian; and chapter ten, by John Haiman, considers Rhaeto-Romance, spoken by about 10,000 people in Alto-Adige and by nearly half a million in the north-eastern part of Italy, near Udine. Each chapter provides a historical introduction to the language under discussion and then deals in more detail with its phonology, morphology and syntax. Concise bibliographies and references to sources are also provided.

398 **AIS, atlante linguistico ed etnografico dell'Italia e della Svizzera meridionale.** (AIS, a linguistic and ethnographic atlas of Italy and southern Switzerland.)
Karl Jaberg, Jakob Jud, edited by Glauco Sanga. Milan: Unicopli, 1987. 2 vols. maps. bibliog.

Volume one contains an Italian translation of the original German introduction to the monumental *Sprach-und Sachatlas Italiens und der Südschweiz* by Karl Jaberg and Jacob Jud, published between 1928 and 1940. Translated by Serenella Baggio, it offers a full explanation of the phonetic symbols employed in the Atlas and a key to all the numbers referring to places in the maps which are included in it. Volume two consists of a large selection of the linguistic maps contained in the original Atlas, photographically reduced. Essentially they are lexical tables in which each map supplies a very large sample of dialect equivalents to a standard Italian word. Map number forty-five, for instance, illustrates the dialect forms for *ragazzo* 'boy', beginning in the North-West and listing terms such as *mat, tus, bagay, ragas, monello, gwaglione, karusu, picciottu, pitsinnu* and many others.

History

399 **L'italiano letterario: profilo storico.** (Literary Italian: a historical outline.)
Gian Luigi Beccaria, Concetto Del Popolo, Claudio Marazzini. Turin: UTET, 1989. 218p. bibliog.

A clear and concise history of the literary language, from its origins to contemporary authors, such as Carlo Emilio Gadda and Italo Calvino. Each chapter deals with an entire century except for the first one which is devoted to the origins of Italian (approximately 900 AD to 1200) and except for one other chapter which is devoted to Dante. Latin quotations are provided with an Italian translation in a footnote.

400 **Etruscan.**
Larissa Bonfante. London: British Museum Publications, 1990. 64p. bibliog.

This is a non-technical introduction to the language of the Etruscans, who lived in central Italy from at least 700 BC to the first century BC. Etruscan inscriptions, many from bronze mirrors, are discussed and interpreted. The final chapter is devoted to the Oscan language, as represented by bronze tablets from Agnone. Two appendices, one of Etruscan names, the other a glossary of Etruscan words, are followed by a section on 'further reading' and by the index to the volume.

401 **L'italiano: elementi di storia della lingua e della cultura.** (The Italian language: elements of the history of the language and culture.)
Francesco Bruni. Turin: UTET, 1984. 482p. 5 maps. bibliog.

As well as tracing the development of Italian from Latin, and considering early Italian texts and the problems of contemporary Italian, this book devotes considerable attention to Italian dialects and to texts produced by semi-literate people. It is fully illustrated and each chapter is provided with an accurate and up-to-date bibliography. At the end of the book there is an index of the most important words studied in the text, since the book was intended as a complement to the *Grande Dizionario della Lingua Italiana* published by UTET (q.v.). There is also a detachable, detailed, coloured map of Italian dialects at the end of the volume. A paperback edition without the numerous illustrations is also available.

402 **Storia della lingua italiana.** (A history of the Italian language.)
Edited by Francesco Bruni. Bologna: Il Mulino, 1989-94. 6 vols.

Each volume is a monograph written by a different author on the history of the language in a given period. For instance, the volume on the 15th century, *Il Quattrocento*, is by Mirko Tavoni and the two volumes dedicated to *L'Ottocento* are by Luca Serianni. The series is aimed at university students and each volume is informative and up to date.

403 **Storia linguistica dell'Italia unita.** (A linguistic history of united Italy.)
Tullio De Mauro. Rome-Bari: Laterza, 1993. 2nd ed. 594p.

This book first appeared in Italy in 1963 and provoked wide consensus and bitter criticism at the time. It represented a new way of looking at linguistic history which took much more into account what used to be called 'external history'. Considerable evidence was taken from social history, from the history of education and from the general history of Italy. It discussed some fundamental changes which had occurred in Italy since the time of unification, such as: the movement from a high level of illiteracy to its virtual disappearance; the learning of Italian on the part of people who spoke only their own dialects; and the emergence of 'popular' Italian. The book is divided into two sections, the second dealing with 'documents and evidence'.

404 **The languages of Italy.**
Giacomo Devoto, translated by Louise Katainen. Chicago; London: University of Chicago Press, 1978. 357p. maps. bibliog.

An authoritative treatment of the earliest languages in the Italian peninsula, which considers traces of Mediterranean words, Indo-European influences, and non-Indoeuropean 'mysteries', such as Etruscan, through to the pre-Latin and Celtic languages to Latin and Italian. The fragmentation that took place at the fall of the Roman empire gave way to a variety of influences from 'external' languages such as Longobard or Byzantine Greek. The emergence of dialects and the social varieties of Italian are discussed with constant reference to historical facts up to the political unification of Italy and the following century. The period covered by the book ranges from approximately 6000 BC to the 1970s.

405 **Nuovo manuale di storia della lingua italiana.** (A new textbook on the history of the Italian language.)
Miklós Fogarasi. Florence: Le Monnier, 1990. 2nd rev. ed. 312p. bibliog.

This book, written for foreign university students, is a clear and very sound introduction to the history of the Italian language. It covers historical grammar and the evolution of Italian and of its dialects. Part three is more technical and provides a concise history of 'sounds and spelling' and part four is concerned with the evolution of vocabulary. Part five considers the evolution of morphology and part six presents a history of syntactic structures. The book concludes with some considerations on the literary language. A bibliography and a word index complete the volume.

406   **From Latin to Italian: an historical outline of the phonology and morphology of the Italian language.**
        Charles H. Grandgent.   New York: Russell & Russell, 1955.
        Reprinted, 1971. 191p.

Originally published in 1927, this is dated, but has some historical value for its treatment of the development of Italian from Latin. It may be useful to note that Italian, according to this book, is still 'the literary and official language ... as pronounced by cultivated Florentines', which many would dispute today. The terminology used is sometimes obsolete and not always easy to understand for the non-initiated.

407   **History of linguistics.**
        Edited by Giulio C. Lepschy.   London: Longman, 1994- . 2 vols.
        bibliog.

First published as *Storia della linguistica* in Bologna by Il Mulino (1990-94), this original work deals with linguistics in China and in India as well as with Jewish and Arab linguistics and the Greek and Latin tradition. It is mentioned here because the sections on Mediaeval and Renaissance linguistics (written by specialists like Edoardo Vineis, Alfonso Maierù and Mirko Tavoni) contain much material which is relevant to the history of linguistics in Italy. Volume three in the Italian edition also contains a whole chapter devoted to Italian linguistics and dialect studies. The English edition will eventually consist of five volumes.

408   **A linguistic history of Italian.**
        Martin Maiden.   London: Longman, 1995. 320p. bibliog. (Longman
        Linguistic Library).

Maiden concentrates on the internal history of the language but also considers dialects, varieties of usage, and cultural and social factors. He takes into account the contribution of current linguistic methods to the study of Italian grammar.

409   **The Italian language.**
        Bruno Migliorini, T. Gwynfor Griffith.   London: Faber, 1984. 2nd ed.
        553p.

A recast version of the first full-length history of the Italian language published by Bruno Migliorini in 1960. Each chapter deals with the development of literary Italian from popular Latin and the earliest documents of 'proto-Italian', dated 960 AD, to the 1980s. The chapters are arranged chronologically by century – one is devoted to Dante and his views on language – and in each the main lexical and grammatical innovations are listed, with a section on the influence of foreign elements in Italian. It is still the standard textbook of its kind, and the best reference in this area available in English.

410   **Italic, Latin, Italian: 600 BC to AD 1260.**
Ernst Pulgram.   Heidelberg: Carl Winter, 1978. 400p. 3 maps. bibliog.
This is the book for those who want to know about the ancient languages of Italy. It is
more specialized than Pulgram's *The tongues of Italy: prehistory and history*
(Cambridge, Massachusetts: Harvard University Press, 1958. Reprinted, New York:
Greenwood Press, 1969), and contains a number of short texts largely from
inscriptions in Pre-Latin languages (such as Ligurian, Lepontic, Raetic). Chapter two
deals with Italic languages (such as Oscan and Umbrian which existed along with
Latin). Part two deals with Latin from its earliest documents up until the point at which
it becomes 'Old Italian' which is dealt with in the final section of this book up until the
age of Dante. A word-index completes the book. For a much more concise, but very
up-to-date treatment of this subject see chapter seven, 'Latin and the Italic Languages'
in *The major languages of Western Europe*, edited by Bernard Comrie (q.v.).

411   **The history of linguistics in Italy.**
Edited by Paolo Ramat, et al.   Amsterdam: John Benjamins, 1986.
364p. bibliog. (vol. 33 of Studies in the History of the Language
Sciences; series III of Amsterdam Studies in the Theory and History of
Linguistics Science).
Each of the fifteen essays collected here, in English, French, German and Italian, is
provided with a summary; the essays deal with different theories or 'responses' to the
Italian vernacular, in particular from Dante to the present-day. The collection
recommends itself for its critical and up-to-date approach to Humanists' concepts of
'Latin, Grammar and Vernacular' and to individual 16th-century lexicographers.
Trends of Italian linguistics in the early 19th century are surveyed, with two other
essays on Giacomo Leopardi and Carlo Denina, and on late 19th-century figures
(Manzoni, De Amicis). Major figures like B. Terracini and G. Devoto in the 20th
century are also discussed. Y. Malkiel surveys in a masterly fashion 'Romance and
Indo-European linguistics in Italy'.

412   **Grammatica storica della lingua italiana e dei suoi dialetti.** (A
historical grammar of Italian and its dialects.)
Gerhard Rohlfs.   Turin: Einaudi, 1969. 3 vols. bibliog.
These three volumes, which are devoted to phonetics, morphology, and syntax and
lexis respectively, discuss a large variety of linguistic phenomena, with reference to
their Latin origin. Words deriving from Germanic languages, or from Greek or Arabic
are also referred to. The content of the books is divided into numbered paragraphs
referring to a linguistic phenomenon or to a grammatical category. Originally
published in German, this is the largest Italian historical grammar which draws
numerous examples from a wide variety of Italian dialects. In this sense its coverage
is larger than that of the more modern work by P. Tekavčić, *Grammatica storica della
lingua italiana*, Bologna: Il Mulino, 1980, 3 vols.

413   **Storia della lingua italiana.** (A history of the Italian language.)
Edited by Luca Serianni, Pietro Trifone.   Turin: Einaudi, 1993-94.
3 vols. bibliog.
This is the most comprehensive history of Italian available today. It is not organized
chronologically but according to themes, and important issues within the discipline.

Volume one, bearing the somewhat mysterious title 'I luoghi della codificazione' (The places of encoding) contains a discussion of the birth of the history of the language in Italy and the reasons why it started later than in other countries; its first fully-fledged history was published by Bruno Migliorini in 1960, as a symbolic celebration of the millennium of the Italian language. Lexicography, grammar, and spelling are then covered. A whole chapter is devoted to theoretical discussions on the Italian language, dating from Dante to the unification and very briefly up to 1985. An original section is also devoted to language and the Church. Literary prose and verse are dealt with in a chronological order and volume one is concluded by a chapter on the language of tragedy. Volume two is devoted to the relationship between the written and spoken language, including the language used in the theatre and in the cinema. Volume three goes back to the 'origins' of Italian and then deals with regional vernaculars up to approximately the 15th century. The relationship between foreign languages and Italian is also discussed here. Although the information contained in these volumes can be dispersive and uneven, the highly up-to-date references provided in the footnotes make it a very valuable work.

414   **La questione della lingua.** (The debate about the Italian language.)
    Maurizio Vitale.   Palermo: Palumbo, 1978. 2nd ed. 800p. bibliog.

The 'Questione della lingua' is an ongoing debate in Italian history and considers such issues as whether vernaculars are comparable to Latin, 'what type of Italian should be used in literary prose?', 'what is a proper name for the language: Tuscan, Italian, Florentine, Courtly?' and 'What models should be used in the written language'. The debate became particularly heated in the 16th century but it continues in certain forms even today when, for the first time it can be said that the majority of Italian people do actually use Italian normally in everyday situations and not one of the very numerous dialects which have existed for centuries. This book outlines the main points of the debate, century-by-century, with reference to the main authors who published tracts on it and including an extensive bibliography. The second part of the volume is devoted to an anthology of critical writings: fifty-five short passages from Dante to P. P. Pasolini.

Grammars

415   **The Italian language today.**
    Anna Laura Lepschy, Giulio Lepschy.   London: Hutchinson, 1991.
    2nd ed. 248p. bibliog.

After a short chapter devoted to 'Italian today' the book discusses the development of Italian from Latin and the 'questione della lingua', a debate which started in the 16th century about which type of language should be used in literary texts. Chapter three is an extremely clear and up-to-date introduction to Italian dialects with a summary of their main phonetic features. A few examples from dialect texts are also provided. Chapter four deals with geographical and social varieties of Italian. The second part of the work is a reference grammar of contemporary educated Italian, and considers specific points of advanced grammar, such as the position of adverbs or the use of prepositions, in a way which reflects contemporary Italian usage. A bibliography, a table of phonetic symbols, and an index complete the volume.

416　**Grande grammatica italiana di consultazione.** (An extensive Italian reference grammar.)
　　Vol. 1 edited by Lorenzo Renzi. 1988. 758p. Vol. 2 edited by Lorenzo Renzi, Giampaolo Salvi, 1991. 943p. bibliog.　Bologna: Il Mulino.

These are the first two volumes of three which will provide scholars interested in the Italian language with an essential modern reference tool. This will be one of the most comprehensive grammars based on generative principles but without the highly formalized notation traditionally associated with the transformational-generative approach. It makes it possible for readers with a relatively small knowledge of linguistics to follow the painstaking discussion of individual grammatical points in contemporary Italian. Volume one deals with the structure of the sentence, noun phrases, pronouns and quantifiers whereas volume two is devoted to verbs, adverbs, adjectives and subordinate clauses. Both volumes are complemented by a full and detailed bibliography.

417　**Grammatica italiana: Italiano comune e lingua letteraria.** (Italian grammar: standard and literary Italian.)
　　Luca Serianni, with Alberto Castelvecchi.　Turin: UTET, 1988. 712p. bibliog.

This is a 'traditional' grammar, and uses mainly written texts to illustrate its rules. This includes newspapers, advertising and occasionally more colloquial forms of Italian. Sometimes referred to as 'prescriptive grammar', it attempts to explain what a contemporary norm is in the usage of the Italian language. The work contains reference to historical facts in the development of Italian and draws upon material collected for the *Grande dizionario della lingua italiana* (UTET) (q.v.), which it accompanies.

Dictionaries

Monolingual, etymological and of names

418　**Dizionario inverso italiano, con indici e liste di frequenza delle terminazioni.** (A reverse index of the Italian language with frequency count and frequency lists of terminations.)
　　Edited by Mario L. Alinei.　The Hague: Mouton, 1962. 607p.

This reverse index, which orders words according to their endings, is one of the earliest experiments with electronic language processing. Covering lexical data in Italian, this volume was still compiled using punch cards.

419   **Grande dizionario della lingua italiana.** (A comprehensive
       dictionary of the Italian language.)
       Salvatore Battaglia.   Turin: UTET, 1961- . 17 vols. (to date).
The latest volume appeared in 1994 and extends from words beginning with ROBB to
ones beginning with SCHI. This is the largest Italian monolingual dictionary which
contains a number of word-forms found in early texts and in regional or semi-dialect
contexts. This is a historical dictionary in which each entry is illustrated by
quotations, usually from literary texts, and arranged in chronological order.

420   **Dizionario etimologico italiano.** (An etymological Italian dictionary.)
       Carlo Battisti, Giovanni Alessio.   Florence: Barbera, 1950-57. 5 vols.
This is still the largest etymological dictionary of Italian. Although some of its
reconstructions of word origins may need updating, it is still a very valuable tool in
this area. It includes numerous references to extremely rare, regional and even dialect
terms, which are sometimes impossible to find in any other Italian dictionary.

421   **Parole degli anni novanta.** (Words of the nineties.)
       Andrea Bencini, Eugenia Citernesi.   Florence: Le Monnier, 1992. 403p.
A list of approximately 5,000 words, collected during the revision of the Devoto-Oli
Italian dictionary (March 1990). Many of these, indicated here by an asterisk, have
not entered current dictionaries, as evidence of the acceleration in the use of
neologisms in present-day Italian. The source of each entry, frequently from
newspapers, is indicated with the date on which it appeared.

422   **Lessico di frequenza della lingua italiana contemporanea.** (A
       frequency lexicon of contemporary Italian.)
       Umberta Bortolini, Carlo Tagliavini, Antonio Zampolli.   Milan:
       Garzanti, 1972. 852p. bibliog.
Various different types of text were used to collect the material on which this lexicon
is based: theatre; fiction; cinema; newspapers; and school-books. After a statistical
analysis 5,356 words were found to be the most frequently used in written Italian at
the time. They are listed here in order of frequency and in alphabetical order. The
problems connected with the collection, the processing of the data and with the
statistics are discussed in the introduction.

423   **Dizionario delle parole straniere in uso nella lingua italiana.** (A
       dictionary of foreign words used in Italian.)
       G. Samuele Carpitano, Giorgio Casole.   Milan: Oscar Mondadori,
       1989. 354p.
A paperback dictionary which lists numerous words of foreign origin, including some
acronyms, along with Latin words and phrases with clear, concise definitions and an
indication of their pronunciation.

424 **Glossario degli antichi volgari italiani (GAVI).** (A glossary of the old Italian vernaculars.)
Edited by Giorgio Colussi. Helsinki: Helsinki University, Helsingin Yliopiston Monistuspalevu, 1982- . 16 vols. (to date).

To date, more than sixteen volumes of this glossary have appeared; the compiler's original aim was to complete it in ten. It includes explanations of rare words with references to the context in which they were found, from texts dating from the origins to about 1300, with the exclusion of texts which belong to the 14th century.

425 **Dizionario etimologico della lingua italiana.** (An etymological dictionary of the Italian language.)
Manlio Cortelazzo, Paolo Zolli. Bologna: Zanichelli, 1979-88. 5 vols. bibliog.

Although not as comprehensive as the *Dizionario etimologico italiano*, since its corpus is based on a concise Italian dictionary published by Zanichelli, this work has the advantage of including bibliographical references for almost each entry, which allows the reader to follow the discussion of sometimes controversial etymologies. A general bibliography is also provided.

426 **Dizionario etimologico dei dialetti italiani.** (Etymological dictionary of Italian dialects.)
Manlio Cortelazzo, Carla Marcato. Turin: UTET, 1992. 404p. bibliog.

This book contains a selected list of words from various Italian dialects with an indication of their origins. Many words concerning food, for example, are of dialect origin, such as *canéderli* 'kind of dumplings' from Trento, deriving from the German *Knödel*, or the Sicilian *cassata* 'cake and ice-cream', probably from the Latin *caseata* 'cheese-cake', or the Piedmontese *ghersìn* and Italian *grissino* 'breadstick' which is a diminutive of *ghersa* 'kind of bread baguette'. The entries run from pages 3-256 and the book concludes with a conceptual index, an etymological index, one of dialect varieties, and a general index.

427 **Dizionario dei cognomi italiani.** (A dictionary of Italian surnames.)
Emilio De Felice. Milan: Oscar Mondadori, 1978. 351p.

Over 14,000 Italian surnames are covered in this dictionary, with numerous cross-references to name variants. It frequently indicates the geographical areas of diffusion of particular surnames as well as their probable origin.

428 **Lessico di frequenza dell'italiano parlato.** (Frequency vocabulary of spoken Italian.)
Tullio De Mauro, Federico Mancini, Massimo Vedovelli, Miriam Voghera. Milan: Etaslibri, 1993. 542p. bibliog.

This is the fruit of a research project sponsored by IBM-Italia and its lists are based on 500,000 words collected from conversations, lectures, telephone calls and similar oral situations in Milan, Florence, Rome and Naples. These were then processed by computer and 15,000 entries were chosen. The actual frequency lists are preceded by an extensive introduction (p. 15-168) with a bibliography. Two computer disks contain the transcript of all the conversations in a compact format.

429 **Il grande dizionario Garzanti della lingua italiana.** (The large Garzanti dictionary of Italian.)
Milan: Garzanti, 1987. 2,268p.

One of the most up-to-date monolingual dictionaries which includes numerous neologisms without neglecting old and highly literary or technical terms. The pronunciation of each main entry is clearly indicated as well as any grammatical peculiarities, or irregular forms. It is one of the few dictionaries that lists prefixes and suffixes, such as *anti-*, *bi-*, *bis-*, *iper-*, or *-accio*, *-ente*, *-ante*, as independent entries. Nomenclature tables and lists of abbreviations complete the volume.

430 **Dizionario di toponomastica.** (A dictionary of place-names.)
Giuliano Gasca Queirazza, Carla Marcato, Giovan Battista Pellegrini, Giulia Petracco Sicardi, Alda Rossebastiano. Turin: UTET, 1990. 720p. bibliog.

The first dictionary of Italian place-names to deal with the whole of the country rather than with individual regions (like D. Olivieri's *Toponomastica lombarda*, or S. Pieri's *Toponomastica della Valle dell'Arno*). All the names of Italian communes, as reported in the *Annuario del Touring Club Italiano 1985*, are included, making it the largest dictionary of its genre in Italy, and one of the most accurate at providing, or at least attempting to provide, an explanation of the origin of place names. An interesting feature of this dictionary is that some of the words which are frequently used to make up place names have been listed as separate individual entries, in italics, such as *agello* 'small field' and *poggio* 'hillock'. Names of Italian regions and rivers are also included. Information about dates at which certain place names have been changed or modified by decree is also provided.

431 **Dizionario italiano ragionato.** (An analogical dictionary of Italian.)
Edited by Angelo Gianni, et al. Florence: G. D'Anna Sintesi, 1988. 2,017p.

An innovative monolingual dictionary which helps the advanced learner to find words connected with the main entry, which are not only morphologically derived from it, but also etymologically connected. For instance, a word like *donna* 'woman' will be found under *duomo* 'cathedral', both connected with the Latin, *domus*. Explanations of individual words are original, clear and up to date. A paperback edition is also available.

432 **Vocabolario della lingua italiana.** (A dictionary of Italian.)
Istituto della Enciclopedia Italiana. Rome: Istituto della Enciclopedia Italiana, 1986-94. 4 vols. (vol. 3 in two tomes).

An up-to-date, comprehensive monolingual dictionary which combines accuracy of definition and clear layout with original illustrations, some of which are in full colour. Volume four contains a series of addenda, among which appear words or abbreviations such as CD-ROM (pronounced *siddi-ròm*) and *ipertesto* 'hypertext'. Indexes of names, of tables, and a thematic index complete the last volume.

433 **Le parole della gente: dizionario dell'italiano gergale.** (People's
     words: a dictionary of Italian slang.)
     Gianfranco Lotti.   Milan: Oscar Mondadori, 1992. 519p.

The titlepage of this dictionary adds a caption to explain that it includes words
ranging 'from the comic medieval to the contemporary youth language'. The claim is
justified and a large number of popular or vulgar Italian words and phrases are
included. The list of authors and works quoted testifies to the time span covered. In
the last few pages there is an 'alternative lexicon of human anatomy' listing a great
deal of metaphors, euphemisms and vulgarisms with reference to parts of the body.

434 **Dizionario della lingua italiana.** (A dictionary of the Italian
     language.)
     Fernando Palazzi, edited by Gianfranco Folena with Carla Marello,
     Diego Marconi, Michele A. Cortelazzo.   Turin: Loescher, 1992.
     2,046p.

A new, completely revised and recast edition of one of the most popular dictionaries
in Italian schools (since 1939, with new editions in 1957 and 1973). It combines a
large number of words which could be found in literary works of the past as well as
clear definitions of modern and contemporary terms, and provides the etymology and
the date of first documentation for every word. An outline of Italian grammar is also
provided in an appendix.

435 **Toponomastica italiana.** (A study of Italian place names.)
     Giovan Battista Pellegrini.   Milan: Hoepli, 1990. 559p. 8 maps.
     bibliog.

This is an excellent handbook by the leading authority on Italian place-names. After
an introduction to the methodology of studying place-names and an overview of
place-names deriving from pre-Latin languages, the author enters into a more in-
depth consideration of their origins; chapter three deals with Latin elements, chapter
four with Arabic, Germanic and Slav; chapters five to seven with names derived from
people, from plants and animals, and names of rivers and mountains. The final
chapter covers names which are influenced by the peculiar location of a city area, by
the names of roads, of saints and of local populations. An extensive bibliography, a
glossary of technical terms and a full index of place names complete the volume.

436 **Sinonimi e contrari.** (Synonyms and antonyms.)
     Giuseppe Pittano.   Bologna: Zanichelli, 1988. 863p.

This is one of the standard dictionaries of synonyms in Italian. It supplies a variety of
synonymic choices for one given word including colloquial ones. More entries are
included in the present, 'major' edition than in other smaller or 'concise' editions
which are also available. The vocabulary is up to date and the layout is clear and
pleasant.

140

437 **Frase fatta capo ha: dizionario dei modi di dire, proverbi e locuzioni.** ('Meaningful clichés': a dictionary of phrases, proverbs and expressions.)
Giuseppe Pittano. Bologna: Zanichelli, 1992. 351p. bibliog.

Proverbial phrases and expressions found in newspapers or in other publications may be difficult to explain as some are very old and may be connected with popular or folk knowledge. Others derive from the Bible or from other works of literature, and some are linked to recent political events. Many of these phrases are explained in this book, frequently with reference to etymology or to their source.

438 **Dizionario degli anglicismi nell'italiano postunitario.** (A dictionary of anglicisms in post-unification Italian.)
Gaetano Rando. Florence: Olschki, 1987. 254p. bibliog.

Anglicisms and americanisms are listed in this dictionary, with reference to their sources. This makes it possible to trace the date of their first appearance in an Italian context. Numerous acronyms and technical terms are included, some of which disappeared in common usage soon after their arrival. Some of the most interesting terms borrowed from English are the ones known as 'calques', made up of elements which already existed in Italian but with a new meaning. The best-known examples of this are 'grattacielo' for 'skyscraper', or 'ragazza squillo' for 'call-girl'.

439 **Dizionario della lingua italiana.** (Dictionary of the Italian language.)
Niccolò Tommaseo, Bernardo Bellini. Milan: B.U.R., 1977. 20 vols.

A paperback reprint of a great Italian dictionary which provides a wealth of information on rare, literary, and common terms. It first appeared in 1865, and this edition has an introduction by a great philologist like Gianfranco Folena.

440 **Il neoitaliano: le parole degli anni ottanta.** (Neo-Italian: the words of the eighties.)
Sebastiano Vassalli. Bologna: Zanichelli, 1991. 2nd ed. 282p.

First published in 1989, this is no ordinary dictionary of neologisms. Written by one of the most interesting contemporary Italian writers, the entries are lively and witty. The explanations are usually much longer than in a normal dictionary, and sometimes trace the history of a particular expression or provide considerable information from various other sources. The entry for *Rambo*, for example, lists films and other sources before giving a detailed and vivid description of a male Rambo and of a female one. The eighties are always referred to as 'the banal eighties', in a parodic reference to the roaring twenties.

441 **Il nuovo Zingarelli: vocabolario della lingua italiana.**
Nicola Zingarelli, 11th ed. edited by Miro Dogliotti, Luigi Rosiello.
Bologna: Zanichelli, 1986. 2,256p.

This dictionary, though still bearing the name of its founder who first published it in 1922, is a completely revised and new edition, with a better layout than earlier editions. It contains approximately 127,000 entries, 65,000 etymologies and 4,300 illustrations and is a popular, and generally reliable reference work which is going to be updated every year.

Bilingual and scientific

442   **Biologia e medicina: biology & medicine: dizionario enciclopedico di scienze biologiche e mediche: italiano-inglese/inglese-italiano.**
Bologna: Zanichelli, 1990. 1,719p.
The Italian-English section has over 27,000 entries and over 30,000 sub-entries. The English-Italian section has over 30,000 entries. Many entries have etymological references which facilitate in some cases the understanding of the term. There are over 200 illustrations, over 300 formulas and 46 appendices with abbreviations and international symbols.

443   **Dictionary of shipping terms: Italian-English and English-Italian.**
Peter R. Brodie.   London; New York; Hamburg: Lloyds of London Press, 1988. 171p.
A reference book for chartering brokers, port agents and ship operators. The principal areas covered are: voyage and time-charters; documentation, including bills of landing; ship-types and their gear; ports, their equipment and facilities; cargoes and their packaging; and geographical and weather features.

444   **International dictionary of building construction: English-French-German-Italian.**
Angelo Cagnacci Schwicker.   Milan: Technoprint International, 1972. rev. ed. 1,261p.
Terms included in this dictionary cover: principles of mathematics; mechanics; soil and foundation engineering; stone structure; bridge construction; building tools; implements and machinery; hydromechanics; aerotechnics; and architecture. The dictionary contains a list of Italian terms at the end with reference to the numbered entry in the main text.

445   **Dictionary of the Italian and English languages.**
Edited by the Centro Lessicografico Sansoni, General editor, Vladimiro Macchi.   Florence: Sansoni, 1985. 2nd ed. 2 vols.
Originally published by Sansoni-Harrap as the Standard Italian and English-Italian dictionary in four volumes in 1973, this revised and enlarged edition appears in two volumes of 1,645 pages (English-Italian) and 1,520 pages respectively. It is the most comprehensive and reliable English-Italian and Italian-English general dictionary for the serious translator or scholar. This edition contains a large number of idiomatic expressions.

446   **Collins Sansoni Italian dictionary: English-Italian; Italian-English.**
Edited by the Centro Lessicografico Sansoni, General editor, Vladimiro Macchi.   Florence: Sansoni, 1988, 3rd ed. 2,277p.
This is a bilingual dictionary in one volume which has always been rated highly in specialist journals. Its level of accuracy is high and it covers a considerable amount of words for a dictionary of its size.

447   **A new dictionary of economics and banking: English-Italian /
Italian-English.**
Livio Codeluppi.   Milan: Cisalpino-Goliardica, 1989. 1,466p.
A dictionary sponsored by the prestigious Bocconi University in Milan, with up-to-
date and comprehensive coverage of general financial terminology and economics,
banking and data-processing.

448   **Dizionario delle scienze e delle tecnologie elettroniche.** (A
dictionary of electronic sciences and technologies.)
Antonio Colella.   Milan: Editrice il Rostro, 1988. 759p.
This dictionary includes tables and nomenclature on telecommunications, electro-
medical equipment, chemistry, biology, mechanics, and mathematics. Over 40,000
terms are covered in the two sections, and the dictionary has 120 illustrations, 80
tables, 1,100 abbreviations, and 37 conversion tables.

449   **Dizionario visuale italiano-inglese.** (An Italian-English visual
dictionary.)
Edited by Jean-Claude Corbeil, Ariane Archambault.   Bologna:
Zanichelli, 1993. 896p.
Originally published in French in Canada by Editions Québec/Amérique, Montréal,
this volume is a modern attempt to produce an English-Italian visual dictionary. It
contains extremely clear, pleasant and effective colour illustrations. Occasionally the
translation of terms is influenced by the original edition and some American terms
have been retained in the English translation. The work contains a total of 50,000
words, 3,500 pictures, illustrating 600 subjects, grouped in 28 chapters. Each section
or chapter is colour-coded. *The Oxford-Duden pictorial Italian and English
dictionary* also appeared in 1995 (Oxford: Oxford University Press).

450   **Dizionario giuridico / Law dictionary.**
Francesco De Franchis.   Milan: Giuffré, 1984. 1,545p.
This looks more like a law treatise than a dictionary. The text is in Italian with an
extensive bibliography included in the introductory section. The dictionary includes
English and American terms for which thorough explanations are provided, with
useful cross-referencing.

451   **Dizionario di informatica: inglese-italiano.** (A dictionary of
computer sciences: English-Italian.)
Michel Ginguay, Italian edition edited by F. A. Schreiber.   Milan:
Masson, 1992. 3rd ed. 242p.
The Italian edition of a classic reference dictionary originally published as the
French/English *Dictionnaire d'informatique*. It covers approximately 16,000 words
and 2,200 abbreviations.

452 **Il Gould Chiampo: dizionario enciclopedico di medicina inglese-italiano/italiano-inglese.** (An encyclopaedic dictionary of medicine: English-Italian/Italian-English.)
Bologna: Zanichelli, 1988. 2,256p.

This is the Italian edition based on the *Blakiston's Gould medical dictionary* published in the United States by the McGraw-Hill Book Company. It is an encyclopaedic dictionary with a distinguished list of contributors. The contents include twenty-six anatomical plates, and tables of arteries, bones, muscles, nerves, synovial joints and ligaments, veins, chemical constituents of blood, and comparative blood test values.

453 **McGraw-Hill, dizionario enciclopedico scientifico e tecnico inglese/italiano, italiano/inglese. (From the McGrawHill dictionary of scientific and technical terms, 1974).** (An encyclopaedic technical and scientific English-Italian, Italian-English dictionary.)
McGraw-Hill, Zanichelli. Bologna: Zanichelli, 1980. 2,062p.

A fully-illustrated dictionary with the English section arranged in the form of an encyclopaedia. Each English entry has an Italian equivalent and is followed by an explanation in English. The Italian-English section is more concise and is organized as a straightforward Italian-English dictionary. It includes about 90,000 terms defined in English, covering approximately 102 specialist sectors. Various tables and appendices are included. There is an appendix in Italian on units of measure and international graphic symbols, as well as short biographies of scientists and technologists.

454 **Dizionario tecnico: technical dictionary: English-Italian-Italian-English.**
Giorgio Marolli. Milan: Hoepli, 1991. 12th ed. 1,960p.

A classic technical dictionary, this has begun to show its age. The twelfth edition did not fulfil expectations as far as coverage of a large number of new technical terms was concerned.

455 **Il nuovo dizionario Hazon Garzanti: inglese-italiano/italiano-inglese.** (The new Hazon Garzanti English-Italian/Italian-English dictionary.)
Milan: Garzanti, 1990. 2,429p.

This is the latest offspring of a successful dictionary (originally produced by Professor Mario Hazon and colleagues connected with Bocconi University in Milan). It is a comprehensive general dictionary in a single volume grouping together about 270,000 words.

456 **Economics & business: dizionario enciclopedico economico e commerciale: inglese/italiano-italiano/inglese.**
Ferdinando Picchi. Bologna: Zanichelli, 1986. 1,333p.

This dictionary is largely for Italian users and provides full explanations in Italian for each entry on insurance, banking, commerce, economics, management, business and

144

accountancy terms. The Italian/English section is much shorter (pages 1,122-312) and Italian terms are provided with a straightforward English translation.

457 **Nuovissimo dizionario commerciale.** (A new commercial dictionary.)
Giuseppe Ragazzini, Giancarlo Gagliardelli. Milan: Mursia, 1983. 813p.
One of the earliest dictionaries to deal with commercial and financial vocabulary, this is still useful and more compact than others.

458 **The Cambridge Italian dictionary.**
General editor, Barbara Reynolds. Cambridge, England: Cambridge University Press, 1962. 897p. vol. 1, Italian-English; vol. 2, English-Italian, 1981. 842p.
One of the largest bi-lingual dictionaries. Volume one has a fairly distinctive literary bias whereas volume two is wider in scope and uses more examples. Unfortunately, however, it contains a number of misprints. A medium-sized, one-volume version, completely revised was later published as: *Cambridge-Signorelli Italian-English, English-Italian dictionary*, edited by Mariangela Pappini Fontanelli and supervised by Barbara Reynolds. Cambridge; Milan: Cambridge University Press and Signorelli, 1985. 2,276p.

459 **Dictionary of computer science: dizionario di informatica: English-Italian-German-French; Italian-English, German-English, French-English.**
Otto Vollnhals. Milan: Jackson, 1993. 2nd ed. 1,270p.
This lexicon of approximately 20,000 words covers hardware, software, information processing, personal computers, word processing, circuit technology and related fields. A new edition is due to appear in 1995.

460 **West's law & commercial dictionary (in five languages).**
Zanichelli-West. Bologna: Zanichelli, 1988. 1,842p.
This is an encyclopaedic dictionary which contains main entries in English, defined in English and with a succinct translation into German, French, Spanish and Italian. The second part is a straightforward Italian-English dictionary of law terms and phrases.

How to find out about Italy.
See item no. 25.

Lingua e dialetti italiani. (Italian language and dialects.)
See item no. 1044.

Bibliografia della linguistica italiana. (Bibliography of Italian linguistics.)
See item no. 1058.

The year's work in modern language studies.
See item no. 1069.

Teaching materials for Italian.
See item no. 1047.

I vocabolari delle parlate italiane. (Dictionaries of Italian dialects.)
See item no. 1072.

Religion

461 **Italia cattolica: fede e pratica religiosa negli anni novanta.** (Roman
    Catholic Italy: faith and religious practice in the 1990s.)
    Edited by Giuseppe Brunetta, Antonio Longo.   Florence: Vallecchi,
    1991. 479p.

This book results from the first comprehensive investigation into the religious
practices of Italians. The two editors, both sociologists, provide a summary of their
questionnaire-based findings in the introduction. The contents of the book are then
divided into three parts. The first provides the statistical evidence of Italians' views
on such topics as popes, the Bible, their own sins and the Church's mission. The
second part includes a great variety of essays by secular and religious scholars; these
range from the development of priesthood and various religious practices to the
relationship between women and religion. The final part consists of a collection of
interviews with scholars, politicians and writers. The tendency towards secularization
appears to contrast with persisting traditional views and practices, especially among
the middle-aged and elderly population.

462 **Madonnas that maim: popular Catholicism in Italy since the
    fifteenth century.**
    Michael P. Carroll.   Baltimore, Maryland; London: The Johns
    Hopkins University Press, 1992. 202p. 3 maps. bibliog.

The popular Catholicism which is the object of this study refers 'to all beliefs
associated with supernatural beings that have been legitimated by the Church (at least
at the local level)'. The relationship among the main three cults (the Madonna, the
Saints, and Christ) is first investigated. The first two cults occupy a higher position in
popular Catholicism and they are discussed in greater detail in two chapters. Carroll
then focuses on some of the darker aspects associated with both madonnas and saints
in Italy. The regional differences in such metacults between northern and southern
Italy are surveyed, and certain features of southern popular practices analysed.
Finally, general observations on the psychology of Italian Catholicism are made, with
sections on masochism both in males and females. The book contains tables and

figures with representations of sanctuaries, sacred images, maps and religious pamphlets.

463   **Fra Lega e Chiesa.** (Between the Northern League and the Roman Catholic Church.)
Roberto Cartocci.   Bologna: Il Mulino, 1994. 221p.

The Italians' sense of identity and social integration seems to have been lost in the political and cultural crisis of the 1990s. Cartocci argues that the two forces which are attempting to provide a solution are the Northern League and the Roman Catholic Church. He suggests that the former has successfully challenged the State in the name of local loyalties grafted on small entrepreneurship. The latter, thanks to its effective organization and symbolic legacy, projects itself as the only critical voice against the atomization of social life induced by capitalism, now that the socialist utopia has gone. The traditional role of the Church in Italian society is explored as the background to this argument in two informative and captivating chapters. The tendency towards secularization is also investigated.

464   **Some call it providence: Don Orione and the little work of divine providence.**
Stephen Clissold, foreword by Cardinal Hume, introduction by Malcolm Muggeridge.   London: Darton, Longman & Todd, 1980. 198p.

Luigi Orione was born in Tortona (Piedmont), in 1872. His father was a road paviour and his mother was a pious woman. Luigi had an early vocation, became a priest, and began his mission by setting up a boarding school for deprived children in Tortona (the 'little work'). Soon he established a similar institution in Sicily. Don Orione became likened to a modern St. Francis of Assisi and congregations he inspired flourished in Europe, North and South America (where he spent a long time), Africa and Australia. He died in 1940 and the proceedings towards beatification began in the 1960s. The life of this simple and lovable man is told with much sympathy by Clissold with frequent references to the general historical events as background to his narrative.

465   **Religione e chiesa in Italia.** (Religion and the church in Italy.)
Franco Garelli.   Bologna: Il Mulino, 1991. 271p.

The relationship between Roman Catholicism and society in Italy is considered here through the study of religious practices, the church structure, the presence of religious institutions involved in welfare and education, and the role of religion-inspired associations active in various fields. Garelli's main argument is that Roman Catholicism is still deeply rooted in Italian society, despite the undergoing process of secularization. This, it is also pointed out, contributes to the stabilization of the socio-political system and also reflects the contrasting features of Italian society. The question of religion and modernity in Italy is discussed in general terms in the first, introductory chapter, which also includes some reference to the presence of other religious faiths in the peninsula.

466   **She died: she lives.**
      Maurus Green OSB.   London: New City, 1989. 173p.

First published in 1977 under the author's pseudonym of George Francis, this is the hagiographic story of Maria Orsola Bussone, a teenager who died by accident while on a group holiday in 1970. The author, a Benedictine monk, heard an edifying account of the girl's religious devotion, accepted the view that she knew more about God than many professionally religious people, and went to her native mountain village near Turin to collect first-hand testimonies about her life. The result is a picture of a community in which traditional religious values are adopted by the younger generation and adapted to new forms of expression. Maria Orsola was an enthusiastic and prominent figure in the evangelical movement and music-making for the local community. She was a model student and a generous friend. The contents of her diary helped to make her story known beyond the village and when Pope John Paul II visited Turin in 1988, Maria Orsola was referred to as 'an example for youth to follow'.

467   **Padre Pio: his life and mission.**
      Mary F. Ingoldsby.   Dublin: Veritas Publications, 1978. 175p.

A devout Roman Catholic and a devotee of Padre Pio, Ingoldsby has written an interesting, if partial, history of the famous Capuchin friar. Born in a poor peasant family near Benevento (Naples region), he possessed – the author writes – 'the quite exceptional charisms of bilocation, prophecy, the gift of tongues, the power of healing, while hundreds if not thousands can testify to the extraordinary fragrance which emanated from his bleeding wounds and from his whole person'. The wounds were the stigmata which appeared on Padre Pio's flesh in 1918, and had no little importance in the powerful attraction and awe he inspired. His early life is described systematically; the latter period is illustrated through various topics, such as 'his charismatic gifts'; 'the Devil's assaults'; 'witnesses to the stigmata'; and 'his holy death'.

468   **La politica vaticana e l'Italia, 1943-1978.** (Vatican politics and Italy, 1943-1978.)
      Sandro Magister.   Rome: Editori Riuniti, 1979. 499p.

Thirty-five dramatic and traumatic years are studied here through the influence of the Vatican and the Roman Catholic Church upon Italian political development: from the collapse of fascism (and Pope Pius XII) to the election of the Polish Pope John Paul II (only mentioned in the preface). The focus is on the three reigning popes during those decades: Pius XII; John XXIII; and Paul VI. The changing religious attitudes of Italians in the wider setting of political, economic and social events provides the background. It is interesting that the projected end of the book coincided with Pope Montini's death and the first election of a non-Italian pope for centuries.

469   **For God and neighbour: the life and work of Padre Pio.**
      Anthony Pandiscia.   Slough, England: St. Paul Publications, 1991. 174p.

This is the most recent in a series of biographies of the Capuchin monk who is now on his way to beatification. The book is divided into two parts. Part one consists of thirty-four short chapters describing the life and work of Padre Pio. Some of them focus on the extraordinary events which contributed to the friar's fame: the stigmata;

the 'mysterious perfume' people scented in his vicinity; and bilocation. Opposition and criticism to Padre Pio from within the Catholic Church are treated with contempt. Among the visitors to the monk was Aldo Moro, the Christian Democrat leader and most famous victim of the Red Brigades; it appears that 'Padre Pio made a prophecy to Moro which was tragically fulfilled'. Part two is only a few pages long and assembles testimonies by more or less famous people on their encounters with the Padre. Pictures and a biographical sketch of the friar are included.

470 **La Chiesa nella società contemporanea.** (The Roman Catholic Church in contemporary society.)
Guido Verucci. Rome-Bari: Laterza, 1988. 494p. bibliog.
A subtitle indicates that contemporaneity is used here to mean: from the end of the First World War to the Second Vatican Council. Although the study concerns the relationship of Roman Catholicism and society at large, a great deal of attention is devoted to Italy and the Vatican. The book is divided into chronologically ordered chapters dealing with: the early post-(Great) war years; Pius XI and the rise of fascism; the Church *vis-à-vis* the economic crisis in the 1930s and totalitarian regimes; World War II and its aftermath; the revival of Catholicism in the 1940s and 1950s (with most interesting considerations on the role of the Vatican and political struggle in Italy); the reign of John XXIII and the first phase of the Second Vatican Council; and Pope Paul VI and the conclusion of the Council.

Comrades and Christians: religion and political struggle in communist Italy.
See item no. 482.

Black madonnas: feminism, religion and politics in Italy.
See item no. 527.

Italy.
See item no. 539.

The Catholic-Communist dialogue in Italy.
See item no. 550.

Catholic collaboration in Italy.
See item no. 566.

Nineteenth-century European Catholicism.
See item no. 1060.

Printed Italian vernacular religious books: 1465-1550.
See item no. 1061.

Social Anthropology

471 **The moral basis of a backward society.**
Edward C. Banfield, with the assistance of Laura Fasano Banfield,
photographs by the author.   Glencoe, Illinois: The Free Press, the
University of Chicago, Research Centre in Economic Development
and Cultural Change, 1958. 204p.

This is a pioneering, classic anthropological study of a poor southern Italian village,
fictitiously named Montegrano, in the region of Basilicata. It is a fascinating
investigation of the cultural, psychological and ethnical conditions in the life of
villagers, showing their inability 'to act together for their common good or, indeed,
for any end transcending the immediate, material interest of the nuclear family'. This
condition is called 'amoral familism'; it represents the core of Banfield's thesis and is
still debated by scholars on southern Italy, even if the original hypothesis is
misunderstood. Banfield did not argue that the excessive strength of the family
inhibited the enforcement of the law of the State; he emphasized the negative
consequences of the fragmentation of social bonds within the village social system.
There are some fine black-and-white photographs and statistical tables.

472 **The broken fountain.**
Thomas Belmonte.   New York: Columbia University Press, 1979.
151p.

The title refers to a fountain in the shape of a lion's head and a sea shell, which was
smashed by children, hence the name of 'Fontana del Re', which the author applied to
the district of Naples where he conducted his research. This is a study of the poor
people of Naples, written not without human empathy by an American anthropologist.
The result is a lively picture of the 'fashion-wise, street-wise and urbane' Neapolitan
poor. 'They are not provincial – Belmonte writes – they live close to the gates of
power in the wards of a great city, but unlike proletarians, they are not integrated into
the political and ideological currents of mass culture'; their existence is submerged in
a 'crude, loud, pushy world where the moral order is exposed as a fraud which
conceals the historical ascendancy of cunning and force'. These are the concluding

significant observations of this fascinating journey through the individual and collective lives of Neapolitan slum dwellers.

473 **Montevarese: a study of peasant society and culture in southern Italy.**
Jan Brögger. Bergen, Norway; Oslo; Tromsö, Norway: Universitetsforlaget, 1971. 160p. 2 maps. bibliog.

This is an anthropological study of a peasant community in the Aspromonte mountains of Calabria. Montevarese is the fictitious name of the village where the field research was carried out. The aims of the book are twofold: to explain the local social forms as the result of aggregate behaviour; and to show the relationships of such forms with aspects of traditional Mediterranean culture, as well as with the broad Italian traditions. After surveying the agricultural organization and land use of the Montevarese district, Brögger explores social mobility, kinship and family structure (with interesting observations on marriage and 'female seclusion'). The forces of integration are then considered, with an emphasis on the Calabrian version of the Sicilian mafia. Finally, a short epilogue addresses the issue of migrant labour, which turns peasants into workers. The book includes tables, figures and drawings.

474 **Chi siamo: la storia della diversità umana.** (Who we are: a history of human diversity.)
Luca and Francesco Cavalli Sforza. Milan: Mondadori, 1993. 405p. maps. bibliog.

Likely to soon appear in English, this work contains interesting information concerning the ancient inhabitants of Europe and of Italy based on genetic research, in which Luca Cavalli Sforza is a leading specialist. It also shows that it is impossible to study one culture in isolation without relating it to others and to their remote ancestry. The existence of an Indo-European group of languages, for example, is confirmed by genetic research as originating in Anatolia where agriculture is likely to have begun. There are also sections specifically devoted to research on Italy, such as the one on emigration in a mountain valley near Parma.

475 **Torregreca: a world in southern Italy.**
Ann Cornelisen. Basingstoke, England; London: Macmillan, 1980. 335p.

Torregreca is the fictitious name of the village in Basilicata where the American-born author spent many years, sharing and observing the lives of the inhabitants, 'who struggle today, as they have for three thousand years, to wrest an existence from the rocks and clay that make up their world'. Individuals are portrayed with subtlety and empathy; family relations, work practices, values and ways of life are examined with insight; landscapes, places and buildings are described with accuracy and conciseness. Chapters are constructed around loose themes which develop into a tapestry of events (such as religious practices), or characters (such as Chichella, a woman who had 'little to show on except the story of her own life'). Chapter eight, in particular, is a fascinating journey into 'prophecies, witches, and spells' – and reminds one of Carlo Levi's classic book, *Christ stopped at Eboli*. The book first appeared in 1969.

476 Flight from Torregreca: strangers and pilgrims.
Ann Cornelisen. Basingstoke, England; London: Macmillan, 1980. 304p.

This is a story of the author's visits to emigrants from Torregreca, the fictional name of a southern Italian village on which she wrote her previous book (q.v.). Her companion for the journeys was Chichella, a local woman and old acquaintance of the writer, who had relatives in Germany. Most of the book concerns visits to Germany, although in the last part some *torresi* living in Turin are also visited. The emigrants' stories are intertwined with Cornelisen's memories of them in Torregreca. Personal details are conveyed in a captivating narrative style, with vivid dialogues, full of sensitivity and perceptive observations. In her final comment, Cornelisen writes that 'with all its brutalities and its discriminations and its wrenches, emigration has given my *torresi*, at least, the only chance they ever had or ever will have for a decent life'.

477 Land and family in Pisticci.
John Davis. London: The Athlone Press, University of London; New York: Humanities Press, 1973. 200p. 2 maps. bibliog.

This classic study in social anthropology covers the town of Pisticci (in Basilicata) as well as the surrounding hamlets and rural centres. An introductory chapter provides information on the cultural and structural characteristics of the district. Marriage and the property arrangements which go with it are observed closely: 'Dowry and marriage settlements – Davis writes – are complementary transactions, negotiated to achieve equality between spouses and to set them up as independent adults'. Families, kinship and the neighbourhood receive much attention. The following topics are also discussed: the distribution of land; the forms of employment; case studies of family structures in relation to land distribution; effects of modernization programmes; and a concluding and resuming chapter on 'Land tenure, kinship and social structure'. Several appendices supply documentary information, while tables, graphs and plates enhance the text.

478 Emigration in a south Italian town: an anthropological history.
William A. Douglass. New Brunswick, New Jersey: Rutgers University Press, 1984. 283p. 2 maps. bibliog.

This is a competently-researched, engaging study of the causes and consequences of emigration in Agnone, a town in the mountainous region of Molise. Douglass shows how 'several factors in Agnone's remote and recent history preconditioned the townspeople for emigration'. Particularly interesting are the pages dedicated to the mediaeval characteristics of that community and the challenge of modernity during the 19th century. At the beginning of the 20th century, Agnone saw internal dissension and class conflict exasperated by the effects of massive emigration. New waves of emigration occurred after the Second World War. This history bears heavily on the present, in that 'Agnone is on the brink of becoming a community of the middle-aged and elderly, precluded, on biological grounds alone, from sustaining even its currently sharply reduced populace for another generation'.

479   **Life and politics in a Venetian community.**
Robert H. Evans.   Notre Dame, Indiana; London: University of Notre
Dame Press, 1976. 228p. 2 maps. bibliog.

Santa Maria, the village at the centre of this study, is a small community on the slopes
of the Euganean hills, in the Veneto region. The changes in the village life,
particularly in the field of politics, are considered with an inquisitive and sympathetic
eye. Evans presents an overview of the region's history before annexation to Italy
(1866); the political development from that date to 1951 is then surveyed. This is
followed by three chapters which analyse, respectively: the demographic movements
and the economic structure; the important role of the family, and broader forms of
communal relations; and the no less important influence of the Church in political and
social spheres. A final chapter covers elections, administration and decision-making
processes in the 1960s. The parochial views of the past, Evans argues, were gradually
dispelled, but great value was still attributed to a communal sense of belonging.

480   **Cultural disenchantments: workers peasantries in northeast Italy.**
Douglas R. Holmes.   Princeton, New Jersey: Princeton University
Press, 1989. 238p. 2 maps. bibliog.

The subjects of this study are the people of Friuli, a north-eastern region of Italy
which has a strong rural tradition, but which has also been deeply changed by small-
scale, diffuse industrialization. Historical and ethnographical data are blended here,
with the focus on the concept of 'peasant-worker society'. It is around this concept
that socio-economic relations are investigated. The notion of 'cultural disenchantments' is at the base of the analysis of cultural issues throughout the book. Two
chapters consider the structure of land tenure and agrarian politics, followed by
insights on folk consciousness and industrialization. Finally, attention is paid to the
autonomous political movement which 'strives not only to stem new onslaughts of
disenchantment, but to retrieve remnants of ancient cultural ideas and ethnic
practices'.

481   **Urban life in Mediterranean Europe: anthropological
perspectives.**
Edited by Michael Kenny, David I. Kertzer.   Urbana, Illinois;
Chicago; London: University of Illinois Press, 1983. 338p. bibliog.

The authors of the essays contained in this volume discuss urban development and
social life in Mediterranean Europe. Despite the variety of the contributions, a
persistent theme throughout is the lifestyle of migrants and the urban poor. In part
one, Kertzer focuses on Italian urban development and urban geography, and surveys
some of the social research carried out on city life. In part two, W. A. Douglass writes
about migration in Italy. After a short overview of pre-Second World War emigration
and a regional demographic profile, the author examines the adaptation of rural
migrants to city life. In part three, T. Belmonte offers a concise case-study on the
'contradictions of social life in subproletarian Naples'. His major informant lamented
'the failure of trust in a world where class, money, and the rules of the market game
have had ample time to invade all the inner sanctums of social life'.

82   **Comrades and Christians: religion and political struggle in communist Italy.**
David I. Kertzer.   Cambridge, England: Cambridge University Press, 1980. 302p. bibliog.

The political and religious attitudes of people in a peripheral working-class, communist-led district of Bologna are studied here. The competition between the two dominating subcultures, the Roman Catholic and the communist, is analysed and their 'worlds' are examined through various organizations and socio-political participation. The communist policy towards the Church, and the latter's attitude towards the Communist Party (PCI) are explored, with the focus on the socially marginal groups of southern immigrants and the poor component of the local population. Although the dominant force in the district is the PCI, the communists did not succeed in replacing the Church as the authority in charge of the rites of passage. This, Kertzer argues, is the result of the conciliatory posture of the PCI, which inhibited a determined assault on the zealously guarded area of Church influence over the masses.

83   **Family life in central Italy, 1880-1910: sharecropping, wage labour, and co-residence.**
David I. Kertzer.   New Brunswick, New Jersey: Rutgers University Press, 1984. 250p. 3 maps. bibliog.

A thorough study of family households in a village community near Bologna (Bertalia), over a thirty-year period of major socio-economic change. The investigation aims at understanding the causes of certain forms of co-residence in relation to various other factors. One of the findings was that 'sharecroppers lived in complex family households much more commonly than agricultural day labourers', and that, more generally, 'all occupational categories [...] showed significantly higher proportions of complex family households than are found in much of western Europe'. A major factor of change induced by progressive urbanization and industrialization was the undermining of sharecropping and the increased number of waged labourers, which 'affected the co-residential situation of the youngsters, who became less likely to co-reside with their uncles, aunts, and cousins'. The book contains several statistical tables and graphs and the methodology of historical household study is discussed in the appendix.

84   **Family, political economy, and demographic change: the transformation of life in Casalecchio, Italy, 1861-1921.**
David I. Kertzer, Dennis P. Hogan.   Madison, Wisconsin: The University of Wisconsin Press, 1989. 270p. 2 maps. bibliog.

This work is an interesting experiment in interdisciplinary study, resulting from the co-operation between an anthropologist-historian and a sociologist-demographer. In the six decades considered here, from Italy's unification to the advent of fascism, the demographic and social change in the farming community in Casalecchio (near Bologna) is thoroughly explored. The transformation of an agrarian society into an increasingly urban and industrial environment provides the general canvass for the investigation. The economic development was compounded with political and social changes. Population mobility, family household, marriage patterns and the fall of fertility rate, are all topics upon which the authors focus. In their conclusion, some important generalizations are offered on people's behaviour changes which were induced by great social changes in western society. There is an appendix on Casalecchio's archival sources and their systematic use.

485 **Political institutionalization: a political study of two Sardinian communities.**
Francesco Kjellberg.   London; New York; Sydney; Toronto: John Wiley, 1975. 146p. bibliog.

The two communities involved in this study are Arzana and Portoscuso. Arzana is situated in the central mountainous area of Sardinia, in the province of Nuoro and Portoscuso is a former fishing village with some intensive agriculture and tourism-led growth; located in the southern part of the island, in the province of Cagliari, the latter was the maritime outlet of a major mining district, now virtually closed down. The first half of the study is devoted to an analysis of the social structure and public activity in the two communities. The second half deals with the political organization and focuses on people's participation and the political leadership. Three common tendencies are noted: a 'deprivatization of political relations'; the gradual establishment of more articulated political forms; and the emergence of a political elite. There are graphs and statistics and an appendix outlines Sardinia's economic and social conditions.

486 **The house that Giacomo built: history of an Italian family, 1898-1978.**
Donald S. Pitkin.   Cambridge, England: Cambridge University Press, 1985. 243p.

This is the story of Giovanni and Giulia Tassoni, their daughter, Maria, and her husband (Giacomo Rossi), and their descendants and circles of friends. The Tassonis' slow and painful ascent from grinding poverty (in Calabria and then near Rome) is told with empathy and measure. The family acquired a house in serious need of repair at the end of the war; all family members worked on it in their spare time until they were able to move in. Pitkin demonstrates how 'the pattern of household growth followed by household dissolution in the service of forming other new households constituted the only adaptive strategy for those who, like Giulia and Giovanni, lacked the resources upon which to build a more enduring familial structure'. There is a fascinating interplay between family structure and land tenure, between sexual division of labour and the concept of honour, between kinsmen and strangers, and between formal and popular religiosity.

487 **The walled city: a study of social change and conservative ideologies in Tuscany.**
Jeff C. Pratt.   Gottingen, Germany: Edition Herodot, RaderVerlag, 1986. 311p. 1 map. bibliog.

This contribution to the understanding of post-war changes in Italian society is based on a field study in Montepulciano and Monte Amiata. The image of the walled city, so typical in the Tuscan landscape, is adopted here as the symbol of corporateness and unity, of class harmony rather than class conflict. Nevertheless, it is argued that such a symbol no longer corresponds to reality, if ever there was such a correspondence. The Catholic ideology, as propelled by the Christian Democratic Party in the early post-war years, is examined (a selection of posters of cold-war propaganda is included): it stressed the values of a hierarchical and organic society, centred around the family and the community. The gradual decline of this ideology is then analysed, alongside its replacement by a more egalitarian and individualistic conception of social relations. Decades of massive rural exodus and economic diversification provide the background to the change.

488 **Long live the strong: a history of rural society in the Apennine mountains.**
Roland Sarti.   Amherst, Massachusetts: The University of
Massachusetts Press, 1985. 282p. 1 map. bibliog.

A fascinating study of one particular village (Montefegatesi) in the heart of the Tuscan Apennines, where the author's ancestors lived before emigrating to America at the end of the 19th century. The village is perched on a mountaintop and surrounded by countryside 'more picturesque than productive'. The story centres around the years from the very turn of the century to the Second World War, although there are frequent references to previous periods and events, while the conclusion surveys the post-war conditions. The study is based on personal experience, elderly people's reminiscences, and scholarly research. The changing patterns of occupations, the old and (relatively) new forms of social life, are carefully observed, as is the role of the Church and fascism. What emerges is a picture of resilience and adaptability.

489 **Culture and political economy in western Sicily.**
Jane Schneider, Peter Schneider.   New York; San Francisco; London:
Academic Press, 1976. 256p. 3 maps. bibliog.

History, sociology and political anthropology are the perspectives of this important study. The authors trace the historical transition of Sicily from major exporter of wheat and animal products, to a land of great emigration and economic decline. Arranged in chronological order, the work is divided into two parts. In the first part the authors look into the changing economic role of Sicily in historical world-systems and evaluate the social and political consequences. The second part concentrates on the transformation during the 19th and 20th centuries. The concept of 'broker capitalism' is introduced here to emphasize the political as well as the economic nature of marginal entrepreneurs. The mafia itself, it is argued, falls within this category. Some fine illustrations are included in the text.

490 **Shepherds, workers, intellectuals: culture and centre-periphery relationship in a Sardinian village.**
Peter Schweizer.   Stockholm: Stockholms Studies in Social
Anthropology, 1988. 246p. 1 map. bibliog.

The village concerned in this study is Basilada, located on a mountain ridge stretching across Sardinia. Schweizer spent over a year there and the resulting study describes the three main social categories indicated in the title and their ways of life. It is set in the wider context of national-regional relationships and focuses on local politics (with the stress on the replacement of clientelism by a right-wing cleavage), the variety of leisure and recreational activities, and the forms of associational and ceremonial life. Shepherd culture is shown to provide an important source of symbolism, against which local intellectuals try to distance themselves by emphasizing their own link with urban and national culture, a situation which 'generates considerable ambivalence'.

491 **Three bells of civilization: the life of an Italian hill town.**
Sydel Silverman. New York; London: Columbia University Press,
1975. 263p. 1 map. bibliog.

The main theme of this anthropological study is the interdependence between urban
and rural traditions and patterns of life in a fairly common Italian hill town:
Montecastello di Vibio, in Umbria. Civil life there is centred around a landowning,
professional and commercial class which is supported by agriculture in the
surrounding area. The members of that class control resources and power, play a civic
role in local government and promote communal activities. This is the backbone of a
distinct *civiltà*, intended here as 'an ideology with elite overtones, consistent with a
social structure dominated by an elite [which] also affects the lower strata of the
population and the life of the town as a whole'. The chapters cover such topics as the
mezzadria system, the context of power, festivals, the life cycle and the heritage of
the town. There are statistical tables and pictures.

492 **Patrons and partisans: a study of politics in two southern Italian
Comuni.**
Caroline White. Cambridge, England; London; New York;
Melbourne; Sydney: Cambridge University Press, 1980. 197p. 5 maps.
bibliog.

The two neighbouring villages of Trasacco and Luco, in Abruzzo, are studied here by
a social anthropologist. The focus is on the evolution of the relationship between the
peasant population and their 'access to the means of subsistence'. The main argument
is that this changing relationship greatly influences the way in which peasants see and
confront the world. In particular, the political conduct is examined: in Luco the
Communist Party was strong and its character is described as a form of 'proto-
socialist, collective individualism'. Trasacco, instead, was dominated by the Christian
Democratic Party and 'patro-clientelism' relations represented the political
framework. The comparative nature of this study is organized in four parts: an
introduction on the political and economic background; the two case-studies of
Trasacco and Luco; and a conclusion. Two glossaries complete the volume.

Social Conditions

Social classes

493 **Social structure in Italy: crisis of a system.**
Sabino S. Acquaviva, Mario Santuccio, translated from the Italian by
Colin Hamer.   London: Martin Robertson, 1976. 236p. bibliog.

This work offers an analysis of Italian society and looks at the root causes of the
crisis of the mid-1970s. It was written when the post-war domination of the Christian
Democratic Party appeared to be seriously challenged by a growing and confident
Communist Party, and when the economic system was undermined by international
havoc and trade-union militancy at home. The main thesis is that in order to
understand contemporary Italian society and its political system, it is necessary to
consider the country's historical development. The endemic underdevelopment at the
time of national unification (mid-19th century) was the cause of subsequent
distortions and imbalances. Part one surveys the division of the working population
by economic sectors and the relationship between the various social strata and the
forces and relations of production. Part two consists of a study of legitimization and
distribution of power.

494 **Contemporary Italian sociology: a reader.**
Edited and translated by Diane Pinto.   Cambridge, England:
Cambridge University Press; Editions de la Maison des Sciences de
l'Homme, 1981. 234p.

A well-selected anthology of writings by leading Italian sociologists, this aims to
show that the authors' analyses of the social and economic imbalances in the 1970s
touch upon crucial problems of Italian society. It also refers to more general questions
affecting all countries which pursued rapid modernization in the post-war period. An
introduction by Pinto surveys the political and economic development of Italian
society from 1945 to 1980, and emphasizes the role of sociological research in the
major areas of study. The four major areas which correspond to the four parts of the
book are: the labour market; social classes; social actors and politics; and dualism, the

Welfare State and market economy. The contributors are: M. Barbagli, F. Ferrarotti, M. Paci, E. Pugliese (part one); C. Donolo, A. Pizzorno (part two); A. Melucci, E. Reyneri (part three); and L. Balbo, M. Paci (part four). V. Capecchi provides a final essay which is more theoretical in character.

Social problems, the mafia and organized crime

495 **Mafia, peasants and great estates: society in traditional Calabria.**
Pino Arlacchi, translated by Jonathan Steinberg.   Cambridge, England: Cambridge University Press, 1983. 212p. 1 map.

This is a study of the economic and social structure of one of the poorest regions in southern Italy, seen from an empirical perspective (from the mid-19th century to the 1950s). Arlacchi selected three 'area-types' for his analysis: the relatively rich and dynamic plain of Gioia Tauro; the 'Marchesato' of Crotone with its great estates and landless labourers; and the hilly district around Cosenza with its static peasant society. One chapter is dedicated to each of the three areas. The conclusion of the research is that those three areas were 'distinct, autonomous and notably complex socio-economic systems [. . .] Each seemed to be endowed with its own peculiar phenomenology and its own particular mechanism of equilibrium and change'.

496 **Mafia business: the mafia and the spirit of capitalism.**
Pino Arlacchi.   Oxford: Oxford University Press, 1988. (First English translation published by Verso in 1986.) 239p. 1 map.

A compelling account of the transition from the old type of *mafioso* to the contemporary entrepreneurial *mafioso*. The first part of the book surveys the traditional nature of the mafia up until the Second World War; credit is given here to scholars such as H. Hess, A. Blok and the Schneiders. The second part describes the effects of post-war social change upon the patterns of mafia power and behaviour. Part three offers an account of the present situation in which 'the mafia and the *mafiosi* have ceased to play the role of mediators, and have devoted themselves to *capital accumulation*'. It is stressed, therefore, that a qualitative transformation has taken place. In a final chapter added to the English version Arlacchi includes an afterword based on a paper prepared for a 1985 United Nations conference on 'the prevention of crime and the treatment of offenders'. Statistical tables and reproductions of documents are included.

497 **The mafia of a Sicilian village, 1860-1960.**
Anton Blok, with a foreword by Charles Tilly.   Cambridge, England: Polity Press, in association with Basil Blackwell, 1988. 293p. bibliog.

First published in 1974, this is a masterly work. The author is an anthropologist, but also reveals a capacity as a social historian. Blok has made a study of a village community in western Sicily, where he lived for two and a half years in the 1960s, and given it the fictional name of Genuardo. There are two parts; in the first, Blok describes the physical, social and economic environment, before he concentrates on the history and development of the mafia. The social structures which kept it thriving are analysed. The emphasis on the social network within which the *mafiosi* operate, and their connection with the sources of political power, lead Blok to conclude that 'government-sponsored reforms and interference with the very conditions that generates mafia often merely helped to enlarge the scale on which *mafiosi* operated. [. . .] Their inroads into the framework of the Christian Democrat Party and that of the expanding regional administration are cases in point'.

498   **Men of respect: a social history of the Sicilian mafia.**
        Raimondo Catanzaro, translated by Raymond Rosenthal.   New York: The Free Press, 1992. 246p.

This is an excellent study of the origins and development of the mafia, in which it is argued that there is continuity between the traditional rural *mafiosi* of the 19th century and the flaunting criminals of today. The mafia has always been flexible enough to adapt to any political change, and indeed able to take advantage of such changes. With reference to the recent successes of the State against the mafia, Catanzaro cautiously concludes that 'trials and repressive activities can inflict a severe defeat on the mafia, but they are not enough to eradicate it'. The book is divided into three parts dealing, respectively, with the general characteristics of the criminal phenomenon, its genesis and (in greater detail) its evolution. The final chapter is devoted to the contemporary 'entrepreneur of crime' and contains a plan showing the intricate network of companies owned by a leading mafia family.

499   **King of the mountain: the life and death of Giuliano the bandit.**
        Billy Jaynes Chandler.   Dekalb, Illinois: Northern Illinois University Press, 1988. 262p. bibliog.

Salvatore Giuliano was a Sicilian bandit who became a legend and inspired writers and film directors; this is the only scholarly work on his life. It is not a full biography, however, since it begins with the incident that turned Giuliano from a black-marketeer into an outlaw. His subsequent story of violence and bravado, until his cousin's betrayal which cost Giuliano's life, is accurately pieced together. Chandler also explores the background to that individual story, setting it in the context of war-time Sicily, the manipulative movement for Sicilian independence, the tense political climate of the immediate post-war years, the pervasive presence of the mafia, and the ambiguous role played by the forces of law and order. The last chapter contains some considerations on traditional rural banditry. Some fine photographs are included.

500   **Men of honour: the truth about the mafia.**
        Giovanni Falcone, with Marcelle Padovani, translated from the French by Edward Farrelly.   London: Fourth Estate, 1992. 172p.

This book appeared first in France in 1991 (Padovani is the Rome correspondent of the *Nouvel Observateur*) and was published in English soon after the murder of Judge Falcone, which occurred in May 1992. A brief foreword refers to the assassination, and the immediate reactions are sketched in a concise chronology of events. The book is the result of twenty conversations between Padovani and Falcone, whose voice speaks directly throughout. There is plenty of first-hand information on the mafia's structure, working methods and violence, but this is mainly a testimony of the courage and determination on the part of true 'men of honour', such as Falcone (and his friend and colleague Paolo Borsellino, who was also murdered in 1992) to fight against the mafia and the political power with which mafia is associated. An appendix provides the long list of names of leading *mafiosi* and a diagram shows the operative structure of the mafia.

501 **The Sicilian mafia: the business of private protection.**
Diego Gambetta. Cambridge, Massachusetts; London: Harvard University Press, 1993. 335p. 2 maps. bibliog.
The central thesis of this well-documented and cogently argued study is, in Gambetta's own words, 'that the mafia is a specific economic enterprise, an industry which produces, promotes, and sells private protection'. A deep-seated ideology combined with political expediency and an outgrowth of anti-liberal legal thinking brought the State and mafia to a bargaining position, rather than set it on a collision course. The result was the undermining of the legitimacy of the State and the destruction of southern society. This elegantly written book provides an innovative approach to the understanding of the mafia, and consists of three parts. Part one considers the market, the resources and the structure of the 'protection industry' and part two expands on this, touching upon the origins and organization of the 'industry'. Part three explores the issues of dispute settlement, and orderly and disordered markets. Two appendices provide the etymology of the mafia and descriptions of mafia rituals.

502 **Trust: making and breaking cooperative relations.**
Edited by Diego Gambetta. Oxford: Blackwell, 1988. 246p. bibliog.
Theoretical and historical approaches characterize the essays included here, which address the issue of success and failure in co-operation in a variety of political and economic contexts. A chapter by the editor discusses the Italian mafia. 'Mafia' here is used in a broad sense, so as to also include *camorra* and *'ndrangheta*, which thrive in Campania and Calabria, respectively. What is common to those regions and Sicily Gambetta argues, is that 'people do not cooperate when it would be mutually beneficial to do so; they compete in harmful ways; and, finally, they refrain from competing in those instances when they could all gain considerably from competition'. A historical survey of southern Italy focuses on the effects of Spanish domination. Attention is then paid to Sicilian mafia, which, 'while exploiting and reinforcing distrust, has been able to maintain itself for over a century'.

503 **Mafia and mafiosi: the structure of power.**
Henner Hess, translated from the German by Ewald Osers. Westmead, England: Saxon House; Lexington, Massachusetts: Lexington Books, 1973. 233p. 1 map. bibliog.
A well-written (and translated), thoroughly documented study of the mafia, showing its development in western Sicily through the roles played by individuals and the network of relationships around them. These relationships are to a large extent maintained by means of violence, the threat of violence and fear of violence Collectively, this produces general attitudes of deference, respect and also honour and represents the basis upon which mafia can be seen as an organization, with a division of labour among its members and a hierarchical pattern of authority. After an introductory chapter on the Sicilian social and political background, three important

chapters deal, respectively, with: the origin, career and legitimization of the *mafiosi*; the structure of their groupings (*cosca*, *partito*, and faction); and the functions of *mafiosi* behaviour (protective, mediatory and economic). A short chapter addresses the issue of *mafiosi* and American gangsters. The original Italian quotations are contained in the appendix.

504   **The honoured society: the mafia conspiracy observed.**
Norman Lewis.   Bath, England: Cedric Chivers, 1973. 254p. 1 map. bibliog.

Lewis argues that the ancient mafia, which had the function of protecting the peasants, merged with the backward Sicilian feudalists who 'had stood between the King of Spain's Viceroy and justice, had deluded the foolish Bourbons, tamed the socialism of Garibaldi, made a laughing-stock of parliamentary democracy, and done a profitable deal with Fascism'. In the last stage of the Second World War, this mafia-feudalist combination was revived by the Allies (notably the Americans) for tactical benefit in their advance on Sicily, and eventually became 'a reservoir of right-wing voters'. The nature, the scope and the means of the 'honoured society' are explored by Lewis in a flowing narrative style. There is some emphasis on leading characters such as Dr Melchiorre Allegra and, above all, Don Calogero Vizzini. The manipulation and eventual disposal of Salvatore Giuliano, the Bandit, is also considered in great detail.

505   **The mafia and politics.**
Michele Pantaleone.   London: Chatto & Windus, 1966. 255p. bibliog.

The author is a Sicilian who fought against the mafia all his life. The historian Denis Mack Smith points out in the preface that nobody did more than Pantaleone to bring about the Italian Parliament's decision to appoint a Commission to investigate the mafia. The book is mainly concerned with the old, traditional mafia, from its origins in the feudal estates of central and western Sicily to its development in the first half of the 20th century. It emphasizes the role of the mafia in post-war Italy as a tool against the political struggles of Sicilian peasants. The work is full of illuminating episodes on the connection between the mafia and political power, and presents a fascinating gallery of *mafiosi*, from 'Lucky' Luciano to Don Calogero Vizzini. The book concludes with the hope that the Commission of Inquiry would 'strike at the very root' of the mafia. The voluminous evidence it produced, however, remained virtually a dead letter.

506   **Mafia wars: the confessions of Tommaso Buscetta.**
Tim Shawcross, Martin Young.   Glasgow: Fontana/Collins, 1988. 320p. bibliog.

First published by Collins under the title *Men of honour* (1987), this is the story of a high-ranking member of the Sicilian mafia who betrayed the code of silence of that criminal organization, and set in motion a chain of events which are still hitting the headlines in the 1990s. It is also the story of the courageous and determined people who fought against the mafia, often losing their lives in the struggle. Both the Sicilian and American mafias are studied, but the emphasis is placed on the Italian side of the story. A wide range of sources are used and the research includes extensive investigations in Brazil. The historical development of the mafia and its shift of interest to the narcotics trade is well documented. A chapter deals with the assassination of General Dalla Chiesa (1982), only a few months after his appointment as prefect of Palermo. It is suggested that Buscetta has a lot more to say.

507   **The mafia encyclopedia.**
      Carl Sifakis.   New York; Oxford: Facts on File, 1987. 367p.
This encyclopaedia is not as comprehensive as the title suggests, since it deals only with the Italian-American mafia, with the addition of its Jewish connection. After an introduction which sets the issue of organized crime in America in its context, the encyclopaedic section begins with the 'Chicago mob leader', Accardo. It ends with the 'New Jersey boss', Zwillman. Most entries are, indeed, about individuals, but there are also more general items, such as 'Buckwheats: painful murder methods'; 'Charity and the mafia'; 'Contract: murder assignment'; and also 'Sex and the mafia', in which it is stated that '*mafiosi* have three advantages most men do not enjoy: 1) they have considerable money to lure women with; 2) if married, their work keeps them out at all hours of the night or even away from home for days at a time, with alibis; 3) they rarely need alibis anyway since their wives are expected to ask no questions'.

508   **The mafia: the long reach of the international Sicilian mafia.**
      Claire Sterling.   London: Grafton, 1990. 493p. 1 map. bibliog.
The complicated story of the mafia is told here by an investigative journalist who has been living in Italy for a long time. The first half of the book examines the development of mafia activity, in Sicily and abroad, up until the 1970s. The second half concentrates on people and events of the last twenty years, when any remaining romantic notion of *cosa nostra* was superseded by virtually uninterrupted violence. The book reveals the real extent of the mafia's influence in Italy and around the world and argues that law enforcement agencies failed 'to look for information in their own archives, to communicate and compare notes', and thus have been largely ineffective. The book includes a map showing the location of the main mafia 'families', a chronology (up to 1988), a partial list of victims, and several photographs, mainly of *mafiosi*.

Family

509   **Italian family structure.**
      Nicholas J. Esposito.   New York: Peter Lang, 1989. 192p. bibliog.
The title promises more than the book delivers, but as an anthropological study of the rural southern Italian family, this is a well-documented and well-argued work. After a comprehensive and concise survey of the relevant literature, it is argued that the extended family is still alive and effective in southern Italy. A chapter on the history of southern Italy shows the complex influences that can affect family life: serfdom; latifundium; patronage and clientelism; taxation; and poor government. Roman Catholic ethics are considered to be a factor in the traditional attitudes which pervade the husband-wife relationship and unfaithfulness is marginal and divorce rare; parent-child relations appear equally reassuring. Interesting considerations are made on

Italian immigrant families in the United States where 'familist' values have survived, although the tendency for their descendants is to share more and more the values of American society.

510 **The family in Italy: from antiquity to the present.**
Edited by David I. Kertzer, Richard P. Saller. New Haven, Connecticut; London: Yale University Press, 1991. 400p. bibliog.

Historians and anthropologists provide a wide range of contributions on the history of the family, enabling the reader to identify continuities and changes from ancient Rome to today's Italy. One essay (by E. Cantarella) embraces the whole period in dealing with the development of adultery law, but most contributions examine specific topics, such as 'The cultural meaning of death' in the ancient Roman family (B. Shaw), or 'Choosing a spouse among nineteenth century central Italian sharecroppers' (L. Tittarelli). In one case, stimulating geographical comparisons are made ('Property, kinship and gender: a Mediterranean perspective', by C. B. Bettell). The regional diversity within Italy is emphasized, together with other general aspects, such as gender ideologies, the impact of Church and State, and property transmission. There are three parts to the work: 'Antiquity'; 'The medieval fulcrum'; and 'The modern period'.

511 **Reunion in Sicily.**
Jerre Mangione. New York: Columbia University Press, 1984. 278p.

A recollection of the author's second visit to Sicily, in the immediate post-war period. Despite the fact that his parents had emigrated to the United States at the turn of the century, Mangione had maintained fairly close ties with his Sicilian relatives. His first visit, in the 1930s, was overshadowed by the political climate of the time; now he was in a better disposition of spirit to observe and describe social life and customs in the island. This is a perceptive and witty journal, mellowed by the distance in space and time from the actual visit to the time of writing. The conditions of poverty in which Sicilians lived is vividly evoked, as is their dignified attitude of endurance towards it. Mangione is a fine story-teller and captures his human characters with brief, incisive commentary.

512 **Mediterranean family structures.**
Edited by J. G. Peristiany. Cambridge, England; London; New York; Melbourne: Cambridge University Press, in association with the Social Research Centre, Cyprus, 1976. 414p.

The section devoted to Italy consists of two essays, written by Tullio Tentori and John Davis. Tentori offers a case-study of the family in the southern town of Matera (Basilicata), surveying the evolution of the social structure in the 19th century and up to the 1950s. He underlines the condition of poverty and class separation and also argues that, contrary to what is normally thought, the family in the Materan community lacks cohesion. Davis offers an account of changes in the rules for the transmission of property in Pisticci (also in Basilicata) from the early 19th century to the 1960s. He shows how an increasingly urban orientation influences the patterns of marriage gifts, dowries and investments, and concludes with general observations on social change and the transmission of property.

Housing

513　**Housing in Italy: urban development and political change.**
Thomas Angotti.　New York; London: Praeger Publishers, 1977.
108p. bibliog.

During the 1970s organized movements voiced their anger against an outmoded legal and financial framework for housing and urban planning in Italy. The author concurs with such sentiments and his study can be seen as a vindication of what he sees as justified anger. An introduction establishes the political background. Chapter one surveys the working of the housing system, while the ensuing chapter focuses on Rome, with examples of illegal building, urban redevelopment and the planning of a new urban quarter. Chapter three returns to an analysis of the mass movements and applies it to case studies in Milan and Turin. The final chapter considers the major reform proposals (which were responsible, incidentally, for the passing of the Fair Rent Act of 1978) and includes case studies on Bologna and its surrounding region. An appendix extends a concise series of case studies to some southern cities (Naples, Taranto, Catania and Palermo). There are many statistical tables.

The new Italians.
See item no. 23.

Fascism and the mafia.
See item no. 237.

Italian family matters.
See item no. 525.

Italy.
See item no. 539.

The mafia and clientelism.
See item no. 582.

Mafia: a select annotated bibliography.
See item no. 1076.

Health and Welfare

514 **The State in capitalist Europe: a casebook.**
Edited by Stephen Bornstein, David Held, Joel Krieger.   London:
George Allen & Unwin, 1984. 175p. bibliog.
Empirical studies and theoretical reflections are the dominant thread of this book. A
chapter by R. C. R. Taylor offers a review of state intervention in health care in
Britain and Italy, with some references made also to the United States. The different
solutions to the problems of cost and efficiency are surveyed. Emphasis is placed on
the role of trade unions in affecting national policies, but also on the 'changing
patterns of economic development and changes in the composition of the labor force
which define the terrain over which those political actors [the unions] negotiate'. Two
Italian documents are presented here: extracts from the Italian National Health
Service Law (1978) and a description of one local health service (for the town of
Terni, in Umbria, but wrongly attributed here to Tuscany) in 1979.

515 **The politics of mental health in Italy.**
Michael Donnelly.   London; New York: Tavistock; Routledge, 1991.
151p. bibliog.
The segregating role of traditional mental institutions and the very concept of mental
illness were called into question during the 1960s and 1970s. Donnelly argues that the
Italian experience merits particular attention because it produced 'a radical mental
health movement of unprecedented strength and breadth' and also because 'this
movement succeeded in legislating the abolition of the mental hospital'. There is an
overview of the international context and the historical background of Italian
psychiatry. The pilot experiments conducted in Italy in the 1960s are surveyed, and
the enactment and implementation of the sweeping new Law Number 180 (1978) is
examined. Patients were to be released into the community (which came to mean back
into their families). In fact, it is pointed out that Law Number 180 produced mixed
results. Interesting documents from the movement of 'Democratic Psychiatry' are
included in the appendix.

516 **[The Welfare State in] Italy.**
Maurizio Ferrera. In: *Growth to limits: the western European Welfare States since World War II.* Vol. 2. Edited by Peter Flora. Berlin; New York: Walter de Gruyter, 1986, p. 385-499.

The introductory section of this important study provides a historical overview of the welfare system in post-war Italy, from the 'missed opportunity' in 1948 to the wave of reforms in the 1970s. Four parts follow, all of which are both highly informative and analytical. The range of benefits and the rise of the welfare clienteles are first examined. Then, the achievements and shortcomings of the system are evaluated, with some attention paid to the redistribution of resources and underdevelopment in the South. Next, a set of issues are tackled and explained: from the impact of demographic change to the relationship between welfare record and types of government coalitions. The last part deals with current conflicts and future prospects and includes an interesting appraisal of the intellectual debate on the subject. Statistical tables and graphs illustrate the essay, which is complemented by an appendix on 'Pension politics and pension policy in Italy', by Ezio Maestri.

517 **AIDS in Italy: emergency in slow motion.**
David Moss. In: *Action on AIDS: national policies in comparative perspective.* Edited by Barbara A. Misztal, David Moss. New York: Greenwood Press, 1990, p. 135-66.

AIDS was first diagnosed in Italy as early as 1982, but the recognition of the threat was extremely belated, a failure which was a likely contributory factor to the rapid expansion of the lethal virus. Ultimately, the authorities were forced to acknowledge that 'a true state of emergency' existed. Moss persuasively argues that the initial perception of AIDS in Italy, as it was virtually affecting only homosexuals in a metropolitan environment, aggravated the difficulty of effective intervention. He also shows that the slow acquisition of knowledge by the authorities regarding the exact broader profile of HIV infection and AIDS incidence, was largely due to the fragmentation of institutional responsibilities. Finally, it is noted that 'the legally liminal – and politically insignificant – positions occupied by the major risk groups have weakened pressures for more rapid action'.

518 **Evolution and implementation of the Italian health service reform of 1978.**
Mark McCarthy. London: Chadwick Press, 1992. 392p. 1 map. bibliog.

This is the only major work in English on the Italian National Health Service (*Servizio Sanitario Nazionale*, SSN), established in 1978. It is a comprehensive and thorough investigation, based on a wealth of sources. Some comparisons between the British and Italian health systems are drawn; for instance, it is pointed out that whereas 'Britain has sought to depoliticise the regional and local tiers, these are dominated by local politicians in Italy'. After an introduction to Italy's modern history and political system, two chapters are devoted to a review of general literature on health care and the development of health services in Italy. The following two chapters examine the structure, resources and special services of the SSN. McCarthy then surveys the general health of the Italians, before providing an evaluation of the system. On balance, it is stated that the Italian health reform of 1978 has been a success.

519 **Psychiatry in transition: the British and Italian experiences.**
Edited by Shulamit Ramon, with Maria Grazia Giannichedda.
London: Pluto Press, 1991. 2nd ed. 288p. bibliog.

Contributions by many Italian and British psychiatrists, psychologists and academics
are gathered in this volume for a comparison and assessment of the achievements and
failures of the two countries' experiments on community mental health. In particular,
attention is directed towards the reforms in the 1970s and the closure of large mental
hospitals. Part one describes the experiences of the two systems and emphasizes
similarities and differences. In particular, a perceptive section is devoted to gender
and ethnicity in the context of mental health. Part two considers the objectives of a
real change in the two countries and the processes by which such change could be
achieved. In an interesting postscript, F. Ongaro Basaglia discusses psychiatric
reform as a reflection of Italian society.

The Italians: how they live and work.
See item no. 3.

Italy today: social picture and trends, 1984- .
See item no. 5.

Women and Feminism

520 **Women and Italy: essays on gender, culture and history.**
Edited by Zygmunt G. Barański, Shirley W. Vinall.   Basingstoke,
England; London: Macmillan, in association with the University of
Reading, Graduate School of European and International Studies,
1991. 304p. bibliog.

The richness of this book can best be conveyed by the full list of authors and short
titles. Part one consists of: A. Cento Bull, 'Lombard silk-spinners in the nineteenth
century'; L. Caldwell, 'Film and fascist concern with motherhood' and 'Italian
feminism: some considerations'; L. Cheles, 'Images of women in the graphic
propaganda of the Italian neo-fascist party' (with plates); and G. Lepschy, 'Language
and Sexism'. Part two contains: S. W. Vinall, P. S. Noble, 'Adultery in the
Decameron and the *Heptameron*'; M. Günsberg, 'The portrayal of women in the
Italian Renaissance epic'; V. R. Jones, 'Women in Alessandro Manzoni's *I promessi
sposi*'; and S. Wood, 'Elements of irony and reversal in Moravia's *L'amore
coniugale*'. Finally, part three covers: L. Kroha, 'Matilde Serao: an introduction' and
'Matilde Serao's *Fantasia*'; U. Fanning, 'Serao's use of the female double'; and M.
Serao, 'The woman in the black dress and with the red coral brooch' (translated by U.
Fanning).

521 **Feminist experiences: the women's movement in four cultures.**
Susan Bassnett.   London: Allen & Unwin, 1986. 194p. bibliog.

The four cultures indicated in the title are those of the United States, the (former)
German Democratic Republic, Italy and Britain. Their collection is connected with
the author's biography ('a cosmopolitan childhood') and the result is this interesting
comparative study, in which the changing patterns of feminist thought are examined.
One chapter is devoted to each country and in the concluding section Bassnett points
out that 'in contrast to the subtle changes taking place in private, the public
organization of women's movements reflects the social context in which they
emerge'. In the section on Italy the author focuses on violence, as a disturbing
phenomenon both within the feminist movement and against it from outside. The

concomitant process of theorization on the role of women in society is outlined in the setting of Italian tormented history, and the highly ideological character of political debate – notably in the 1970s.

522 **Little girls: social conditioning and its effects on the stereotyped role of women during infancy.**
Elena Belotti Gianini, collectively translated from Italian by Lisa Appignanesi, Amelia Fletcher, Toshiko Shimura, Sian Williams and Jeanne Wordsworth.   London: Writers and Readers Publishing Cooperative, 1975. 158p.

This is a minor classic of feminist literature. Originally published in Italy for Italians, and with systematic references to Italian experiences, the book contains stimulating observations on the prejudices and preconceptions which condition the upbringing of girls, preparing them for a life of submission. The case histories to which the author refers are related with insight and affection. In a perceptive introduction, Margaret Drabble notes that different emphases would have been required if the book had been written in an English or American context, but also adds that 'this book is a plea that we should think about what we are doing, rather than blindly perpetuate the mistakes of our mothers and fathers'.

523 **Education of Italian Renaissance women.**
Melinda K. Blade.   Mesquite, Texas: Ide House, 1983. 83p.

Given the title one would expect a rather more thorough discussion of the subject than is contained in this book. This is in fact a rather modest work based on the author's MA thesis (University of San Diego, 1975). It does, however, provide an elementary outline of the education of women during the 15th and 16th centuries, with a basic bibliography.

524 **Italian feminist thought: a reader.**
Edited by Paola Bono, Sandra Kemp.   Oxford: Basil Blackwell, 1991. 458p. bibliog.

An extensive and comprehensive collection of writings, most of which appear here in translation from the original Italian versions which were published in books, magazines and journals. An introduction touches on the various cultural dimensions of Italian feminism, surveys the legacy of the past, and considers the contemporary debates. The contents are divided into two parts and fifteen chapters, part one of which outlines the Italian feminist groups, while part two deals with the changing context of Italian feminism. A large number of pieces are included here; particularly interesting is the analysis of abortion and sexual violence, with writings from the early 1970s to the mid-1980s. This useful book also contains a list of women's centres in Italy (with the year of foundation), a chronology of national and international events which were relevant to women (1965-86), a repertory of the Italian feminist journals, and an exhaustive bibliography.

525 **Italian family matters: women, politics and legal reform.**
Lesley Caldwell. Basingstoke, England; London: Macmillan, 1991.
164p. bibliog.

This well-informed and thought-provoking work outlines the socio-political context of 'the woman question', focusing on the political and cultural significance of the Catholic Church and Communist Party policies. The author then concentrates on three crucial areas of state regulation: divorce and family law; abortion; and working mothers. Two chapters are devoted to the first issue, tracing the historical roots of the question and using this as a background to the 'post-war history' of the relevant legislation, which culminated in 1970 with the Divorce Law, and in 1974 with the referendum upholding that law. Abortion was legalized (or 'decriminalized' as the Italians used to say) in 1978, marking the apex of the Italian feminist movement, and, again, the attempted repeal of the law was defeated by a referendum three years later. In the conclusion, the influence of legislation in strengthening the position of women is reiterated. The bibliography is exhaustive.

526 **Liberazione della donna: feminism in Italy.**
Lucia Chiavola Birnbaum. Middletown, Connecticut: Wesleyan
University Press, 1986. 353p. 1 map. bibliog.

The history and the interpretation of Italian feminism are the two basic ingredients of this comprehensive and thoughtful book. The 'empowerment of women' (the author's own definition of feminism) is examined against the background of a polarized Italian culture of Catholicism and communism. There are three parts. Part one provides the historical background, with anthropological considerations of women in the Mediterranean setting, and surveys the role of women in Italy from the 19th century up to 1968. This date marks the beginning of the modern feminist movement in Italy, to which part two is devoted. The work is not in chronological order but is split into topics such as feminism and marxist theory, literature and feminist cultural revolution, the Italian women's union (UDI), and feminist opposition to violence *vis-à-vis* the issues of violence and peace. A short part three concludes this study with further reflections on the variety of Italian feminists. The book is interspersed with photographs, reproductions of posters and drawings.

527 **Black madonnas: feminism, religion and politics in Italy.**
Lucia Chiavola Birnbaum. Boston, Massachusetts: Northeastern
University Press, 1993. 273p. 1 map. bibliog.

Popular religiosity, the women's movement and liberation theology are the three intertwined themes running through this book. It consists of self-contained chapters of impressive scholarly breadth, ranging from the metaphor of black madonnas and peasant rituals in the Middle Ages, to analyses of specific worships (such as that of the 'black madonna of Siponto', in Apulia), and 19th-century carnivals in Sicily. One of the main arguments of the book is that black madonnas in Italy imply multicultural liberation theology and politics. Their iconographic and ritual evidence suggests that this ancient goddess continues to have a significant meaning in today's Italy. This is the subject of the last chapter-essay, in which it is noted that 'one sign of the contemporary cultural revolution in Italy is the emergence of women artists in touch with conscious or unconscious ancient memories'. Some iconographic illustrations are included.

528   **Visions and revisions: women in Italian culture.**
Edited by Mirna Cicioni, Nicole Prunster.   Providence, Rhode Island;
Oxford: Berg, 1993. 238p. 1 map. bibliog.

In the words of the editors, 'this volume is an attempt to offer Italianists recent research [. . .] into the literary and social processes through which "women" have been constructed in Italian culture since the Middle Ages'. There are two distinct parts. Part one looks into their literary and artistic heritage, and contains contributions by F. Coassin, D. Cavuoto (on Francesca da Rimini), S. D. Kolsky, N. Prunster, M. Baker (on women in C. E. Gadda's novels), W. Musolino, and P. Di Cori (on photographic representations in the early 20th century). Part two deals with women in society and feminism; the contributors here are P. Carroli, L. Chiavola Birnbaum, F. Bimbi (on the transformations of female identity), L. Passerini (on the women's movement in Italy and the events of 1968), P. Dagnino, and T. Lagostena Bassi (on violence against women). The variety of contents and approaches provides a stimulating cross-cultural collection of scholarly but readable studies.

529   **Women and trade unions in eleven industrialized countries.**
Edited by Alice H. Cook, Val R. Lorwin, Arlene Kaplan Daniels.
Philadelphia, Pennsylvania: Temple University Press, 1984. 327p.
bibliog.

Bianca Beccalli provides the contribution for Italy, arguing that 'a mobilization of working women with strong feminist overtones developed in the mid-1970s, awakening in the trade union movement an interest in the "woman question" that had not been felt for some years'. Until then, even working women themselves regarded the masculine and feminine 'worlds' as separate entities, at work as well as at home, while the unions were perceived as part of the masculine 'world'. The author provides an outline of the structural trends and political traditions in women's employment in Italy, emphasizing the working-class militancy, trade-union renewal and feminist mobilization within the unions. For all this progressive change, however, it is pointed out in the conclusion that sexual segregation of the workforce continued, in a context of increased women's employment in tertiary activities, at the expense of manufacturing, where unions are stronger.

530   **Women of the shadows.**
Ann Cornelisen, photographs by the author.   Basingstoke, England;
London: Macmillan, 1976. 246p.

The author lived for many years in southern Italy and has dedicated this book to a portrayal of the humble and strong peasant women, mostly from Basilicata. Some beautiful photographs are interspersed throughout the text and the final chapter, 'A life cycle', consists entirely of images. The first chapter looks upon the condition of women as they perform communal functions together, and yet remain separate. The following chapters contain central characters: these are the people who take the important decisions, 'but don't have to talk about it in the Piazza', as their men do, as one woman tells Cornelisen. The author has witnessed the transformation of southern village life in the 1950s and 1960s, when most able-bodied men migrated either to northern Italy or abroad and this can be seen in the text.

531 **How fascism ruled women: Italy, 1922-1945.**
Victoria De Grazia.   Berkeley, California; Oxford: University of
California Press, 1992. 350p.

This is an exploration of the experience of women under Mussolini's dictatorship; it is also a study of fascist sexual politics in the broader context of Italian society, and highlights 'how an avowedly fascist regime handled the entry of women into the age of mass politics in the wake of World War I and during the hard times of the 1930s'. The book offers both a synthesis and an interpretation. After an introductory chapter, the following topics are explored: the liberal legacy of the State's neglect of issues concerning women and motherhood; the dictatorship's and women's redefinitions of the meaning of childbearing; family life and the new duties towards the State; growing up and the ideals of girlhood; the public presence of women and the perception of the regime and the Catholic Church; and women and political culture, with particular attention to the effects of warmongering in the late 1930s and during the war.

532 **Women workers in fifteen countries: essays in honour of Alice
Hanson Cook.**
Edited by Jennie Farley.   Ithaca, New York: ILR Press, Cornell
University, 1985. 195p.

The common theme of this collection of essays is the situation of women in advanced industrial countries. With reference to Italy, Bianca Beccalli points out that 'the decade 1973 to 1983 saw dramatic changes in the relationship between women and work, with the reversal of the long-term decline in women's labour force participation'. It was a change connected with the profound transformation of Italian culture and society. Beccalli first outlines the history of women's work in post-war Italy, stressing the persistent weakness of the policies oriented towards equality, while protective policies prevailed. On the 1977 equal opportunities law the author comments that it did not provide for positive action on behalf of women and concludes that for the purpose of bringing about equality in the workplace, the State is an unreliable partner.

533 **Women of the Mediterranean.**
Edited by Monique Gadant, translated from the French by A. M.
Berrett.   London; Atlantic Highlands, New Jersey: Zed Books, 1984.
196p.

A collection of essays showing the ways in which feminist ideologies and practices are articulated in the different social realities of Mediterranean countries and regions. The editor notes in her introduction that, unlike other areas, Italy is split internally by the very difference which separates the northern industrialized countries and the southern relatively underdeveloped ones. Maria Minicucci offers a contribution on the condition of women in a Calabrian village. She argues that women there have a much more important role than it would appear, since they 'occupy a key position in the reproduction strategy of the society', as becomes evident from the study of kinship structures. Readers may be interested to know that the book also contains an essay by the authoritative Italian writer Rossana Rossanda; it concerns the general issue of polarization of male and female cultures.

534   **Journeys among women: feminism in five Italian cities.**
Judith Adler Hellman.   Cambridge, England; Oxford: Polity Press, in
association with Basil Blackwell, 1987. 276p. bibliog.

Italian feminism in the last two decades, Hellman argues, emerged in opposition to
both the traditional conservative political forces of Italian society and the traditional
left. A general introduction considers the historical context and the relationship
between the movement for women's rights and the parties of the left. The main body
of the book then consists of five case-studies in as many cities: four in the north and
one in the south. The subtitles are indicative of the local characteristics of the
movement there: Turin (a workers' city); Milan (a cosmopolitan city); Reggio Emilia
(a 'red' city); Verona (a 'white' city); and Caserta (the deep south). The common
features of feminism in the five cities, as well as the differences, are underlined,
together with an assessment of the degree of success. Special attention is paid to the
transformation of UDI (the women's union close to the ex-Communist Party).

535   **The lonely mirror: Italian perspectives on feminist theory.**
Edited by Sandra Kemp, Paola Bono.   London; New York:
Routledge, 1993. 251p.

A companion book to *Italian feminist thought: a reader* (q.v.), edited by the same
authors. Whereas the earlier project involved extracts from books and articles from
journals, the present work is a collection of essays by Italian (women) scholars
centred around 'the female body (individual or collective, silent or speaking)'. The
contents are divided into four parts, each with distinct disciplinary and
methodological approaches: language, literature, and semiotics (with contributions
from P. Magli, N. Fusini, V. Papetti, M. Mizzau and M. Cambon); psychoanalysis
(with essays by S. Montefoschi, M. G. Minetti and S. Vegetti Finzi); history (with
writings by G. Pomata and A. Buttafuoco); and philosophy (with pieces by A.
Cavarero, A. Putino, and G. Bonacchi). Kemp's informative introduction includes an
interview with Bono on Italian feminism and the conceptualizations it has produced.

536   **Sex and power: the rise of women in America, Russia, Sweden,
and Italy.**
Donald Meyer.   Middletown, Connecticut: Wesleyan University
Press, 1987. 721p.

Part one contains a chapter on Italy which focuses on the country's late and patchy
industrial development and its significance for women. In part two the section on Italy
surveys 'the opportunities and obstacles, the conflicts and dilemmas' shaping the
Italian women's consciousness of themselves (with emphasis placed on the fascist
period, and the influences of marxism and Catholicism). Finally, in part four the
attention is selectively directed to individual writers, philosophers and film-makers,
ranging from Sibilla Aleramo and D'Annunzio (for his 'self-created masculinity'),
Gramsci (for his abstractions), to Rossellini's, Fellini's and Pasolini's films. In his
conclusion, Meyer notes that 'Italian women endured their perpetuation of
backwardness, not because of the patriarchy vested in Italian life, but because of the
inability of Italian leaders to get a powerful Italian economic machine running'.

537 **Women's movements of the world: an international directory and reference guide: a Keesing's reference publication.**
Edited by Sally Shreir. Harlow, England: Longman, 1988. 384p.

The percentages of women throughout the world who are employed in the national workforce differ sharply: Italy is close to France (around thirty-six per cent), with a higher percentage than Spain (twenty-nine per cent), but a much lower figure than the United Kingdom (forty-three per cent), Japan (forty-nine per cent) and the United States (sixty-five per cent). Such simple and interesting comparisons can be quickly made by looking through the pages of this directory, which features almost two hundred countries. Particular attention, in the introduction to Italy, is paid to the important legislation of the 1970s (on divorce, marriage and abortion). It is also noted that in that decade 'a surge of feminist activity revolved around campaigns to change the abortion and rape laws, and improve women's status in general'. The main part of the section on Italy is devoted to the list of women's associations and their publications. Details on their aims and objectives are included, together with their ideological orientation and affiliation.

538 **Donna: women in Italian culture.**
Edited by Ada Testaferri. Ottawa: Dovenhouse, 1989. 316p.

This is a collection of twenty-three short essays. The majority of them are gathered in the first part, devoted to 'Women as agents of change': it includes a most varied set of contributions, ranging from an entirely theoretical piece by L. Hutcheon (on feminism and post-modernism) to studies of well-known Italian modern and contemporary writers (M. Corti, E. Morante, L. Cavani, N. Ginzburg, A. Banti, G. Deledda, and A. Vivanti) as well as little-known authors of past centuries. The smaller second part examines 'Images of women in Italian literature'. The idea of 'the feminine' is surveyed here in the works of such famous male writers as Dante, Machiavelli, Leopardi, Manzoni and Pirandello. No general conclusion is attempted, and it would probably be an impossible task anyway. Only a vague hint in the laconic preface by the editor suggests that the book 'draws attention to the centrality of women's issues in the Italian culture'.

539 **Italy.**
Maria Weber. In: *The politics of the second electorate: women and public participation.* Edited by Joni Lovenduski, Jill Hills.
London; Boston; Henley, England: Routledge & Kegan Paul, 1981, p. 182-207. bibliog.

The author outlines the history of Italian women's political activity, from the end of the 19th century to the 1970s. The personalities of Anna Maria Mazzoni and Anna Kuliscioff are first examined. This is followed by: an outline of women's condition under fascism; their position in the party political spectrum of the Italian republic; their relationship with the Catholic Church and the Christian Democratic party (DC); and the issue of women and the labour market. The last sections concentrate on the debates of the 1970s, which covered such subjects as divorce, abortion, family law and the women's liberation movement. The voting behaviour of Italian women during that decade is also analysed, with particular attention paid to the transfer of votes from the DC to the Communist Party.

540   **The clockwork factory: women and work in fascist Italy.**
      Perry R. Willson.   Oxford: Clarendon Press, 1993. 291p. bibliog.

This is an important study of an Italian engineering firm during the fascist era, considered from a feminist point of view (half of its workforce was female). The firm, *Magneti Marelli*, was located near Milan and established in 1919. It soon became 'one of Italy's industrial giants and arguably the most modern firm of its day', following American-inspired methods of management. The study first analyses the setting of the 'scientific' management before exploring the following topics: the composition and mobility of the workforce; gender and work roles; welfare provisions and leisure activities; and the women's political attitudes and their contribution to the Resistance. A complex picture emerges in which emancipation and repression are combined, suggesting that 'only by taking into account the gendered nature of inter-war Italian society can historians hope to reach a fuller understanding of this period'. Statistical tables are included in the appendices.

Three generations of Italian American women.
See item no. 367.

Workshop to office: two generations of Italian women in New York city.
See item no. 370.

The sexual division of labour: the Italian case.
See item no. 742.

Italian women writing.
See item no. 858.

Malafemmina: la donna nel cinema italiano. (Tarts: women in Italian cinema.)
See item no. 861.

Gender and sexuality in Renaissance and Baroque Italy.
See item no. 1074.

Politics

General

541 Italy: republic without government?
Percy A. Allum.   London: Weidenfeld & Nicolson, 1973. 267p.
1 map. bibliog.

This title became a cliché and is still quoted in current books on Italian politics. The reader interested in this subject will find Allum's analysis fascinating and in many ways still relevant to an understanding of today's Italy. The book is divided into three parts: Italian society; civil society; and the Italian State. Part one outlines the historical, social and economic background, emphasizing the pervasive nature of the 'Southern Question'. Part two deals with the Catholic Church, political parties (with the focus on the practice of patronage), and interest groups. Part three examines the various institutions of the state system: executive and legislative; public administration and the military; the judiciary; and local regional government.

542 Politics and society in post-war Naples.
Percy A. Allum.   London: Cambridge University Press, 1973. 410p.
3 maps. bibliog.

Allum presents a masterly sociological study of Neapolitan post-war society, its people, politicians and politics. A vast range of sources is investigated, from official documents to secondary publications and direct interviews. The study's focus is on the relationship between political power and society; its main conclusion is that the regional case-study is just a variant of a more general political system of patronage, 'bossism' and the 'political machine', expressions used with reference to two famous local political leaders and patrons: Achille Lauro and Silvio Gava (and his son Antonio). 'The central argument of this study – the author concludes – is that the politics of the constituency is to be understood in the light of a particular political system – the southern system – which operates as a sub-system within the national one'. Several tables are provided.

543   **Culture and conflict in post-war Italy: essays on mass and popular culture.**
Edited by Zygmunt G. Barański, Robert Lumley.   Basingstoke,
England; London: Macmillan, in association with the University of
Reading, Graduate School of European and International Studies,
1990. 346p. 1 map. bibliog.

This book contains essays by various English and Italian authors. They are divided in
five parts but broadly focus on the crisis of popular traditions in a society facing the
emergence of mass culture. The first part deals with Italian history, culture and
language, and includes, correspondingly, essays by P. Ginsborg, G. Nowell-Smith,
and G. Lepschy. Essays in the second part examine religion, politics and social
movements, with writings by P. A. Allum, D. Forgacs, and R. Lumley. The third part
concerns mass culture and intellectuals, and the authors are Z. G. Barański, D. Robey,
and I. Chambers. The fourth part covers cinema and design, and contains items by S.
Gundle and P. Sparke. Finally, the fifth part focuses on television and its development
from public monopoly to private enterprise; here the contributors are U. Eco, G.
Richeri, P. Schlesinger, M. Wolf, C. Wagstaff, and L. Curti.

544   **The government and politics of contemporary Italy.**
Dante Germino, Stefano Passigli.   New York; Evanston, Illinois;
London: Harper & Row, 1968. 212p. bibliog.

Conceived as an introduction to the politics of contemporary Italy in the 1960s, this
book retains some value as a clear exemplary study of the Italian political system
during the first two decades of Italy's post-war history. It first outlines the historical
background and the fascist era; the republican constitutional framework is then
analysed, before the working of the political system is considered. This is examined
in two chapters which deal, respectively, with the polarized character of the system,
and with policy-making and the representation of interests by political parties and
interest groups. The two subsequent chapters focus on the administrative tradition
(with a flash-back to the 19th century and the impact of fascism) and the post-war
administrative structure. The final chapter discusses the issue of Italian communism.
There are some graphic illustrations and tables which show election results (1946 to
1963) and the political spectrum.

545   **Italy.**
Norman Kogan.   In: *Politics in western Europe.*   Edited by G. A.
Dorfman, P. F. Duignan.   Stanford, California: Stanford University
Press, Hoover Institution Press, 1991, p. 265-95. bibliog.

The political changes which unexpectedly occurred in Europe at the end of the 1980s
prompted the editor to reissue an updated version of this book, whose first edition
appeared in 1988. New chapters have been added, and contributions have been
updated. Kogan provides a lucid and thorough introduction to the Italian political
system, outlining the governmental structures, the character and role of political
parties, and foreign relations. The focus is on contemporary political, economic and
social issues, with particular attention paid to the defeat of terrorism in the 1970s by
the Italians' manifestations of solidarity towards their institutions, preferring 'Italian
parliamentary democracy, with its defects, to a leap into the dark'.

546 **Italy in transition: conflict and consensus.**
Edited by Peter Lange, Sidney Tarrow. London: Frank Cass, 1980.
186p.

The 1970s were a decade of turbulent change in Italy's political, economic and social landscapes. Leading political scientists (and one economist) offer their views on that period here. A. Parisi and G. Pasquino provide an introductory piece on the changes in electoral behaviour; M. Salvati surveys the relationship between economics and politics; A. Martinelli writes on the post-war relations between the main employers' association and the dominant Christian Democratic Party (DC); G. Pasquino focuses on the DC ('A party for all seasons'); P. Lange analyses the dilemmas of the Communists in the 1970s; and D. Hine contributes with an essay on the Socialist Party ('surviving but not reviving'). The last two chapters tackle more general issues: G. Di Palma considers the possible reforms of the State; and S. Tarrow addresses the central question: 'crisis, crises or transition?', and argues that 'the transition [had] already begun'.

547 **Interest groups in Italian politics.**
Joseph LaPalombara. Princeton, New Jersey: Princeton University Press, 1964. 452p. bibliog.

Some thirty years after its appearance this important study still provides useful insights into the working of Italian politics, which has been characterized in its post-1945 settlement by weak governments and strong interest groups. These are defined here as 'any aggregation of interacting individuals who manifest conscious desires concerning the authoritative allocation of values'. Several such interest groups are considered, but major attention is paid to *Confindustria* (the Confederation of Italian Industry) and the Catholic Action. Analytical chapters explore the groups' interaction with the legislature and the bureaucracy (placing the emphasis on *clientela* and *parentela* connections). Other chapters describe the social, political and governmental context. One significant conclusion notes the shifting nature of the political elite, depending also on the types of groups mobilized.

548 **Democracy, Italian style.**
Joseph LaPalombara. New Haven, Connecticut; London: Yale University Press, 1987. 308p.

This is a major work of synthesis by a foremost expert on Italian politics. Apart from all the problems which have affected Italy for so long (such as insecure historical past, social cleavages and political fragmentation, sharp conflicts and forms of violence) LaPalombara has a clear message: 'contrary to appearances, and despite what so many Italians would have us believe, Italian democracy is alive and thriving'. He knows very well that the all-intrusive presence of the parties ('party-ocracy') has gone too far, but – paradoxically – he considers it a sign of strength (if 'Italian style') rather than a disturbing weakness. All aspects of political life are explored (civil society, political parties, elections, ruling class, and government), and all negative features are optimistically turned into objects for praise. Such a cheerful viewpoint, however, did not have to wait long to be disproved by events.

549 **Parliament and democratic consolidation in southern Europe: Greece, Italy, Portugal, Spain and Turkey.**
Edited by Ulrike Liebert, Maurizio Cotta. London; New York: Pinter, 1990. 278p. bibliog.

From the evidence shown here it appears that the parliamentary role in the five countries considered has recently been strengthened. M. Cotta's essay on Italy is entitled 'The "centrality" of parliament in a protracted democratic consolidation'. The transition from fascism to democracy is surveyed, with particular attention paid to the drafting of the Republican Constitution (1947). The subsequent development of Parliament is investigated in its characteristics as an 'incremental process of step-by-step institutional integration'. The Community Party was also an active participant in this process. On the whole, therefore, conflictual tensions diminished, but this also contributed to a deceleration of the pace of change in the political system.

550 **The Catholic-Communist dialogue in Italy: 1944 to the present.**
Rosanna Mulazzi Giammanco. New York; Westpoint, Connecticut; London: Praeger, 1989. 171p. bibliog.

This book is based on extensive study of the documents of the Italian ex-Communist Party (PCI), the Vatican, and their supporting groups. The author argues that 'the theoretical elaborations made by these organizations of their roles and goals in society are ex-post facto rationalizations necessitated by changes that the organizations could not control'. The problematic nature of the 'dialogue' between the PCI and the Church is emphasized, if only because the term has been used with different and even contradictory meanings. A particularly interesting chapter is devoted to the 'four dialogues' originated, respectively, by the Vatican Ecumenical Council II, the Catholic journal *Testimonianze*, the class choice of ACLI (the Italian Christian Workers Association), and the small radical groups including 'Christians for socialism'. These new left groups are listed in the appendix, together with the dialogue publications.

551 **The promised land: peasant struggles, agrarian reforms, and regional development in a southern Italian community.**
Thorkil Ørum. Copenhagen: University of Copenhagen, Akademisk Forlag, 1985. 261p. 4 maps. bibliog.

In this study the author focuses on Melissa, a small village in the Calabrian mountains which gained recognition in 1949, when a peaceful occupation of fallow land was confronted by the armed police, and some peasants were killed, thus precipitating a nationwide general strike and land occupations in many parts of southern Italy. The background of those events is effectively explored in a historical context. The agrarian reform of 1950 is then analysed, and the last chapter deals with Italy, the south, and Melissa from 1950 to 1980. It is argued that the agrarian communities were forgotten in the 1960s, when industrialization of the south was the fashionable policy. The failure of this strategy became obvious in the 1970s: emigrants returned, but appeared to have lost the old political consciousness and desire to organize and fight to change their living conditions. There are many statistical data and photographs.

552 **Italian politics: a review: vol. 1.**
Edited by Robert Leonardi, Raffaella Y. Nanetti. London;
Wolfeboro, New Hampshire: Pinter, 1986. 188p.

This is the first of an important series of annual volumes (in both Italian and English versions) which can be found annotated here individually (q.v.). Each book outlines the main political events of the year concerned (1985 in this case), and contains essays on relevant topics. Introduced by S. Tarrow, the present book is divided into two parts: politics and institutions. Part one includes essays by P. Corbetta and A. Parisi (the 1985 local government election); P. Lange (the 1985 referendum on wage indexation); S. Hellman (the Italian Communist Party towards its 17th Congress); J. Chubb (the Christian Democratic Party); and R. Catanzaro (the perennial question of the Mafia). Part two contains writings by D. Hine (the Craxi premiership); G. Pasquino (the debate on institutional reform); S. Ferrari (the new Concordat between Italy and the Vatican); F. J. Piason (the 'Achille Lauro' affair and Italian foreign policy); and R. Mannheimer and G. Sani (electoral trends and political subcultures).

553 **Italian politics: a review: vol. 2.**
Edited by Raffaella Nanetti, Robert Leonardi, Piergiorgio Corbetta.
London; New York: Pinter, 1988. 185p.

This review covers the major political, social and economic events in Italy during 1986. The list of contributors and their topics is as follows: V. Della Sala (the use of decree legislation by the Craxi government); S. Magister (tensions within the Catholic organizations and within the Church); J. Barth Urban (the Communist Party's 17th Congress); D. A. Wertman (the 17th Congress of the Christian Democrats); P. Ceri (nuclear power after Chernobyl); M. B. Miller (liberalization of financial markets); P. Bianchi (Fiat's acquisition of Alfa Romeo); A. Z. Guttenberg (debate on the administrative amnesty on illegal building); L. Gray and P. Miggiano (Italian defence policy and Libya); P. Barrera (military service and reform); and C. Marletti (the political parties' control of mass media). A chronology of the political events concerning Italy in 1986 is included at the beginning of the volume.

554 **Italian politics: a review: vol. 3.**
Edited by Robert Leonardi, Piergiorgio Corbetta. London; New
York: Pinter, 1989. 201p.

The contents of the present volume refer to events and debates of 1987, and an appropriate chronology is included. Of particular interest: E. Balboni writes on the end of Craxi's government; G. Di Federico contributes on the referendum on the civil liability of judges, and P. V. Uleri on the broader issue of the 1987 referenda; L. Bordogna deals with the fragmentation of trade unions; and R. Cagiano de Azevedo and L. Musumeci comment on the new immigration to Italy. There are also essays on the three main political parties *vis-à-vis* the general election held in that year (G. Bibes and J. Besson, on the Christian Democrats; D. Sassoon, on the Communists; and M. Rhodes, on the Socialists), on the Italian navy's participation in the Nato operation in the Persian Gulf, and, finally, on the 'political messianism' of the Catholic Popular Movement (L. Accattoli).

555 **Italian politics: a review: vol. 4.**
Edited by Raffaella Nanetti, Raimondo Catanzaro.   London; New
York: Pinter, 1990. 220p.

A chronology of political events in 1988 is followed by a short survey of that year by
the editors. The following topics are then discussed: the new law on the institutional
reforms of government (P. Barrera); the characteristics and limitations of the new
finance bill (F. Cavazzuti); Italian preparedness for the further step towards European
integration (P. Bianchi); the continuing crisis of the Italian steel industry, and a case
study of the steel mill near Naples (A. Pichierri and A. C. Masi, respectively); the
election of the new president of the industrialists' Confederation, Sergio Pininfarina
(L. Lanzalaco); the political evolution of the Neo-Fascist Party, and the condition of
the Communist Party (G. Tassani and G. G. Amyot, respectively); the issue of law
reform on sexual violence (T. Pitch); mafia and anti-mafia in Sicily (F. Sabetti); and
the deployment of Nato's F-16 combat aeroplanes in Calabria (D. Price, Jr.).

556 **Italian politics: a review: vol. 5.**
Edited by Filippo Sabetti, Raimondo Catanzaro.   London; New York:
Pinter, with the Istituto Cattaneo, Bologna, 1991. 161p.

Presents a chronology of the political events of 1989, followed by ten essays; the first
of which is written by the editors about the impact of that year's portentous events in
Italian politics. In addition, M. Caciagli and M. J. Bull contribute with essays on the
Christian Democratic and the Communist Party, respectively. G. Pasquino reflects on
the crisis of the De Mita government; G. Colombo comments on the new code of
criminal procedure; D. Moss tackles the issue of AIDS in Italy; while anti-pollution
policies and politics are investigated by D. Alexander. The equally broad theme of
concentration trends in the media is the subject explored by P. P. Giglioli and G.
Mazzoleni. The volume concludes with an analysis by J. Barth Urban of Gorbachev's
state visit to Italy and the Vatican, and a survey by L. Bardi of the Italian vote in the
third election for the European Parliament.

557 **Italian politics: a review: vol. 6.**
Edited by Robert Leonardi, Fausto Anderlini.   London; New York:
Pinter, with the Istituto Cattaneo, Bologna, 1992. 211p.

Improving on the previous volumes of this useful series (q.v.), a statistical appendix
by S. Romani is added in this edition. The contents, however, are as varied and
interesting as in the volumes one to five. After a chronological table of the political
events of 1990, and an introduction by the editors, the following authors provide
essays: G. Pasquino, on the electoral reform referenda; L. Vandelli, on the new law of
local government (setting up 10 'metropolitan areas'); C. Cardia, on the financing of
Church activities; D. Hine, on the Italian presidency of the European Community;
D. I. Kertzer, on the 19th Congress of the Communist Party, and F. P. Belloni, on the
party's road to dissolution; D. Woods, on the equally highly topical issue of the
regional 'Leagues'; A. Mastropaolo, on 'machine politics and mass mobilization in
Palermo'; P. Segatti, on the revamped student protest; and P. Lanfranchi, on soccer in
Italy and the World Cup.

558 **Italian politics: a review: vol. 7.**
Edited by Stephen Hellman, Gianfranco Pasquino. London; New
York: Pinter, with the Istituto Cattaneo, Bologna, 1992. 240p.

The political events of 1991 are listed and selectively commented upon with essays
by leading political scientists and other experts. After an introduction by the editors:
P. McCarthy discusses the referendum which reduced the preferential votes in
parliamentary constituencies; F. Ferraresi investigates the 'secret structure
codenamed Gladio'; E. Balboni chronicles the bitter constitutional battle between the
President of the Republic (Cossiga) and the judiciary; Hellman comments on the
difficult birth of the Democratic Party of the Left (ex-Communists); the crisis of the
main trade union (CGIL) is analysed by C. A. Mershon; and A. Becchi considers the
story of political entanglement in the post-earthquake reconstruction in Irpinia. Other
contributions examine organized crime (F. Sabetti), the privatization of public
companies (F. Cavazzuti), Catholic pacifism and the Gulf War (M. Donovan), the
papal encyclical 'Centesimus Annus' (J. Zucchi), and immigration (D. Woods).

559 **Italian politics: a review: vol. 8.**
Edited by Stephen Hellman, Gianfranco Pasquino. London; New
York: Pinter, with the Istituto Cattaneo, Bologna, 1993. 228p.

A chronology of Italian political events which covers 1992 and an introduction by the
editors are followed by essays on the following: the general election of April 1992,
and the demise of the political system (J. Besson and G. Bibes); the election of
Scalfaro as the new president of the Republic (V. Della Sala); the rise of the Northern
League (R. Leonardi and M. Kovacs); the crisis of the Socialists (M. Rhodes), and
that of the Christian Democrats (M. Follini); the eruption of the *tangentopoli*
('bribesville') scandal in Milan (D. Della Porta); the unending mystery of the Ustica
airline disaster (G. Salvadori); the no less dramatic stepping up of criminal activity by
the mafia (R. Catanzaro); the loosening of the link between the employers'
confederation and Christian Democracy (L. Mattina); Italian foreign policy in a
changing Europe (J. W. Holmes), and Italy *vis-à-vis* the Maastricht Treaty (P.
Daniels). A statistical appendix compiled by S. Romani completes the volume.

560 **Italian politics: ending the First Republic.**
Edited by Carol A. Mershon, Gianfranco Pasquino. Boulder,
Colorado; San Francisco; Oxford: Westview Press, published in co-
operation with the Istituto Cattaneo, Bologna, 1994. 224p.

This collection of essays continues an eight-volume series of reviews on Italian
politics (q.v.) and deals with 1993, for which a chronology of major Italian political
events is provided. The introduction by the editors is followed by contributions on the
Ciampi government (G. Pasquino and S. Vassallo); the launching of a broad left
alliance (M. Rhodes); the end of the Christian Democratic Party (D. A. Wertman); the
referendum to amend the electoral legislation (P. Corbetta and A. M. L. Parisi); the
important new electoral laws (R. S. Katz); Italian intervention in Somalia (O. Croci);
an update on mafia and politics (D. Della Porta and A. Vannucci); the abolition of the
wage-indexation mechanism (R. M. Locke); and the restructuring of State television
(G. Mazzoleni). A statistical appendix, edited by R. Salvato, is also included.

561   **The end of post-war politics in Italy: the landmark 1992 elections.**
Edited by Gianfranco Pasquino, Patrick McCarthy.   Boulder,
Colorado; San Francisco; Oxford: Westview Press, 1993. 187p.

The 1992 election delivered heavy losses to the Christian Democrats and the ex-
Communists, and big gains to the Northern League. This portentous event is analysed
here by leading experts in the context of the demise of the post-war political
equilibrium. G. Pasquino contributes with an introduction on the crisis of the old
order and an essay on Cossiga's resignation from the Presidency of the Republic
while D. A. Wertman and P. McCarthy examine the crises of the Christian Democrats
and the former Communists, respectively. D. Hine writes on the Socialist Party's
stability at the polls but hints at the dire consequences following the revelations of
corruption. P. Ignazi surveys the outcome of the election in minor parties, while R.
Mannheimer discusses the various strands in the electorate of the Northern League.
Finally, an essay on the changes by G. Sani and one on the Amato government by S.
Hellman precede P. McCarthy's conclusion on the 'inching towards a new regime'.

562   **Italy today: patterns of life and politics.**
Edited by Luisa Quartermaine, with John Pollard.   Exeter, England:
University of Exeter, 1985. 114p.

Various aspects of Italian society are considered here. L. Quartermaine first
underlines the tension between cultural uniformity and diversity. M. Slater then
studies the relationship between socio-economic changes and political transformation,
and suggests that a constant feature has been the juxtaposition of Catholicism and
socialism. J. Eisenhammer offers a fine analysis of economic decisions in the State-
supported steel industry, motivated by political perspectives. P. Furlong deals with
the changing role of the Vatican in Italian politics, and argues that the background to
that role is more complex than is commonly perceived, because of regional
differences and signs of autonomy in civil society. G. Pridham focuses on the
characteristics of government coalitions and shows that under the surface of
instability and confusion, complicated processes are at work, involving actions at
local and national levels. Finally, J. Walston writes on the nature and development of
political patronage and *clientelismo* in Calabria.

563   **Political authority in a Sicilian village.**
Filippo Sabetti.   New Brunswick, New Jersey: Rutgers University
Press, 1984. 293p. bibliog.

The problem of political authority in Sicily is fundamentally a problem of social
organization and the collective response to the pursuit of individual opportunities. A
village in western Sicily (under the fictitious name of Camporano) is selected as a
microcosm for this study. Two centuries of history are compressed here and shown to
be representative of a story of continuity. By the middle of the 19th century, Sabetti
argues, 'the shift from the Bourbon to the Savoy monarchy did not fundamentally
alter the institutional arrangements that governed agricultural and communal affairs'.
Nor were they substantially altered by subsequent and more recent developments,
which were dominated by the mafia and the Christian Democratic hegemony.
However, Sabetti adds that, by the late 1970s, 'the struggle between [these] two
groups still provided possibilities for a majority of villages to be part of the larger
political community without foreclosing opportunities to act as an autonomous local
community'.

564 **Contemporary Italy: politics, economics and society since 1945.**
Donald Sassoon. London; New York: Longman, 1986. 269p. bibliog.

This is a comprehensive and authoritative work on post-war Italy. As the author assumes no prior knowledge of Italian politics on the part of the reader, the result is a readable, highly-informative book which covers a variety of complex issues peculiar to Italian society. Organized in three parts, the first of these deals with the economic policies of successive governments. Essential data and statistics on finance, industry, agriculture and patterns of employment, with reference to regional differentiation and social strata, are provided. Part two considers social groups including women, youth, the Church, trade unions, and the mass media, while the third part provides detailed information about institutions, the electoral system, government, parliament, local authorities, and political parties. The book also examines such issues as the mafia, the 'southern question', and the role of the secret services and the P2 masonic lodge in attempting to destabilize Italian democracy.

565 **Italy: a difficult democracy: a survey of Italian politics.**
Frederic Spotts, Theodor Wieser. Cambridge, England; London;
New York; Melbourne; Sydney: Cambridge University Press, 1986.
328p. 1 map. bibliog.

Italy's paradoxes, it is stated at the beginning of this excellent study, 'are symptomatic of a singularly intricate and sophisticated political society' which appears to be almost ungovernable but manages to muddle through. This study was written before the real, comprehensive turmoil began, but it will help the reader to understand the subsequent crisis. After an initial section on the political context, four chapters are devoted to the politial parties, with an emphasis on the three main actors: the Christian Democrats; the Communists; and the Socialists. Well-informed chapters on parliament, government and public administration follow. The last part of the book addresses such specific issues as terrorism, plots and the mafia; the economic transformation; the problem of the south; the changing relations between Church and State; and Italy's foreign policy. Various tables on political and economic data are included in the appendices.

566 **Catholic-Communist collaboration in Italy.**
Edited by Leonard Swindler, Edward James Grace. Lanham,
Maryland; New York; London: University Press of America, 1988.
173p.

The editors have gathered together a collection of assorted materials on the history, theory and practice of dialogue (rather than collaboration) between Catholics and Communists. With the exception of the brief introduction by Swindler on the 'ground rules' for such dialogue, which was written specifically for this book, all contributions were written at the end of the 1970s. Thus, they reflect the political climate in Italy, wherein the Communist Party (PCI) supported the government and was inspired by the strategy of 'historical compromise'. A general background to the Christian-Marxist dialogue is provided by Swindler and precedes a comprehensive essay by Grace on the Italian case. This is followed by various contributions, mostly by Italian Catholics who held important positions in the PCI. The indirect correspondence of 1976 between the bishop of Ivrea (Luigi Bettazzi) and the PCI general secretary (Enrico Berlinguer) is also included along with documents on the ensuing polemical debate.

567 **Stars, stripes, and Italian tricolor: the United States and Italy, 1946-1989.**
Leo J. Wollemborg, foreword by Richard N. Gardner. New York; Westport, Connecticut; London: Praeger, 1990. 320p. bibliog.

The author of this work is an Italian-born American writer on international relations and on Italian politics who resettled in Italy after the end of the war. Throughout, he makes systematic reference to his own innumerable pieces, with frequent inclusions of self-quotations. The contents are arranged in a chronological order, with emphasis placed on particular events and circumstances which contributed to the United States government focusing its interest on Italian affairs. In the chapter on the Carter administration's policy towards Italy, wide extracts from the document on Eurocommunism and Italy are published for the first time. The book forms a highly informative chronicle, as Wollemborg knew and interviewed virtually every Italian political leader and United States ambassador in Rome. One former such ambassador writes in the foreword that 'US-Italian relations for most of the last forty years have been dominated by questions of domestic Italian politics rather than by foreign policy questions'.

Political system

568 **Semiperipheral development: the politics of southern Europe in the twentieth century.**
Edited by Giovanni Arrighi. Beverly Hills, California; London; New Delhi: Sage, 1985. 279p. bibliog.

Part one of this work considers 'the formation of the southern European semiperiphery' while part two covers the post-war transition, including two essays centred on Italy. The first is by Peter Lange and examines the country's post-war experience. For all its contradictions, with both advanced and relatively backward regions, it is admitted that Italy did shift from 'semiperiphery' to 'core' development, but that the legacies of the recent and uneven transition, and the effects of the economic international crisis represent serious constraints in Italy's world-system position. Sydney Tarrow contributes with a comparative essay on the crisis of the late 1960s in Italy and France. The crisis of France was political, it is argued, whereas in Italy it coincided with the completion of the country's transition to mature capitalism. The transition became more apparent during the cycle of protest in the late 1960s and early 1970s.

569 **Representation in Italy: institutionalized tradition and electoral choice.**
Samuel H. Barnes. Chicago; London: The University of Chicago Press, 1977. 187p.

Barnes's analysis is based on a survey he carried out during the Italian electoral campaign of 1968. Three blocs of voters are identified: middle-class and peasants, for whom religion (Roman Catholicism) is an important common element in their electoral choice (Christian Democratic Party); left-wing network, based on union-

187

affiliated respondents; and a residual bloc including those who could not identify with either the first or second groups. The analysis contains interesting information on the different levels of political knowledge, types of participation and perceptions of the political parties. The conclusion is that the electoral stability of Italian voters was founded on 'institutionalized tradition', that is to say, on the two traditional sub-cultures based around religious and working-class voters.

570   **Faction politics: political parties and factionalism in comparative perspective.**
Edited by Frank P. Belloni, Dennis C. Beller.   Santa Barbara, California; Oxford: American Bibliographical Center; Clio Press, 1978. 472p.

Two theoretical chapters provide both an introduction and a conclusion to this book. The section in-between consists of a number of empirical case-studies, divided into three categories, according to the political system to which they belong: dominant-party systems; alternating-party systems; or single-party systems. Italy falls into the first category and Belloni investigates the structure and role of factions in two parties: the Christian Democratic Party (DC) and the Italian Socialist Party (PSI). It is argued that a dominant-party system tends to encourage factionalism and that a further factor, as far as the DC is concerned, is that this party seeks to represent all elements of society. Belloni concludes that 'DC factions constitute an almost self-contained system of organised competition for power in the Italian polity'. Less attention is paid to factionalism within the PSI.

571   **Patronage, power, and poverty in southern Italy: a tale of two cities.**
Judith Chubb.   Cambridge, England: Cambridge University Press, 1982. 292p. bibliog.

This is a major study of clientele politics in southern Italy. It focuses on the bases of local power in Palermo, and in the third and shorter section of the book compares the situation there with the second city referred to in the subtitle, Naples. Chubb examines the roots of clientele power in part one; and in part two she analyses the social bases of the power machine in Palermo. The mafia is considered in its business-like role, and against the background of urban poverty and political control. The fundamental problem, Chubb argues, is that a certain process of change and modernization occurred without development, thus 'creating a modern society in terms of models of consumption and, most importantly, of expectations, but without providing the productive base to sustain those levels of consumption'. Consequently, large areas of the Mezzogiorno became dependent for survival on various forms of State assistance through the mediation of the dominant party, the Christian Democrats. The book contains several tables, figures and a statistical appendix.

572   **Surviving without governing: the Italian parties in Parliament.**
Giuseppe Di Palma.   Berkeley, California; London: University of California Press, 1977. 300p.

It may be surprising that this book can still be useful for the study of Italian politics twenty years after the author began to draft it (1973), if only for historical reasons rather than current interest. At that time Italy presented 'a most explosive mix of soaring inflation and economic recession'. Italy in the 1990s is faced with different, but no less explosive problems. A postscript written after the Communist Party's success of 1976 emphasized that an era of Italian politics had come to an end, since 'all governing formulas that made possible thirty years of muddling through [had] been exhausted'. The book is concerned with those thirty years, and studies the low performance of the system through an analysis of the working of Parliament, the legislative output, and the relationship between Government and the party system.

573 **Social change and transformation of the State in Italy.**
Carlo Donolo.   In: *The State in Western Europe.*   Edited by Richard
Scase.   London: Croom Helm, 1980, p. 164-96.

This essay provides an analysis which combines the approaches of both sociologists and political scientists. Donolo underlines three main points: 'The crucial historic break with the past represented by the forming of the Republic' at the end of the Second World War; the belated capitalistic development; and the fragmentary configuration of Italian public institutions, as a consequence of the spoils system which regulates Italian politics at government level. Donolo emphasizes the role of the dominant Christian Democratic Party in post-war Italy, in transforming the State into 'an extended political system' managing capital accumulation. Consequently, any reform of the State resulted in a reform of the model of economic development.

574 **Modern Italy: representation and reform.**
Paul Furlong.   London; New York: Routledge, 1994. 295p. 3 maps.
bibliog.

In the author's own words, 'this is a study of how public policy is made in Italy, and about the practical results of these processes in some key policy areas'. It is both descriptive and analytical. Part one presents the policy framework and considers the historical and cultural context, the constitutional setting, the State machinery, the workings of parliament and government, and issues concerning parties and interest groups. Part two examines the implementation of economic and industrial policies. In the final chapter, which provides some interesting insights on the more recent dramatic changes in Italian politics, Furlong writes that 'for better or worse, the opportunity now presents itself to seek to redraw the established institutional boundaries so as to include as appropriate those traditional groups previously excluded [from representation] and the new groups whose rise has contributed to the decay of the old constraints'.

575 **Patterns of political participation in Italy.**
Giorgio Galli, Alfonso Prandi.   New Haven, Connecticut; London:
Yale University Press, 1970. 364p.

The authors summarize the main findings of one of the earliest extensive studies of Italian political life, carried out in the 1960s. Many tables and figures are contained in the main body of the text, which concentrates on the Christian Democratic Party and the Communist Party, but also considers some more general topics. The conclusion refers to a notable anomaly in the Italian political system: the split of mass participation between the Catholic and the Socialist-Communist sub-cultural poles. This, it is argued, created a situation of stalemate, with one party in a permanent position of command (the Christian Democrats) and the main opposition party (the Communists) confined to the margins of the system.

576 **Regionalism in France, Italy and Spain.**
Edited by M. Hebbert, H. Machin. London: International Centre for
Economics and Related Disciplines; London School of Economics,
1984. 127p.

The discussion on Italy is a concise contribution by Sabino Cassese, entitled 'Italy: a
system in search of an equilibrium'. It is argued that the relationship between the
centre and the regions is characterized by overlapping responsibilities, and hangs
together in an unstable balance. The effective mechanism which secures the
connection is the pervasive role of the party system and the strong cohesion of the
periphery around the centre. It is also worth pointing out that most essays included in
this collection contain references to cross-national aspects of regionalism. In
particular this is the case in respect of the types of conflicts between regions and the
centre *vis-à-vis* economic development. The last chapter (by V. Wright) provides a
comparison of the three national experiences and concludes that 'unstable
equilibrium' appears to be an appropriate formula for all of them.

577 **Governing Italy: the politics of bargained pluralism.**
David Hine. Oxford: Clarendon Press, 1993. 388p. 1 map. bibliog.

This is an outstanding study of the Italian political system. It is argued that 'the
ability of the parties to aggregate demands and respond to them by offering voters
clear policy choices is limited'. The fragmentation of political parties, the role of
lobbies, and the complex institutional procedures ensure that no single institution
dominates. After surveying the legacy of the past, and the economic and social
features, Hine examines the party system and organization, the constitutional
framework, the characteristics of parliament and government (both central and local),
and the administrative structure. The final chapter is devoted to the European
Community dimension of Italian government. After the shocking outcome of the 1992
election, the results of the expected institutional reform are 'likely to be slow to
emerge'. The book contains tables and useful appendices on the leading politicians
since 1945.

578 **The nature of the Italian party system: a regional case study.**
Geoffrey Pridham. London: Croom Helm, 1981. 283p. 1 map.
bibliog.

The central theme of this book is the process of fundamental change which occurred
in Italian party politics during the 1970s, as a consequence of unprecedented mobility
in voting behaviour, and resulting in the challenge by a stronger Communist Party to
the traditionally dominant Christian Democratic Party. After a general historical and
comparative chapter, the study focuses on Tuscany, discussing the internal and
external relationships of the two main political parties, and their development and
roles in that region. Various factors of change and continuity are considered, and their
significance is evaluated. Sensibly, Pridham concludes that 'predictions about the
future of the party system in Italy are hedged with greater uncertainty than ever
before'. However, only a decade later the system entered what (at the time of writing)
appears to be a true terminal crisis.

579 **Political parties and coalitional behaviour in Italy.**
Geoffrey Pridham. London; New York: Routledge, 1988. 443p.
bibliog.

A ponderous theoretical study of coalition politics, based on a vast knowledge of the relevant secondary literature and on empirical research. It represents an important contribution to the understanding of Italian politics, where coalition governments have been the rule (and the necessity) since the end of the Second World War. Political parties are seen as the central dynamic agents in the coalition formations, but they are also seen as the link betwen political structures and society, and as subject, therefore, to a variety of pressures which reflect on short-term coalition problems. The first part of the book discusses coalition theory and its relevance to the Italian case. The second, third and fourth parts deal with a conceptual framework which, among others, takes into account the historical, institutional and motivational dimensions, and the complex power relations within and among parties, between national leadership and the periphery.

580 **Parliamentarians and their constituents in Italy's party democracy.**
Geoffrey Pridham. In: *Representatives of the people?*
Parliamentarians and constituents in western democracies. Edited by Vernon Bogdanor. Aldershot, England; Brookfield, Vermont: Gower, 1985, p. 151-65.

Pridham argues that the difference ('even separateness') between formal procedures and informal processes is much greater in Italy than in other west European countries. The informal channels, it is also maintained, provide 'a better understanding of the complexities of the Italian system'. After general considerations on the institutional structure, and the electoral and party system, the author examines the two-way relationship between the parliamentary representatives and their constituents: the upward and downward vertical links. The role of the *partitocrazia* (the pervasiveness of party power in all aspects of public life in Italy) is then explored and pessimism is declared with respect to the likelihood of electoral reform.

581 **The beliefs of politicians: ideology, conflict, and democracy in Britain and Italy.**
Robert D. Putnam. New Haven, Connecticut; London: Yale University Press, 1973. 309p.

This is a highly conceptual, comparative study of political culture in Britain and Italy, researched through interviews with various politicians. As the author explains, his enquiry 'lies at the juncture of two important approaches to the study of politics': the elite theories, and the focus of ideology and political context. After a chapter concerning the methodology used in the empirical aspect of the research, the investigation is divided into three parts entitled, respectively: 'Ideology and politics'; 'Politicians and conflict'; and 'Politicians and democracy'. Each part highlights certain topics and draws comparisons between the two countries. For instance, Putnam argues that, when it comes to democratic ideals, 'the British value liberty and accept equality; the Italians value equality and accept liberty [. . .]. In Italy dissent is tolerated less because tolerance is thought morally right than because it is thought politically necessary'.

582 **The mafia and clientelism: roads to Rome in post-war Calabria.**
James Walston. London; New York: Routledge, 1988. 265p. bibliog.
Walston makes a broad analysis of how far a system of large-scale patronage rooted in southern Italy – and which feeds the mafia – impinges on national politics. The study focuses on two provinces of Calabria: Reggio (where the Calabrian version of the mafia, called *'ndrangheta* is strong) and Cosenza (where it is weak). Walston examines the growth of clientelism in relation to the distribution of public resources, and a wide range of material (including interviews) is used to present a historical, political, social and geographical view of a complex situation. The ethics of State intervention under such conditions is briefly discussed. The relationship between local and national politics, and how far clientelism and mafia have contributed to the development of the two main government parties – Christian Democracy and the Socialist Party – is also assessed.

583 **Italy: the politics of uneven development.**
Raphael Zariski. Hinsdale, Illinois: Dryden Press, 1972. 360p. bibliog.
The focus of this thorough study of Italian politics is the contrast between the modernization brought about by urbanization and industrialization, and the relatively backward political system. This is a contrast which has in many ways sharpened since Zariski produced his work. The relationship between rapid economic and social change, and an archaic political system is the main theme of this book. A brief historical background introduces the analysis of the following topics: political socialization; participation and recruitment; political culture; local and national politics; the party system; groups, interests, and cleavages; the policy-making process; Italian courts and judges; and Italy's role in world affairs. There is cautious optimism in the conclusion, in which it is noted that some positive reformist tendencies at the time had a good chance to strengthen. Nevertheless, the subsequent decades were to prove possibly more contradictory than the previous ones.

584 **Italy.**
Raphael Zariski. In: *Politics in western Europe*. Edited by M. D. Hancock, D. P. Conradt, B. G. Peters, W. Safran, R. Zariski. Basingstoke, England; London: Macmillan, 1993, p. 293-332.
Zariski first sets the discussion in the context of Italian politics by surveying the country's modern history, socio-economic background, religion, education and political culture. The four subsequent sections are introduced by questions which they then attempt to answer: where is the power? (the high degree of regional devolution is emphasized); who has the power and how did they get it? (the election results from 1946 to 1992 are examined, and particular attention paid to the main parties and the electoral system); how is power used? (the issues of policy formulation and implementation are covered); and what is the future of Italian politics? (the elements of strength and weakness are highlighted, with reference to institutional reform). An appendix supplies cross-national statistics, ranging from per capita gross domestic product to consumer prices, unemployment rates, life expectancy at birth and religious adherents by denomination.

Political parties

General

585 **The Italian party system (1945-1980).**
Paolo Farneti, edited by S. E. Finer, Alfio Mastropaolo. London:
Pinter, 1985. 200p. bibliog.
This book was only in its first draft when Farneti was killed in a car accident at the
age of forty-four. An edited version soon appeared in Italian and with minor
amendments became the present version, namely the first book written in English to
provide a detailed survey of how the Italian party system has evolved since the end of
the war. The three main parts of the book relate political parties to Parliament, the
electorate, and the social context. Farneti discusses the complexities of coalition
politics, the cultural cleavages, the ideological distance between and within different
parties, and election shifts. He revisits some traditional interpretative models of
Italian politics and suggests the formula of 'centripetal pluralism'. The fundamental
idea is that the social and political centre – the basis for any government majority – is
not a homogeneous and cohesive area, because it reflects the tensions of both the right
and the left.

586 **Western European political parties: a comprehensive guide.**
Edited and compiled by Francis Jacobs. Harlow, England: Longman,
1989. 730p.
In the chapter on Italy there is a preliminary emphasis on the country's Constitution,
followed by a historical review of political events from 1861 (when Italy was united)
to the mid-1980s. A section on the main features of the current political system (with
a table of election results from 1948 to 1987) precedes the comprehensive survey of
the different political parties, with information on their membership, history and
policies. Attention is also paid to regional parties and to the characteristics of their
regions. In particular, South Tyrol (Trentino Alto Adige) is discussed with its four
local parties (of which the *Südtiroler Volkspartei* is relatively well-known), as are
Trentino, Sardinia and Val d'Aosta. The new regionalist parties which emerged in the
1980s are also noted although for some of them the subsequent remarkable
development will require a substantial revision of this chapter.

The left

587 **The Italian Communist Party: the crisis of the popular front
strategy.**
Grant Amyot. London: Croom Helm, 1981. 252p. bibliog.
This constitutes a thorough study of a double, interrelated failure: firstly, the failure
of the Italian Communist Party (PCI) to provide an effective contribution to the
development of an evolutionary strategy for the working class; and secondly, the
failure of the leftist tendency within the PCI to challenge the conservative strategy of
the leadership. The origins of the Eurocommunist ideology (adopted by the PCI in the

early 1970s) are examined and regarded as the development and adaptation of the popular front policy pursued by the Comintern in the 1930s. This increasingly moderate line, Amyot argues, was 'the major factor explaining the de-radicalisation of the PCI'. It resulted in a crisis of hegemony which in turn became a political crisis in the late 1970s, with the collapse of the 'historic compromise'. Yet, once again, the Communist left was unable to assert itself. A vast and useful bibliography is included.

588   **Party democracy: politics in an Italian socialist federation.**
       Samuel H. Barnes.   New Haven, Connecticut; London: Yale
       University Press, 1967. 279p.

The Italian political landscape has already changed so much in the 1990s that anything dating back thirty years now sounds like prehistory. This is particularly relevant when referring to the Socialist Party (PSI), which underwent a deep transformation under Craxi in the 1980s and was much affected by the crisis of the 1990s. However, as a study of post-war Italian politics this is a book worth noting. It presents an inquiry into the functioning of democracy in modern society, focusing on the internal politics of one provincial federation of the PSI in Tuscany (Arezzo). Chapters with empirical evidence of political behaviour are associated with sections discussing the theoretical framework and the interpretation of the findings. The context of national and local politics is also outlined. Barnes argues that 'there are factors that encourage internal party democracy in the PSI federation and others that frustrate it'.

589   **Moscow and the Italian Communist Party: from Togliatti to**
       Berlinguer.
       Joan Barth Urban.   London: I. B. Tauris, 1986. 370p. bibliog.

This is the only comprehensive study of the relationship between the Italian Communist Party (PCI) and the Soviet Union: it covers a period of some sixty years and is based on exhaustive research. Part one focuses on the emergence of Togliatti as the undisputed party leader in the late 1920s. Part two refers to the years between the late 1920s and the early 1940s when the organizational alliance between the PCI and other Resistance groups revealed a sharp departure from Moscow's wartime directives. Part three considers the search for an Italian independent road to socialism, first under Togliatti's notion of 'polycentrism' and then with Berlinguer's concept of 'new internationalism' and the plans for a Eurocommunist strategy. Part four tackles the Soviet-PCI rift in the 1970s, emphasizing the PCI's challenge to Moscow's 'revolutionary credentials'. An analytical survey of the sources used concludes the book.

590   **Communism in Italy and France.**
       Edited by Donald L. M. Blackmer, Sydney Tarrow.   Princeton, New
       Jersey: Princeton University Press, 1975. 651p.

This collection of excellent critical essays focuses more on Italy than on France while at the same time providing a comparative perspective. The differences between Italy and France, as well as those within Italy itself are analysed, and a picture of the complex varieties of 'communism' is presented. The work is divided into five parts in the first of which Blackmer examines the Italian Communist Party (PCI) in the post-Second World War period. The second and third parts deal, respectively, with the communist politicians and with local party politics; S. Tarrow, R. Putnam, A

Stern and P. Lange write on the PCI. The fourth part concentrates on alliance strategies, especially those formulated by the PCI in its attempts to establish hegemony – that is, at widening its influence over social strata other than the traditional working classes and labour movement. Contributions also come from S. Hellman, G. Sani and P. Weitz before, finally, Tarrow draws some comparative conclusions.

591 **The politics of Eurocommunism: socialism in transition.**
Edited by Carl Boggs, David Plotke. London; Basingstoke, England: Macmillan, 1980. 480p.

The contributions in this work are all by writers who share socialist leanings, although their views on Eurocommunism differ. Chapter one considers the strategic origins and perspectives of the phenomenon of Eurocommunism; it includes one essay on Italian communism, by J. Barkan. She stresses the growing dissatisfaction among the rank-and-file towards the party's strategy of moderation and compromise. Chapter two deals with the communist parties and popular movements; it contains two essays on Italy: 'Terrorism and the Italian left', by S. Cowan, and 'The feminist challenge', by A. Buttafuoco. Chapter three concerns the international setting, containing one study on Italy by P. Joseph, 'American policy and the Italian left'. Other contributions include only minimal references to Italy. Finally, chapter four focuses on the prospects of Eurocommunism, regarding the role of Italian communists as central; it includes two general essays by the editors.

592 **The theory and practice of Italian communism.**
Alastair Davidson. London: Merlin Press, 1982. 302p.

As the first of two intended volumes on Italian communism, this book roughly covers the same period as the massive five-volume history of the Italian Communist Party (PCI) by Paolo Spriano (not available in English). Davidson's scope, however, is in a sense wider: his study looks outside the party and into the lives of the working class. The book is divided into three unequal parts. In the first the author considers the background of the class struggles, organization and debates in the 1890s and up until the First World War. Part two, the main component of the book, deals with the 1920s. It focuses on the establishment of the PCI, the political developments in the face of defeat by fascism and on the contrasting policies pursued by the Third International. The figure of Gramsci, both before and after incarceration, is dominant. Finally, Davidson examines the theory and practice of Italian communism in the last period of the old PCI (1935-42).

593 **The Italian left in the twentieth century: a history of the socialist and communist parties.**
Alexander De Grand. Bloomington; Indianapolis, Indiana: Indiana University Press, 1989. 182p. bibliog.

The author brings together recent scholarly works on Italian socialism and communism, and explores the ways in which both traditions dealt with the problem of gaining power, as well as the ways they dealt with each other. The ten chapters, divided into two parts, are arranged in a strict chronological order. Part one spans a period of almost one hundred years: from the origins of the socialist movement at the time of Italy's unification to the fall of fascism. Part two deals more analytically with the subsequent forty years. Ultimately, De Grand writes that 'despite bitter defeats, the achievement of the Italian left has been considerable. In a land where, historically, things change only to remain the same, the revolution that would bring about a socially and economically modern Italy did occur – but in a totally unexpected form'. A united left, it is argued, may blend moral idealism and pragmatism.

594 **Renewing Italian Socialism: Nenni to Craxi.**
Spencer M. Di Scala.   New York; Oxford: Oxford University Press, 1988. 336p. bibliog.

This is a very comprehensive study covering sixty years of the history of the Italian Socialist Party (PSI). The period stretches from the 1920s through the 1930s and fascism to the Second World War, the Resistance, the post-war struggles, and the formation of Christian Democrat-led governments to the PSI's entry into government coalitions from 1963 onwards. The international context is also reviewed, especially the impact on Italian socialist politics of the cold war, the revolts in Hungary and Czechoslovakia, as well as that of student unrest in the late sixties, the scandals and corruption in high places, and the development of terrorism, both right- and left-wing. Less interesting are the final chapters, devoted to the PSI under Craxi, possibly because under his leadership the party was prolific with statements and sterile with ideas – unless these were reiterations of the principle to stick to power as long as possible, and however possible.

595 **Communist and Marxist parties of the world.**
General editor, Roger East.   Harlow, England: Longman, 1990, 2nd ed. 596p. bibliog.

The concise, opening section of this repertory provides an historical overview, with the inclusion of extracts from important documents. The main body of the volume deals with the communist and marxist parties all around the world. For each country there is a brief introduction which puts the relevant parties in perspective. Seven pages are dedicated to Italy, four of which are devoted to the Communist Party (PCI). At the time this work was written, the PCI had just begun the discussion on its new name and emblem, so that these dense pages can be regarded as a sort of obituary of the old party. Short references are made to some other parties, namely: Democrazia Proletaria; Gruppi dei Comunisti Rivoluzionari; Partito Comunista Unificato d'Italia; and Autonomia Operaia. Some attention is finally devoted to three terrorist organizations: the Brigate Rosse (with more details), the Partito Comunista Combattente, and Prima Linea.

596 **Socialist parties and European integration: a comparative history.**
Kevin Featherstone.   Manchester: Manchester University Press, 1988. 366p. bibliog.

Theoretical issues are touched on in the introduction and conclusion, while the main body of the book consists of a survey of the socialist parties in all the countries of the European Community. Italy is unique, it is pointed out, in that it has not one but two parties affiliated to the Socialist International: the Socialist Party (PSI) and the Social Democratic Party (PSDI). This is a reflection of past disputes and domestic political pressures and constraints, not least the presence of the (former) Communist Party. Featherstone offers a balanced survey of those developments, and concludes by saying that 'both the PSI and the PSDI are likely to continue to be at the forefront of socialist support for integration in the future [. . .]. Transnational party co-operation serves to protect their limited domestic positions and to offer an alternative guide to the Italian public'.

597   **Southern European socialism: parties, elections and challenge of government.**
Edited by Tom Gallacher, Allan M. Williams.   Manchester; New York: Manchester University Press, 1989. 292p. bibliog.
Part one of this volume contains chapters on case studies and part two develops common conceptual themes in the different political systems. The chapter on the Italian Socialist Party (PSI), in part one, is written by David Hine. He argues that, compared with the other socialist parties considered here, the PSI is the exception because it failed to show a dramatic increase in support throughout the 1980s. This was despite the flamboyant role played by its leader, Bettino Craxi, who was also Prime Minister between 1983 and 1987. A partial explanation for this was the persistent strength of the Communist Party. Another reason was that the PSI was handicapped by its long partnership in a basically conservative government dominated by the Christian Democrats. Only 'the gamble of major electoral or institutional reform – Hine concludes – will enable the PSI to escape' from the apparent fate of becoming a 'catch-all party of the centre'.

598   **The Italian Communist Party: Gorbachev and the end of 'really existing socialism'.**
Stephen Gundle.   In: *Western European communists and the collapse of communism.*   Edited by David S. Bell.   Providence, Rhode Island; Oxford: Berg, 1993, p. 15-30.
Gundle first explores the difficulties encountered by the Italian Communist Party (PCI) during the 1980s and suggests that they were the result of failed renovation. The Gorbachev challenge was met with much sympathy by the PCI, which had a long history of dissociation from, and criticism of Soviet communism. Yet despite this, the democratic legitimacy of the PCI was still questioned in the late 1980s, if only because of the party's reluctance to condemn its own Stalinist past. Only one year after becoming the new PCI leader, Occhetto took the opportunity of the collapse of the Berlin Wall and the crisis of 'really existing socialism', to push through a process of radical reform of the party, involving the change of name (*Partito Democratico della Sinistra*) but also arousing fierce opposition and an eventual split. Gundle concludes that 'renovation has been achieved but only at great cost in terms of influence and cohesion'.

599   **Italian communism in transition: the rise and fall of the historic compromise in Turin, 1975-1980.**
Stephen Hellman.   New York; Oxford: Oxford University Press, 1988. 274p. bibliog.
Hellman closely observed the development of the Italian Communist Party (PCI) throughout the 1970s, mainly in Turin. The book focuses on the 'transitional crisis' affecting – and ultimately undermining – the PCI in the second half of the decade. 'Transitional crisis' is defined as 'a watershed which challenges at least several, and perhaps all, of the major dimensions of party activity: doctrinal, strategic, organizational, and behavioral'. The first two chapters establish the context of the

PCI's crisis, emphasizing the party's ambiguous character as a cadre party with qualities of mass appeal. Analytical chapters on general issues then alternate with chapters on the Turin case-study. It is argued, in conclusion, that a middle-of-the-road course was probably the only viable option for the PCI, with the risk of abandoning any broader vision of a radical transformation of society. There are tables, graphs and a list of PCI relevant documents.

600   **The Italian road to socialism: an interview by Eric Hobsbawm with Giorgio Napolitano of the Italian Communist Party.**
      Eric Hobsbawm, translated by John Cammett, Victoria De Grazia.
      London: The Journeyman Press, 1977. 122p.

The interview was carried out in two phases: first, in October 1975; then, in March 1977. In between those two dates, the Italian Communist Party (PCI) achieved its greatest electoral success (over thirty-four per cent of the total vote). Furthermore, as from the summer of 1976, the PCI began to support the government, considered by many to be the first acknowledged step towards the realization of 'historical compromise'. At the roots of that strategy was Togliatti's idea of an 'Italian road to socialism'. In fact, at the time that idea was influencing other European Communist parties and was known as 'Eurocommunism'. The interview is divided into five parts focusing, respectively, on the development of the PCI from the mid-1940s to the end of the 1960s; the PCI's position *vis-à-vis* the crisis of the 1970s; the international context of that crisis; the 'Italian road to socialism'; and an assessment of the PCI standing after the 1976 electoral success.

601   **The communist parties of Italy, France and Spain: post-war change and continuity: a casebook.**
      Edited by Peter Lange, Maurizio Vannicelli, with a foreword by
      Stanley Hoffman.   London: George Allen & Unwin, 1981. 386p.
      bibliog.

A collection of documents showing the separate development of the three communist parties from the end of the Second World War to their common declaration and strategy of Eurocommunism. The material is presented in five thematic parts and arranged (within each part) in a chronological sequence. The theme of part one is 'national roads to socialism': Togliatti and Berlinguer are the main sources for the Italian Communist Party (PCI). Part two concentrates on 'alliance policy' and various items concern the complex approach by the PCI. Part three focuses on the party structure, with relevant excerpts from reports by several PCI leaders. Parts four and five deal with the international dimension of the communist movement: the former contains some of the most important documents of the entire collection, including Togliatti's interview of 1956 with *Nuovi Argomenti* and his 'testament', the 1964 Yalta Memorandum.

602   **The Italian Communist Party, 1976-81: on the threshold of government.**
      James Ruscoe.   London: Macmillan, 1982. 293p. bibliog.

Ruscoe commences with an account of the great electoral success of the Communist Party (PCI) in 1976. But only four years later the PCI was on the defensive and isolated. The main cause of such a reversal of fortunes, the author argues, was that the

PCI leaders underestimated the inefficiency of the State machinery and their excessive restraint in pushing for the Communist alternative. The reformist programme became paralysed after Aldo Moro's assassination, and the Christian Democrats were encouraged to look towards the Socialist Party for support, now that under Craxi the party was showing signs of revival, with a strong anti-communist flavour. This approach was vindicated by the PCI's electoral losses in 1979 and 1980. The abandonment of the 'historic compromise' left the PCI without a valid strategy. At the end of the book there is a very useful glossary of Italian current political expressions.

603   **The Italian communists speak for themselves.**
Edited by Donald Sassoon.   Nottingham, England: Spokesman, 1978. 196p.

In his introductory essay on the European strategy of the Italian Communist Party (PCI), Sassoon argues that the party's original hostility developed into a plan aiming at the disengagement of western Europe from the constraints of power blocs and the strengthening of solidarity among the western European Communist parties (Eurocommunism). The following selected pieces included in the book reflect the title more closely. The contributions are extracts from official PCI documents and articles and they focus on the international framework, economic policies, the 'historic compromise' and other 'new ideas'. Most items are by E. Berlinguer; two are by G. Napolitano, and one each by A. Reichlin, G. Amendola, L. Longo, and P. Ingrao.

604   **The strategy of the Italian Communist Party: from the resistance to the historic compromise.**
Donald Sassoon, foreword by E. J. Hobsbawm.   London: Pinter, 1981. 259p. bibliog.

Part one of this volume covers the years 1944-55 and discusses the Communist Party (PCI)'s strategy in the Resistance, the formation of a 'mass party', the period of difficult coalition government and the subsequent years of opposition. Part two deals with the years 1956-64: from the Hungarian crisis to Togliatti's death. The main topic considered here is the PCI's concept of 'polycentrism' and structural reforms. Part three (1964-80) constitutes rather an extended conclusion, with interesting insights on the PCI's 'Eurocommunism' and 'historical compromise'. As Hobsbawm writes in the foreword, 'Sassoon's book is based not only on an impressive command of the sources and literature, but also on a considerable first-hand knowledge of both Italy and its Communist Party, and on an understanding [. . .] of the complexities of both'.

605   **The Italian Communist Party: yesterday, today, and tomorrow.**
Edited by Simon Serfaty, Laurence Gray.   London: Aldwych Press, 1980. 256p. bibliog.

A collection of essays by a variety of scholars, all at one time or another associated with the Johns Hopkins Centre of Advanced International Studies, in Bologna. The aim of the compilation is to offer an introduction to the history and policies of the Italian Communist Party (PCI), at a time when it was attracting much attention both in Italy and abroad (especially in the United States). Although the contents are mainly descriptive, different views emerge – none of which anticipates the relatively rapid decline of the party. In the first part the PCI's strategy from Gramsci to Berlinguer is investigated, with contributions by the editors, F. Mancini, E. Di Nolfo, and G.

Pasquino. Part two covers the PCI's foreign policies and the response from the United States, the USSR and western Europe, and includes essays by A. M. Gentili and A. Panebianco, C. Terzi, R. E. Osgood, M. M. Harrison, G. Luciani and G. Sacco, and P. Hassner.

606 **Italian communism: the escape from Leninism.**
Cris Shore. London; Concord, Massachusetts: Pluto Press, 1990. 246p. bibliog.

The research for this book involved intensive fieldwork (mainly in Perugia). The first part deals with the structure and cultural identity of the Italian Communist Party (PCI), by examining the historical development of its ideology and organization. The post-war success, it is argued, was due to three factors: the independence from the Soviet Union; the development of its own strategy ('the Italian road to socialism'); and the party's strong social role within Italian society. The vanguard (or autocratic) role of the leadership is scrutinized in the second part. The topic lends itself to a more theoretical discussion of the PCI's 'awkward Leninist legacy of democratic centralism'. Although democratic centralism and pluralist democracy are incompatible, the PCI appeared to square the circle, in that democratic centralism was employed by a farsighted leadership to orchestrate the progressive changes which a more conservative mass membership was reluctant to inspire.

607 **Peasant communism in southern Italy.**
Sidney G. Tarrow. New Haven, Connecticut; London: Yale University Press, 1967. 389p. bibliog.

Tarrow carries out an investigation of political development and comparative communism, with important theoretical contributions to both fields of research. His central argument is that the communist ideology of southern peasants in the immediate post-war years was adopted 'as an ideology of liberation in a backward society', but soon became 'an ideology of backwardness in contact with that society'. The first chapters discuss the economic, social and political setting. An analysis of the communist party follows, with emphasis placed on the difference between the votes, structure and leadership, in the north and south. The last chapters provide the conceptual explanations and focus on the 'ideology of backwardness', the 'mobilization of peasants', and their subsequent demobilization caused by the new structure of power, based on the Christian Democrats' dominance and the use of the resources of the State through patronage. There are many statistical tables.

The centre

608 **Italian Christian democracy: the politics of dominance.**
Robert Leonardi, Douglas A. Wertman. Basingstoke, England; London: Macmillan, 1989. 280p. bibliog.

The Christian Democratic Party (DC) had been in power since 1945, without any interruption when this book appeared. Even when the Prime Minister belonged to an allied party, the DC was the dominant force of the governing coalition. The DC's political foundations and development in power are competently examined, with the emphasis on the factional nature of the party, its organization and electorate. The issue of the Church's role in Italian society and its relationship to the State is also considered. The main characteristics of the DC, as summarized in the final chapter, are: anti-communism, moderatism, catholicism, and a multi-class base. The authors conclude by writing that 'the DC's unparalleled record among parties in Western democracies [. . .] is very likely to be extended well beyond the late 1980s'. In fact, by 1995 the DC had disintegrated, and its main relic – renamed *Partito Popolare Italiano* moved to the opposition in 1994. However, this does not diminish the validity of this study in the 'politics of dominance'.

609 **The politics of faction: Christian Democratic rule in Italy.**
Alan S. Zuckerman. New Haven, Connecticut; London: Yale
University Press, 1979. 252p. bibliog.

Two introductory chapters establish the conceptual and theoretical framework which is to be employed for this study of the Christian Democratic Party (DC). The starting point is the political competition which leads to the emergence of a political elite. This is structured like a pyramid, built upon and bound together by chains of personal ties which are technically known as 'clientelistic factions' and 'political clienteles'. The changing forms of such clienteles in contemporary Italy are then discussed, but the main body of the text focuses on the development, electoral results and organization of the DC. The subsequent two chapters connect the case of that party to the theoretical framework established at the beginning by looking into the nature of factions and assessing their influence in policy-making. Some stimulating general questions are raised in the two final chapters, namely: the future of DC's clientelistic rule and comparisons on a cross-national perspective.

The right

610 **Neo-fascism in Europe.**
Edited by Luciano Cheles, Ronnie Ferguson, Michalina Vaughan.
London; New York: Longman, 1991. 300p. bibliog.

Two essays on the Italian neo-fascist party (*Movimento Sociale Italiano*) are included here. R. Chiarini provides a historical profile of the MSI, in which he emphasizes both the persistence and the limited importance of the party's appeal (around five per cent). The deradicalization of politics in the 1980s induced the MSI to shift its strategy from radical and total opposition to the system to focusing their initiatives on particular issues, such as the reform of the State. The self-image of the MSI through its own posters is the topic developed by Cheles in the second essay on that party. Thirty-two posters are reproduced. The argument sustained is that until around 1970 the MSI posters resorted to traditionally fascist images; the style then diversified, borrowing images ranging from Renaissance iconography to the fashionable graphics of the radical left, while the connection with the fascist era was made through allusive motifs.

611 **Stefano Delle Chiaie: portrait of a black terrorist.**
Stuart Christie. London: Anarchy Magazine, Refract Publications,
1984. 183p. bibliog.

This sketchy biography of a notorious neo-fascist is interwoven with a survey of Nazism in the post-war world. Suspected to have taken part in various terrorist activities in Italy, Delle Chiaie found refuge abroad, first in Spain and then in Latin America, where he was still hiding when this book was published. Called 'the black pimpernel' because of his elusiveness, he was arrested in Venezuela in 1987 and extradited to Italy, where he was accused and tried for 'subversive association'. He was eventually released because of 'insufficient evidence' in 1990. This is a useful, if fragmentary, study of right-wing subversion in Italy and worldwide. The several chapters contained in the book are broken down further into many shorter sections, interspersed with a large number of photographs of rather poor quality. The bibliography is slim.

612 **The radical right: a world directory: a Keesing's reference publication.**
Compiled by Ciarán Ó. Maoláin. Harlow, England: Longman, 1987. 500p.

Italy receives less attention here than either France or Germany, let alone the United Kingdom. This is only partly justified by the relatively little importance of the Italian parties and movements which openly state their right-wing stance. In fact, the influence of the radical right in post-war Italy is much greater than those organizations appear to exercise, because of the intricate network of more or less hidden connections they have with State departments (especially in the area of security and intelligence). However, the eight pages dedicated to Italy do contain comprehensive and detailed references on various right-wing organizations, from the parliamentary party of the right (*Movimento Sociale Italiano*) to movements based on political journals (such as *Il Borghese* and *Diorama Letterario*). An exhaustive list of defunct organizations is also provided, together with brief notes on a myriad of small, mainly local movements.

613 **After Mussolini: Italian neo-fascism and the nature of fascism.**
Leonard B. Weinberg. Washington, DC: University Press of America, 1979. 88p.

Until the publication of this concise book, Italian neo-fascism had been largely ignored by British and American scholars. After an introduction to the nature of fascism, Weinberg charts the history of neo-fascism in post-war Italy. He traces its origins in the meeting of two different streams of former followers of Mussolini: the southern conservative people who were at first attracted by Guglielmo Giannini's short-lived movement *L'uomo qualunque*, and those who had remained loyal to Mussolini's Social Republic and began to resurface in 1946. The subsequent debate on renewal and continuity, and the contrasting condition of isolation and openings are lucidly surveyed. In the conclusion, Weinberg discusses the relationship between Italian neo-fascism and fascism in general, and argues that the political direction of the former (and similar movements elsewhere) is 'a reflection of the different external stimuli to which they are exposed in diverse national contexts'.

Elections

614 **[Electioneering in] Italy.**
Stephen Gundle. In: *Electioneering: a comparative study of continuity and change.* Edited by David Butler, Austin Ranney. Oxford: Clarendon Press, 1992, p. 173-201. bibliog.

After outlining the static characteristics of electoral campaigning in Italy during the 1950s and 1960s, Gundle focuses on the process of change which manifested itself in the late 1970s and gathered momentum throughout the 1980s. These innovations involved 'an altered mass media system, a reduction in the output of conventional activism, a more assertive press, recourse to outside professional assistance by the parties and a greater emphasis on leadership'. The 'Americanization' of Italian politics through the brash images of television was pioneered by the entrepreneur and media magnate Berlusconi, through his private TV network. At the root of his 'spectacularization' of electoral campaigning – Gundle points out – stood Italy's social and political changes. We know that this tendency has achieved full development in the 1994 electioneering, when Berlusconi himself 'took the field' as a leading contender and the catalyst of the right-wing spectrum.

615 **Italy at the polls, 1983: a study of the national election.**
Edited by Howard G. Penniman. Durham, North Carolina: Duke University Press, 1987. 216p.

The third and last volume of a series on Italian elections, produced by the American Enterprise Institute for Public Policy Research (AEI). A concise introduction highlights the main features of the previous two elections (1976 and 1979), and the government changes which preceded the 1983 election. A full background picture of post-war Italian elections is offered in the first nine chapters, by Norman Kogan. The subsequent chapters consider such topics as the electorate, the political parties, the unions, and the mass media, with contributions by G. Sani, D. A. Wertman, M. Fedele, K. R. Nilsson, R. Leonardi, C. A. Mershon, W. E. Porter, and J. LaPalombara (who emphasizes the ambiguity of the electoral result). Appendices provide information on the process of government formation in Italy and some technical electoral details.

Political theory

616 **Modern Italian social theory: ideology and politics from Pareto to the present.**
Richard Bellamy. Cambridge, England: Polity Press, in association with Basil Blackwell, 1987. 215p. bibliog.

This is the first clear and comprehensive English-language survey of the development of social and political theory in modern Italy. The intellectual tradition and the social and economic conditions of the country provide the context for the study of six major thinkers, with a chapter dedicated to each of them: Vilfredo Pareto; Gaetano Mosca;

Antonio Labriola; Benedetto Croce; Giovanni Gentile; and Antonio Gramsci. Each chapter contains a biographical outline of the relevant thinker, a discussion of theory and an examination of the application they made of their own theories to the understanding of Italian society. Two concluding chapters deal, respectively, with the post-war debate on the left (centred on Bobbio, Della Volpe and Togliatti) and some general remarks on social theory and political action. A useful glossary contains notes on Italian terms, politicians and minor political theorists to whom frequent reference is made in the text.

617 **Gramsci and the Italian State.**
Richard Bellamy, Darrow Schecter. Manchester; New York: Manchester University Press, 1993. 203p. bibliog.

Unlike most of the many books written on Gramsci, which are more interested in his works for what they can add to the debate on Marxism, this study returns the famous founder of the Italian Communist Party (PCI) to his historical context. To this end, the authors examine the contemporary debate on the nature of the Italian State, and its influence on Gramsci's thinking. They argue that Gramsci's Marxism was strongly influenced by the particular social and political condition of Italy. A biographical outline of the thinker is followed by six chapters on his political apprenticeship, the *biennio rosso* (1919-20), the establishment of the PCI and the struggle against fascism (1921-26), and his Prison Notebooks. The last topic is analysed in great detail and is covered in three chapters, devoted, respectively, to: historical materialism and Croce's historicism; the concepts of hegemony, State and party; and the issue of the *Risorgimento* and the new order.

618 **Italy: society in crisis/society in transformation.**
John Fraser. London; Boston; Henley, England: Routledge & Kegan Paul, 1981. 307p. bibliog.

Fraser presents a Marxist analysis of Italian society and politics in the light of classical 'crisis theory' and its more refined versions. The Italian case offered a good example for such study, as the country was going through a serious economic and social crisis during the 1970s, at a time when it appeared that a political transformation was also taking place, with a successful Communist Party. Fraser takes into account the theoretical foundations of the left's response to the Italian crisis. Basically these can be reduced to two forms: those of the revolutionary-subversive, and the bureaucratic-organized one. The *Autonomia* movement (who had Toni Negri as one of its leaders) represented the first strand, while the second found its advocate in the Communist Party. A brief first part deals with the theoretical framework, whereas a more substantial second part articulates the Italian crisis.

619 **Italian fascism: from Pareto to Gentile.**
Edited and introduced by Adrian Lyttelton, translated from the Italian, unless otherwise indicated, by Douglas Parmee. London: Jonathan Cape, 1973. 318p. bibliog.

This collection of translated writings on the ideological roots of fascism begins with the famous encyclopaedia entry on *Fascismo*, written by Mussolini in collaboration with Gentile. It also includes: excerpts from Pareto's works; extracts from a speech by Papini; an article by Prezzolini; various items by Corradini; an extract from a novel written by a painter (Soffici); D'Annunzio's *Letter to the Dalmatians* (1919); a few pages from *The defeat of Socialism* (1918), by Lanzillo; Marinetti's Futurist Manifesto and a newspaper article; Malaparte on 'Mussolini and national syndicalism'; writings by Alfredo Rocco, from 1914 to 1926; and an extract from Gentile's *The origins and doctrine of Fascism* (1934). In his introduction Lyttelton underlines the cultural poverty of fascism, and the 'uneasy symbiosis' produced by the official doctrine, in which 'incompatible schools of thought were united only in their dislike and fear of free discussion and reasoned argument'.

Political and social movements

620 Revolutionary and dissident movements: an international guide.
Edited by Henry W. Degenhadt.   Harlow, England: Longman, 1988.
466p.

For each of the 170 countries included in this volume there is a short introduction outlining its history and politics. In the nine-page section which concerns Italy, it is stated that because of a notable reduction of terrorist activities, 'by 1987 Italy had introduced a lenient prison regime for [repentant] convicted terrorists, who were permitted to take social leaves of absence from prison'. The following right-wing movements are surveyed: *Nuclei Armati Rivoluzionari*; *Ordine Nero*; *Avanguardia Nazionale*; *Ordine Nuovo*; and *Propaganda Due* (that is, P2). In addition, several more left-wing groups are included: three pages are given over to the *Brigate Rosse* while the other notable subversive organizations are: *Nuclei Armati Proletari*; *Prima Linea*; *Colonna Walter Alasia*; *Autonomia Operaia*; and *Potere Operaio*. A brief reference is also made to the German-speaking independence movement in South Tyrol.

621 Italy.
Giovanni Lodi.   In: *International social movement research: a research annual: vol. 3: peace movements in Western Europe and the United States.*   Edited by Bert Klandermans.   Greenwich, Connecticut; London: Jai Press, 1991, p. 203-24. bibliog.

In his contribution on the Italian peace movement Lodi argues that peace mobilization in his country went through three distinct phases. In the first stage the early post-war movement coincided with the most dramatic period of the 'Cold War' (1948-52) at which time the Communist Party was the dominant force behind it. The second phase (1968-72) was influenced by the student movement and their criticism of the American intervention in Vietnam; Catholic forces were influential here, as well as a wide range of other groups. The third phase (1981-85) was a reaction to the installation of 'Euromissiles', some of which were set up in eastern Sicily. The essay focuses in particular on the first phase, analysing the structure of the Italian peace movement at that time, and its mobilization strategies. A series of conclusive points suggest that the Italian movement provides interesting indications 'as to the nature of emergent forms of collective action'.

622   **States of emergency: cultures and revolt in Italy from 1968 to 1978.**
       Robert Lumley.   London; New York: Verso, 1990. 377p. bibliog.

This is an excellent and comprehensive social and intellectual history of contemporary Italy. It deals with the rise of the student movement in the late 1960s, which emerged from a crisis in Italian society and its institutions, the failure of the State educational system to meet the challenges of a modern society, and the parallel growth of unrest in the labour movement especially in northern Italy. The author then goes on to describe the rise of extreme left-wing violence, the red brigades, the feminist movement, and lastly, of *sinistrese*, a slang language peculiar to left-wing dissenters. The four separate parts deal, respectively, with: the origins of the 1968-69 crisis; the students' movement; the workers' movement; and the social movements and protest in the 1970s. There is a glossary of organizations, and a fine collection of cartoons and various illustrations, arranged in such an order as to provide 'the story in pictures'.

623   **Democracy and disorder: protest and politics in Italy, 1965-1975.**
       Sidney Tarrow.   Oxford: Oxford University Press, 1989. 400p.
       bibliog.

Tarrow produced this account of the social movements in Italy at a time of general crisis and amid hopes of regeneration. The decade under consideration saw the expansion of mass politics and this in itself is regarded by Tarrow as a positive and lasting phenomenon. Part one outlines a theoretical approach to the origin and manifestation of protest cycles. Part two deals with the students' movement, the workers' movement, and the religious movements. Part three focuses on the new 'extra-parliamentary' left, in general, and on two groups in particular (*Potere Operaio Toscano* and *Lotta Continua*). Part four draws some conclusions. Firstly, it is noted, some protest groups chose the path of institutionalization, while others opted for violence. Secondly, it is pointed out that even young democracies such as Italy 'can have extraordinary power to adapt to protest cycles'. Several tables and graphs are included.

The Church and Christian movements

624   **Chiesa e Stato: Church-State relations in Italy within the contemporary constitutional framework.**
       P. Vincent Bucci, with a foreword by Herbert J. Spiro.   The Hague:
       Martinus Nijhoff, 1969. 132p. bibliog.

The first chapter of this rather fragmentary but interesting book analyses the debate on the insertion of the 1929 Lateran Pacts into the Republican Constitution, which took place at the Constituent Assembly in 1947. Next is a study of the controversial case of the 'Bishop of Prato', who in 1956 loudly condemned as 'public sinners' two young people whose wedding had taken place only before the civil authorities. The ensuing trial offered fresh interpretations of the Church-State relations. The equally complex question of non-Catholic confessions is then discussed, under the general category of freedom of religion. A survey of the pre-war background and post-war development is followed by a consideration of some conflictual cases, involving a Pentecostal group, an American missionary of the Church of Christ, and an Italian evangelical minister. Bucci criticizes the constitutional recognition of the Lateran Pacts which secured a privileged position for the Catholic Church.

625 **Italy and the Vatican: the 1984 Concordat between Church and State.**
Maria Elisabetta De Franciscis.   New York; Berne; Frankfurt; Paris: Peter Lang, 1989. 349p. bibliog.

De Franciscis first provides a historical perspective on the subject by surveying relations between the Church and State in Italy from the unification of the country (1861) to the 1929 Lateran Accords. The slow revision process is then considered, from the moment in which the Accords were incorporated into the Italian Republican Constitution (1947), to the time when the necessity of a revision was accepted by both parties. Three major chapters contain the analysis of the 1984 Concordat. The author argues that the new Concordat is more than a revision, in that it aims at redressing the balance of mutual influence between Church and State by establishing a more thorough separation; it also provides the basis for a more equal relationship between the State and the other religious denominations. Appendices include the text in English of the 1984 Concordat and political cartoons on the history of Church and State relations in Italy.

626 **Church and State in Italy, 1850-1950.**
Arturo C. Jemolo, translated by David Moore.   Oxford: Basil Blackwell, 1960. 344p.

This book is one of the classic studies of Church-State relations in Italy, spanning a century of dramatic changes: the unification of the country and the conflict with the Pope; the gradual entry of Catholics into Italian politics; the rise of fascism and the 1929 Lateran Pacts; and the hegemony of the Christian Democratic Party after the Second World War. Jemolo's work of synthesis is still unrivalled for comprehensiveness and lucidity. The version annotated here is the well-translated version of an abridged edition of the original study. After a survey of the background during the *Risorgimento*, the narrative follows a strict chronological order. The longest chapter is devoted to the fascist era, with many details and subtle analysis. A brief postscript, on the period 1958-59, mentions the election of Pope John XXIII, of whom it is said that 'unlike his predecessor, [he] may intend to make less use of the authority of the Holy See'.

627 **Christian democracy in Italy: 1860-1960.**
Richard A. Webster.   London: Hollis & Carter, 1961. 229p. bibliog.

First published in the United States under the title of *The cross and the fasces* (1960), this is a study of Catholic movements in Italy during the one hundred years following the unification of the country. The first part examines the Christian democratic movements and their failures, up until 1929, when the Vatican and Mussolini's government signed the Lateran Pacts. The rise and fall of the Popular Party (1919-26) is competently treated. The second part draws on primary sources to analyse the revival of Catholic movements from 1929 to the end of the war. An epilogue comments on the success of the Christian Democratic Party after 1945 and enables

Webster to conclude that 'when the political climate is right, Catholic movements can shape Church-State relations to the advantage of the Church'. Two appendices provide supplementary information on the programmes of the movements (1899-1948), and the electoral situation of Catholic parties (1919-48).

Corruption

628   God's banker: an account of the life and death of Roberto Calvi.
Rupert Cornwell.   London: Victor Gollancz, 1983. 260p.

Cornwell was the Italian correspondent for the *Financial Times* when the story of the banker Roberto Calvi turned into high drama, culminating in his death by hanging under Blackfriars Bridge in London. The author's controlled, professional style is applied to what he calls 'an uncommonly complicated tale'. The beginning of Calvi's career is outlined and the entanglement between politics, economics and the Vatican presence is lucidly investigated. A long list of characters are introduced as the story becomes more complex and murky, including the Vatican's financier Michele Sindona (whose bankruptcy contributed to Calvi's demise), and Licio Gelli, the 'Venerable Master' of the mysterious freemason lodge at the centre of a political scandal in the early 1980s. Calvi's death, which remains a mystery, is dealt with swiftly, as are the subsequent events. The book is illustrated with some photographs.

629   Spider's web: Bush, Saddam, Thatcher and the decade of deceit.
Alan Friedman.   London; Boston: Faber & Faber, 1993. 455p.

Although Italy does not appear in the title of the book, it was very much a part of the 'spider's web' admirably undone by Friedman. In fact, the whole story of deceit and corruption which provided Saddam Hussein with the money to purchase all sorts of weaponry, began within the secret rooms of the *Banca Nazionale del Lavoro* (BNL). The miscalculated and illegal series of operations were solicited by President Reagan and implemented through the bank's representative office in Atlanta. The BNL is not an irrelevant institution: for some time, it was the leading Italian bank and part of the state-controlled credit system. It was only when the BNL's enormous losses were exposed that the international scandal broke, a scandal 'that would eventually lead investigators to question the secret policies and actions of Presidents Reagan and George Bush, Prime Minister Margaret Thatcher, and leading members of Italy's political class'. Many documents are reproduced in the appendix.

630   The Calvi affair: death of a banker.
Larry Gurwin.   Basingstoke, England; London: Macmillan, 1983. 250p. bibliog.

The first half of this book illustrates Calvi's triumphant career, which came to a halt when he refused to help his early mentor, the bankrupt financier (and mafia-associate) Michele Sindona. Sindona's *vendetta* was able to hit the target because in his path to glory Calvi had made some shadowy deals. Events precipitated further when his name was also involved in the scandal of the scheming freemason lodge, P2. Calvi was then arrested, but soon released, after which he decided to go abroad and was eventually found hanging under Blackfriars Bridge in London. The second half of the book concerns Calvi's death and the inquiry. Attention is paid to the odd circle of friends who had accompanied Calvi to London, and to a financial institution belonging to the Vatican. An 'open verdict' was returned by the jury at the inquest although at the end of 1992 the Italian judiciary decided to re-open the case. There is a good selection of photographs.

631   **The moneychangers: how the Vatican Bank enabled Roberto Calvi to steal $250 million for the heads of the P2 Masonic Lodge.**
Charles Raw.   London: Harvill, 1992. 520p.

The long subtitle expresses exactly the subject of this lengthy volume. It is a meticulous and thorough new investigation of the saga of power and corruption surrounding the still quite mysterious death of Calvi. The fact that money figures are indicated in dollars, normally in units of millions, demonstrates the international dimension and magnitude of the affair. The intricacies of the affair are unravelled in a readable manner, and moral condemnation is equitably distributed. If 'the main beneficiaries of the fraud were the heads of the P2 masonic lodge, Licio Gelli and Umberto Ortolani', Raw demonstrates that it was the American archbishop Paul Casimir Marcinkus who provided the mechanism which enabled Calvi to divert something like a quarter of a billion dollars. Several documents (mostly in Italian) are reproduced in the appendix.

Terrorism and violence

632   **The Red Brigades and left-wing terrorism in Italy.**
Edited by Raimondo Catanzaro.   London: Pinter, 1991. 216p.

This publication contains an account of some of the main results of a wide-ranging research programme on left-wing terrorism in Italy. The specific characteristics of Italian terrorism are mentioned in the editor's introduction: its duration in time; the mixture of right- and left-wing orientations; and the 'existence of a succession of different generational waves of militants in the armed struggle'. Among the contributors, S. Tarrow provides a study of 'Violence and institutionalization after the Italian protest cycle'. A historical profile of the Red Brigades is offered by G. C. Caselli, and their political ideology is investigated by Luigi Manconi. C. Novaro discusses a different subversive group, *Prima Linea*, presenting it as a case-study of social networks and terrorism. Finally, Catanzaro provides an interpretation of political violence through an analysis of interviews with some fifty ex-terrorists. An appendix with an interview-outline, and a glossary complete the book.

633   **The De Lorenzo gambit: the Italian coup manqué of 1964.**
Richard Collin.   London: Sage, 1976. 68p.

Giovanni De Lorenzo was the General Commandant of the *Carabinieri* (a corps of the Italian army, which also performs the tasks of a police force) in the summer of 1964, when he made plans to topple the government and round up political and trade-union leaders of the left. De Lorenzo's career and ambitions are outlined by Collin, who sets the story in the context of the political changes of the early 1960s (establishment of a centre-left government) and the economic and ministerial crisis of the summer of 1964. The failure of the plot was partly due to the lack of support by the army, and partly to the reaction of the politicians who quickly managed to establish a new and relatively effective government. Collin is perceptive in pointing out that the De Lorenzo affair was only a revealing episode of a disturbing condition of Italian democracy and its enemies within.

634   **The revolutionary mystique and terrorism in contemporary Italy.**
      Richard Drake.   Bloomington, Indiana; Indianapolis, Indiana: Indiana
      University Press, 1989. 218p. bibliog.

The ideological origins of Italian terrorism are emphasized in this study. In what is arguably a rather schematic approach, Drake maintains that left- and right-wing violence was the manifestation of 'forces [which had] declared war on Italy's liberal political institutions and culture'. In fact, the emergence of the two 'faces' of Italian terrorism in 1969-74 is dealt with in the first chapter. The Red Brigades dominate the subsequent seven chapters, which range from their surging phase (1975-77), the kidnapping and murdering of Aldo Moro (1978), to their defeat in the early 1980s. Nevertheless, a chapter is also devoted to the case of Toni Negri's movement (*Potere Operaio*). A glossary includes many extreme movements of the left and right.

635   **The heart attacked: terrorism and conflict in the Italian State.**
      Alison Jamieson, with a foreword by Richard Clutterbuck.   London;
      New York: Marion Boyars, 1989. 306p.

This is a vividly-told story of Italian terrorism in the 1970s, centred on the kidnapping and murder of Aldo Moro. The background to the Italian political crisis during that decade is only sketched, but the author offers a readable account of a very complicated affair. In Jamieson's view the defeat of terrorism was due to the cumulative effects of the anti-terrorist laws of 1979-82, and in particular the inducements provided for 'repentant terrorists'. However, she also mentions the importance of mass rejection of violence by the Italians. The conclusion that 'the world of the Italian armed struggle begins and ends with myth' is rather simplistic but the reader will find most interesting appendices, including the transcription of an interview with Adriana Farandola, a female terrorist.

636   **Days of wrath: the public agony of Aldo Moro.**
      Robert Katz.   London; Toronto; Sydney; New York: Granada, 1980.
      352p.

This is the story of the kidnapping, captivity and assassination of Aldo Moro by the Red Brigades in 1978. It is based on reports in the Italian press, Moro's letters (those which were known at the time Katz wrote the book), documents released by his captors, and interviews. The account was written in 1979, when the kidnappers and murderers were still at large and subsequent works on Italian terrorism provide more comprehensive accounts. Notwithstanding, this truly Italian tragedy offers Katz large scope to exercise his journalistic narrative technique spiced with dramatic style. The book will have more appeal to the general reader (with preference for sensational thrillers) than to the scholar. A chronology of the period between the day of the kidnapping and that of the autopsy is added, as are two diagrams of the actual kidnapping, an 'organizational chart' of two Red Brigade columns, and ten photographs.

637 **Red Brigades: the story of Italian terrorism.**
Robert C. Meade, Jr. Basingstoke, England; London: Macmillan, 1990. 301p. bibliog.

A well-researched and forcefully-argued study of the 'years of lead' in Italy, when the prolonged economic and social crisis was further aggravated by widespread political violence, both from the extreme right and the extreme left. The account begins with the involvement of the future founders of the Red Brigades in the students' turmoil of 1968. Their ideological background and development is outlined, emphasizing their utopian dream of transforming society by resolute actions. All major events involving the Red Brigades are analysed, from their first steps in the use of violence to the kidnapping and killing of Aldo Moro, to the subsequent emergency legislation and the defeat of the Red Brigades. Mead indicates that Italy's traumatic socio-economic transformation with its crisis of values, a tradition of strong left-wing ideology and right-wing violence, and the failure of the system to produce a credible alternative were all factors in the development of the terrorism.

638 **Political violence and terror: motifs and motivations.**
Edited by Peter H. Merkl. Berkeley, California; London: University of California Press, 1986. 380p. bibliog.

In part one, R. Drake discusses the origins of the radical right in contemporary Italy, focusing on the creative thinker Julius Evola, whose ideology developed in response to certain social and political characteristics of 20th-century Italy. In the second part, two contributions are relevant to Italy: L. Weinberg, on left- and right-wing terrorism in the peninsula; and G. Pasquino and D. Della Porta, on interpretations of Italian left-wing terrorism. Weinberg argues that historical and cultural preconditions made Italy vulnerable to political violence, but that the democratic State survived and indeed was strengthened. Pasquino and Della Porta survey and analyse the main sociological and non-sociological explanations of left-wing violence. The former look into either collective choice, or faults with the system whereas the latter emphasize individual psychopathologies.

639 **The politics of left-wing violence in Italy, 1969-85.**
David Moss. Basingstoke, England; London: Macmillan, 1989. 317p.

The distinctiveness of left-wing violence in Italy, Moss argues, lay in the internal divisions in both camps: those who here, only reluctantly, are called 'terrorists', and their opponents. Only a few of the former were prepared to take up armed struggle; as for the latter, their lack of a common view on the categorization of political violence inhibited any determined response at a national level. The main argument of the book is that 'neither the users of violence nor their opponents in fact had, or managed to construct, authoritative centres with the power and authority to define by fiat the issues of "armed struggle" and "terrorism" respectively'. The argument is developed by focusing on the patterns of recruitment and mobilization against political violence in politics, the judiciary, the forces of law and order, and among the workers' movement. There are some statistical tables and plates, mostly of courtroom scenes.

640 **The Moro affair and the mystery of Majorana.**
Leonardo Sciascia, translated by Sacha Rabinovitch. London; Glasgow; Toronto; Sydney; Auckland: Paladin Grafton Books, 1991. 175p.

The first and larger part of this book is devoted to the chronicle and comment on the kidnapping, 'trial' and murder of Aldo Moro by the Red Brigades in Spring 1978. The gripping story is recreated from Moro's letters, his captors' press releases, newspaper reports and speeches. This is a distinguished writer's denunciation of the ambiguous, if not callous, behaviour of the Italian ruling politicians who did not do all that was possible to save Moro's life. The whole affair, Sciascia elegantly and passionately argues, showed 'the imperceptible waning of any eagerness to find Aldo Moro'. The second, shorter part of the book discusses another Italian mystery, also based on facts, which is: the disappearance of a Sicilian nuclear physicist in 1938. Again, Sciascia queries the official account of Majorana's disappearance and sees him as a morbid, retiring man who symbolizes the ethical crisis of science.

641 **The Moro morality play: terrorism as social drama.**
Robin Erica Wagner-Pacifici. Chicago; London: The University of Chicago Press, 1986. 360p. bibliog.

As the author states in the preface, 'this is a book about many things'. In the first place, the kidnapping and assassination of Aldo Moro in 1978 is thoroughly investigated as a case-study of 'the ways in which a society "constructs" a social and political crisis and the roles that individuals and institutions play (or try to play) in this construction'. In addition, however, it is also a study of Italy in the late 1970s and of terrorism in general. The pervading analytical approach is to view the whole story and the wider context as a dynamic mix of reality and representation of events: terrorism as 'social drama' and theatrical self-consciousness. It is argued that a fundamental ambiguity can be shown by the dualism 'tragedy and melodrama': the former aiming at encouraging audience empathy with the victim, the latter excluding the audience from authentic identification with the victim.

642 **The rise and fall of Italian terrorism.**
Leonard B. Weinberg, William Lee Eubank. Boulder, Colorado; London: Westview Press, 1987. 155p. bibliog.

The authors explain that 'Italian terrorism appears to have been less like that experienced by other industrialized democracies and more like the sort of violence experienced in the 1970s by such fragile democracies as those of Argentina and Turkey'. However, they do admit that, unlike the case of the latter countries, Italy's democratic system was preserved, as there was no military intervention. The book consists of a concise survey of Italian terrorism, with an initial chapter on its causes, set against social, economic and political explanations. The two subsequent chapters deal, respectively, with 'black terrorism' and 'red terrorism', between 1969 and 1984. Other chapters discuss the sociological portrait of terrorists, the various forms of attacks and violence, and the response of the State.

643 **Puppetmasters: the political use of terrorism in Italy.**
  Philip Willan.   London: Constable, 1991. 375p.

A well-researched book, this forcefully argues that Italian terrorism was manipulated by political masters. In his introductory notes Willan writes that 'the Italian secret services played a crucial role in both the rise and the fall of Italian terrorism'. He also notes that a real reform of military intelligence never took place. The main text begins with the still unexplained background of the Bologna bombing of 2 August 1980, surveys the previous decade of widespread violence and terrorism, focuses on the P2 masonic conspiracy (and its connection with the United States), the recently emerged 'Operation Gladio' (NATO stay-behind network in Italy), and the long history of cover-up for this and similar schemes and attempted coups. A great deal of attention is then centred on the kidnapping and murder of Aldo Moro, and on the Red Brigades which 'having arisen from the left, had been allowed to operate in order to discredit the left'.

Italian first! From A to Z.
See item no. 1.

The Italians: how they live and work.
See item no. 3.

Alcide De Gasperi.
See item no. 331.

Mattei: oil and power politics.
See item no. 333.

Fra Lega e Chiesa. (Between the Northern League and the Roman Catholic Church.)
See item no. 463.

Comrades and Christians: religion and political struggle in communist Italy.
See item no. 482.

Culture and political economy in western Sicily.
See item no. 489.

Patron and partisans.
See item no. 492.

Men of respect: a social history of the Sicilian mafia.
See item no. 498.

The mafia and politics.
See item no. 505.

Black madonnas: feminism, religion and politics in Italy.
See item no. 527.

Italy.
See item no. 539.

Constitution and Legal System

644　The government of republican Italy.
John Clarke Adams, Paolo Barile.　Boston, Massachusetts; New
York; Atlanta, Georgia; Geneva, Illinois; Dallas, Texas; Palo Alto,
California: Houghton Mifflin, 1972. 3rd ed. 248p. 1 map. bibliog.

This is a clearly-written, classic text-book, which, first published in 1961, provides a
comprehensive and perceptive description of the Italian system of politics and
government. It consists of carefully titled chapters, which means that it can be easily
consulted as a reference source on various relevant topics. Two geographical and
historical chapters offer a concise background, with an emphasis placed on fascism.
The book then covers the following topics: the constitution; parliament; the president
of the republic; the council of ministers; the constitutional court; the administration;
local government; the judicial system; the party system; elections (with fine examples
of the electoral mechanism which lasted until the reforms of the early 1990s); the
economy; labour; and social security. A final chapter encompasses the broader issue
of Italy as a liberal democracy.

645　Italy: practical commercial law.
Roberto Barbalich.　London: Longman, 1991. 212p.

Provides a straightforward and comprehensive guide to Italian commercial law. A
concise survey of the Italian legal system and its characteristics is offered in the
introduction; the following thirteen chapters then outline the different subject areas of
commercial law and include specific information on the main topics involved.
Chapter one ('Industrial and intellectual property'), for example, deals with: patents;
trademarks; copyright; trade secrets; confidential information; and licensing. Other
general areas covered by the various chapters are: competition; setting up and running
a business; mergers and acquisitions; establishing agencies; distribution; franchising;
property and succession; employment and immigration; tax and banking; insolvency;
debt; and environmental and planning law.

646   **The Italian legal system.**
G. Leroy Certoma.   London: Butterworths, 1985. 520p. bibliog.
The book is divided into five parts, part one of which outlines the historical development of the system, the characteristics of the legal profession, and the divisions, sources and sphere of application of Italian law. Part two deals with public law and explores such topics as the constitutional system, the resolution of disputes, and criminal law. Part three consists of two chapters, one on civil law and one on commercial law, while two special areas are surveyed in part four: labour law and environmental law. A short final section offers indications as to how to research Italian law and supplies a wide bibliography, consisting, necessarily, almost entirely of items in Italian. Italian legal expressions are systematically indicated, together with their corresponding English words, and an explanation of the difference is given when required. An updated edition of this valuable book would be welcome.

647   **Consumer legislation in Italy: a study prepared for the EC Commission.**
Gustavo Ghidini.   Wokingham, England: Van Nostrand Reinhold, 1980. 108p.
This is part of a series of books on consumer legislation in the countries of the European Community. Ghidini outlines the general deficiencies of consumer protection in Italy in the first chapter. More specific issues are tackled in the subsequent sections, namely: the consumer and prices; consumer information, advertising and sale promotion; safety and quality of products and services; consumer credit; and standard contract clauses. The final chapter evaluates the means of law enforcement in the interest of the individual consumer. Despite the unsatisfactory characteristics of the Italian legal system in this field, the conclusion points out that a growing awareness of these problems is resulting in improved legal means to protect the consumer and the environment.

648   **Business law guide to Italy.**
Maisto & Misiali, Milan law firm.   Wiesbaden, Germany: CCH Europe, 1992. 441p. bibliog.
In this guide comprehensive information is provided about the Italian legal system, with emphasis placed on aspects connected with business and international transactions. Particular attention is also paid to relevant domestic issues such as labour law and environmental regulations. After an introduction on the Italian political structure and legal system, the book covers the following topics in a concise and effective style: exchange control; importing into Italy; business organizations; taxation (a particularly detailed section); accounting; banking and finance; insurance; real estate; investment incentives; sales and distribution; labour law; intellectual property; anti-trust law; judicial power (which focuses on the court system and arbitration); protection of the environment; and personal business. There is also a useful glossary.

649 **Italian law of companies, labour enterprise and economic organization: the Italian civil code, book five.**
Translated, annotated and with an introduction by V. G. Venturini.
Deventer, The Netherlands: AE. E. Kluwer, 1967. 245p.

The Italian Civil Code dates back to 1942, surviving Italy's defeat in the Second World War and the collapse of fascism. With minor amendments it is still the fundamental civil law of the country. The Code's fifth section, which is considered here (Book Five, articles 2060 to 2642) establishes the ground rules and legal definitions of companies, labour relations and enterprise organization. Venturini's introduction outlines the historical and legal background of the Civil Code; the bulk of the book then consists of the translation of the relevant section, with frequent footnotes mainly referring to subsequent integrating legislation. An analytical index relates the items to the corresponding articles of the Code.

650 **Italian company law.**
Piero Verrucoli. London: Oyez, 1977. 218p.

Despite the innumerable pieces of legislation that have modified Italian company law since the publication of this book, the fundamental characteristics of that system have not changed, and Verrucoli's work therefore still serves a useful purpose. It presents the main features of Italian commercial law in a concise and clear narrative form, with continuous but unintrusive references to the relevant legislation (in most cases the Civil Code). The five chapters of the work cover the following areas: a classification and description of civil and commercial companies; the various features of public companies (this is an extensive chapter); private companies; the procedures for winding up public and private companies, including the cases of dissolution, bankruptcy and other insolvency proceedings; and mergers, divisions and conversions of companies.

651 **The Italian penal code.**
Edited and translated by Edward M. Wise, in collaboration with Allen Maitlin. Littleton, Colorado: Fred B. Rotham; London: Sweet & Maxwell, 1978. 249p.

An integral translation of the Italian penal code (which came into force in 1931), as part of the American Series of Foreign Penal Codes, promoted by the New York University School of Law. A historical background is provided by the editor in his introduction. At the end of the war a committee to revise the penal code was set up but its suggestions were not acted upon. Subsequent proposed reforms fared no better. Lingering conservatism towards established institutions was one cause, but Wise argues that there were other, special reasons, notably, the code's technical merits of being 'closely coordinated with other laws such as the laws on public safety and the Code of Criminal Procedure which came into force at the same time'. However, the latter code was reformed in 1989 and perhaps the penal code will also, at last, be revised.

Italian first! From A to Z.
See item no. 1.

Italy.
See item no. 9.

Living in Italy.
See item no. 16.

Law dictionary.
See item no. 450.

The law and practice relating to pollution control in Italy.
See item no. 775.

Administration and Local Government

652 **Bureaucrats and politicians in western democracies.**
J. D. Aberach, R. D. Putnam, B. A. Rockman, with the collaboration
of T. J. Anton, S. J. Eldersvelt, R. Inglehart.   Cambridge,
Massachusetts; London: Harvard University Press, 1981. 308p.
bibliog.

This collective and comparative study is based on interviews with some 1,400 senior
servants and politicians in the United States, Britain, France, Germany, Italy, the
Netherlands and Sweden. The differences and similarities between the systems in the
different countries are considered first; then the guiding concepts and methods of
study are indicated. The interaction between bureaucrats and politicians is
subsequently explored and their ideological frame of mind assessed. There are
frequent and systematic references to Italy; for instance, on such topics as educational
attainment, geographical origin and social class, career mobility and the role of the
elites, party preferences and ideals. Sometimes the Italians are singled out, as is the
case with the particularly illiberal attitudes of their civil servants. But the main,
general discovery is 'the peculiar effects of American political institutions, which
seem to blur the differences between bureaucrats and politicians that are so sharp in
Europe'.

653 **Centre-local relations in Italy: the impact of the legal and political
structures.**
Bruno Dente.   In: *Centre-periphery relations in western Europe.*
Edited by Yves Mény, Vincent Wright.   London: George Allen &
Unwin, 1985, p. 125-48.

The author begins by surveying the major changes in the relations between central
and peripheral government in Italy, which were introduced in the 1970s. This process
is labelled 'institutional incrementalism', because of the gradual emergence of an
extensive series of new agencies to provide for representation in the local political
system. Italian centre-local relations, it is argued, are built within a framework in
which 'the main points of reference are the administrative rule, the existence of

rong national parties and the need for clientelistic consensus'. All three aspects
ontribute to contradictory tendencies, because – paradoxically – they may lead to the
rengthening of either centralization or local autonomy, as a result of a tradition of
rong central government and a tendency to fragmentation of political power. The
reation of regional governments, it is also pointed out, has changed more the form
han the substance of the centre-periphery relations.

54 **The Italian prefects: a study in administrative politics.**
Robert C. Fried.   New Haven, Connecticut; London: Yale University
Press, 1963. 343p. bibliog.

refects in Italy are the central government's agents in the territorial subdivision of
he State called 'province'. Their responsibility is to see that the government policies
re implemented at local level. Fried's book is over thirty years old, but it still
epresents one of the best studies of the historical development of prefects, and the
nly comprehensive work on this subject in English. The prefectoral system has not
ubstantially changed since the book appeared, despite the establishment of the
egions as semi-autonomous bodies in the 1970s, and the reorganization of the system
arried out in the early 1980s. The historical approach enables the author to address
he more general issue of the development of Italian public administration under
arying political, social and economic conditions.

55 **Red Bologna.**
Max Jäggi, Roger Müller, Sil Schmid, with an introduction by Donald
Sassoon, photographs by Otmar Schmid, and translated from the
German by Aidan Clark.   London: Writers & Readers, 1977. 207p.

assoon's introduction sketches the political and economic development and
mbalances in post-war Italy, and suggests that the well-run city of Bologna, led by
he Communists, offered a valid model of transition to socialism, for Italy as a whole.
The nine chapters which form the book focus on various aspects of Bologna's
dministration. In particular, Schmid deals with the historical background, urban
lanning and health policies; Jäggi concentrates on traffic policy, work and consumer
olicy; and Müller explores the areas of education, social policy and the provisions
or old people. A final section consists of an interview with the then mayor of the
ity, Renato Zangheri. Each chapter is full of factual information and includes several
mall photographs of Bologna's people in their every day activities.

56 **The civil service in liberal democracies: an introductory survey.**
Edited by J. E. Kingdom.   London; New York: Routledge, 1990.
220p. bibliog.

he countries involved in this comparative study are: Great Britain; Canada; France;
reland; Italy; Sweden; The United States; and West Germany. R. E. Spence
ontributes on Italy with an informed and lucid survey of the Italian civil service.
After a historical and political introduction, the study turns to a consideration of the
tructure of government, and the recruitment, career patterns and accountability of
ureaucrats. The failure to reform the civil service is stressed in the conclusion, which
lso points out how this is only part of a broader crisis of decision-making and
aralysis of the political system. Only a stable and stronger government, it is argued,
ould successfully undertake such reform.

657 **The regional reform in Italy: from centralized to regionalized State.**
Robert Leonardi. In: *The regions and the European Community: the regional response to the Single Market in the underdeveloped areas.* Edited by Robert Leonardi. London: Frank Cass, 1993, p. 217-46.

Leonardi first outlines the history of the relationship between regions and the nation-state, from 1862 to 1970, when the constitutional provisions for decentralization began to be implemented with regional elections. The author then surveys the two subsequent phases to decentralization: the first was dominated by national government and administrative elites, and took place between 1970 and 1972; the second phase was characterized by parliamentary control and developed between 1973 and 1977, when effective legislation for regional devolution was introduced. This is followed by a discussion on the unresolved problems of Italian regionalism, with particular reference to the issue of the southern regions and their economic conditions. The final section emphasizes the need to strengthen the regional reform *vis-à-vis* the move towards a more integrated Europe.

658 **Making democracy work: civic traditions in modern Italy.**
Robert D. Putnam, with Robert Leonardi, Raffaella Y. Nanetti.
Princeton, New Jersey: Princeton University Press, 1993. 228p. 5 maps.

This is an important work, resulting from a systematic empirical study of the Italian regions, and aimed at providing theoretical answers to the fundamental question of why some local democratic governments succeed, while others fail. The opportunity for the study was offered by the establishment of fifteen new regional governments in 1970. After a description of the ensuing two decades of institutional development, the focus is on the different performances of the regions and on their causes. The level of economic development is only one factor; the main explanation of good performance, Putnam argues, is the level of 'civic community resulting from a complex historical process of social co-operation based on active citizen participation, trust and tolerance'. Thus, for instance, Emilia-Romagna outperforms Calabria. This 'social capital', Putnam concludes, cannot be easily built, 'but it is the key to making democracy work'. The text is interspersed with figures and tables.

659 **Between centre and periphery: grassroots politicians in Italy and France.**
Sidney Tarrow. New Haven, Connecticut; London: Yale University Press, 1977. 272p.

Tarrow's study is based on a series of interviews with the mayors of several French and Italian towns and cities. It is presented in three parts. The first deals with the concept of 'periphery', the development of political linkages in contemporary Italy and France, and the different results of 'national-local policy allocation' in both countries. The second part concentrates on the roles and strategies of the mayors as grassroots leaders: their policy brokerage; administrative and political activism; and the nature of clientelism. The final part offers a comparison of the structure of grassroots politics and assesses the relationship between overall political integration and fragmentation in the two countries. Both the similarities and the differences in the two systems are stressed. Several tables provide information on the empirical data.

The government of republican Italy.
See item no. 644.

Armed Forces and Defence

660 Army, State and society in Italy, 1870-1915.
John Gooch.   London: Macmillan, 1989. 219p. bibliog.

Narratives and analyses are combined in this well-researched study of the Italian army in the period between the completion of the *Risorgimento*, with the annexation of Rome, and Italy's entry into the First World War. It was not a time of glory for the army, nor had the Piedmontese army experienced much success in the period beforehand. Indeed, the situation was to remain constant thereafter. The merit of the book is that, as the title indicates, it is not about narrow military history, but about the relationship between politics and military organization. The central argument focuses on the military's isolation from politics, resulting in low professionalism and inefficiency. The Italian army, Gooch writes, was politically 'the servant of the State but regarded the crown as its true master. Professionally it bore old-fashioned Piedmontese attitudes into the twentieth century. Socially it mistrusted the Italian masses as volatile and unreliable'.

661 Italian army handbook, 1940-43.
Edited by W. Victor Madey.   Allentown, Pennsylvania: Game, 1984. 176p. 3 maps.

This is a pocket-sized, oblong-shaped, abridged version of the original handbook produced by the United States Military Intelligence Service in 1943. Illustrations and maps were added to this edition, whose contents follow the same structure as the complete manual, with six sections dealing with: recruitment and mobilization; organization; tactics; ranks and identification; armament and equipment (the largest part of the book); and the air force. Graphic information on uniforms and insignia is contained at the end of the volume, which also includes coloured plates not to be found in the original handbook.

662   Italian tanks and fighting vehicles of World War II.
Ralph Riccio.   Henley-on-Thames, England: Pique, 1975. 96p.
bibliog.

This booklet is full of technical information and pictures of Italian tanks, self-propelled guns and armoured cars, with an emphasis on the various types of tanks. A brief section on the designation of tanks explains, for instance, that M 13/40 stands for a medium tank of 13 tons introduced in 1940. Weight categories, however, did not correspond to either the Allied or the German categories so that the heaviest Italian tank, the P40, compared only to Allied and German medium-weight tanks (26 tons). Also included is a historical outline of Italian armoured vehicles, and the organization of armoured units and divisions. All vehicle types are listed and illustrated with many details on their specifications. Appendices offer further technical information on unit numbering, organization and tank battalions.

663   The Italian Navy in World War II.
James J. Sadkovich.   Westport, Connecticut; London: Greenwood
Press, 1994. 379p. bibliog.

This is a well-researched and interesting contribution to historical revisionism. The author persuasively argues that the Italian Royal Navy (as with all branches of the Italian forces during the Second World War) has been either neglected or grossly maligned, when judged in terms of the Axis effort in the Mediterranean. The work is divided into ten chapters. Sadkovich first writes about the building of the Navy and then provides detailed accounts of all its engagements with the British counterpart. Special attention is paid to air operations over Malta. Ultimately, the authors shows 'that the Italians performed well despite their handicaps, and that they were primarily responsible for tying down the bulk of British power in the Mediterranean basin for thirty-nine long months'. There are numerous tables and some effective illustrations. While no similarly stimulating book has been written on the Italian army, it is worth mentioning Frank McMeiken, *Italian military aviation* (Leicester: Midland Counties Publications, 1984. 288p. bibliog.). This is an illustrated guide to the current and past organization and equipment of the Italian Air Force.

664   Politics and security in the southern region of the Atlantic Alliance.
Edited by Douglas T. Stuart.   Basingstoke, England; London:
Macmillan, 1988. 210p. bibliog.

Luigi Caligaris, who writes the section on Italy, argues that only in the 1980s was there an open discussion of the country's defence problems. Therefore, after a background introduction, he concentrates on the relevant debate and on the efforts to restructure the Italian armed forces. Various aspects of the Italian defence problems are then discussed, with insistence on the traditional lack of interest in the issue shown by politicians as well as ordinary people, an attitude that is criticized here but hardly analysed. Rather simplistically, Caligaris concludes that to achieve modernization of the armed forces 'it is essential first to get decision-making right at both the political and military levels. If this were achieved, the rest would follow suit'. What 'the rest' should be, in today's post-Cold War world, is, of course, another matter.

665 The politics of the Italian army: 1861-1918.
John Whittam.   London: Croom Helm, 1977. 216p. bibliog.

Whittam demonstrates how ambitious Italian governments have periodically plunged one of the least militaristic of societies into aggressive wars. The first section of the book begins with the unification of Italy and considers the Piedmontese army of the preceding decade, as well as its transformation into the Italian army. The second part covers the army interventions in the following decade (against southern brigands and for the annexation of Venice and Rome), further reforms and the role of the military in the complex diplomatic game of the 1880s. The last part opens with the army and the crisis of Italian society in the late 1890s, the role of Giolitti and the Libyan war. I concludes with Italian neutrality, the country's intervention in the First World War and the recovery from the trauma of defeat at Caporetto.

Italy and the European Defence Community, 1950-54.
See item no. 675.

Foreign Relations

566 **Successful negotiations: Trieste 1954: an appraisal by the five participants.**
Edited by John C. Campbell. Princeton, New Jersey; Guildford, England: Princeton University Press, 1976. 182p. 2 maps.
The settlement of 1954, by which Trieste was returned to Italy and Istria given to Yugoslavia, is chosen as a model of successful diplomatic negotiation in solving one of the classical territorial disputes in European history. The final bilateral agreement between the two countries, however, was only signed in the year of this book's publication. An introduction by the editor provides a historical background to the problem. The main body of the book then consists of the memories of the five participants at the 1954 negotiations, held in London. The Italian representative was Manlio Brosio. The conclusion draws attention to the factors which contributed to the success of the negotiations: from the fortunate timing to the quality of the diplomats involved, and to sheer good luck. For all these reasons, it is argued, a similar success could not easily be replicated elsewhere.

567 **Italy and EC membership evaluated.**
Edited by Francesco Francioni. London: Pinter, 1991. 239p. bibliog.
There are four parts to this volume. The first concerns economic policies and contains contributions on monetary, agricultural, environmental, and fiscal policies. The second addresses the question of Italy's foreign relations. The third part is devoted to the political and legal systems; the topics covered here concern the impact of EC integration on the Italian form of government, on the political system, and on the legal and fundamental rights in Italy (written by Francioni himself). Finally, part four consists of one contribution on the relationship between the Community's objectives and Italy's social policies. In some cases the authors provide a description, rather than an evaluation of changes introduced in Italy. When they do assess the costs and benefits for Italy, it appears that the expected gains outweigh the losses. A general conclusion by the editor would have been useful.

668   **Securing peace in Europe, 1945-62: thoughts for the post-cold war era.**
Edited by Beatrice Heuser, Robert O'Neill. Basingstoke, England; London: Macmillan, in association with St. Antony's College, Oxford, 1992. 355p.

There are two contributions on Italy. The first, by A. Varsori, emphasizes the role of the United States in shaping Italy's foreign policy between 1948 and 1955. The aim was to help the Christian Democratic Party and its allies to keep the communists and socialists at bay. However, Italy's membership of Nato was a difficult choice for the country's government, despite the obvious limited role it would be expected to play in the Alliance. Italy's attitude remained lukewarm in those years although it warmed to the idea later. C. Nuti, in the second piece, outlines the Italian defence strategies in the early 1950s by evaluating Italy's support to the nuclear policies formulated by the Alliance. Three turning points are indicated: the development of tactical weapons; the installation of new missiles in southern Italy; and the debate on the 'multilateral force'. The Italian government systematically showed 'a keen interest in being included in any form of nuclear sharing'.

669   **The United States and Italy.**
Henry S. Hughes. Cambridge, Massachusetts; London: Harvard University Press, 1979. 3rd enlarged ed. 326p. bibliog.

The title is somewhat misleading, as this is a survey of Italian history, rather than a study of the relationship between the United States and Italy. It is only as a way to introduce his story that Hughes refers to the two countries, and only to warn his American compatriots about their misplaced views of Italy and the Italians. The author dismisses the widely-shared fear in the United States that the Italian Communist Party's success in the first half of the 1970s represented a threat to the West. Hughes shows a fine perception of Italy's political development, but he welcomes so much the 'historical compromise' that he is carried too far and sees it as the path towards conciliation between Catholicism and Communism. Most of the book is devoted to post-1945 Italy; the preceding chapters deal with the legacies of history. There is a statistical appendix and a section on suggested reading (mainly on books published in the United States).

670   **The politics of Italian foreign policy.**
Norman Kogan. New York: Praeger; London; Dunmow, England: Pall Mall Press, 1963. 178p.

The underlying argument of the book is that the internal environment dominated Italy's political decisions affecting its foreign policy. Hence, the stress is on the Italian political system as a whole, whilst the analysis centres on the ways in which such a system could orient the questions of foreign policy. This approach dictates the structure of the book, with the first part devoted to the general background and political behaviour. The large second part covers the sources of political power and their impact on foreign policy and the final, shorter part focuses on the perspectives of Italian foreign policy. The subservient position of Italy towards the United States is emphasized, and it is argued that this position is more indicative of the weakness of political leadership deriving from the 'fractured' nature of Italian society, rather than a persuasive commitment to an alliance with America.

671 **The United States and Italy, 1940-1950: the politics and diplomacy of stabilization.**
James E. Miller. Chapel Hill, North Carolina; London: The University of North Carolina Press, 1986. 356p. bibliog.

A carefully and widely-researched study of the process by which the United States became involved in Italian politics from the dramatic moment of the landing in Sicily of the Allied forces in July 1943. It is argued that from their previous reluctance to play any significant role in Italy's political development, the United States proceeded to impose their vision of post-war settlement and stability. Miller's conclusion is that 'American intervention, especially after 1950, was often needless meddling in the internal affairs of a nation whose commitment to democratic stabilization of Italy between 1940 and 1950 was a positive achievement, because the Italians were free to build a better society within the framework of a democratic State'.

672 **The American Constitution as a symbol and reality for Italy.**
Edited by Emiliana P. Noether. Lewiston, New York; Queenston, Ontario; Lampeter, Wales: The Edwin Mellen Press, in association with Pirandello Lyceum Press, 1989. 163p.

The bicentenary of the American Constitution was commemorated in this collection of papers presented at a symposium held in 1987 at Harvard University. Two themes were pursued: the influence of Italian political theorists, from Machiavelli to Beccaria, on the Founding Fathers of the American Constitution; and the influence of the American Revolution and Constitution on Italy and the Italians. The general historical setting is provided by the editor's introduction to the collection. M. D'Addio, K. Preyer and A. Grab discuss the influence of Italian thought on the Founding Fathers; E. Tortarolo deals with the interesting case of Philip Mazzei, an Italian immigrant close to Jefferson; G. Butta, E. P. Noether, E. Morelli and R. Grew offer contributions on the Italians' view of the United States, during the 19th century; and finally, F. J. Coppa concentrates on 'American constitutionalism and the separation of Church and State in Italy'.

673 **The United States, Italy and NATO, 1947-52.**
E. Timothy Smith. Basingstoke, England; London: Macmillan, 1991. 232p. bibliog.

This is a study of the United States' policy towards Italy in the early years of the cold war. The focus is on the American decision to include Italy in Nato, and the transformation of Italy into a rearmed member of the western camp. The United States security interests in Italy are considered *vis-à-vis* the existence of a strong communist party in that country. The reasons for the inclusion of Italy in Nato and the reactions to it (both in Italy and elsewhere) are explored in the light of rearmament and the militarization of American foreign policy. The United States debate on the revision of the peace treaty with Italy concludes this study. An interesting point is made at the end, when it is argued that the United States military and strategic influence over Italy weakened the impulse toward reform there and also 'led to the belief that security was attainable only through military strength'.

674 **Alto Adige – South Tyrol: Italy's frontier with the German world.**
Mario Toscano, edited by George A. Carbone. Baltimore, Maryland;
London: The Johns Hopkins University Press, 1975. 283p. 1 map.

This book is based on wide research and the personal recollections of the author, a
distinguished diplomatic historian who was also an Italian delegate at meetings with
Austrian representatives at the United Nations' general quarters. The main objective
of the book is the analysis of the De Gasperi-Gruber Agreement of September 1946,
and the consequent protracted discussion and controversial application. There is also
a historical account of the disputed region, with special attention devoted to its
annexation to Italy at the end of the First World War, the development during the
fascist period, and the changes introduced from the *Anschluss* to the end of the
Second World War. The events of the late 1960s are chronicled by the editor. It may
be noted that the 1969 Italian-Austrian package provided the basis for the 1972
Autonomy Statute, but was only implemented in 1992.

675 **Italy and the European Defence Community, 1950-54.**
Antonio Varsori. In: *Shaping post-war Europe: European unity and
disunity, 1945-1957.* Edited by Peter M. R. Stirk, David Willis.
London: Pinter, 1991, p. 100-11.

Varsori argues that Italy's attitude towards the Cold War was ambiguous, because the
country's membership of Nato was 'perceived by many Italian moderate anti-
Communist leaders and diplomats as an unpleasant necessity'. Not surprisingly,
therefore, the European Defence Community project aroused suspicion among Italian
leaders, which put them in a dilemma, since they were full-hearted supporters of
European political integration. There was no reaction from Rome when the French
parliament sank the defence project. In any case, Varsori concludes, Italy's role
throughout the process had been a minor one.

Stato dell'Italia. (The state of Italy.)
See item no. 7.

Ethnics in a borderland.
See item no. 359.

The 1891 New Orleans lynching and US-Italian relations.
See item no. 377.

**Stars, stripes and Italian tricolor: the United States and Italy, 1946-
1989.**
See item no. 567.

Italian foreign policy, 1918-1945.
See item no. 1051.

Economy

General

676 **An introduction to the Italian economy.**
Kevin Allen, Andrew Stevenson. London: Martin Robertson, 1974.
300p.

This is a comprehensive monograph on the development and persistent problems of the Italian economy, up until the early 1970s, when the post-war model of economic growth in the western world came to a halt. The authors provide an excellent descriptive and analytical study, commencing with an introduction and overview of Italy's pre-war economy and the early post-war recovery. After a general discussion on the two distinct periods of growth (1950-63 and 1964-72), the following topics are considered: the balance of payments; labour markets, labour costs and industrial relations; the short-term management of the economy; the problem of the south and the southern development policies; and the State holding sector and its role. There is an appendix containing further information on the political development and a postscript on the problems arising from the 1973-74 crisis: it is argued that the potential for long-term growth would remain.

677 **Saving and the accumulation of wealth: essays on Italian household and government saving behaviour.**
Edited by Albert Ando, Luigi Guiso, Ignazio Visco. Cambridge, England: Cambridge University Press, 1994. 408p.

This book contains the main results of a research project launched by the Bank of Italy in 1989. The purpose of the project was to investigate the numerous and complex factors underlying decision-making pertaining to saving in Italy. As Antonio Fazio, the Governor of the Bank of Italy, points out in his foreword, the Italian experience is of particular interest and concern, as it combines a strong propension to private saving with a huge public debt. The contents of the report are divided into three sections focusing, respectively, on 'Saving trends, government deficit and demographic changes', 'Life-cycle saving and precautionary motives' and

'Borrowing constraints, inter-generational transfers and bequests'. Some contributions are highly technical and riddled with mathematical formulations, while others are quite readable and informative. There are many tables and graphs, and two appendices discussing the methodology of the survey and statistical data.

678 **The Italian economy: heaven or hell?**
Edited by Mario Baldassarri. Basingstoke, England; London:
Macmillan; New York: St. Martin's Press, 1994. 222p.

How the 'new economic miracle' of the late 1980s could be transformed into the serious crisis of the early 1990s (with sky-rocketing national debt, surging unemployment and the devaluation of the currency) is the conundrum the editor tackles in the introduction. The following five essays, each written by distinguished economists, highlight various aspects of the predicament. F. Giavazzi and L. Spaventa cover the effects of inflation and disinflation. I. Cipolletta and A. Heimler deal with technological change and growth, in highly technical and obscure terms. S. Micossi and F. Trau examine the role of monetary and financial policies in industrial restructuring. D. Gressani, L. Guiso and I. Visco contribute with an abstruse analysis of disinflation, using the econometric model of the Bank of Italy. Finally, the editor and M. G. Briotti conclude with an interesting study of the public debt. The essays are full of statistics and graphs.

679 **Review of Economic Conditions in Italy.**
Banca di Roma. Rome: Banca di Roma, 1947- . quarterly.

An important quarterly journal containing analyses by leading Italian economists and up-to-date factual information on the Italian economic trends. The volumes are normally divided into: articles devoted to specific sectors or topical issues of the Italian economy; 'Notes and Comments' on contingent events and debates; book reviews; and a final, particularly useful section with bibliography cards on relevant publications. The last volume of each year contains an annual double index, by author and by subject. Sometimes issues are entirely dedicated to special topics, such as (to name some items dealt with in the early 1990s) the industrial census, the labour market, unemployment, and the reforms of monetary and financial markets in Italy.

680 **The recent performance of the Italian economy: market outcomes and state policy.**
Edited by Carluccio Bianchi, Carlo Casarosa. Milan: Franco Angeli,
1991. 309p. bibliog.

The eighteen essays written by Italian economists and gathered here, fall into six distinct sections: Macroeconomic policy and the pattern of economic growth; Export-led growth and trade performance; Uneven development; The labour market dynamics; Economic development and industrial strategies; and Monetary, exchange and Common Market policies. Some contributions contain complex econometric analyses, but on the whole it is an approachable book for the general reader. Two essays included in the first section are of particular note: one is on the Italian experience as an export-led economy (by A. Graziani); the other is an informative survey of the Italian economy in the 1970s and 1980s (by C. D'Anna and B. Salituro). Within the context of the European Community the last section also contains two important contributions: on Italy and the European Monetary System (by S. Vona), and on Italian agriculture and the Common Market policy (by G. Balestrieri).

681   **The irregular economy: the 'underground' economy and the 'black' labour market.**
      Bruno Dallago.   Aldershot, England: Dartmouth, 1990. 202p. bibliog.

Although some form of 'irregular economy' has always existed in regulated economic systems, there is now a new type of such phenomena: it is a much more dynamic, albeit 'hidden', component of economic development, based on rational decisions. The objective of the book is to compare the 'irregular economies' of different economic systems, focusing on the labour market. Examples are taken from two large countries with abundant natural resources (the United States and the former Soviet Union) and two medium-size economies (Italy and Hungary). The author first defines the terms used, providing facts and interpretations. Secondly, attention is addressed to the labour market. Finally, Dallago returns to general issues, namely the working of economic systems containing an irregular sector. An extensive bibliography contributes to make this book an important reference source on a subject affecting the Italian economy so profoundly.

682   **'The Economist' guide: Italy.**
      London: The Economist Books, Hutchinson, 1990. 256p. 1 map.

Intended 'first and foremost for business people travelling in Italy', this is also a useful book for a more general readership. After a brief introduction outlining Italy's post-war political and economic development, there is an overview consisting of highly informative briefings on topics ranging from the business, economic and political scenes, to business and cultural 'awareness'. The second half of the book constitutes a travel guide to a dozen main cities (including plans) with basic information on the relevant regions. It explains how to arrive at various destinations, how to get about, and what is worthy sightseeing. A large amount of information is provided on hotels and restaurants. On the former, readers are warned not to expect 'Teutonic efficiency or Scandinavian standards of cleanliness'. A short section with sundry practical advice completes the guide.

683   **Italy: country profile: 1992-93.**
      The Economist Intelligence Unit.   London, 1992. 50p. 1 map.
      bibliog.

An accurate source of information which appears in updated versions every year. It provides a most useful survey of the country's political and economic background, including an outline of the Constitution, the election results (from 1983 to 1992), health and social security. More detailed sections are devoted to the economy, with a general picture of the current conditions and specific information on the national accounts, employment, wages and prices, agriculture, energy, manufacturing, transport and communications, finance, foreign trade and balance of payments. Most sections contain statistical tables. A companion, quarterly publication to the *Country profile* is the *Country report*, also published by the Economist Intelligence Unit to monitor Italy's political, economic and business conditions.

684 **The underground economies: tax evasion and information distortion.**
Edited by Edgar L. Feige.   Cambridge, England: Cambridge University Press, 1989. 378p.

Feige deals with the still relatively uncharted territory of the economy's informal sector. Part two of the book examines the western developed countries and contains a wide-ranging contribution on Italy by B. Contini. He notes that the existence of a substantial irregular economy was at first detected as a result of an unlikely decline in the labour force participation rate. He then surveys the various manifestations of the phenomenon, from multiple job holding to the diffusion of work-at-home cottage industry and other forms of irregular working practices. An estimate of the size of the 'hidden' Gross National Product is proposed, based on data up to the late 1970s. It is then added, however, that such official figures probably underestimate the importance of the Italian underground economy, despite an attempt to make them more reliable.

685 **High public debt: the Italian experience.**
Edited by Francesco Giavazzi, Luigi Spaventa.   Cambridge, England; New York; Melbourne; Sydney: Cambridge University Press, 1988. 260p.

This book contains the text of papers presented at a conference held near Rome in 1987. Its topic was 'surviving with high public debt', and referred to Italy. Significantly, by the time the book appeared, the editors had removed the first two words, showing less confidence in the future of an Italian economy burdened by enormous government deficits. A comparative essay on various periods and countries affected by high public debt is written by A. Alesina. The following contributions resort to complex and technical language, but their conclusions can be understood by the general reader. They are: G. Tabellini, on monetary and fiscal policy with a high public debt; M. Pagano, on public debt and financial markets; A. Giovannini, on capital controls and public finance; and A. Bollino and N. Rossi, on public debt and households' demand for monetary assets. Each paper is followed by a brief discussion and there are several tables and graphs.

686 **Growth and structure in the economy of modern Italy.**
George H. Hildebrand.   Cambridge, Massachusetts: Harvard University Press, 1965. 475p. bibliog.

Hildebrand's book remains one of the best studies of Italy's economic development from 1945 to the 'economic miracle' of the early 1960s. Empirical data and sustained argument are interwoven throughout the ponderous volume, with frequent references to historical and institutional aspects. The author's guiding principle is that 'economic affairs are part of a larger system of behaviour whose determining forces are broad in compass, including as they do the nation's history, its culture and institutions, and even its geography'. The study is divided into three parts. Part one reviews the 'Italian miracle', examining monetary policies pursued in the late 1940s, and various aspects of the 'long boom': output, prices, savings, investment, foreign balance and money supply. Part two considers the labour market and discusses the issues of unemployment and wages. Finally, part three deals with the dual character of the Italian economy.

687 **Italy: a study in economic development.**
Vera Lutz, with a foreword by Frederic Benham, Muriel Grindrod.
London; New York; Toronto: Oxford University Press, 1962. 342p.
2 maps. bibliog.

Written at the peak of the Italian 'economic miracle', this book aroused as much interest as controversy. For the first time the dualistic nature of Italian economic development was studied as an interdependent system. A major cause in that imbalance, Lutz argued, was the excessive wage claims by the trade unions. The different consequences of those distortions on the large and small firms was emphasized. Attention was also devoted to the backwardness of southern Italy: here Lutz suggested that natural emigration, rather than capital investment induced by artificial incentives, would contribute to lasting economic growth. The importance of Lutz's book was recognized, but it was also pointed out that it was a descriptive, rather than a diagnostic study. There are three parts dealing, respectively, with Italy's economic dualism, the southern problem, and an assortment of special topics (such as wages and labour costs).

688 **Growth and territorial policies: the Italian model of social capitalism.**
Raffaella Y. Nanetti.   London; New York: Pinter, 1988. 183p.
bibliog.

This is the first comprehensive attempt in English at analysing the relationship between small-size firms and institutional devolution in Italy. Nanetti argues with other observers that the turning point was 1968-69, when challenges and demands forced significant changes in all aspects of Italian society. The author argues that the post-war period should be divided into two phases. Phase one (1945-69) was characterized by the dominant role of the State as policy-maker for the creation of basic infrastructures and the development of human resources. In the second phase (from 1970 onwards) regional governments assumed the primary role of meeting the needs of local economic and social interests. This is the background against which the diversified system of production, largely based on the diffusion of small enterprises, should be seen. A range of policies is considered, to show this development of Italy's 'social capitalism'.

689 **OECD Economic Surveys: Italy.**
Organisation for Economic Co-operation and Development.   Paris:
OECD, 1961- . annual.

These are informative yearly reports on Italy's economic conditions, containing many statistical tables, diagrams and a full chart with international comparisons of basic statistics. A general survey of recent developments and prospects is contained in each volume; from year to year topical features are then highlighted. The 1992-93 volume, for instance, focuses on the descent into recession, the widening of labour market slack and imbalances, the reduced wage and price inflation, and the improvement of the external balance. Macro-economic policies and prospects are examined, and a special section is devoted in this issue to the drive for privatization and structural reform. Finally, each volume contains some general conclusions.

690 **Italy: the sheltered economy: structural problems in the Italian economy.**
Fiorella Padoa Schioppa Kostoris, translated by John E. Powell.
Oxford: Clarendon Press, 1993. 258p. 1 map. bibliog.

The role of the public sector in the Italian economy has always been impressive and used to be praised as a major factor of the Italian 'economic miracle'. This is no longer so. In fact, the main aspect of this well-researched study is a censorious judgement on such interventionist policies: the author argues that much of the public action in the Italian economy is irrational, inconsistent and counter-productive. Firstly, she examines the causes of market failure, notably: the existence of pure public goods, externalities, natural monopolies, imperfect information and market incompleteness. Secondly, the following main areas of State intervention are investigated: the policies towards the south; industrial restructuring; employment; private investment; the welfare system; taxation; and the public debt. Legal deregulation and privatization is the recommended therapy to achieve higher rates of growth. There are continuous references to scholarly studies and many statistical tables.

691 **Monetary policy, fiscal policy and economic activity: the Italian experience.**
Edited by Francesco Spinelli, Giuseppe Tullio.   Aldershot, England: Gower, 1983. 103p.

The essays contained in this volume address the issue of the monetary and fiscal policies adopted by the Italian authorities in response to the external and internal shocks to which the country's economy was subjected during the 1970s. The traditional use by the Italian policy makers of monetary policy as a tool for short-term stabilization (mainly through credit rationing or credit expansion) is criticized for the negative side effects it entails. The first three chapters are devoted to monetary policy and are written, respectively, by D. E. W. Laidler; S. Calliari, F. Spinelli and G. Verga; and A. Penati and G. Tullio. Chapter four deals with fiscal policy and is by G. Tullio. It should be warned that all essays are dense and often full of jargon and technical formulations.

692 **The Italian economy.**
Donald C. Templeman.   New York: Praeger, 1981. 362p. bibliog.

This is an impressive work by an economist who manages to write about complex issues without resorting to technical jargon. There are two distinct but complementary parts. The first deals with the economic institutions and trends; in particular, the following macroeconomic variables are examined: labour cost; growth; employment; inflation; and international trade. Part two focuses on the levers which the authorities can use to achieve their economic targets: taxation; monetary policy; exchange control; and wage, price and employment policies. At the end of the troubled 1970s the signs of economic recovery were there, with a notable increase in productivity and a restored balance of payments. Nevertheless, some negative features remained, and in particular inflation and unemployment, which were both on the rise again. Strangely, no mention is made of Italy's entry into the European Monetary System (1979), which contributed to contain inflation. There are many statistical tables, mostly with data from 1960 to 1978.

693 **Italy chooses Europe.**
F. Roy Willis.   New York: Oxford University Press, 1971. 373p.
1 map. bibliog.

Despite the abundant and at times turbulent waters which have flowed under the European bridges since its publication, this book still offers useful insights to the readers and scholars of contemporary Italy. The first part chronicles the political and economic history of post-war Italy in the light of the country's strong European connections. The second part is thematic and examines Italy's eagerness to be part of a more integrated western Europe through an analysis of: the economic sectors; the demographic issue and the related problem of the south; the leading industrial companies and the pressure groups in industry and agriculture; the trade unions' view of the European Common Market; and the position of the main political parties, both in government and in opposition.

Regional and local

694 **Small firms and industral districts: the experience of Italy.**
Sebastiano Brusco.   In: *New firms and regional development in Europe.*   Edited by David Keeble, Egbert Wever.   London; Sydney; Dover, England: Croom Helm, 1986, p. 184-202. bibliog.

First of all, Brusco outlines and analyses the three models of small firms in Italy: the traditional artisan; the dependent sub-contractor; and the small firm in industrial districts. It is noted that the recent enormous spread of industrial decentralization has strengthened the second and third models. The author then deals with such general topics as the relationship between small firms and economy of scale, the pattern of regional variations in the characteristics of Italian small firms and industrial districts, and the role of local government in the development of such industrial districts.

695 **Return migration and regional economic problems.**
Edited by Russell King.   London; Sydney; Dover, England: Croom Helm, 1986. 276p. bibliog.

The impact of return migration on the economic conditions of the regions of origin is explored here through case-studies involving various countries. Italy has the lion's share, with three contributions which specifically consider its case. R. King, A. Strachan and J. Mortimer write about the emigrants returning to southern Italy, mainly from Germany and Switzerland. E. Saraceno investigates the occupational resettlement in relation to the regional development of Friuli-Venezia Giulia. L. Took deals with 'Land tenure, return migration and rural change in the province of Chieti'. The general conclusion, shared by all contributors, is that the effect of return migration depends to a large extent on the economic environment of the area in which people resettle. The editor provides an introduction on the various interpretative models of return migration, with an exhaustive bibliography.

696 **Return migration and rural economic change: a south Italian case study.**
Russell King, Jill Mortimer, Alan Strachan, Anna Trono. In: *Uneven development in southern Europe.* Edited by R. Hudson, J. R. Lewis. London; New York: Methuen, 1985, p. 101-22. 2 maps. bibliog.
An Apulian village in the provice of Lecce (Leverano) is chosen for this case-study, in which the economic behaviour and impact of returned migrants is examined. It is suggested that recent returnees differ from those belonging to older generations, who used to be blamed for economic problems and described as 'uneconomic, bourgeois petty traders interested only in big, villa-style houses'.

697 **The regions and European integration: the case of Emilia-Romagna.**
Edited by Robert Leonardi, Raffaella Y. Nanetti. London; New York: Pinter, 1990. 205p.
This is a case-study of the politics, economics and institutional developments in Emilia-Romagna between 1970 and 1990. It consists of a collection of papers, several of which are written by the two editors (either jointly or separately). Other contributors are: S. O. Garmise and R. J. Grote, on the economic performance; P. Bianchi and G. Gualtieri, on the industrial districts; N. Bellini, on the relationship between politics and economics; and also by Bellini, with M. G. Giordani and F. Pasquini, is an essay on the business service centres. The final chapter, again by the two editors, evaluates the prospects of the region within the European Community; they argue that the successful model of the region should enable it to compete effectively in a more integrated open market. There are several statistical tables and figures.

698 **Regional policies in Italy for migrant workers returning home.**
Annalisa Signorelli. In: *'Nation' and 'State' in Europe: anthropological perspectives.* Edited by R. D. Grillo. London; New York; Toronto; Sydney; San Francisco: Academic Press, 1980, p. 89-103.
This contribution to Grillo's book offers insights from research which was initiated by the Italian region of Apulia, as the emergence of the problems concerning returning emigrants became apparent during the economic crisis of the early 1970s. Back in Italy, they were likely to be unemployed, underemployed, or precariously occupied and contributing to the 'submerged economy'. The condition of marginality of emigrants in general is emphasized, as is their doomed attempt to seek change through individual rather than collective action. It was the latter strategy that the Apulian region tried to foster, and which is considered as a case-study here.

699 **Planning in Europe: urban and regional planning in the EEC.**
Edited by R. H. Williams. London: George Allen & Unwin, 1984. 190p.
After an introduction by the editor, in which he sets the contributions in context and outlines the evolution of planning systems in Europe, a series of essays follow for each country, in order of their entry into the EEC. The chapter on Italy is written by

S. Bardazzi. He indicates the importance of the basic planning law, which goes back to 1942, and the changes which occurred during the 1960s and 1970s. The fundamental role of the communes is emphasized, although it is also added that they have more formal than substantial power. Transfer of power from regions to communes only started in the late 1970s and took place within the framework of the old and inadequate laws on planning. The types of plan are described and it is finally pointed out that specific regional planning instruments were developed by the regional councils.

700   **Planning and urban growth in southern Europe.**
Edited by Martin Wynn.   London; New York: Mansell, 1984. 210p.

Outlines the history of urban planning and city development over the past two centuries in five countries: Greece; Italy; Portugal; Spain; and Turkey. The chapter on Italy is written by Donatella Calabi. It is a concise survey, starting with the early ideas of urban planning at the beginning of the 19th century, under the influence of the French. Planning legislation throughout that century is considered, with examples of city growth from 1850 to 1918. Calabi then discusses Italian planning under fascism, during the post-war reconstruction, and its new development in the 1960s and 1970s. Finally, the case of contemporary Rome is briefly addressed. Calabi stresses that planning thought and practice had relatively little impact on the process of urban growth. The results of speculative and uncontrolled development are a sad reality. The essay is well illustrated with maps and pictures.

The South

701   **The Italian Mezzogiorno: development or decline?**
Bela Butalia.   New Delhi: ABC Publishing House, 1985. 199p.
bibliog.

This is an eminently readable account of the perennial Italian 'southern question' written by an Indian scholar. An introductory first chapter charts the historical background up to 1950, when the Agrarian Reform was launched and the *Cassa per il Mezzogiorno* was set up. The impact of such plans for the development of the south is then surveyed and the reasons for their failure are examined. The subtle links between political power, corruption and criminal groups are also explored, before Butalia focuses on southern emigration. A concluding chapter discusses the alternative models for development proposed in Italy and emphasizes the fact that new ideas have recently emerged, which question industrialization as the necessary road to development and progress. Agriculture, the author argues, ought to be revived and channelled into new forms of production. An extract from the 1948 'Italian Long-term Economic Programme' appears as an appendix.

702 **The northern question: Italy's participation in the European Economic Community and the Mezzogiorno's underdevelopment.**
Adrian Nicola Carello. Newark, Delaware: University of Delaware Press; London; Toronto: Associated University Press, 1989. 213p. 2 maps. bibliog.

The conceptual basis of Carello's book is provided by a brief section in which political power is highlighted as the cause of distorted economic development. The historical perspective is addressed in the second part: it is argued that from the unification of the country to its involvement in the European Community (EC) the dominant position of the north-western regions of the peninsula was strengthened at the expense of the south. The issues of the EC's integration and Italy's position in the international division of labour follows. Finally, Carello addresses the cultural theme of the relationship between the EC's unbalanced integration and the Mezzogiorno's underdevelopment, concluding that 'the participation of an Italy under its current ruling class in an EC dominated by other States economically [in fact, the reference is to Germany and France, but also northern Italy and – from outside the EC – the United States] exacerbates the Mezzogiorno's underdevelopment'.

703 **The awakening of southern Italy.**
Margaret Carlyle. London; New York; Toronto: Oxford University Press, 1962. 147p. 1 map. bibliog.

A classic, passionate and optimistic account of the transformation of southern Italy after the Second World War, encouraging the belief that 'the worst features of degrading poverty [would] soon disappear with the growth of improved agriculture, some degree of industrialization and the removal to other parts of Italy and abroad of part of the surplus population'. An overview of the people and life in general in the south is provided initially. The attention is then directed to agriculture and the government's development policy, which is followed by sections on individual regions: Calabria; Apulia and Basilicata; Sicily; and Sardinia. The conclusions in the final chapter stress the 'awakening' of the south. The government and government-sponsored agencies are praised for the successful implementation of the agrarian reform and the channelling of special funds.

704 **Relevance and nature of small and medium-sized firms in southern Italy.**
Alfredo Del Monte, Adriano Giannola. In: *New firms and regional development in Europe.* Edited by David Keeble, Egbert Wever. London; Sydney; Dover, New Hampshire: Croom Helm, 1986, p. 275-98. bibliog.

This chapter consists of two sections. First of all, the authors survey the development of small firms in southern Italy, pointing out their characteristics and peculiarities in respect of similar firms in the northern half of the country. Secondly, there is a discussion of the obstacles to growth for local firms in less advanced districts. It is noted that such growth was significant in the 1970s and that to a large extent it was the result of the regional industrial policy pursued at the beginning of the decade. This was more relevant in the case of some industries (metal products, mechanical, electrical, and car manufacturing) than in the case of others (clothing and footwear). Several statistical tables are included.

705 **State and regions in the regional policy for southern Italy: ten lectures.**
Francesco Forte, with the collaboration of Domenico Miele.   Naples: Guida, 1979. 466p. 9 maps. bibliog.

The text of ten lectures on regional planning in southern Italy is offered here both in the original Italian and in its English translation. The first three lectures survey the regional policies pursued in the 1950s, with an emphasis on the 1957 Act which launched a policy of industrialization. The following two lectures concern the relationship between national planning and the policy of regional development, as was debated in the 1960s. The remaining five lectures focus on the 1970s, when devolution to regional governments was implemented, with consequent changes to the strategy for southern development. Particular attention is paid here to two pieces of legislation: Law N.853 (1971) and Law N.183 (1976).

706 **The Italian State and the underdevelopment of south Italy.**
Robert Wade.   In: *'Nation' and 'State' in Europe: anthropological perspectives.*   Edited by R. D. Grillo.   London; New York; Toronto; Sydney; San Francisco: Academic Press, 1980, p. 151-69.

This is a survey of the positive changes and persistent problems experienced by southern Italy in the 1970s, to which Wade applies the centre-periphery model in order to explain why general development was not achieved. He argues that 'what took place in the South [is] a "reflexive", dependent type of development, reflecting the interests of the owners and managers of Italian big capital, in the North'. Wade explains that there was a political as well as an economic dimension, in that the government strategy to invest most of the State holding companies' new capital in the South was the response to the persistent failure of employment to increase there in the 1950s, despite the heavy emigration at that time. This created a potential threat to social order.

707 **Social literature on the southern Italian problem.**
Marilyn Yanick Gaetani.   Naples: Giannini, 1981. 321p. bibliog.

In this book the author deals with the works of sociologists and literary figures who have investigated the socio-economic and political aspects of the 'Southern problem' – that is the relative underdevelopment of the lower half of the Italian peninsula. The first part looks back at the past, focusing on the fascist era and its influence on the south and on southern literature. The second, largest part is concerned with the revived debate in the immediate post-war years, with particularly interesting observations included in the chapter entitled 'Southern Italy in transition'. The final part is devoted to the social literature in subsequent years, when the emphasis was on industrialization and urbanization. A glossary is added at the end of the volume.

State intervention and planning

708 **Regional and subregional planning in Italy: an evaluation of current practice and some proposals for the future.**
F. Arcangeli. In: *Regional planning in Europe.* Edited by Ray Hudson, Jim R. Lewis. London: Pion, 1982, p. 57-84. 1 map. bibliog.

Tendencies towards decentralization and devolution in several European countries were characteristic of the 1970s and Italy was no exception. Arcangeli first describes the statutory framework and methodology of planning there, before offering some general hypotheses on regional and subregional planning. This is followed by three case-studies of strategic planning in Milan, Turin and Venice. The conclusion stresses the different ways in which Italian regions have approached planning and their relationship with the smallest local authorities (the communes). It also discusses a common problem they all face: the lack of effective institutional bodies between regions and communes.

709 **Public enterprise.**
Edited by Domenicantonio Fausto, Gustavo Minervini. Naples: Liguori, 1983. 214p.

This volume contains the papers presented at an Italian-Polish symposium held in Warsaw in 1981. Among the fourteen contributions, the following are worth mentioning as they focus on Italy: G. Minervini discusses the main features of public enterprises in Italy (the text is in French); F. Martorano outlines the relationship between State enterprise and joint stock companies; S. Stammati examines, in a substantial paper, the role of the government in the running of public enterprises (in French); an analysis of the structure of Italian State enterprises is provided by S. Cattaneo (also in French); O. Gobbato considers public enterprises as a policy tool in the inter-war years; S. Sciarelli covers the organizational structure and management strategies of State holding companies; and finally, D. Fausto deals with the system of financing Italian public enterprises.

710 **State, market, and social regulation: new perspectives on Italy.**
Edited by Peter Lange, Marino Regini. Cambridge, England: Cambridge University Press, 1989. 295p. bibliog.

Presented at a conference held in Italy in 1986 on State intervention in the economy, the selection of ten papers contained in this volume are divided into four sections: 'Models of regulations' (with contributions by G. Pasquino, B. Dente and G. Regonini; and S. Stefanizzi and S. Tarrow); 'Regulation of the economy' (with essays by M. Ferrera; E. Reyneri; G. A. Epstein and J. B. Schor); 'Industrial relations and its actors' (G. P. Cella; A. Chiesi and A. Martinelli); and 'The welfare state' (with papers by M. Paci; and E. Gramaglia). Two particularly interesting contributions are those by Epstein and Schor, on the divorce between the Bank of Italy and the treasury, and by Paci, on the combination of public and private in the Italian welfare system. The editors conclude by pointing out that the outcome of the patterns of regulation only rarely reflects the policy-makers' intentions, because of conflicts among the interested parties.

711 **Italy: the politics of planning.**
Joseph LaPalombara, preface by Bertram M. Gross. Syracuse, New
York: Syracuse University Press, 1966. 184p. bibliog.

Only at the beginning of the 1960s did the Italian government contemplate the idea of
economic planning. The fact that it came to nothing does not detract from this
interesting study of that attempt. The origins of such a policy are considered,
emphasizing some of the political implications. This is followed by an overview of
the ways in which the Italian authorities intervened in the economy from the time of
the country's unification up until the 1950s. There is a section on the establishment
and working of the largest State-holding companies and the Southern Development
Fund. Three major chapters then deal, respectively, with the debate on planning, the
criteria and machinery to be set up, and the main problems associated with such
policies. Finally, two chapters discuss more general issues, ranging from the
relationship between interest groups and national economic planning, to some of the
problems facing it.

712 **Twenty-five years of special action for the development of**
Southern Italy.
Gisèle Podbielski. Milan: Giuffrè Editore, 1978. 222p. bibliog.

Podbielski provides a general account of the State intervention in the South, from its
beginning in 1950s to the mid-1970s, when major changes were introduced, giving
more responsibility to the regions for the formulation and implementation of
development policies. Part one of the book deals with the objectives, institutions and
instruments of special intervention in the South, emphasizing the historical
background, the main phases of intervention and providing a statistical survey of the
Southern Fund (*Cassa per il Mezzogiorno*). In part two the results of that intervention
are evaluated. The lack of policy co-ordination and integration into longer-term
programmes and priorities is noted, and the hope is expressed that such development
policies may acquire greater coherence within the framework of the regulations of the
European Regional Development Fund. The volume is rich in statistical tables.

713 **Italian public enterprise.**
Michael V. Posner, Stuart J. Woolf. London: Gerald Duckworth,
1967. 160p.

At the time of publication, this book was intended to offer lessons that could be
learned from the Italian experience of public enterprise. The Labour government in
Britain had just set up the IRC (Industrial Reorganization Corporation) on the lines of
the Italian IRI (*Istituto per la Ricostruzione Industriale*). The Corporation did not last
long, but this study is still valuable for the clarity with which the original role of State
enterprises in Italy is surveyed and analysed – from the early post-war years to the
end of the 'economic miracle'. A comprehensive description of the nature and growth
of the public sector is followed by a detailed outline of the methods for raising funds
and their implications. The relationship between State enterprise investment and the
general pattern of economic growth in Italy is also investigated. Several tables are
included in the appendix.

714 **Economic development in retrospect: the Italian model and its significance for regional planning in market-oriented economies.**
Allan Rodgers. Washington, DC: V. H. Winston, 1979. 208p.

The author is an economic geographer with an interest in the theory of regional development. Economic duality in Italy, consisting of a generally dynamic north and a relatively backward south, provides an attractive case-study because of the various initiatives the Italian government launched in the 1950s to reduce that imbalance. They were somehow sustained throughout the three following decades, which are examined here. The main thrust of the book is concerned with the impact such development plans had on the industrialization of the south, with considerations of the socio-economic changes induced by that intervention. The analysis is articulate, coherently explained and richly complemented with statistical tables and figures. Rogers maintains that despite its limited success, the Italian case offers interesting food for thought to other countries where there are starkly different patterns of development – that is, to virtually all countries.

715 **Regional development policy and administration in Italy.**
M. M. Watson. London: Longman, 1970. 110p. 4 maps.

The regional problem this book addresses is that of southern Italy, which attracted much attention after the Second World War. This well-informed study examines the policies pursued by the Italian government in the 1950s and 1960s. The foundations for action laid in the first post-war decade are discussed, with emphasis on the establishment of the *Cassa per il Mezzogiorno* (Southern Development Fund). The switch towards industrialization, rather than continuing to invest in the infrastructure, is then considered in the context of the theories of economic development and the emergence of the European Common Market. The regions with a high degree of autonomy are also considered closely; in particular, the Sardinian 'renaissance' policy is singled out and analysed as a model of regional planning.

716 **Creating capitalism: the State and small business since 1945.**
Linda Weiss. Oxford: Basil Blackwell, 1988. 272p. bibliog.

Stemming from a study of the small-firm economy in Italy, this book develops into a theoretical discussion on industrialism and capitalism in general, and draws some practical lessons. The first part focuses on the Italian case and argues that 'Italy's small business economy expanded and prospered because it had something its European counterparts lacked: a highly sympathetic state'. The ideological background and the political struggles which contributed to that result are then explored. The second part deals with the theoretical implications of the Italian case-study. Firstly, an attempt is made to extend the analysis of the state's role in shaping capitalism to other countries (namely, Germany, France and Britain). Secondly, Weiss concludes that the Italian model can be imitated: big business and micro-capitalism can co-operate and thrive, provided the state encourages such a climate of co-operation, which must also involve the trade unions.

Italian first! From A to Z.
See item no. 1.

Italy.
See item no. 9.

Finance, Banking and External Trade

717 **Conventions for the avoidance of double taxation with respect to taxes on income.**
Milan: Banca Commerciale Italiana, 1981. 1,375p.

This is a collection of the texts of agreements on double taxation drawn up between Italy and other States. The Italian text is accompanied by the English text, together with that of the other languages in which the agreement was signed (if different from English). The Convention between Italy and the United Kingdom was first signed in 1960 and amended in 1969. That between Italy and the United States dates back to 1955. A general model of such conventions, in French, is included, together with two address lists of foreign diplomatic and consular representatives in Italy, and Italian diplomatic and consular legations abroad.

718 **A central bank between the government and the credit system: the Bank of Italy after World War II.**
Giangiacomo Nardozzi. In: *Central banks' independence in historical perspective*. Edited by Gianni Toniolo. Berlin; New York: Walter de Gruyter, 1988, p. 161-96. bibliog.

The first half of the title concisely indicates the main characteristic of the Bank of Italy since the war. The large majority of Italian banks, the author notes, 'are owned, directly or indirectly, by the State or by local public authorities'. The issue of the independence of the Central Bank, therefore, acquires a poignant relevance for its important role as supervisor of the credit system. Nardozzi outlines the implication of the 1936 Banking Act which, with some subsequent amendments, still applies. The evolution of the system is surveyed, focusing on its relationship with the government, the long period during which Guido Carli was the Governor of the Bank of Italy, and the changing strategy introduced by his successor, Paolo Baffi. A final section considers the monetary policy pursued by the Bank until the early 1980s and argues that it enjoyed considerable freedom in the formulation and implementation of monetary policies throughout.

719   **Italy: tax and investment profile.**
Reconta Touche Ross.   New York: Touche Ross International, 1988.
58p.

A useful booklet by the well-known multinational organization specializing in public
accounting, tax and management consulting. Reconta Touche Ross, the Milan-based
member firm, provides an effective companion for foreigners intending to set up a
business in Italy. A brief chapter on the general features of the country is followed by
sections containing relevant details on investment factors, exchange controls and
establishing a business. Taxation is dealt with in greater detail.

720   **Using bank services in Italy.**
Touche Ross International.   London: Touche Ross International,
1980. 42p.

Although financial regulations have undergone fundamental changes in the last
decade or so, this booklet is still useful for the general description it provides of the
Italian banking system and its workings. It outlines the main services provided by the
Italian banks: from money transmission and related services to borrowing from banks,
placing funds short-term, and general foreign business. The emphasis is on the
commercial banks and the 'special credit institutions', which have an important role
in Italy's financial market and whose operations are strictly controlled by a web of
regulations. The characteristics of the two most popular forms of short-term
government securities (BOT and CCT) are illustrated. The booklet would have been
more valuable if it contained an Italian-English glossary of the relevant terms.

721   **The monetary approach to external adjustment: a case-study of
Italy.**
Giuseppe Tullio.   Basingstoke, England; London: Macmillan, 1981.
127p. bibliog.

The five fairly independent essays contained in this volume concern the Italian
balance of payments and exchange rate in the post-war period. Tullio studied at the
University of Chicago and his approach follows the neo-monetary credo which
became the trade mark of that university. The five topics covered are: a survey of the
theories in Italian economic thought; the fluctuations in the Italian balance of
payments between 1951 and 1973; the Italian monetary policy pursued in the years
1960-78; the fluctuations in the exchange rate of the lira and the Swiss franc in
1973-78; and some empirical findings on the 'speed of adjustment of the capital and
the current accounts to money market disturbances'. There are graphs, tables and less
digestible mathematical formulations.

Industry

722 Guide to Italian motor cycles.
Cyril J. Ayton. Feltham, England: Temple Press, 1985. 156p.

The author points out in the foreword that 'this book [. . .] purports to be no more than a partial selection, for review, made from many machines currently and previously on offer. The very latest have not been commented on; nor the earliest'. Nevertheless, it is a very comprehensive guide, arranged in alphabetical order of models and manufacturers: from Aermacchi to Vespa. In fact, the two most famous scooters (Lambretta and Vespa) are included in a gallery otherwise dominated by Benelli, Bianchi, Ducati, Garelli, Gilera, Laverda, Morini, Moto Guzzi and MV Agusta. Various black-and-white photographs accompany the entries, and at the end of each the specification is given.

723 Industrial policy in Italy, 1945-90.
Edited by Mario Baldassarri. Basingstoke, England; London: Macmillan-St. Martin's Press, 1993. 333p.

Published in association with the Italian journal *Rivista di Politica Economica*, this volume provides a mixture of analysis, proposals and conclusions. The book is divided into three uneven parts. Part one includes two broad surveys of industrial policies, the first is general and theoretical (by P. Ranci), and the second is an empirical assessment of post-war achievements (R. Prodi, D. De Giovanni). In the larger second part, F. Coltorti and P. Leon consider various aspects of the relationship between private and public enterprise; G. M. Gros-Pietro and P. Bianchi discuss large and small firms; and M. D'Antonio and M. Tenenbaum respectively examine industrialization in southern Italy and territorial development in the central-northern half of the country. Finally, part three consists of a paper by B. Lamborghini and C. Sacchi on innovation and competitiveness.

724 **Made in Italy: small-scale industrialization and its consequences.**
Michael L. Blim. New York; Westport, Connecticut; London:
Praeger, 1990. 288p. bibliog.

This study is based on one unnamed town in the Marche region. Two introductory
chapters are dedicated to the period between 1881 and 1945. In the following four
chapters, the post-war industrial development is analysed and the connection between
politics and economics rightly emphasized. Shoe workers and small artisans, Blim
argues, easily identified with the local Communist Party, in towns as well as in the
region as a whole. The civic betterment schemes, however, were gradually
undermined by the darker side of small-scale economic growth, with a new middle
class 'acquiring the symbolic capital [. . .] to pursue its class project of social and
political dominations'. In times of economic difficulties small factories are closed
without consulting their employees, thus jeopardizing the social fabric based on
household and tightly-knit communal values.

725 **Technology and enterprise in a historical perspective.**
Edited by Giovanni Dosi, Renato Giannetti, Pier Angelo Toninelli.
Oxford: Clarendon Press, 1992. 415p.

This collection stems from a conference organized by the Italian Association of
Business History, which included some papers concerning Italian firms and industry.
P. P. Saviotti discusses 'R & D imitation and innovation at Montecatini'. G. Sapelli
provides an interesting view of Italian industrial development involving technical
change, micro-economic evolution and growth; in particular, the author points out
that 'a few of the weaknesses that the Italian system of innovation reveals also
manifest the power of the common obstacles which late-coming countries must
overcome'. F. Malerba deals with the growth of research and development in Italian
industry in an international perspective. Finally, G. Sirilli contributes with an
overview of the transfer of international technology, with special reference to Italian
firms.

726 **Small firms and industrial districts in Italy.**
Edited by Edward Goodman, Julia Bamford, with Peter Saynor.
London; New York: Routledge, 1989. 273p. 7 maps. bibliog.

The eleven essays contained in this volume deal with both conceptual and empirical
aspects of the role of small firms in Italy. M. Bellandi writes about the role of Italian
small businesses in the development of manufacturing industry (and also about the
concept of the industrial district according to Alfred Marshall). G. Rey offers a profile
and analysis of such firms for the years 1981-85. A. Amin contributes with a concise
general article and with a study of small footwear firms in Naples. The geography of
industrial districts is the subject of F. Sforzi's essay while the relationship between
small firms and political subcultures is considered by C. Trigilia. M. Russo deals with
ceramic tile production and technical change and the industrial structure of Ravenna
is examined by M. Pezzini. Finally a contribution on the conceptual foundations of
industrial economics, by G. Becattini concludes the volume.

727 **The amazing Bugattis.**
Edited by Malcolm Haslam. London: Heinemann, 1979. 84p.

The story of three generations of one family is sketched here through the life and works of Carlo Bugatti (1856-1940), his sons Rembrandt (1885-1916) and Ettore (1881-1947), and his grandson Jean (1909-1939). It is also a story of fine and applied arts, from furniture to motor cars, through to sculpture. P. Garner contributes an essay on Carlo, 'the child prodigy of the decorative art in Italy in the last decades of the nineteenth century'. M. Harvey writes about Rembrandt, who produced 'some of the greatest animal sculptures of modern times'. H. Conway elaborates on Ettore's superb combination of art and mechanics, culminating in the manufacturing of possibly the most handsome cars ever conceived and made. Conway also writes on Jean's talent as a coachwork designer, whose untimely accidental death (while testing a car) brought to an effective end this family story. Illustrations are an important part of the book.

728 **The industrial geography of Italy.**
Russell King. London; Sydney: Croom Helm, 1985. 332p. 37 maps. bibliog.

This is an excellent survey of Italian industrial geography. It is rich in information, well written and shows a keen perception of the regional variations in manufacturing activities. Three approaches characterize this study, which is divided into as many parts. In part one the temporal approach provides the background to Italy's industrial development, with reference to natural and human resources, the historical build-up and the growth of industry. Part two is informed by a sectorial approach: here the main sectors of industry are explored, with an emphasis on fuel and power; textiles, clothing and footwear; and the metallurgical engineering, and chemical industries. Part three employs the spatial approach and offers an effective picture of regional contrasts, covering northern, central and southern Italy.

729 **The Italian multinationals.**
Edited by Fabrizio Onida, Gianfranco Viesti. London; New York; Sydney: Croom Helm, 1988. 186p. bibliog.

The result of extensive research on the internationalization of Italian industry, this book examines Italian direct investment and ventures abroad in manufacturing, oil and mining. Onida writes on the patterns of international specialization and technological competitiveness in the Italian manufacturing industry. Viesti contributes with three essays, ranging from the size and trends of Italian investment abroad to the strategies and the general characteristics of Italian multinationals. The other writers are: C. Schieppati, on the geographical and sectoral features of Italian investment abroad; G. Balcet, on an enquiry concerning Italian non-equity ventures abroad; and S. Mariotti, with a comparison between Italian investment at home and abroad. The editors suggest, at the end, that Italy will rapidly expand its role as an international investor. Profiles of twenty major Italian multinationals are included in an appendix.

Italy.
See item no. 9.

Italy.
See item no. 13.

Mattei: oil and power politics.
See item no. 333.

Agnelli and the network of Italian power.
See item no. 334.

Cultural disenchantments: workers peasantries.
See item no. 480.

The clockwork factory: women and work in fascist Italy.
See item no. 540.

Interest groups in Italian politics.
See item no. 547.

Industrial conflict resolution in market economies.
See item no. 755.

The structuring of labour markets.
See item no. 764.

Transport

730 **Le barche di Venezia – The boats of Venice.**
Edited by Giancarlo Fullin, text by Riccardo Pergolis, drawings by
Ugo Pizzarello, translation into English by Patricia Coales, Riccardo
Pergolis.   Venice: Cooperativa Editoriale "L'Altra Riva", 1981.
190p. 1 map. bibliog.

In this bilingual, large-size book a highly informative text is combined with most
attractive drawings and illustrations. Historical notes on the development of the
various boats accompany technical details on measurements, types of wood used and
the (Venetian) names of the many different components. The *gondola* is given
prominence with chapters on its construction techniques, historical background and
development, but many other Venetian boats are also accurately described and
illustrated. These are: the *sandolo*, and its variations known as the *mascareta*, the
s'ciopon, and the *puparin*; the *topo* and its associate, the *topa*; the *sanpierota*; the
batela, in its two versions of *batela buranela* and *batela a coa de gambaro* (prawn-
tailed *batela*); the *caorlina*; the *batelon*; and the *peata*. A variety of boats from the
past and carnival boats are also portrayed. A fascinating chapter on the Venetian style
of rowing contains an extensive quotation from John Ruskin's *The stones of Venice*.
Finally, sixteen folded boat plans are included, in which the main boats are presented
in their various sections, with measurements in metres, Venetian feet and English
feet.

731 **Italian State railways steam locomotives.**
P. M. Kalla-Bishop.   Abingdon, England: Tourret Publishing, 1986.
122p.

A large-format and condensed encyclopaedia of Italian steam locomotives from the
beginning of the 20th century until the 1980s. It also includes electricity-driven
machines within the range of Low Voltage Direct Current Motive Power. A wealth of
technical details and specifications are supplied, to accompany the numerous plates
and drawings. The official classification of the locomotive stock provides the
arrangement of the vast material collected here, and the criteria adopted are clearly

outlined in an historical introduction to the Italian State railways. Railway museums in Italy are mentioned, thus contributing to the value of the book as a unique source of information for those interested in the history of Italian transport, as well as for train enthusiasts.

732   **The Italian airships.**
Giuseppe Pesce.   Modena, Italy: Mucchi, 1983. 109p. bibliog.

This is a reduced version in English of the original Italian book, and consists of two parts. In the first, there is a list of all airships built in Italy (nearly 100, from 1905 to 1931), with technical details and notes (normally indicating their employment, often connected with First World War operations). Secondly, Pesce includes a photographic survey of airships, crews and other documents. Each illustration is accompanied by informative captions in Italian and English, providing such details as: 'the Italian army, first in the world, used dirigibles in war, during the Italian-Turkish campaign in Libya, 1912'. Another, less directly bellicose Italian record of this type of transport was the first and only attempt to build an airship controlled by air jets. Indeed, it was the very last airship constructed in Italy (1931).

The Italians: how they live and work.
See item no. 3.

Agriculture

733 **Italia rurale.** (Rural Italy.)
Edited by Corrado Barberis, Gian Giacomo Dell'Angelo. Rome-
Bari: Laterza, 1988. 526p.

Three concise essays introduce the reader to the social, cultural and economic post-
war changes in the Italian countryside. A common conclusion among them stresses
the new perception and appreciation of rural life in a predominantly urban and
industrial – indeed, post-industrial – Italy. The bulk of the text then consists of a
collection of fascinating case-studies which reveal an unexpected variety of changing
realities throughout the peninsula. The contributions are by scholars and writers, and
cover topics which range from the tourism-oriented 'new rurality' in the Aosta Valley
and the culinary richness of Umbria, to the densely populated countryside around
Rome, and the impact of the new FIAT plant at Termoli (Molise), to the 'little
California' district in one of the poorest regions of the country (Basilicata).

734 **Storia dell'agricoltura italiana in età contemporanea.** (History of
Italian agriculture in the modern age.)
Edited by Piero Bevilacqua. Venice: Marsilio Editori, 1991. 3 vols.
maps.

This is the best up-to-date collection of studies by leading scholars on many aspects
of Italian agriculture during the past two hundred years. The first volume considers
the physical background and the systems of production, working practices, housing,
tools and machinery, and the use of animals. The second volume concerns the forms
of land tenure, social classes and the structure of rural families. The third volume
deals with markets, institutions and peasant culture. Among the notable contributions
in the last volume are F. De Filippis and L. Salvatici with their piece on Italian
agriculture and the European Common Market; F. Fabbri's examination of the co-
operative movement; and S. Lanaro, who significantly entitles his essay: 'From
peasants to Italians'. An attractive and varied visual gallery of plates is inserted at the
centre of each volume.

735   **Breve storia dell'agricoltura italiana, 1860-1970.** (A brief history of
      Italian agriculture, 1860-1970.)
      Camillo Daneo.   Milan: Arnoldo Mondadori, 1980. 237p. bibliog.
A century of rural life is studied here in the light of the general history of united Italy.
The central argument is that in many ways the structural characteristics of agriculture
have survived not so much as a consequence of 'natural' causes, but as a result of
decisions reflecting political circumstances. Much attention is paid to the modes of
production and to the living conditions of peasants. There are also insights on the
relationship between the social stratification in agriculture and that concerning the
expanding industrial and urban setting. This is a well-informed and perceptive history
of the diminishing importance of agriculture in contemporary Italy and the near-
disappearance of the 'peasant world'.

736   **L'agricoltura italiana tra sviluppo e crisi, 1945-1985.** (Italian
      agriculture between development and crisis, 1945-1985.)
      Guido Fabiani.   Bologna: Il Mulino, 1986. 2nd ed. 411p.
This is arguably the best study on the transformation of post-war Italian agriculture.
The relationship between economic and social aspects is investigated, while the
consequences of the European Community's agricultural policies are aptly discussed.
The 'difficult and incomplete' process of modernization throughout decades of
evolutionary changes in Italian society as a whole is surveyed and analysed, with the
support of a wealth of statistics and graphs. The book is divided into eight chapters,
of which the first two explore the constant characteristics and long-term tendencies of
change. The early post-war years are then considered, before a discussion of the
agrarian reform of the 1950s. The following decade is then explored, with the
addition of a chapter on trade (edited by F. De Filippis). The two final chapters deal,
respectively, with the 'Common Agricultural Policy' and the most recent
developments.

737   **Information and innovation on farms in central Italy: a study in
      Lazio and Umbria.**
      Colin Fraser.   Langholm, Scotland: The Arkleton Trust, 1984. 126p.
The object of this study, as the author points out, is 'to discover how farmers in Lazio
and Umbria inform themselves about technical and economic matters, how they use
existing agricultural information and extension services, and what opinion they hold
about these services'. Detailed personal interviews with farmers, agricultural
authorities, and producers' organizations were conducted. A television programme
about agriculture, *Linea Verde* (Green Line) was singled out and analysed in the
context of the relationship between the media and the rural world. The conclusion
reached was that many farmers wanted wider access to technical and economic advice
and that more intense local television programmes would be welcome. Two
appendices deal with the farmers' survey and questionnaire; a further appendix
consists of a map of the two regions concerned, and the location of interviewees.

738 **Annuario dell'Agricoltura Italiana.** (Yearbook of Italian
   Agriculture.)
   Istituto Nazionale di Economia Agraria (INEA).   Bologna: Il Mulino,
   1947- . annual.

These yearbooks have remained one of the best sources of information on al
economic and policy aspects of Italian agriculture for the past fifty years. The forma
has changed throughout this long period, but it has been standardized since Il Muline
took over publication of the volumes for the Rome-based INEA. In general, a first
section dealing with the agricultural contribution to the national economy is followec
by a section on public policy and financing in agriculture. The relevant factors o
production are then considered, while the final and more detailed part surveys specific
sectors of production, processing and marketing of agricultural products. The
summaries in English at the end of each chapter are a very useful innovation. Many
statistical tables are included.

739 **Italian agriculture in figures: 1988.**
   Italian Ministry of Agriculture and Forests.   Rome: Istituto Nazionale
   di Economia Agraria, 1989. 72p.

An official booklet with an outline of the Italian agricultural sector, this is divided
into three sections which provide: an analysis of economic trends (with data on value-
added production, employment, productivity, food consumption, prices and costs, and
foreign trade); a structural analysis (on the number, type and size of farms, livestock,
labour and forestry); and legal and administrative considerations (with an emphasis
on the regional authorities). It is full of statistical tables and figures. There is also a
glossary and a list of useful addresses on national and regional institutions concerned
with agriculture. Readers may find more recent editions, as it is the stated intention of
the Ministry to periodically update this booklet.

740 **Storia della politica agraria in Italia dal 1848 a oggi.** (History of
   agrarian policies in Italy from 1848 to the present.)
   Giuseppe Orlando.   Rome-Bari: Laterza, 1984. 210p. bibliog.

The contents of this work are arranged in a rigid chronological order. The first four
chapters deal with agrarian policies during the second half of the 19th century while
the remaining five chapters concern the present century and two, in particular, provide
a good survey of the relationship between fascism and the rural world; the last chapter
concisely covers the post-war period. The author argues that the *laissez-faire* attitude,
which dates back to the years preceding the unification of Italy, continued to inform
and shape the policy of intervention in agriculture. An interesting historical appendix
provides a comparative study of state intervention in agriculture in some European
countries during the 19th century. A list of the main (and cited) acts concerning
agriculture and commercial treaties is also included.

Italy.
See item no. 9.

Enciclopedia agraria italiana.
See item no. 112.

Montavarese: a study of peasant society.
See item no. 473.

Employment

741   Educating for unemployment: politics, labor markets, and the school system: Italy, 1859-1973.
Marzio Barbagli, translated by Robert H. Ross.   New York:
Columbia University Press, 1982. 414p. bibliog.

Originally published in Italian over twenty years ago, this book was instantly acclaimed as a major study in the fields of sociology and social history. The narrative focuses on the relationship between education (at its highest levels) and society, and the main thesis is that Italian secondary schools and universities produce more certificate and degree holders than the economic system could easily and profitably absorb. This chronic imbalance is traced by Barbagli as far back as the 1880s. The particular characteristics of Italian economic development – namely, its slowness until the 1950s and its dualistic nature throughout – together with the limited opportunities it offered, perversely strengthened the demand for self-promotion by means of education. The book is divided into several chapters following a chronological order. The translator provides useful information with an introduction and three appendices. There are also various statistical tables and graphs.

742   The sexual division of labour: the Italian case.
Francesca Bettio.   Oxford: Clarendon Press, 1988. 293p. bibliog.

The sexual division of waged labour in Italy is comprehensively analysed here, and the implications for female employment and pay are appropriately studied. Historical evidence as well as contemporary empirical data are used. While the focus of the case-studies and the statistical analysis of job divisions based on gender is on the manufacturing sector, the wider implications of sex-based segmentation in the employment and pay of women are considered with reference to the entire economy. In the conclusion, Bettio underlines the two dominant factors in such sexual division of labour, as far as Italy is concerned: '(1) the relative cheapness of the female supply, on account of women's secondary income role, and (2) women's subordinate status'. Statistical analyses with theoretical considerations and empirical data are supplied in four appendices.

255

743   **Farm workers in Italy.**
Enrico Pugliese.   In: *Uneven development in southern Europe.*
Edited by R. Hudson, J. R. Lewis.   London; New York: Methuen,
1985, p. 123-39. 4 maps. bibliog.

The question posed at the outset is whether the Italian farm workers are 'agricultura
working class, landless peasants, or clients of the Welfare State', such is the
uncertainty produced by the recent social, political and economic changes in rura
Italy. The strategies of the agricultural union are outlined and set in context. The
conclusion reached is that Italian farm workers now waver between two poles: the
'clients of the Welfare State' and the 'agricultural working class'; it is also that
in the past this group wavered between two other poles: the 'agricultural working
class' and the 'landless peasants'.

744   **Beyond employment: household, gender and subsistence.**
Edited by Nannette Redclift, Enzo Mingione.   Oxford: Basil
Blackwell, 1985. 362p. bibliog.

The common theme of this collection of essays is the crisis of traditional forms of
employment. Some contributions concentrate on general conceptual issues while
others consider specific regional cases. To the latter category belong two essays
which are of relevance to the present bibliography. Mingione examines southern Italy
as a case of 'social reproduction of the surplus labour force', employing a theoretical
approach in the first half of the essay and an empirical one in the second. It is argued
that the informal sector of the economy tends to expand, but fails to ensure the
survival of the existing surplus population. A more specific study of Naples is
provided by G. Pinnaro and E. Pugliese. They analyse a situation of social resistance
to the working and living conditions existing in the informal sector and underline how
the reproduction of these conditions is also the result of State intervention policies.

745   **Child labour in Italy: a general review.**
Marina Valcarenghi.   London: Anti-Slavery Society, 1981. 96p.

Officially, no child under the age of fifteen works in Italy. The reality is different.
This forcefully argued study is based on research conducted a long time ago, but
illegal child labour is still evident in Italy, probably in similar proportions. The author
investigates the extent of such a labour market, together with the interrelated causes
of child labour, the relevant legislation and the types of accidents children at work are
likely to suffer. Next she considers child labour in Naples and puts forward some case
histories. The final section consists of a transcription of interviews which were
conducted by the author with officials expert on child labour (judges, labour
inspectors and trade unionists). The conclusion stresses the fact that illegal child
labour 'is deeply rooted in the socio-economic reality of Italian life'. The appendix
includes extracts from the legislation on the subject (in Italian) and statistical tables.

The Italians: how they live and work.
See item no. 3.

Italy today: social picture and trends, 1984- .
See item no. 5.

Montevarese: a study of peasant society.
See item no. 473.

Italy.
See item no. 539.

The clockwork factory: women and work in fascist Italy.
See item no. 540.

Business and
Co-operatives

746 **The Italian co-operative movement: a portrait of the Lega
Nazionale delle Cooperative e Mutue.**
John Earle.   London: Allen & Unwin, 1986. 226p.

This is the only comprehensive study of the Italian co-operative movement in
English. First of all, Earle considers the origins and early achievements of the
movement, before moving on to survey the changes made under fascism and the
renewal after the Second World War. Profiles of the three main organizations follow:
the left-wing *Lega* of the subtitle, the Catholic Co-operative movement, and the
moderate *Associazione* – a division along ideological lines which is also reflected in
the trade-union movement. The largest part of the book consists of a detailed
description of how co-operatives actually live and operate in different parts of the
country. The lion's share is taken up by the *Lega* in Emilia-Romagna. There is also an
outline of the initiatives abroad, and it is with a consideration on how Italian co-
operation can be a model of democratic development for third world countries, that
the book concludes.

747 **Doing business in Italy.**
Dalbert Hallenstein.   London: BBC Books, 1991. 160p. 5 maps.

'Learning Italian is absolutely fundamental to operating successfully in Italy', writes
the author. He then outlines the appearances and realities of that contradictory
country. The topics treated in the book are indicated by the laconic chapter titles: the
Italians; the South; the North; the bureaucracy; successes; hiccups; things Italian;
social life; survival pack. There are informative sections at the beginning of each
chapter, as well as references to the direct experience of British expatriates and
companies. The last chapter ('Survival pack') contains guidance to consultants and
setting-up agencies (mainly in Milan and Rome), the police, political parties, the
banks and the associations for English-speaking expatriates (among which is the
Italian Cricket Association, based in Rome).

748 **Italian entrepreneurs: rearguard of progress.**
Edith Kurzweil. New York: Praeger, 1983. 221p. bibliog.

Based on interviews with sixty entrepreneurs of medium-size companies, this is a study intended to test Schumpeter's idea of entrepreneurs as innovators, rather than managers and supervisors. Kurzweil found that her respondents showed a high capacity to react to specific conditions, namely: the adverse events of the 1970s, and the looming participation of the Communists in government. Fourteen chapters address both general and particular issues, such as: the historical background to the changes in life-style during that decade; women as entrepreneurs; industrial relations; entrepreneurs and political parties; and bureaucracy and local authorities. The final chapter sets the empirical study in the context of relevant theories. The resourceful adaptability of Italian entrepreneurs is praised. Several tables are included, together with the two questionnaires used, in the appendix.

749 **Business cultures in Europe.**
Edited by Collin Randlesome. Oxford: Heinemann, 1990. 319p. bibliog.

In his chapter on Italy William Brierley points out that three factors strongly influence the country's business environment. The first concerns the size and importance of the State sector and the concomitant importance of politics and client-patron relationships. The second is the large number of family concerns, and hence a preoccupation with social values including, but also beyond those of, the profitability of the enterprise. The last is the scale of the small firms sector, which requires for its survival a final balanced mix of both highly co-operative and highly competitive attitudes. The author then focuses on: government; the law; finance; the labour market; the trade unions; education, training and development; small business; and the European 'single market'.

750 **The performance of Italian producer co-operatives.**
Alberto Zevi. In: *Participatory and self-managed firms: evaluating economic performance.* Edited by Derek C. Jones, Jan Svejnar.
Lexington, Massachusetts: Lexington Books, 1982, p. 239-51. bibliog.

In his essay Zevi first provides a historical overview of the Italian producer co-operatives, with an emphasis on the post-war decades. The organization and structures of the co-operatives are then discussed, and the focus here is on large manufacturing and construction co-operatives during the late 1970s. Various aspects of these firms are examined, and their behaviour is compared to that of conventional companies. Finally, the results of the study are compared with those of similar investigations on other types of co-operatives. One of Zevi's concluding remarks points out that 'in many producer co-operatives job security for membership seems to be an important objective, even if it is at odds with maximizing per-worker income of existing members'.

Business law guide to Italy.
See item no. 648.

Industrial democracy in Italy: workers co-operatives and the self-management debate.
See item no. 756.

Labour Movement and Trade Unions

751 **Visions of emancipation: the Italian workers' movement since 1945.**
Joanne Barkan.   New York: Praeger, 1984. 266p.
Part one of this book provides a good survey of the Italian trade-union movement from 1945 to the early 1980s, set against the changes in political and economic development. Barkan emphasizes: the 1969 watershed, with its new demands and forms of struggle; the new union of the 1970s and terrorism; and the beginning of the 1980s when the labour movement was again divided and on the defensive. A particularly interesting chapter is devoted to 'Feminism, working-class women and the unions'. Hard facts are systematically accompanied by perceptive analysis. In part two some of the protagonists speak for themselves, as the author reproduces the contents of interviews with FIAT workers, trade unionists, managers and politicians in Turin. The interviews deal with people's daily lives, past experiences and hopes for the future. The book is illustrated with old and contemporary photographs.

752 **Politics and ideology in the Italian workers' movement.**
Gino Bedani.   Oxford; Providence, Rhode Island: Berg, 1995. 365p. bibliog.
This important study fills a gap in scholarly works written on Italian contemporary society. The development of the Italian trade-union movement during the past fifty years is illustrated with clarity, knowledge and insight. The underlying background of the changing roles of the Catholic and Communist subcultures, which so much influenced the workers' unions, is consistently taken into account in the six parts which make up this study. The immediate post-war years ('From unity to secession') are first examined. The 1950s are then considered and defined as 'years of division and rival ideologies'. Two parts are devoted to the 1960s, commencing with 'the rediscovery of common ground' and then focusing on 'the unforgettable autumn of 1969' and the general, important issues it raised. The consequences of those momentous events are examined next, with particularly interesting observations on the relationship between the unions and society at large. Finally, the 'crisis and reappraisal' since 1980 are analysed. At the end of a postscript on the dramatic

political development in the 1990s, the author suggests that the main unions 'will once again be called upon to deploy the energies and resources of their considerable historical imagination'. A statistical appendix and a glossary enrich this valuable book.

753 **Labour relations and economic performance.**
Edited by Renato Brunetta, Carlo Dell'Aringa. Basingstoke, England; London: Macmillan, in association with the International Economic Association, 1990. 482p. bibliog.

The second of the three groups of essays gathered here (on trade unions and incomes policies) includes two papers on Italy. The first, by L. Reichlin and M. Salvati, considers the consequences of shifts in union power in the 1970s and 1980s. The authors' thesis is that the change in industrial relations in around 1980 'coincided with or slightly preceded changes in the main trends of employment, unemployment and money supply'. In the second essay, R. Brunetta and C. Carraro look at the incomes policies pursued by the Italian government in the 1980s. Part three concentrates on the relationship between labour flexibility and unemployment. C. Dell'Aringa and C. Lucifora contribute here with a paper on wage determination and trade-union behaviour in Italy. They conclude that there are substantial unexplained wage differentials between industries and occupations. Although some of the above authors employ highly technical models, their arguments can still be followed by general readers.

754 **Labor divided: austerity and working-class politics in contemporary Italy.**
Miriam Golden. Ithaca, New York; London: Cornell University Press, 1988. 270p.

A well-researched study of the Italian labour movement between the late 1970s and early 1980s. The focus is on the policies of the three main union confederations (CGIL, CISL and UIL) and the joint engineering and metal workers' federation (FLM), at national and local levels. For the latter, four northern localities were chosen for investigation: Turin and Pordenone, where radical attitudes prevailed; and Modena and Cuneo, which showed moderation at the national confederation's adopted policy of wage restraint. Particular attention is paid to the Italian Communist Party and to its influence on the labour movement. The background to Italian trade unionism and its political involvement is provided, together with a theoretical framework on union policy orientations.

755 **Industrial conflict resolution in market economies: a study of Australia, the Federal Republic of Germany, Italy, Japan and the USA.**
Edited by Tadashi Hanami, Associate editor, Roger Blanpain. Deventer, The Netherlands: Kluwer, 1984. 322p.

Part three of this work is relevant to Italy and contains three essays. In the first, T. Treu deals with the organization and structure of workers' and employers' unions, the bargaining procedures, individual disputes, and means of settlements. Secondly, M. Boccella provides a study of the postal service administration and a case in which the unions appear 'in the middle of the ford, between bargaining and co-management, old and new'. Finally, Treu and Boccella together consider one particular industry: the (then) State-controlled Alfa Romeo plant at Arese (Milan). Several types of disputes are examined, such as those that arise over grading systems, investment policy, work organization, environmental conditions, temporary lay-off, and disciplinary sanctions. For all the attempts by the opposite sides to find reasonable solutions, a company manager is reported as having said that 'the effort towards rationalization could prove to be irrational in the end'.

756   **Industrial democracy in Italy: workers co-ops and the self-management debate.**
Mark Holmström.   Aldershot, England; Brookfield, Vermont; Hong Kong; Singapore; Sydney: Avebury, 1989. 190p. bibliog.

Holmström is an anthropologist interested in the broad question of self-management, which he investigates here in connection with the workers' co-operative movement in Italy. This is the largest in western Europe and is mostly concentrated in the northern half of the peninsula, especially in Emilia-Romagna, where the author conducted his field research. One of the aims of the study is 'to show what can be learned from the little known Italian experience'. References are made to other countries' experiences, notably Britain, France, Spain and the former Yugoslavia. The conclusions are best conveyed by the observations made on the case of Imola's co-operators who, it is stated, have found 'a way of working together, and earning a good living, in an atmosphere of greater freedom and respect for each other's dignity and personal space than most people'.

757   **Economic crisis, trade unions and the State.**
Edited by Otto Jacobi, Bob Jessop, Hans Kastendiek, Marino Regini.
London; Sydney; Dover, England: Croom Helm, 1986. 295p. bibliog.

Industrial relations in Britain, Germany and Italy are the subject of this collection of papers, which refers to the early 1980s. Part three concerns Italy and contains three essays. M. Dal Co and P. Perulli write about the 1983 agreement between the government, trade unions and employers' associations. They argue that the agreement had little normative value, and was replaced by unilateral intervention by the State in 1984. G. P. Cella and T. Treu focus on intervention itself and its negative (in the authors' view) consequences for industrial relations. Finally, M. Carrieri and C. Donolo consider the wider scene and explore the background to such measures, emphasizing the weaknesses of the trade-union movement and suggesting that the key to understanding the problems lies in the political system.

758   **Technological change, rationalization and industrial relations.**
Edited by Otto Jacobi, Bob Jessop, Hans Kastendiek, Marino Regini.
London; Sydney: Croom Helm, 1986. 283p. bibliog.

Part one outlines some of the general problems of technological change with comparative references to Britain, Germany and Italy. Part two focuses on the car industry, and a contribution by M. Rollier deals with the turning point of autumn 1980, when the Italian unions confronted Fiat management on the question of mass dismissals. A government-sponsored compromise ensued, and intensified technological changes followed, with a recovery in productivity and weakening of the unions. Part three offers a wide range of studies on the impact of economic crisis and plant rationalization upon the unions. There are three contributions on Italy: 'Some current strategy problems of the Italian trade unions', by H. Heine; 'Centralisation or decentralisation? An analysis of organizational changes in the Italian union movement at a time of crisis', by I. Regalia; and 'Social change and the trade union movement in the 1970s', by A. Accornero.

759 **Unions, change and crisis: French and Italian union strategy and the political economy, 1945-1980.**
Peter Lange, George Ross, Maurizio Vannicelli.   London: George Allen & Unwin, 1982. 295p.

Part two of this work deals with Italy. In it, Lange and Vannicelli emphasize the uniqueness of the Italian trade-union movement, with the sense that the political and economic crisis of the 1970s did not undermine the bases of the union unity and general success which had been achieved during and after the strike wave of 1969. Several further chapters cover a wide range of topics: from the post-war rebirth and the difficult 1950s, to the revival in the 1960s (and the apex of the 'hot Autumn' of 1969), from the strategic response to the consequences of the oil crisis in the mid-1970s, to the 'EUR line', when the united Federation (CGIL-CISL-UIL) proposed a moderate platform for national bargaining. The authors persuasively argue, however, that such a significant shift from the line previously pursued should not be overstated, because it incorporated major elements of continuity.

760 **Protest and participation: the new working class in Italy.**
John R. Low-Beer.   Cambridge, England; London; New York; Melbourne: Cambridge University Press, 1978. 285p.

This book is based on a combination of theories, field research and statistical analysis. The 'new workers' (predominantly technicians) of three electronic factories in Milan offered Low-Beer the raw material for his observations, while he was in Italy in 1970-71. At that time there was optimism and enthusiasm *vis-à-vis* progressive change, an atmosphere which influenced the author's perceptions, as he himself admits. The fundamental issue at the centre of this sophisticated study, is the high degree of militancy among those 'new workers', which is attributed here to their social background, rather than to the nature of their jobs or organizations. More general factors were the raising of levels of income and education, and the consequent desire and capacity to articulate demands and expect participation.

761 **Italy: school of awakening countries: the Italian labour movement in its political, social, and economic setting from 1800 to 1960.**
Maurice F. Neufeld.   New York: New York State School of Industrial and Labour Relations, Cornell University, 1961. 590p. bibliog.

This classic study in English of the history of the Italian labour movement appeared at a time of great changes, when the economic leap forward known as the 'Italian economic miracle' was in full swing, and was naturally to transform Italian society. The book is therefore still useful to labour historians for its historical perspective and the wide range of contents it includes. The first five chapters are devoted to the period 1800-1890, and place the emphasis on the decades which followed the country's unification (1861). Three chapters subsequently cover the story up to 1926, the year in which political and trade-union freedom was completely abolished by fascism. The last two chapters deal, respectively, with the fascist regime and with the restored freedom of the labour movement after the end of the war. There are appendices on the structure of the main trade unions and labour relations terminology.

762 **European employment and industrial relations glossary: Italy.**
Tiziano Treu. London: Sweet & Maxwell, Office for Official Publications of the European Communities, 1991. 252p. bibliog.

This is a publication of the European Foundation for the Improvement of Living and Working Conditions (Dublin). Its contents include entries on industrial relations, labour market and employment laws, and areas in which different national practices within the European Community make it difficult to find the corresponding expressions. The glossary proper is preceded by a list of entries, in Italian and English, for cross-reference purposes, and by a survey of the economic and social context of industrial relations in Italy. A set of tables follows, including figures on population, employment, union membership, strike statistics, earnings, indexes of labour costs, productivity and prices. A double index, also bilingual, concludes the volume.

763 **Trade unions of the world, 1992-93: a Keesings reference publication.**
Edited by Martin Upham. Harlow, England: Longmans, 1991. 3rd ed. 579p.

The compact pages devoted to Italy (pages 241-49) offer a relatively extended picture of the development of trade unions since the Second World War, focusing on the three major confederations: CGIL, CISL and UIL. Their strength in the 1970s is underlined, as are their difficulties throughout the 1980s. Also included are sections on collective bargaining and the system of wage indexation (*scala mobile*), which was established after the war and which the unions grudgingly agreed to abandon in two stages, in 1992 and 1993 – as future editions of this useful repertory will indicate. There are also references to the independent 'Base Committees' (COBAS) and other national unions, including the right-wing CISNAL and CISAL.

764 **The structuring of labour markets: a comparative analysis of the steel and construction industry in Italy.**
Paola Villa. Oxford: Clarendon Press, 1986. 420p. bibliog.

Villa combines a theoretical discourse on labour market structures with a thorough empirical investigation into Italian steel and construction industries. After providing a survey of the two advanced theories of the labour market (segmentation and duality), Villa adopts the latter as the framework for her study, and defines the basic hypothesis of that theory as the separation of the markets into two sectors. The different economic and technological conditions that characterize the two sectors are considered, before focusing on the division of labour. The attention then moves to the internal organization of various jobs in the two industries concerned, and the dynamics of labour market structures. Finally, a return to the theoretical discussion calls for a definition of the labour market different from the traditional view. Tables, graphs and figures are included in the text and are supplemented by an extensive statistical appendix.

765   **Employers associations and industrial relations: a comparative study.**
Edited by John P. Windmuller, Alan Gladstone.   Oxford: Clarendon Press, 1984. 370p.

Competently written by T. Treu and A. Martinelli, the contribution on Italy outlines the origins and development of employer associations, with the emphasis on the post-war decades. After mentioning the three main employers' confederations (for industry, commerce and agriculture), the focus is centred on the industrialists' national organization, *Confindustria*. Its structure, strength and rationale are effectively reviewed, with considerations on the limited success of the reform carried out in the 1970s, whose purpose was to enhance the principle of collective leadership. The attention is then switched to the main territorial organization (*Assolombarda*) and the trade federations, such as *Federmeccanica* (engineering) and *Assochimici* (chemicals). Lastly, the industrial relations conduct by the employers is considered, with observations on the strategies pursued in the 1970s, in the wake of the 'hot autumn' of 1969, and the relationship with the dominant political party of government, Christian Democracy.

Women and trade unions in eleven industrialized countries.
See item no. 529.

Statistics

766 **Annuario Statistico Italiano.** (Italian statistical yearbook.)
Istituto Centrale di Statistica. Rome: Istituto Centrale di Statistica,
1878- . annual. maps.

This is the classic yearly compendium of statistics on most aspects of Italy's public
life. As the bulk of information is provided through tables full of figures, only a
rudimentary knowledge of the Italian language is required to make profitable use of
these volumes. Their contents follow a well-established pattern, both in the format
and in the sequence. The main headings cover: Territory, climate and natural
environment; Population; Health and sanitary provisions; Education; Cultural, social
data, and elections; Justice; The workforce; National economic accounts; Agriculture
forestry, fishing and hunting; Manufacturing industry; Building industry; National
trade and tourism; External trade; Transport and communications; Banking, insurance
and finance; Prices; Wages and salaries; Public finance; Family consumption;
Company finances; and International comparisons.

767 **Sommario di statistiche storiche dell'Italia, 1861-1965.** (Summary
of historical statistics of Italy, 1861-1965.)
Rome: Istituto Centrale di Statistica, 1968. 147p.

A century of statistical data on most aspects of Italian public life are included here in
a most useful and comprehensive compendium. The headings included are those
normally provided in the contemporary, yearly statistical volumes edited by the
government-sponsored Central Statistical Office (such as the indispensable *Annuario
statistico italiano* [q.v.]). Concise statistics are offered for: Climate; Population;
Health; Education; Elections; Justice; Agriculture and forestry; Manufacturing and
building industry; Transport and communications; External and internal trade;
Banking and insurance; Prices; The workforce; Wages and salaries; Consumptions
and National economic accounts. An introduction provides an account of the various
different methods used for the collection of statistical data throughout the century.

768 **Economic statistics, 1900-1983: United Kingdom, United States of America, France, Germany, Italy, Japan.**
Thelma Liesner. London: The Economist Publications, 1985. 142p.

General comparisons of the six countries are made in the introductory and concluding sections. The latter contains, in particular, comprehensive tables and charts on the total output, productivity, employment, population trends, age distribution, consumer prices and external trade. A wide range of sources is used for the chapter on Italy, from the Italian Central Statistical Office to OECD and United Nations statistics. The relevant tables are: Gross Domestic Product at constant prices (1900-83); industrial production, index and selected series (1900-83); prices and income (1900-83); population (1901-82); labour market: employment (1929-83); labour market: other indicators (1900-83); and value of exports and imports by country (1900-83). There are also two charts, one on the gross domestic product at constant prices (1926-83), and one on industrial production, selected series (1900-80).

769 **Italian statistical abstract: edition 1991.**
Italian Central Statistical Office. Rome: ISTAT, 1991. 214p. 2 maps.

This is a pocket-size, abridged version in English of the *Annuario Statistico Italiano*, the most comprehensive collection of statistical data on Italy, published every year by the Italian Central Statistical Office (ISTAT) (q.v.). Figures are updated here to 1988 or 1989. The contents are divided into twenty-one sections: Territory and climate; Population and vital statistics; Health care and social security; Education; Culture; Elections; Judicial statistics; Labour force; National accounts; Agriculture, forestry and fishery; Industrial census; Industry (the largest section, with twenty-two tables); Building and public works; Internal trade and tourism; Foreign trade; Transport and communications; Banking and insurance; The monetary and financial markets; Price indexes; Wages and salaries; Financial accounts of the public sector; Household consumption; and Enterprise balance-sheets. It includes colour charts.

770 **Sommario di statistiche storiche: 1926-1985.** (Summary of historical statistics: 1926-1985.)
Italian Central Statistical Office. Rome: ISTAT, 1986. 358p.

A wide-ranging compendium of statistics which is lavish with tables, graphs and figures, but modest with commentary. The volume includes nineteen sections, the smallest is 'Il clima' (the climate) with two tables; the largest is 'I conti economici nazionali' (the national economic accounts) with forty-three tables. Statistics on the country's economic performance form the largest section, with many pages dedicated to agricultural and industrial production, transport and communication, trade and prices (with useful tables for the conversion of the value of the lira). Wage and salaries, on the other hand, are not given much space. Adequate attention is paid to demographic change, health, education, and civil and penal justice. The changes shown throughout the volume effectively quantify the transformation of Italy into a leading industrial country in the sixty years considered.

A history of Italian fertility.
See item no. 344.

Environment

Regional and town planning

771 **Planning the Eternal City: Roman politics and planning since World War II.**
Robert C. Fried. New Haven, Connecticut; London: Yale University Press, 1973. 346p. 6 maps. bibliog.

As a study of Rome's urban development and planning in the 1950s and 1960s, this book is still of great interest, and not only for urban historians. An outline of planning in Rome's past and a survey of Roman society and culture is followed by a comprehensive analysis of planning as related to economic issues, national politics and various interests. In the final section, which discusses the strategies for improving performance, the author mentions, tongue-in-cheek, the planners and builders who were 'most active and vehement in defending the Appian Way district from private development', but who had themselves built villas there. The text is accompanied by statistics and graphs. A useful appendix with the chronology of plan formulations from 1946 to 1970, is included.

772 **Building new communities: New Deal America and fascist Italy.**
Diane Ghirardo. Princeton, New Jersey: Princeton University Press, 1989. 223p. bibliog.

This is a stimulating comparative study of extensive town and community building in Italy and the United States during the 1930s. A chapter on the 1930s in the two countries is followed by two chapters devoted, respectively, to Italian and American new towns. With regard to Italy, a historical context to Mussolini's policies of land reclamation and community building, is provided. The architecture and urban planning is explored, as is the case of the Agro Pontino new towns near Rome. Attention is also paid to similar operations carried out in the Italian colonies. It is noted that fascism was in step with some dominant 20th-century notions of urban and district planning. A short, concluding chapter points out that most Italian new towns flourished, whereas the same could not be said for the American experiment.

Conservation

773 **The death of Venice.**
Stephen Fay, Phillip Knightley. London: André Deutsch, 1976.
190p. 1 map.

The prolonged decay of Venice was dramatically highlighted by the flood which engulfed the city in November 1966. Since then the Italian government has passed numerous acts and allocated huge sums of money for the restoration of Venice, if only to transform it into a vast museum piece. In addition, generous contributions and expertise were donated to the rescue operation from all over the world. Yet, the urgency was not met by an adequate response from the Italian central and local authorities. The authors provide a fascinating but sad study of the neglect and mismanagement, and also of the growing concern (mainly from abroad) for the preservation of the city. The last chapter focuses on the various plans to prevent new floodings, by building movable barriers at the entrances of the lagoon. Alas, none were implemented. The book includes illustrations, especially of aspects of the physical decay caused by air pollution.

774 **Disaster and reconstruction.**
Robert Geipel, translated from Germany by Philip Wagner. London;
Boston; Sydney: George Allen & Unwin, 1982. 202p. 38 maps.
bibliog.

This is an absorbing study of the two earthquakes which hit the region of Friuli (in north-east Italy) in 1976. The four central chapters are devoted, respectively, to a survey of the social character of the disaster area; the relationship between hazard theory and the empirical evidence gathered in Friuli; the earthquake's immediate and longer-lasting effects; and the perspectives of reconstruction. Incidental references are also made to what happened in the Neapolitan hinterland after the 1980 earthquake there. Reconstruction in Friuli was a success but it was a failure in the south. 'What was possible under the more intimate, homogeneous conditions of Friuli – Geipel writes – failed in the environment of a city of more than a million inhabitants, a city characterized by extreme contrasts of rich and poor, social class and stratification'. The book is full of statistical data, maps, graphs and pictures.

775 **The law and practice relating to pollution control in Italy.**
M. Guttieres, U. Ruffolo. London: Graham & Trotman, 1982. 207p.
bibliog.

The first chapter provides background information on the sources of legislation on environmental protection, on the organization of public powers and associated bodies, and on the way the interests of individual citizens are protected. The following six chapters deal with specific types of pollution. Each of these chapters begins with a repertory of the relevant legislation, an indication of the relevant authorities and the various forms of administrative power they can apply. General considerations are interwoven in the technical text. Chapter eight contains information on the 'Control of products', and the final chapter deals with the relationship between the environmental problem and the Italian legal framework. Some remarks on Italian legislation and European Community directives are also made.

776 **Venice preserved.**

Peter Lauritzen, photographs by Jorge Lewinski, Mayotte Magnus, introduction by John J. Norwich.   London: Michael Joseph, 1986. 176p.

As recently as December 1992 Venice was entirely submerged by an exceptional tide: it was a nasty reminder of the city's frailty. However, it was nothing like the major flood of November 1966, after which an international programme of rescue took place. This large-size and richly-illustrated book charts the achievements of that programme, outlining the historical background to both man-made and natural perils along with the various rescue operations. This covered the: restoration of paintings; reparation of churches; and conservation of stonework. In his concluding chapter, the author writes: 'As much as Venetian monuments have been successfully preserved as relics of a glorious past, there is now every hope that Venice's natural environment may be saved by that same combination of international concern and national legislation that has hitherto done so much for the city'. Did he speak too soon?

777 **The superpoison, 1976-1978.**

Tom Margerison, Marjorie Wallace, Dalbert Hallenstein.

Basingstoke, England; London: Macmillan, 1980. 236p.

The superpoison of the title is the dioxin gas which escaped after an explosion at a chemical plant in Seveso, north of Milan, in July 1976. Although the scale of the disaster was much less than the similar accident which occurred in Bophal (India) eight years later, it became a *cause célèbre* in the book of human and environmental miseries, mainly because of its effect on pregnant women, with a high number of miscarriages and malformed births. The local chemical works at the centre of the events was called Icmesa and belonged to the powerful Swiss pharmaceutical firm Hoffmann-La Roche. The book 'is about the way in which the company responsible for the disaster, and the authorities whose duty it was to protect the people, failed and continued to fail to meet the emergency'. The authors also offer a passionate and detailed consideration of the people of Seveso.

Education

778 **International higher education: an encyclopedia.**
Edited by Philip G. Altbach. Chicago; London: St James Press,
1991. 2 vols.

The section on Italy (in the second volume) is by Roberto Moscati and provides
details on the historical trends in higher education in the country. These are
accompanied by up-to-date figures and precede an argument which emphasizes three
aspects of education: the relationship between higher education and the labour
market; the years of crisis and development (1978-88); and the current debate on
reforms. One interesting statistical fact concerns the rapid increase of the percentage
of women in Italian universities: from 44.6 per cent in 1982-83 to 47.2 per cent in
1986-87, with Humanities reaching 80.1 per cent of all female undergraduates. The
conclusion, however, is pessimistic, as far as reforms are concerned. Moscati states
that 'people in privileged positions both inside and outside the University system
continue to resist essential change [. . .] Higher education bureaucrats and academics
continue to look to the past; their conservatism prevents a real modernization of the
system'.

779 **Academic power in Italy: bureaucracy and oligarchy in a national
university system.**
Burton R. Clark. Chicago; London: The University of Chicago Press,
1977. 205p. bibliog.

This is the only thorough study in English of the system of higher education in Italy:
a centralized model which Clark considers to be important because 'it might also
speak to the future experiences of developing societies as well as reveal some
characteristics shared with such advanced neighbours as France and Germany'. The
first chapter provides the historical background to the different Italian universities.
The following chapters then discuss the attempt which was made to establish a
unitary system by bureaucratic means (noting the limited results of this policy), and
the emergence of an alternative form of control: the powerful academic oligarchy.
The last chapter makes some international comparisons and reaches the conclusion

that the mediaeval concept of 'guild' (as a unit of semi-autonomous power and self-organization) so typical of Italian universities, is only a more radical form of the academic system prevailing elsewhere.

780 **Were they pushed or did they jump? Individual decision mechanisms in education.**
Diego Gambetta.   Cambridge, England; London; New York;
Melbourne; Sydney: Cambridge University Press, 1987. 234p. bibliog.

Gambetta offers an analytical study of educational behaviour, focused on the factors influencing individuals' choices at and beyond school-leaving age. Why some pupils leave while others stay on in education is the fundamental question addressed here. The study is based on empirical research carried out in north-west Italy, but both the theoretical framework and the conclusions reached apply to the educational systems in any industrialized country. The first chapter is concerned with theoretical aspects. This is followed by an outline of the Italian educational system, an examination of the 'pushing' and 'pulling' forces which basically depend on the level of cultural and economic resources of the family. The complexity of the variables involved is discussed in a cogent conclusion and there are also statistical appendices.

781 **Higher education in the European Community: student handbook.**
Edited by Brigitte Mohr.   London: Kogan Page, 1990. 6th ed. 516p.

Published on behalf of the Commission of the European Communities, this handbook contains a wealth of information on the higher education systems of EC member countries and on the various schemes planned to implement the programmes of co-operation and exchange. As with other member countries, the chapter on Italy considers the structure of higher education in the peninsula, the system of admission and registration, the requirements in terms of the language of instruction, the forms of financial assistance and scholarship, the regulations on entry and residence. There are also brief sections on the social aspects, such as student employment, services to students, cost of living and accommodation. Appendices include a survey of courses in all institutions, student statistics, a diagram of the education system, and a glossary.

782 **Europe at school.**
Norman Newcombe.   London: Methuen, 1977. 264p.

Newcombe has written a fascinating comparative study of primary and secondary education in France, West Germany, Italy, Portugal and Spain. The book is arranged by topics, rather than by individual countries, but the Italian schools visited by the author (in Cremona and Perugia) provide a wealth of information on education in Italy. The very first chapter, which considers organization, begins with a ditty sung by Italian children. This is followed by an examination of what is actually taught in class and the methods used. Two chapters subsequently explore 'the teacher and his work' (although in Italy it is more likely to be 'hers'). A survey of buildings and equipment follows, and the last chapters are concerned with activities outside the classroom, pastoral care, discipline and regulations (the nine grades of punishment for Italian pupils are duly listed). Appendices focus on curricula, working hours and teachers' salaries.

783 **Progressive renaissance: America and the reconstruction of Italian education, 1943-1962.**
Steven F. White.   New York; London: Garland, 1991. 215p. bibliog.
The book opens with a survey of schooling in Italy up to the Second World War: an authoritarian heritage. White then pays much attention to the period from the arrival of the Allies in southern Italy (1943), to the liberation of the north (1945). Those two years saw an effort by the Allies' Educational Subcommission to expose Italy to wider currents of European and American pedagogy and textbook and curricular reforms were introduced in what became known as 'new progressivism'. However, a counter-reformation took place, coinciding with the reflection on Italy of the Cold War, that is, the influence of conservative catholicism. Elements of renovation and pluralism were only introduced by the early 1960s. The final chapter examines the American intervention in education in a comparative perspective on the three main former Axis countries (Germany, Italy and Japan).

The Italians: how they live and work.
See item no. 3.

Italy today: social pictures and trends, 1984- .
See item no. 5.

Italy.
See item no. 9.

Education of Italian Renaissance women.
See item no. 523.

Educating for unemployment: politics, labor markets and the school system.
See item no. 741.

Higher education and the engineering profession in Italy.
See item no. 786.

The world of learning.
See item no. 1041.

Science and Technology

784   **History of science in Italy.**
Ferdinando Abbri, Paolo Rossi.   *ISIS, An International Review Devoted to the History of Science and its Cultural Influence*, vol. 77 (1986), p. 213-18.

This is a concise but effective review of the history of science in Italy from the early 20th century through to the 1980s. Gino Loria was the first to advocate the history of science as a suitable subject for universities, followed in 1916 by Aldo Mieli who requested the institution of a university chair in the subject. In the 1920s important books were written, although the idealistic philosophy of Benedetto Croce and Giovanni Gentile denied any value to the history of science. After the Second World War a number of periodicals concerning this subject were first published in Italy. The 1960s saw a remarkable increase in scholarly activity associated with the history of science and the collaboration of philosophers of science, scientists and historians of philosophy and of ideas became more common. Further works of importance were published in the 1980s and several university chairs in the history of science were created.

785   **The dominance of nuclear physics in Italian science policy.**
Alberto Cambrosio.   *Minerva* (Great Britain), vol. 23, no. 4 (1985), p. 464-84.

The author discusses the reasons for the dominance of nuclear physics which has always been a favourite science in the research policy of Italy. Such dominance is partly due to the group created around Fermi in the 1920s and 1930s, who produced highly successful research even with relatively small resources. However, it is also connected to the Italian university system in which it is very difficult to change the attitudes of established professors. The article considers the attempts made by more progressive professors to change the ways in which researchers were treated and research financed, especially in the 1960s.

786 **Higher education and the engineering profession in Italy: the**
     ***Scuole* of Milan and Turin, 1859-1914.**
     Anna Guagnini. *Minerva* (Great Britain), vol. 26, no. 4 (1988),
     p. 512-48.

Guagnini offers a detailed and interesting reconstruction of the origins of the
engineering schools in northern Italy, which were later to be called *Politecnici*. In
Lombardy the profession of engineer was recognized as early as 1563, but at the time
of unification (1861) there were no specific training courses. Those which existed in
the universities, such as the one at Pavia, placed the emphasis on the knowledge of
geometry and mathematics. The task of university engineering courses in Italy has
been largely that of preparing for an academic qualification rather than training for a
profession. The situation did not change at the time of the education reform of 1923
and, the author seems to imply, little has changed since.

787 **Science and industry in Italy between the two world wars.**
     Arturo Russo. *Historical Studies in the Physical and Biological
     Sciences*, vol. 16, pt. 2 (1986), p. 281-320.

The author describes the transformation of Italian science from a purely academic
subject to a social activity with an interest in industry. The *Società Italiana per il
Progresso delle Scienze* (SIPS) or Italian Society for the Progress of Science, which
was created in 1907, resumed its meetings after the First World War to discuss the
'present conditions of chemical, electrical and mechanical industries'. The search for
synthetic ammonia, first produced in Germany and necessary for fertilizers, served as
an incentive to a co-operation between science and industry. Russo discusses the
beginnings of the *Consiglio Nazionale delle Ricerche* (National Research Council) in
1923 and considers its role and instrumentalization by the fascist movement in the
1930s. The relationship between fascism and science is thoroughly investigated.

788 **Physics in Italy.**
     Philip Campbell, Sally Croft, Peter Rodgers, Susan Biggin. *Physics
     world*, vol. 6, no. 1 (January 1993), p. 29-51.

The general title refers to a report contained in the central pages of the journal and
encompasses ten separate articles on Italian physics. The first article outlines the
precarious political situation in Italy and its impact on research policy. The second
piece deals with the two main research bodies for physics: an efficient INFN (*Istituto
Nazionale di Fisica Nucleare* [The National Institute of Nuclear Physics]) and a very
slow CNR (*Consiglio Nazionale delle Ricerche* [National Research Council]). Three
short articles are devoted respectively to the synchrotron being built in Trieste, to
space research and to optics research. The next article discusses Italian physics
degrees which are aimed at producing researchers, and points out that a shorter course
to help meet the needs of industry may be soon available. On page 36 there is a report
on Ansaldo, one of the leading technological companies and this is followed by a
discussion of technology transfer and science parks. Two more substantial articles by
Nicola Cabibbio, the president of INFN, and by Carlo Rizzuto, director of the
Interuniversity Consortium for the Physics of Matter, provide names and addresses of
area directors and national projects co-ordinators. The last article is devoted to the
International Centre for Theoretical Physics in Trieste.

789 **An inside view of 50 years of physics.**
Emilio Segrè. *Proceedings of the Royal Institution of Great Britain*, vol. 55 (1983), p. 117-32.

The author offers a personal account of the development of physics in Italy, and especially of nuclear and particle physics. It covers the period up until 1938 when Segrè went to the United States, where he later found himself in the position of an 'enemy alien'. He was in fact one of the few to know secrets that not even the highest government officials knew, 'such as the fact that one could make an atomic bomb with plutonium'. This is a very readable and not too technical account of some of the great discoveries made in physics, written by a pupil and friend of Enrico Fermi, who himself received the Nobel prize for physics in 1959.

790 **Observations on the history of science in Italy.**
Maurizio Torrini. *British Journal for the History of Science* (Great Britain), vol. 21, no. 4 (1988), p. 427-46.

This article represents a critical attempt at reassessing the definition and scope of the history of science in Italy. It includes a discussion of the work of Evandro Agazzi, the main author of *History of science from antiquity to the present: Storia delle scienze dal mondo antico al secolo XVIII, dal secolo XIX al mondo contemporaneo*, vol. 2, Rome, 1984. Torrini then focuses on the views of scholars like Geymonat and Garin, expressed in two conferences between 1966 and 1967, which was a crucial period for this subject. The author is also sharply critical of 'the manneristic description' given by Abbri and Rossi (q.v.) and concludes that the history of Italian science is to be found 'among the historians of philosophy gathered around Dal Prà's' study centre'.

Italian first! From A to Z.
See item no. 1.

Stato dell'Italia. (The state of Italy.)
See item no. 7.

How to find out about Italy.
See item no. 25.

Technology and enterprise in a historical perspective.
See item no. 725.

Technological change, rationalization and industrial relations.
See item no. 758.

Enciclopedia italiana di scienze, lettere ed arti. (Italian encyclopaedia of sciences, letters and art.)
See item no. 1040.

Architecture

791 Palladio.
James S. Ackerman. Harmondsworth, England: Penguin, 1976. 196p.
Originally published in 1966, this is a valuable, short, standard introduction to the work and achievements of Andrea Palladio.

792 Michelangelo architect.
Giulio Carlo Argan, Bruno Contardi. London: Thames & Hudson, 1993. 388p. bibliog. (Originally published in Italian in 1990 and translated by Marion L. Grayson).
In the introduction on Michelangelo as an architect there are numerous incisive statements, such as: 'seemingly conservative but in reality audaciously advanced, Michelangelo was the opposite of Leonardo in thought'. The book then deals chronologically with the artist's work in Florence, between 1516 and 1534, and in Rome, between 1534 and 1546, and with St. Peter's construction and later works (1546-1564). The volume is lavishly illustrated and completed by a detailed index.

793 Cities of childhoods: Italian colonies of the 1930s.
Compiled by Stefano De Martino, Alex Wall. London: Architectural Association, 1988. 88p. bibliog.
Seaside welfare institutions were devised by the Italian authorities to offer communal, open-air life, with sea-water and sun-therapy to children, for their physical and moral development. These institutions date back to the middle of the 19th century, but they were boosted and transformed under fascism, which added demagogic and propaganda policies to the original welfare objectives. Although this interesting book is more concerned with the architectural aspects of the phenomenon (as the many photographs, drawings and plans of buildings show), two introductory essays also emphasize the social, cultural and political implications. The first deals with the origins and history of the colonies, and the second is a brief testimony by Eduardo

277

Paolozzi, the sculptor, who remembers his childhood experience in the colonies as the son of Italian emigrants to Scotland. There are short biographies of the architects and a table providing the historical context (1918-1940).

794 **The architectural history of Venice.**
Deborah Howard. London: B. T. Batsford, 1987. 263p. maps. bibliog.

This is the first paperback edition of the book which was originally published in 1980. It is a sound introduction to the main styles of buildings in Venice, from the early Byzantine to Gothic, early Renaissance to Baroque, Palladianism and Neoclassicism to the present day. The work is informative and readable, although it does contain occasional annoying remarks concerning the origin of place names. For example, it is doubtful whether Rialto, coming from *Rivo Alto* means 'High bank' (Italian *riva*) rather than 'deep canal'. The book is illustrated with numerous ground plans and includes a glossary.

795 **Renaissance architecture in Venice 1450-1540.**
Ralph Lieberman. London: F. Muller, 1982. 144p. 1 map. bibliog.

Lieberman provides a short, fairly general but informative introduction to this book which consists of 103 plates and crisp photographs, all taken by the author and 'organised according to type: churches, family chapels, palace façades, *scuole*, and civic buildings'. Each plate is accompanied by a concise explanation which places it in context.

796 **Studies in Italian Renaissance architecture.**
Wolfgang Lotz. Cambridge, Massachusetts; London: The Massachusetts Institute of Technology Press, 1977. 220p. bibliog.

A collection of essays, most of which have been translated from the German and Italian originals by Lotz. Of particular interest for the history of Italian architecture and town planning are the essays on 16th-century squares and their sequel which discusses the square of Vigevano in Lombardy. The essays concern the following topics: the rendering of the interior in architectural drawings of the Renaissance; notes on the centralized church of the Renaissance; 16th-century Italian squares; the Piazza Ducale in Vigevano: a princely forum of the late 15th century; the Roman legacy in Sansovino's Venetian buildings; Italian architecture in the later 16th century; and three essays on Palladio.

797 **Pienza: the creation of a Renaissance city.**
Charles R. Mack. Ithaca, New York; London: Cornell University Press, 1987. 250p. map. bibliog.

Pienza, in Tuscany, owes its name to Pope Pius II, himself a native of the town previously known as Corsignano, near Siena, who wanted the new city to be an example of an ideal early Renaissance city. This is a comprehensive account of the origin and the building of Pienza, and is well written, readable and informative.

798   **Venetian architecture of the early Renaissance.**
John McAndrew.   Cambridge, Massachusetts; London: The
Massachusetts Institute of Technology Press, 1980. 599p. bibliog.

The text occasionally appears somewhat opaque and this may be explained by the fact
that the author died when the book was nearly finished and that it had to be edited by
a colleague. Nevertheless it devotes detailed attention to the works of 15th-century
and early 16th-century architects such as Antonio Gambello, Pietro Lombardo, and
Mauro Codussi, as well as to all the churches, tombs and *palazzi* built or restructured
in this period. An appendix on the cloisters of St. Zaccaria was added by James
Ackerman.

799   **Bologna.**
Giovanni Ricci.   Bari, Italy: Laterza, 1985. 2nd ed. 192p. maps.
bibliog. (Le Città nella Storia d'Italia).

This book is mentioned as an example of a historical series devoted to most Italian
cities (among the ones already published are Palermo, Florence, Rome, Perugia,
Naples, Milan, Bari, Siena, Turin, Venice, Ravenna, Trieste and Cagliari). Each
volume contains a scholarly introduction to the history of the city, and its physical
development, from its earliest settlement. In the case of Bologna, the first chapter is
devoted to 'Felsina', the Etruscan town, and 'Bononia' the Roman town from which
the modern name is derived. Special attention is paid to the architectural and social
history of the city with a large number of illustrations from 15th- and 16th-century
town plans.

800   **History of Italian architecture, 1944-1985.**
Manfredo Tafuri, translated by Jessica Levine.   Cambridge,
Massachusetts; London: The Massachusetts Institute of Technology
Press, 1989. 269p. bibliog.

This book consists of a collection of essays divided into two parts. The first part
includes ten chapters, either dealing with the general characteristics and trends of a
specific period (between 1944 and 1979), or focusing on the works of leading
architects. The second part, which covers the period 1980-85, consists of five essays
on current issues; one of them is a comprehensive survey of structural transformations
and new experiences in town planning. As a result of the organization of the work the
narrative is fragmentary, with interweaving paths and a combination of description
and evaluation. In the brief, concluding chapter, Tafuri states that 'one discovers that
a few of the now mature ideas are approaching – in spite of the atonality of the music
they intone – a horizon on the confines of habitual intellectual systems'. A central
section contains many illustrations with fine examples chosen throughout the forty
years under consideration.

801   **Index to Italian architecture: a guide to key monuments and
reproduction sources.**
Compiled by Edward H. Teague.   New York; Westpoint, Connecticut;
London: Greenwood Press, 1992. 278p.

Reference to illustrations of approximately 1,800 works of Italian architecture are
included in this guide. They refer to more than eighty major books which are either
wholly or partially on the subject, and which are listed at the beginning of the

volume. The main contents are divided into four parts. Part one is the Site Index, listing architectural works according to their specific location (with Florence, Milan, Rome and Venice taking the lion's share). In parts two, three and four, the same works are referred to according to the following criteria: their architects, engineers and planners; their century and site; and their type and site. Finally, there is a section with a general alphabetical listing of works indexed in the previous parts; the indication of their site makes it possible to refer easily to the Site Index for information on illustrations.

802 Italian baroque and rococo architecture.
John Varriano.   New York; Oxford: Oxford University Press, 1986. 329p. 1 map. bibliog.

An authoritative and well-written book which illustrates the precursors of the Roman Baroque before devoting specific chapters to the great architects who transformed Rome: Francesco Borromini and Gianlorenzo Bernini. The book then moves on to discuss Rococo and Academic Classicisms in 18th-century Rome. An interesting feature of the book is the attention paid to northern and central Italy in the 17th-century with discussion of architecture in Florence, Genoa, Bologna, Venice and Turin. The final section is devoted to southern Italy. A glossary completes the volume.

Italian first! From A to Z.
See item no. 1.

Literature

General

803   **Letteratura italiana: storia e geografia.** (Italian literature: history
       and geography.)
       General editor, Alberto Asor Rosa.   Turin: Einaudi, 1990- . 6 vols,
       plus 2 with biobibliog., dictionary and index.
The title recalls that of a famous collection of essays published by Carlo Dionisotti, in
which for the first time special attention was devoted to the history and to the regional
relevance of Italian literature. This was important, since for a long time literature had
been seen largely as a unified phenomenon emanating from central Italy, and from
Tuscany in particular. This is a collective and massive enterprise in which each
volume is devoted to important issues, such as: vol. 1, 'The man of letters and
institutions'; vol. 2, 'Literature production and consumption'; vol. 3, 'The forms of
the text: theory and poetry: prose'; vol. 4, 'Interpretation'; vol. 5, 'The issues'; and
vol. 6, 'Theatre, music, the tradition of the classics: history and geography: I, the
medieval period; II, the modern period; III, the contemporary period'. It is virtually
impossible to give an outline of its varied contents but generally it is a collection of
authoritative, but uneven, essays, which attempt to present a 'state of the art' view of
the complex history and geography of Italian literature.

804   **Précis de littérature italienne.** (A summary of Italian literature.)
       Edited by Christian Bec.   Paris: Presses Universitaires de France,
       1982. 434p. bibliog.
This is a well-organized book and the layout makes it easy to find relevant material in
the various sections and paragraphs. Each chapter is preceded by a list of critical
studies, in which titles originally written in English are usually given in an Italian
translation. If a chapter is concerned with an individual author (for instance, Petrarch)
there is an accurate biography followed by a discussion of the author's works. The
emphasis is frequently on the ideas expressed in the individual works. In the section
devoted to contemporary literature (1940-80), however, it is somewhat strange to find

titles of books, by Calvino or Sciascia, for example, given in French. The volume, edited by one of the leading Italianists in France, is slightly uneven, since different sections have been written by different contributors, all from French universities.

805   **The Macmillan directory of Italian literature.**
Edited by Peter Bondanella, Julia Conaway Bondanella.   London;
Basingstoke, England: Macmillan, 1979. 621p. bibliog.

The book contains 362 entries arranged alphabetically and cross-referenced, many of which were written by different specialists. This useful reference work purports to be the first concise reference guide to Italian literature in English and written for the English-speaking reader, rather than translated from another language. Most entries are enhanced by a concise bibliography.

806   **Dizionario critico della letteratura italiana.** (A critical dictionary of Italian literature.)
Edited by Vittore Branca.   Turin: UTET, 1989. 2nd ed. 3 vols.
bibliog.

This is one of the best general reference works on Italian literature. Authors and significant literary movements are listed with accurate factual and interpretative entries. Each entry is written by a leading specialist in that field and contains a bibliography of the author's works and of criticism connected with it.

807   **Dizionario della poesia italiana: i poeti di ogni tempo, la metrica, i gruppi e le tendenze.** (A dictionary of Italian poetry: poets from all periods, metrics, groups and trends.)
Maurizio Cucchi.   Milan: Oscar Mondadori, 1983. 419p.

Arranged in alphabetical order, this is a useful general introduction to Italian poets and to groups and literary movements, such as *Crepuscolarismo*, *ermetismo*, *futurismo*, *stilnovo*, and *neoavanguardia*. The appendix by Edoardo Esposito deals with metrical forms and terms, which are also arranged alphabetically.

808   **Italy and the English Renaissance.**
Edited by Sergio Rossi, Dianella Savoia.   Milan: Unicopli, 1989.
265p.

These are the proceedings of a 1987 conference held in Italy. The volume contains fourteen contributions by distinguished scholars covering: Humanism; Guarino and John Colet; Petrarch (translation); Italian sources of Surrey's *Aeneid*; Shakespeare and Johnson; Milton's sonnets; and the *Commedia dell'arte*. The introduction by Sergio Rossi is an up-to-date and comprehensive overview of the relationship between Italy and the English Renaissance, of the contacts that Italian emigrants created in Britain and of the English in Italy. There were approximately 200 Italians living in England in the days of Elizabeth and James I, and during the same period maybe 500 Englishmen went to Italy. Four plates and an index complete the volume.

09   **A history of Italian literature.**
      Ernest Hatch Wilkins.   Cambridge, Massachusetts: Harvard
      University Press, 1966. 2nd ed. 523p. bibliog.
An authoritative, clear and informative overview of Italian literature from its origins
to Benedetto Croce (1866-1952). The introduction examines the background of Italian
literature and refers also to the complex linguistic situation of Italy. Chapters one to
twelve deal with authors from just before Dante to Boccaccio and chapters thirteen to
thirty with 16th-century authors, including Machiavelli and Guicciardini. There are
fifty-two chapters in all, arranged according to a broadly chronological order, and
numerous passages from poetry and prose are provided in English translation.

Dante, Petrarch and Boccaccio

10   **Enciclopedia Dantesca.**
      Edited by Umberto Bosco.   Rome: Istituto della Enciclopedia
      Italiana, 1970-78. 6 vols. bibliog.
Each volume of this work, which is fundamental for a study of Dante, is
approximately 1,000 pages long. All aspects of the poet's life, work, style and
language are dealt with by a large number of specialists from all over the world.
Entries are arranged alphabetically from the preposition '*a*' to the word *zuffa* (brawl),
which appears three times in *Inferno*, and they include names of characters, critics
and writers who are connected with Dante or his works. Many entries have their own
bibliographies. The first five volumes contain the encyclopaedia proper, while volume
six is devoted to Dante's biography and to an analysis of the language and style of his
works according to phonetics, morphology and syntax, sentence organization and
word formation. A further bibliography is supplied on pages 501-618 of volume six,
the latter part of which contains the text of Dante's works, including the controversial
Fiore.

11   **Dante philomythes and philosopher: man in the cosmos.**
      Patrick Boyde.   Cambridge, England: Cambridge University Press,
      1981. 408p. bibliog.
It is rare to find a book dealing with a complex subject which is so clear and
passionate as this one. In his discussion of Dante as a lover of myth (philomythes)
and a lover of knowledge (philosopher), the author manages to express, with lucidity
and rigour, the enthusiasm which must have accompanied many of the lectures on
which the book is based. The book can be used as a refined introduction to Dante's
works.

812 **Boccaccio: the man and his works.**
Vittore Branca. New York: New York University Press, 1976. 341p bibliog.

This is a composite translation of excerpts from Branca's fundamental *Boccacc medievale* (A mediaeval Boccaccio) and from his other studies. It is divided into tw parts (Book I and Book II). Book I contains a detailed, informative and we documented life of Giovanni Boccaccio, written with the enthusiasm of t discoverer. The connection is established between the merchant classes in 14t century Tuscany, their travels, culture, stories and Boccaccio himself. Book II focus on the *Decameron*. The rhythmical structure of its prose is investigated as well as 'contents' defined, in chapter three, as a 'mercantile epic' with numerous referenc to the reconstructions of the affairs of 14th-century Tuscan merchants made t economic historians.

813 **Dante: the critical heritage.**
Edited by Michael Caesar. London; New York: Routledge, 1989. 659p. bibliog.

This is an anthology of critical writings on Dante, from the Letter to Cangrande de Scala (attributed to Dante himself) to Francesco De Sanctis's analysis of the *Divi Comedy* in his fundamental *Storia della letteratura italiana* (History of Italia literature) of 1870. The attention of the editor, who has also written a luc introduction to his selection of criticism, has been concentrated on works produced Britain, France, Germany and Italy, with only small samples from other countri such as the United States of America. The book, which includes three indexes, is useful tool to follow Dante's *fortuna* through the centuries.

814 **Giovanni Boccaccio: an annotated bibliography.**
Joseph P. Consoli. New York; London: Garland, 1992. 284p.

Consoli has divided the material into eleven sections, namely: biography, gene criticism; minor works; the *Decameron*; Latin works; Boccaccio in Italy; Boccacc in other countries; Boccaccio and the classics; Boccaccio and Chaucer; manuscrip and editions; and a bibliography. The starting date for the entries is 1939 sin previous bibliography had been investigated by Vittore Branca in his monument *Linee di una storia della critica al Decameron*. An update to this bibliography, which 'all annotations were prepared with the item in hand', is announced by t author in the introduction. The book is completed by an index of critics, and one subjects.

815 **Bibliografia analitica degli scritti su Dante 1950-1970.** (An analytical bibliography of literature on Dante, 1950-1970.)
Enzo Esposito. Florence: Olschki, 1990. 4 vols.

There are 9,180 entries in this bibliography, the fourth volume of which is complete devoted to indexes. The entries are grouped by subject, into reference work miscellanies and anthologies, biographical works, milieu and cultural tradition. The are also sections on Dante's art, studies on the *Divine Comedy*, Dante's minor wor and on manuscripts, commentaries, translations and criticism. The indexes provide list of the texts and periodicals consulted, of the authors quoted, of subjects and index of contents.

816 **Petrarch, poet and humanist.**
Kenelm Foster. Edinburgh: Edinburgh University Press, 1984. 214p. bibliog.

Foster begins with a discussion of Petrarch's life, divided into periods which refer to his childhood and adolescence, young manhood, the meeting with Laura, the stay in Rome, the middle years, Avignon, Vaucluse, Italy and the later years. The central part of this book is then devoted to Petrarch's *Canzoniere*. This is discussed in chapter two which is subdivided into five sections: from Latin to the vernacular; the contents of the *Canzoniere*, with its three sections; the making of the *Canzoniere*; its metrical forms and stylistic soundings; and rhythm and representation. Chapter three is devoted to Petrarch's philosophy and in particular to four Latin works, namely *Africa*, *De Ignorantia*, *De vita solitaria* and the *Secretum*. The bibliography is divided into Petrarch's works and studies and the book is concluded by indexes of names and of individual poems from the *Canzoniere*.

817 **Dante: the poetics of conversion.**
John Freccero. Cambridge, Massachusetts; London: Harvard University Press, 1986. 328p. bibliog.

This is a collection of seventeen essays, previously published in periodicals and in edited books between 1959 and 1983. Each essay deals with specific episodes or passages in Dante's *Divine Comedy*. The author's approach throws light on such topics as the significance of a single line (like the second essay on 'The firm foot on a journey without a guide'), Dante's use of images and on general issues, such as 'Infernal irony' or 'The significance of the terza rima'. These are readable and absorbing essays based on 'personal meticulous research, and on the use of historical, literary and biblical sources'.

818 **The Cambridge companion to Dante.**
Edited by Rachel Jacoff. Cambridge, England: Cambridge University Press, 1993. 270p. bibliog.

The work contains fifteen essays, including three introductions to the three *cantiche* of the *Divine Comedy*. Also covered are: *Inferno* by John Freccero; *Purgatorio* by Jeffrey T. Schnapp; and *Paradiso* by Rachel Jacoff. The objectives of the book are clearly set out in the introduction: 'This book is designed to provide background information as well as up-to-date critical perspectives for reading Dante. It explores five general areas: Dante's works other than the *Divina Commedia* and their relation to it; the literary antecedents both vernacular and classical, of Dante's poetry; historical considerations, particularly social and political; intellectual background (biblical, philosophical and theological sources); and selected reception history (the commentary tradition and Dante's presence in English language literature)'. A chronological table of important dates at the beginning and a detailed index complete this valuable volume.

819 **Petrarch.**
Nicholas Mann. Oxford: Oxford University Press, 1984. 120p.
bibliog. (Past Masters).
A short, but authoritative introduction to the life, the poetry, and the letters o
Petrarch. A final chapter entitled 'the afterlife' deals with the poet's influence an
with so-called Petrarchism.

820 **Dante as dramatist: the myth of the earthly Paradise and tragic
vision in the *Divine Comedy*.**
Franco Masciandaro. Philadelphia: University of Pennsylvania Press
1991. 239p. bibliog.
The author recognizes that 'an important aspect of Dante's poem is the deep relatio
between drama and ritual, and, correspondingly, between the tragic action of th
pilgrim's journey to Eden and the life of the sacred'. The contents, which ar
organized in six chapters, deal with the nostalgia for Eden and the rediscovery of th
tragic, the garden of the ancient poets, the Paradise of Paolo and Francesca and th
negation of the tragic, the recovery of the way to Eden, rites of expulsion an
reconciliation in Purgatory, the garden of the negligent princes and the earthl
paradise and the recovery of tragic vision.

821 **Dante among the moderns.**
Edited by Stuart Y. McDougal. Chapel Hill, North Carolina;
London: University of North Carolina Press, 1985. 175p.
A collection of essays in which two kinds of appropriation of Dante by the moderns i
clearly explained in the first essay by John Freccero. Dante's fragments can be used
as in T. S. Eliot's case, 'often ironically, in order to shape totally different individua
talents'. The role of Cavalcanti, Dante's friend, is played for Eliot by Ezra Pound
who is here discussed by Hugh Kenner. Other moderns who have 'used' Dante t
some extent are Beckett, Yeats, Wallace Stevens and Auden.

822 **Giovanni Boccaccio.**
Judith Powers Serafini-Sauli. Boston: Twayne, 1982. 173p. bibliog.
Boccaccio's life is considered against the historical background of 14th-century Italy
a period of 'profound upheaval and transformation'. Born in 1313, Boccaccio spen
most of his youth, from around 1327, in Naples where his father was working for
Florentine banking company. He resided there until the age of about twenty-eight. Hi
early works, such as the *Caccia di Diana* (Diana's Hunt), *Filocolo*, and *Filostrate*
(the story of Troilus and Criseida) were written there. Returning to Florence in 1341
Boccaccio wrote the *Ameto*, as well as other poems and his masterpiece th
Decameron which is discussed here in a central chapter (chapter four). The work
written in later years, such as the strongly mysogynous *Corbaccio* are discussed in th
final chapter. The book contains a chronology, a soberly annotated bibliography o
primary and secondary sources and a detailed index.

23 **Renaissance humanism: foundations, forms and legacy.**
Edited by Albert Rabil, Jr. Philadelphia: University of Pennsylvania
Press, 1988. vol. 1, 492p.; vol. 2, 414p.; vol. 3, 692p. bibliog.

is virtually impossible to give an account of such a vast, and impressive piece of
cholarship, but the table of contents will at least give an idea of the scope of these
ooks. Volume one deals with the classical and mediaeval antecedents of humanism
nd with Petrarch and the humanist tradition. Of particular interest is part two of
olume one which is concerned with humanism in the major city-states (Florence,
enice, Milan, Rome, and Naples) before focusing on one of the major figures of
umanism: Lorenzo Valla. Volume two is concerned with humanism in England, with
n essay on women and humanism in England, and with humanism in Spain, France,
ermany, and the Low countries, with a separate chapter on Desiderius Erasmus. It
en considers humanism in Croatia, Hungary, and in the Slavic tradition with special
ference to Czech lands. Volume three deals with humanism and education,
uattrocento Humanism and classical scholarship, Renaissance grammar, poetics,
etoric, history and moral philosophy, humanism and the professions (such as
risprudence), theology and reformation, and humanism and the arts and science.
he third volume concludes with an essay by Paul Oskar Kristeller on 'The cultural
eritage of humanism: an overview'.

24 **De vulgari eloquentia: Dante's book of exile.**
Marianne Shapiro. Lincoln, Nebraska; London: University of
Nebraska Press, 1990. 277p. bibliog.

new translation of Dante's work on eloquence in the vernacular, with a full
troduction and commentary.

25 **A dictionary of proper names and notable matters in the works of
Dante.**
Paget Toynbee, revised by Charles Singleton. Oxford: Clarendon
Press, 1968. 722p.

his has now been superseded by material contained in the *Enciclopedia Dantesca*
.v.) but it is still one of the few reliable reference works on Dante in English.

26 **The poet as philosopher: Petrarch and the formation of
Renaissance consciousness.**
Charles Trinkaus. New Haven, Connecticut; London: Yale
University Press, 1979. 147p. bibliog.

ome chapters of this book were conceived as lectures and they confirm that
Petrarch's work and career as a poet should [not] be thought of and studied
eparately from his role as a humanist'. The five chapters deal with: Petrarch and
lassical philosophy; Petrarch and the tradition of a double consciousness; Petrarch's
ritique of self and society; Theologia poetica and theologia rhetorica in Petrarch's
nvective; and Estrangement and personal autonomy in Petrarch's *Remedies* and in
occaccio's *Decameron*. There are ambivalent features in Petrarch's work and these
an be found in both the philosophy of Graeco-Roman paganism and the theology of
t. Augustine, which is part of a long western tradition of a 'double consciousness'.
he author concludes that Petrarch reverted to 'the single consciousness of a
rotagoras, one of the founders of the rhetorical tradition [. . .]. Petrarch sees the poet

and preacher as inspired by Christian faith, using the literary arts to arouse the mora sense and faith of the dispirited and demoralized man' (p. 112).

827 **Giovanni Boccaccio: Decameron.**
     David Wallace.   Cambridge, England: Cambridge University Press, 1991. 117p. bibliog.

A reliable, concise guide to the reading of Boccaccio's masterpiece. After a detaile chronology and an introduction to the making of the *Decameron*, the one hundre stories are dealt with in a critical and lucid manner according to the themes of the te days in which they were purportedly narrated. The book ends with a short chapter c works written by Boccaccio after the *Decameron*.

Other major authors and themes

828 **Shearsmen of sorts: Italian poetry 1975-1993.**
     Edited by Luigi Ballerini.   Stony Brook, New York: Forum Italicum, 1992. 647p.

In the foreword to this book, Luigi Ballerini explains that 'the year 1975 is convenient *terminus a quo*: it was more or less the year that Italy resumed if no writing [. . .] certainly seeking out and publishing poetry'. This bilingual anthology preceded by critical essays on the influence of Ungaretti (by Luciano Anceschi an Luigi Ballerini), themes in contemporary Italian poetry (by Remo Bodei), aspects language (by Paolo Barbera), the lyric and the antilyric (by Thomas Harrison), th Gruppo '93 (by Filippo Bettini), and some comparison between American and Italia poetry (by Stephen Saltarelli). The anthology is quite extensive and the translation are of good quality. It includes poems by Edoardo Cacciatore, Mario Luzi, Emili Villa, Andrea Zanzotto, Paolo Volponi, Alfredo Giuliani, Amelia Rosselli, Antoni Porta, Nanni Cagnone, Luigi Ballerini, Adriano Spatola, Angelo Lumelli, Cesar Viviani, Biagio Cepollaro, and Sebastiana Comand. An appendix of reviews an biographical profiles completes the volume.

829 **The new Italian novel.**
     Edited by Zygmunt Barański, Lino Pertile.   Edinburgh: Edinburgh University Press, 1993. 261p. bibliog.

A general, up-to-date, critical introduction to the Italian novel today precedes th main body of the book which consists of fifteen chapters written by a team c specialists from England, Scotland and Italy. They cover a large number of significar contemporary writers of fiction, such as: Gesualdo Bufalino; Aldo Busi; Giann Celati; Vincenzo Consolo; Andrea De Carlo; Daniele Del Giudice; Francesca Durant Rosetta Loy; Giuliana Morandini; Roberto Pazzi; Fabrizia Ramondino; Francesc Sanvitale; Antonio Tabucchi; Pier Vittorio Tondelli; and Sebastiano Vassalli. Eac chapter sometimes represents the first attempt to introduce, in English, the mai interests and themes of these contemporary authors in a clear and concise manne The introduction to the whole volume helps to place contemporary Italian narrative i its social and literary context. All quotations from Italian are translated into English and a short bibliography is provided for each author. A detailed index completes the volume.

830   **Torquato Tasso: a study of the poet and of his contribution to English literature.**
C. Peter Brand.   Cambridge, England: Cambridge University Press, 1965. 344p. bibliog.

Approximately two-thirds of the book is devoted to a study of Tasso, and the remaining third to his 'fortune' in England. The narrative is rich in detail but never pedantic and is written in a very clear way. It deals with Tasso's life and letters, with the *Aminta*, the preparation for the epic, and the *Gerusalemme liberata*, with its aftermath, with the lyric and with Tasso's minor works. In part two the author investigates the legend of Tasso's life, and the *Gerusalemme* and *Aminta* in England.

831   **Ariosto.**
C. Peter Brand.   Edinburgh: Edinburgh University Press, 1973. 206p. bibliog.

Although the subtitle of this book reads 'A preface to the "Orlando Furioso" ' it is a standard introduction to the life and works of the great Italian Renaissance poet, Ariosto. The main part of the book is indeed devoted to his poem which is considered among the literary tradition, and then its main themes are investigated. The final chapter is devoted to the fortunes of the *Orlando Furioso*.

832   **Eugenio Montale's poetry: a dream in reason's presence.**
Glauco Cambon.   Princeton, New Jersey: Princeton University Press, 1982. 274p.

This is a personal interpretation of many of Montale's poems, from his first collection *Ossi di seppia* (Cuttlefish bones) of 1925 to the *Quaderno di quattro anni* (A four-year notebook) of 1977. The author emphasizes in the introduction his debt to Montale whose friendship he enjoyed for a quarter of a century. Montale's relationship to philosophy and his personal way of responding to external, including historical, events, are properly exploited and contribute to our understanding of Montale's poetry as a whole.

833   **Postmodern Italian fiction: the crisis of reason in Calvino, Eco, Sciascia, Malerba.**
JoAnn Cannon.   London; Toronto: Associated University Presses, 1989. 139p. bibliog.

This work is mentioned here because it deals with four representative contemporary Italian writers, even if it is debatable whether 'there is a certain postmodernist zeitgeist that the fiction of Malerba, Sciascia, Eco and Calvino does not so much exemplify as help to define'. What brings them together is more a generational interest in the question of literature, and the writer's role in society. The book is in fact a collection of readings on the following works: Leonardo Sciascia's *The death of the Inquisitor* and *The Council of Egypt*; Luigi Malerba's *The serpent* and *What is this buzzing?*; Umberto Eco's *The name of the rose* and Italo Calvino's *Mr Palomar* and *Collezione di sabbia*.

834 **Homage to Moravia.**
Edited by Rocco Capozzi, Mario B. Mignone. Stonybrook, New
York: Filibrary, 1993. 175p. bibliog. (*Forum Italicum* supplement).
This supplement to the scholarly journal *Forum Italicum* contains twelve essays on
Alberto Moravia, four of which are in English and the remainder in Italian. Rocco
Capozzi deals with 'voyeurism and intertextuality as narrative strategies in Moravia's
latest works', and investigates some unexpected experimental aspects of his writings.
Louis Kibler looks at another important side of Moravia's activity in 'Alberto
Moravia as journalist: 1930-1935'. An interesting comparison between two waiters in
Moravia's works allows James D. Le Blanc to discuss his relationship to
existentialism and a fundamental theme is discussed by Howard Moss in 'Moravia
and the middle class: the case of "seduta spiritica" '.

835 **Three modern Italian poets: Saba, Ungaretti, Montale.**
Joseph Cary. Chicago; London: University of Chicago Press, 1993.
2nd ed. 380p. bibliog.
Cary has added an important contribution to our knowledge of three significant, and
diverse, poets. This is not merely an introduction to their works but a collection of
three sensitive short monographs. It contains a general introduction on the so-called
crepuscolari poets (a definition of G. A. Borgese dating from 1911), and on the
futurist reaction to them and to all that was reminiscent of the past. The introductory
chapter is entitled 'Twilight, and the conditions of new day'. The section on Umberto
Saba is perhaps the fullest of the three and contains much material which is original.
The chapters on Giuseppe Ungaretti and Eugenio Montale are also clear, stimulating
and very readable. They combine personal readings on Ungaretti's and Montale's
poetry with reference to their biography and to the milieu in which their work is
rooted. A chronological table is included, and the new edition (the original was in
1969) contains an 'afterword' (1993) on each of the poets.

836 **A Leopardi reader.**
Edited and translated by Ottavio M. Casale. Urbana, Chicago;
London: University of Illinois Press, 1981. 271p. bibliog.
The choice of passages from Leopardi's works, from his letters, poems and prose is
preceded by a general introduction on 'The mind and art of Giacomo Leopardi', in
which the author reviews critical opinions expressed about Leopardi by his
contemporaries. He mentions for example the unpleasant remarks made by Niccolò
Tommaseo, and by more recent critics, with some emphasis on the poet's pessimism.
The translations of Leopardi's passages are of a high standard and some of the poems
manage to retain a good deal of the polished expression of the originals which are
provided in Italian in an appendix.

837 **Alessandro Manzoni: the story of a spiritual quest.**
S. B. Chandler. Edinburgh: Edinburgh University Press, 1974. 139p.
bibliog.
A standard critical work which deals with Manzoni's life, his conversion, his poems,
prose works and his major novel *I promessi sposi* (The betrothed). Manzoni's work
on language are briefly discussed in the final chapter.

838 **Italy and English literature 1764-1930.**
Kenneth G. Churchill. London: Macmillan, 1980. 230p. bibliog.
This work was originally a Cambridge PhD thesis and it is a fundamental source of information on the ways in which British and American writers from Addison to D. H. Lawrence have reacted to or developed a picture of Italy. The interest in classical antiquity and the greatness of Rome, 'a greatness to which they felt themselves, the British ruling classes, to be the rightful and magnificent heirs' (p. 1) gives way to Byron who felt that Italy seemed to be a 'stimulating embodiment of the anguished tension which he felt within himself'.

839 **The humanism of Ludovico Ariosto.**
Vincent Cuccaro. Ravenna, Italy: Longo, 1981. 244p. bibliog.
In the introduction the author reviews a large number of attempts which have been made to define humanism. In the first chapter he then discusses an operational definition of this concept revolving around human dignity. With Florentine Neo-Platonism and the concept of Platonic love and Platonic beauty 'man begins to lose his sense of limit, as Ariosto will frequently point out both in his *Satire* and in the *Orlando Furioso*'. Chapter three treats Ariosto's *Satire* as 'explicit expressions of Ariosto's Humanism' while the following chapters consider a humanistic reading of the *Orlando Furioso* in which Ariosto constantly tempers excesses with reason and moderation.

840 **Italian futurism and the German literary avant-garde.**
Peter Demetz. London: University of London, Institute of Germanic Studies (The 1986 Bithell Memorial Lecture), 1987. 21p.
A clear, interesting study of the relationship between Marinetti, the founder of Italian futurism, and German artists, especially Walden and other attentive readers of his works, such as August Stramm, Alfred Döblin and Johannes R. Becher. Demetz shows the influence that futurist language and images had on German writers and artists between 1909 and 1921, even if the basic futurist idea of 'the demand of literature to grasp the truly vital' came to nothing.

841 **Selected poetry of Andrea Zanzotto.**
Edited and translated by Ruth Feldmann, Brian Swann. Princeton, New Jersey: Princeton University Press, 1975. 344p.
This is an extensive anthology of Zanzotto's poetry, from his earliest collections to *Pasque*. The translations of this notoriously 'difficult' poet, who frequently played with language and meaning, are of a good standard. The book is preceded by a short essay written by Glauco Cambon and is concluded by another by Gino Rizzo on Zanzotto's poetry. A full-length monograph has also been written on this poet. See: Vivienne Hand, *Zanzotto* (Edinburgh University Press, 1994).

842 **Primo Levi as witness.**
Edited by Pietro Frassica. Fiesole: Casalini Libri, 1990. (Proceedings of a symposium held at Princeton University, 30 April-2 May, 1989).
A collection of eleven essays on Primo Levi, some of which are in English and some in Italian. Gian Paolo Biasin's contribution, dedicated to hunger and food in Levi's *Se questo è un uomo* (Survival in Auschwitz, translated by Stuart Woolf) is a model of clarity and of deep understanding of the writer's concerns. Other essays in English

291

include: Raymond Rosenthal 'Translating Primo Levi' and Alexander Stille's 'Primo Levi and the art of memory'.

843 Italo Svevo: a double life.
John Gatt-Rutter. Oxford: Clarendon Press, 1988. 410p. bibliog.

The life of Ettore Schmitz, who preferred to write under the name of Italo Svevo, is investigated in full, with constant reference to Svevo's works. The book is divided into nine parts, each of which deals with approximately six to ten years of Svevo's life. The last chapter, entitled 'Resurrection of Italo Svevo and death of Ettore Schmitz 1923-1928' discusses Zeno as the protagonist of Svevo's novel, with reference to *Senilità*.

844 Strangers at home: Jews in the Italian literary imagination.
Lynn M. Gunzberg. Berkeley, California; Oxford: University of California Press, 1992. 294p.

Gunzberg presents an analysis of the iconography of Italian Jews contained in works of popular literature written by non-Jews from the early 1800s to 1938, which was the year in which fascist racial laws came into force. Novels by Father Bresciani, Carlo Varese, G. A. Giustina and Carolina Invernizio are discussed, together with poetry by the most famous of poets in the Romanesque dialect, G. G. Belli. As a result of the investigation, the prevalent view that anti-Semitism does not exist in Italy, voiced among others by Benedetto Croce and Antonio Gramsci, needs to be revised.

845 The hidden Italy: a bilingual edition of Italian dialect poetry.
Hermann W. Haller. Detroit: Wayne State University Press, 1986. 548p. bibliog.

A large and unique selection of Italian dialect poetry from the early 19th century, which includes major figures such as the Milanese Carlo Porta and the Roman Giuseppe Gioachino Belli, to the present day, when the so-called *neodialettali* or *neovolgari* ('neo-dialect') poets, such as Franco Loi and Albino Pierro are well represented. The latter uses a deliberately individual type of dialect to convey not only expressive nuances but deep contemporary concerns using both short lyrical poems as well as long, narrative ones. The anthology is arranged by region, with short dialect profiles for each, and virtually all the main dialects of Italy are included. The selection is wide, representative and interesting and each text is offered in the original dialect version, in an accurate text, with a good English translation opposite. Texts are annotated and each poet is introduced through a short bio-bibliographical piece.

846 Elio Vittorini.
Joy Hambuechen Potter. Boston: Twayne, 1979. 156p. bibliog.

This is a good introduction to Vittorini's life and works. A chronology is provided at the beginning of the book citing the most important dates in Vittorini's career from his birth in Syracuse, Sicily, in 1908 to his death in Milan in 1966. The complex figure of this largely self-taught writer is outlined in a clear and convincing manner. His contribution to the renovation of Italian literature, his political affiliations, from early fascist to committed 'socialist', are explained with a judicious reference to relevant passages in his works (quoted in English). The arrangement of the book is broadly chronological, covering Vittorini's apprenticeship and interest in fantasy to his more pessimistic outlook. A whole chapter is devoted to his best-known work *Conversazione in Sicilia.*

847   **Calvino's fictions: cogito and cosmos.**
Kathryn Hume.   Oxford: Clarendon Press, 1992. 212p. bibliog.
The author makes a thorough examination of the nature of Italo Calvino's literary enterprise, and finds that the common thread is that 'most of his works show a Cartesian cogito facing the cosmos', the human mind trying to make sense of the universe. After an introductory survey of previous criticism Hume uses a psychological approach to the short story 'Under the jaguar sun' and then focuses on the centrality of *Cosmicomics* for Calvino's work to prove her point. She concludes that Calvino used literature not to give reassuring answers but rather as an invitation to use our own intellectual and creative talents.

848   **Of virgin muses and of love: a study of Foscolo's *Dei Sepolcri.***
Tom O'Neill.   Dublin: Irish Academic Press, 1981. 219p.
This is only the second book in English wholly devoted to Foscolo, the first one being Glauco Cambon's *Ugo Foscolo: poet of exile* (Princeton, 1980). The present work is a detailed textual analysis of Foscolo's most famous poem *Dei Sepolcri*, divided into four chapters after an introduction on its genesis and a discussion of 'the unity of *Dei Sepolcri'*. Many quotations from poetry and criticism are provided in Italian, but without a translation.

849   **Pasolini 1922-1975.**
The Italianist, no. 5 (1985). 161p. Special issue.
This entire issue of *The Italianist*, produced by the Department of Italian Studies at the University of Reading, England, is dedicated to Pasolini, in celebration of the ten years since his death. Six main essays, two shorter critical pieces, two short unpublished passages by Pasolini and a very short, but intense, commemoration by Laura Betti, who uses a quotation from Pasolini's *Teorema*, constitute the volume. The critical essays deal with Pasolini's poems, with his journalism, with his attitude to the Italian language, with the text of St. Matthew's Gospel and with Pasolini's film theory.

850   **Midday in Italian literature: variations on an archetypal theme.**
Nicholas J. Perella.   Princeton, New Jersey: Princeton University Press, 1979. 336p. bibliog.
The theme of noontide, 'with its strong religious and philosophical implications' is analysed in various Italian literary poetical texts. The image of the sun is an obvious major archetypal image and will therefore recur in many texts. It has deep mythological and psychological connotations, the heat of midday also being connected with erotic force. According to the modern philosopher Cornelis Verhoeven 'At noon, clarity, light and heat become something absolute, cease to be functions, are transformed into concrete substances, and replace all other concrete substances. Midday threatens to destroy the world that was built up by the morning'. After an introductory chapter, dealing mainly with the theoretical background, chapter one considers the period 'From Dante to Pindemonte'. It is indicative that the theme becomes more dominant in the following period. The remaining topics considered are: chapter two, 'The nineteenth century'; chapter three, 'Gabriele

D'Annunzio'; chapter four, 'Some twentieth-century voices'; chapter five, 'Giuseppe Ungaretti'; and chapter six, 'Eugenio Montale'. A brief conclusion, is followed by an index which completes the volume.

851 **Ludovico Ariosto: an annotated bibliography of criticism 1956-1980.**
Robert J. Rodini, Salvatore Di Maria.   Columbia, Missouri: University of Missouri Press, 1984. 270p.

The bibliography contains 930 entries arranged according to the alphabetical surname of the authors of the books or articles, many of which are in English. All entries are accurately annotated and cross-referenced when necessary. A subject index and an index of Ariosto's works cited complete the volume.

852 **Pasolini: a biography.**
Enzo Siciliano, translated by John Shepley.   New York: Random House, 1982. 435p. bibliog.

An extensive and passionate biography of Pier Paolo Pasolini, with reference to his poetry, polemical writings and films.

853 **The prettiest love letters in the world: letters between Lucrezia Borgia and Pietro Bembo 1503 to 1519.**
Compiled and translated by Hugh Shankland, wood engravings by Richard Shirley Smith.   London: Collins Harvill, 1987. 112p.

The title of this work is a quotation from Lord Byron who saw some of the letters in Milan and was fascinated by the famous lock of hair, attributed to Lucrezia Borgia. First published in a limited edition as Messer Pietro Mio (Libanus Press, 1985), the book is a collector's item, with wood engravings and borders in imitation of 15th- and 16th-century Italian printing. The introduction is clear and informative on the two correspondents, with a short essential bibliography.

854 **The new Italian poetry: 1945 to the present: a bilingual anthology.**
Edited and translated by Lawrence R. Smith.   Berkeley, California; London: University of California Press, 1981. 483p. bibliog.

This is a significant anthology which groups poets under the following labels: New realism (Fortini, Pasolini, Scotellaro, Giudici, Volponi, Vivaldi, and Pagliarani); New hermeticism (Zanzotto and Erba); and New experimentalism (Risi, Cattafi, Roversi, Majorino, Giuliani, Marmori, Pignotti, Rosselli, Sanguineti, Balestrini, Porta, and Spatola). It is a personal but representative selection of Italian poets up to 1980.

855 **Cesare Pavese: a study of the major novels and poems.**
Doug Thompson.   Cambridge, England: Cambridge University Press, 1982. 292p. bibliog.

This is a critical assessment of Pavese's works, written in a clear, sensible way. The book is divided into thirteen chapters, the first of which is devoted to the world of Cesare Pavese, his early years and his career up until his death in 1950. The other chapters are concerned with his poetry and his narrative works and deal with them in a chronological order. The book also discusses the central role that the idea of personal myth had for Pavese. Other key terms used are symbol, language, style and structure.

856   **Three Victorian views of the Italian Renaissance.**
      Richard Titlebaum, edited by Stephen Orgel.   New York; London:
      Garland, 1987. 198p. bibliog. (Harvard Dissertations in American and
      English Literature).
This is a fine 'essay in the history of ideas' on the conception and misconception of Italian Renaissance by 'the moralist' John Ruskin, 'the aesthete' Walter Pater and the historian John Addington Symonds. The original thesis was presented in 1969.

857   **Interpreting the Italian Renaissance: literary perspectives.**
      Edited by Antonio Toscano.   New York: Forum Italicum, 1991. 207p.
A collection of essays originating from a symposium held at the State University of New York in March 1990. As the editor rightly points out in the introduction 'Interpreting the Renaissance poses a series of apparently insoluble intellectual problems. One soon realizes that what is pervasive in discussions of the Renaissance is a striking lack of *consensus*'. Questions concerning topics such as gender and humanism are also discussed.

858   **Italian women writing.**
      Edited by Sharon Wood.   Manchester, England: Manchester
      University Press, 1993. 168p. bibliog. (Italian Texts).
This is primarily an anthology of short texts by Italian female writers. Texts are in Italian but the introduction is in English and includes short biographies of the authors included. In the order of which they appear, these are: Fausta Cialente; Natalia Ginzburg; Anna Maria Ortese; Elsa Morante; Lalla Romano; Dacia Maraini; Anna Maria Scaramuzzino; Francesca Duranti; Francesca Sanvitale; Sandra Petrignani; Ginevra Bompiani; Marina Mizzau; and Paola Capriolo. Each text is accompanied by succinct notes, and the volume is completed by a good vocabulary list. Some works written by the above writers and many other contemporary novels available in English are summarized in the *Babel guide to Italian fiction*, edited by Ray Keenoy and Fiorenza Conte (London: Boulevard, 1995).

How to find out about Italy.
See item no. 25.

Donna: women in Italian culture.
See item no. 538.

Ludovico Ariosto: an annotated bibliography of criticism 1956-1980.
See item no. 851.

Romanzo storico, d'appendice, di consumo. (Historical, serialized, pulp novels.)
See item no. 1045.

Illuminated manuscripts of the Divine Comedy.
See item no. 1049.

Italian Renaissance poetry.
See item no. 1050.

Dante in America: bibliography 1965-1980.
See item no. 1055.

Critical bibliography.
See item no. 1073.

Cinema

859   **Italian cinema: from neo-realism to the present.**
Peter Bondanella.   New York: Continuum, 1988. 2nd ed. 440p.
bibliog.

An introductory section provides an overview of Italian cinema before neo-realism, to which three chapters are devoted, ranging from the works of its masters (Rossellini, De Sica and Visconti) to the early films by Antonioni and Fellini. The light vein of the 1950s, *Commedia all'italiana*, is then explored, followed by the new narrative dimensions developed by Visconti, Antonioni and Fellini. Sergio Leone and the 'Spaghetti Western' are considered, before the author analyses politics and ideology in Italian cinema (on Pasolini, Bertolucci and others). The final chapter surveys contemporary Italian film-making and 'the new Italian comedy': attention here is concentrated on the films by the two best-known female directors, Cavani and Wertmüller, as well as on those by Scola. Only brief references are made to works by such film-makers as Nichetti, Verdone, Moretti, Troisi, and Avati. Many film stills illustrate the book.

860   **Italian films.**
Robin Buss.   London: B. T. Batsford, 1989. 174p.

The objective of this work is to show how Italian cinema over the course of eight years has depicted Italy and the Italians. There are two parts. Firstly, the author explores films in their relation to themes central to Italian individual and social life. This leads Buss to conclude that the best tradition of Italian film-makers is that, behind an apparent parochial façade, they are open to influence from outside and thus reflect the wider reality of their time. Secondly, a reference guide to some 200 films is provided, arranged under twelve headings: culture; history; fascism and war; politics and religion; the upper classes; the low classes; Rome and the north; Naples and the south; crime and the law; women and the family; childhood and youth; and fantasies. For each film cast credits are given, along with plot synopses. A selection of film stills is included, corresponding roughly to the above categories.

861 **Malafemmina: la donna nel cinema italiano.** (Tarts: women in Italian cinema.)
Patrizia Carrano. Florence: Guaraldi, 1977. 260p.

A passionate analysis of the position and the role of women in Italian cinema. It states that the poor quality that is sometimes visible among Italian actresses is not their fault since it is not a requirement of their job that they be good, professionally trained people; they must simply be eternally young, attractive, and faithful to stereotyped models. Italian cinema more than most seems to have found little scope for good actresses, some of whom have to work in the theatre. The responsibility lies with the industry which has never recognized the basic, heroic, role of women in Italian society.

862 **The body in the mirror: shapes of history in Italian cinema.**
Angela Dalle Vacche. Princeton, New Jersey: Princeton University Press, 1992. 306p. bibliog.

The encounter between cinema and history in Italy is the dominant theme of this perceptive study. Italy's cinematic tradition and style are scrutinized against the background of politics and historicist thought. The national self-image as it appears on the screen is the 'body in the mirror': a dynamic shape which changes in response to political and historical development. Dalle Vacche's work is wide-ranging and conceptually sophisticated, and points out the connections between Renaissance art and Italian cinema. Nine films are selected to support the argument for a 'tradition of quality'. These are: Pastrone's *Cabiria* (1914); Blasetti's *1860* (1933); Gallone's *Scipio Africanus* (1937); Rossellini's *Paisà* (1946); Visconti's *Senso* (1954); Bertolucci's *Spider's stratagem* and *The conformist* (1970); and the Taviani brothers' *Allonsanfan* (1973-74) and *Night of the shooting stars* (1982). Three themes and two points in time are used as parameters: fascism, antifascism and the *Risorgimento*; and the Second World War and 1968.

863 **Spaghetti westerns: cowboys and Europeans from Karl May to Sergio Leone.**
Christopher Frayling. London; Boston, Massachusetts; Henley, England: Routledge & Kegan Paul, 1981. 304p. bibliog.

Frayling presents a study of western films made in various European countries, with much emphasis on the works of Italian directors, notably Sergio Leone. He argues that Italian westerns can be better understood in the context of the European perception of the mythological American genre in film-making. Several critical perspectives are adopted to investigate the 'spaghetti westerns', mainly deriving from sociology, history and film theory. The book is divided into three sections dealing, respectively, with the general context, the critics and their controversy on 'cultural roots', and the major films. In the last section Frayling analyses Sergio Leone's films, first, the *Dollars trilogy*, and then the more ambitious film, *Once upon a time in the West*. The volume includes many illustrations (mainly film stills) and appendices on critical filmography, the cut sequences in Leone's westerns, and the sketchy model by Umberto Eco for 'The Superman formula'.

864 **Fascism in film: the Italian commercial cinema, 1931-1943.**
Marcia Landy. Princeton, New Jersey: Princeton University Press, 1986. 349p. bibliog.

The author notes that much of the ordinary film production of the 1930s has been dismissed as escapist, and attention has been directed instead either to the overt fascist propaganda works, or to the few quality films which signalled the emergence of the neo-realist aesthetic. Nevertheless, Landy argues that the neglected films 'deserve attention because in them one finds images, attitudes, and values that can help to alter, expand and redefine the nature of fascist ideology'. The first of two sections focuses on the representation of youth, of men and of women in a variety of genres. The second section looks into historical film, comedy and melodrama, with the emphasis on the representation of the family, work and leisure. A large number of film directors and their works are considered and compared.

865 **The Italian cinema.**
Pierre Leprohon, translated from the French by Roger Greaves, Oliver Stallybrass. London: Secker & Warburg, 1972. 256p. bibliog.

This is a relatively old, but still useful history of Italian cinema, since it provides a well-documented account of its early days. The first four chapters are devoted to the fifty-year period before the appearance of neo-realism, during the Second World War. They are rather short, but full of information on the role of *dive* (or goddesses), their passions, and the spectacular historical epics, to which the poet and aesthete D'Annunzio somehow contributed. Before the First World War, Italy was a leader in the world film markets. The rhetoric and grandiose style, however, laid the foundations for the fascist cinema. The period of neo-realism is competently surveyed and followed by a concise study of the 1950s through its masters: the more mature works by Rossellini and De Sica are considered, together with the early films of Fellini and a variety of minor directors. The last chapter explores the cinema of the 1960s. There is a useful biographical dictionary.

866 **Passion and defiance: Italian films from 1942 to the present.**
Mira Liehm. Berkeley, California; London: University of California Press, 1984. 396p. bibliog.

1942 was the year of Visconti's *Ossessione*, which began the splendid season of neo-realism in Italian cinema. After a preliminary chapter on Italian film-making before that turning point, there is an engaging discussion of neo-realism, which follows through the works of Rossellini, De Sica, Zavattini, Visconti, and minor directors. The historical, political and cultural contexts, as well as the encounter between films and literature, are emphasized. The uneven production of the 1950s and the 'glorious sixties' is then considered. In the latter decade, mature works by such masters as Antonioni and Fellini (as well as the enduring Visconti) were accompanied by the emergence of the new Italian cinema (including Pasolini, Rosi, Bertolucci, and the Taviani brothers). The changing image of the film world during the 1970s and early 1980s is then explored and seen as the product of Italy's unstable political conditions. The book contains a selection of film stills.

867 **Struggles of the Italian film industry during fascism, 1930-1935.**
Elaine Mancini.   Ann Arbor, Michigan: UMI Research Press, 1985.
298p. bibliog. (Studies in Cinema, no. 34).

This is a revised edition of a doctoral thesis submitted to the University of New York in 1981. The author states that during the period 1930-35 the film industry in Italy can be said to be 'essentially separate from Fascism itself'. Among its protagonists there were a few anti-fascists, like Emilio Cecchi, as well as members of the Fascist Party, such as Alessandro Blasetti. In 1930 the first full-scale Italian talking picture was made and in chapter two, after a survey of the silent-film period, the author includes a discussion of Pirandello's only complete script (written in 1930 and translated in full in an appendix). Chapter three focuses on the activities of the Cines studio (eventually destroyed by fire in 1935). The fourth chapter deals with the work of Alessandro Blasetti and his impact on the Italian film industry whilst chapter five concentrates on LUCE, 'the state controlled company for the production of newsreels, documentaries, and educational materials'.

868 **Italian film in the light of neorealism.**
Millicent Marcus.   Princeton, New Jersey: Princeton University
Press, 1986. 443p. bibliog.

The impact of neo-realism on Italian cinema up to the early 1980s is studied here through selective analyses of exemplary films. The thesis of the book is that 'neorealism constitutes *la via maestra* of Italian film, that it is the point of departure for all serious post-war cinematic practice, and that each director had to come to terms with it in some way, whether in seeming imitation (the early Olmi), in commercial exploitations (the middle Comencini), or in ostensible rejection (the recent Tavianis)'. The contents are arranged in four parts: neo-realism proper (Rossellini, De Sica and De Santis); transitions (Comencini, Fellini, Visconti and Antonioni); return to social commentary (Olmi, Germi, Pasolini and Petri); and fascism and war reconsidered (Bertolucci, Wertmüller, Rosi, the Taviani brothers and Scola).

869 **Film-making by the book: Italian cinema and literary adaptations.**
Millicent Marcus.   Baltimore, Maryland; London: The Johns Hopkins
University Press, 1993. 313p.

The meeting between literary and cinematic culture in post-war Italy is analysed through an interpretation of some leading directors and their experiences in adapting literary works. Five directors are studied through two of their films: Visconti (*The earth trembles* and *The Leopard*); De Sica (*Two women* and *The garden of the Finzi-Continis*); Pasolini (*The gospel according to Matthew* and *Decameron*); the Taviani brothers (*Padre padrone* and *Kaos*); and Fellini (*Casanova* and *The voice of the moon*). Theoretical considerations are provided, drawing on semiotics, psycho-analysis, feminism, and ideological criticism; however, Marcus points out that her working hypotheses do not embrace 'any one [of such methodologies] as a totalizing theoretical explanation'.

870 **The new Italian cinema: studies in dance and despair.**
Rick T. Witcombe.   London: Secker & Warburg, 1982. 294p.

The Italian cinema of the 1960s and 1970s is explored here through a selective study of leading directors, arranged by themes rather than in chronological order. Film-makers with artistic affinities are 'paired', with the exception of the final, broader chapter. The themes and relevant names (some of which are misspelt) included are: 'Exile and exasperation: Antonioni and Ferreri'; 'Distance and didactics: Bellocchio [not Bellochio] and Cavani'; 'Forms as fatherscape: Bolognini and Bertolucci'; 'Fable and phenomena: Pasolini and Fellini'; 'Debate and denunciation: Rosi and Petri' [not Petrie]; 'Peasant perspectives: Olmi and the Tavianis'; 'Terminus and tantrum: Visconti and Wertmüller'; and 'During the devolution: Brusati, Brass, Giuseppe Bertolucci, Peter Del Monte and Nanni [not Nano] Moretti'. Film stills and photographs of directors at work are included.

Food and Drink

871 **Burton Anderson's guide to the wines of Italy.**
Burton Anderson.   London: Mitchell Beazley, 1992. 408p. 16 maps.
This is a revised and expanded version of the original book published in 1982 (*The Mitchell Beazley pocket guide to Italian wines*). It is probably the best reference book for finding one's way around the labyrinth of Italian wines. The guide includes more than 2,000 individual wines and producers, with maps of the wine-growing districts and information on local specialities. The journey begins in the Val d'Aosta and comes to an end in Sicily, visiting all twenty Italian regions, as well as San Marino. An oenological profile of each region is followed by information on recent vintages, an exhaustive list of their wines (with quality ratings), producers, and a concise survey of their main dishes and recommended restaurants. Introductory sections include a glossary, notes on wine temperatures, laws and labels, and grape varieties.

872 **Pleasures of the Italian table.**
Burton Anderson.   London: Viking, 1994. 318p.
This is a pleasant and personal account of some of the most interesting natural Italian regional foods, or ingredients. It is written by a journalist who has been living in Italy for a number of years. Each chapter is devoted to a celebration of absolute excellence in one specific field: white truffles from Alba in Piedmont; Tuscan bread; pasta; extra virgin olive oil from Tuscany; Neapolitan pizza; Parmesan cheese; wine in Abruzzo; culatello 'the king' of cured hams in the foggy region near Parma which may be threatened by European law; risotto; Florentine steak; traditional balsamic vinegar from Modena; and last but not least, caffè espresso produced in Sicily. Addresses of shops or remote restaurants where excellence can be found are listed at the end of each chapter. A general introduction and an index complete the volume.

873   **Italian regional cooking.**
Ada Boni, translated from Italian by Maria Langdale, Ursula Whyte.
London: Nelson, 1969. 300p.

This is arguably still the best collection of recipes from Italy. Although the book is without a general introduction, each of the fourteen chapters is preceded by a survey of the culinary characteristics of the region concerned (including wines and cheeses). The regions covered are: Piedmont; Lombardy; Veneto; Liguria; Emilia-Romagna; Tuscany; Umbria-The Marches; Rome-Latium; Abruzzo-Molise; Naples-Campania; Calabria-Lucania; Apulia; Sicily; Sardinia. Appetizing photographs and a selection of recipes accompany the narrative text. The very first and last entries might provide the starter and the dessert of many unforgettable meals: Piedmontese *crostini di tartufi bianchi* (sliced toasted bread with truffles, butter, lemon and parmesan cheese) and Sardinian *biscottini con il miele* (honey cookies).

874   **The talisman Italian cook book.**
Ada Boni, translated and augmented by Matilda La Rosa, introduced
by Professor Mario A. Pei.   London; Sydney: Pan, 1975. 320p.

The full literal translation of this standard national cook book for Italians would be: the talisman for happiness. It appeared in Italy in 1928 and was first translated into English in 1950. The present edition is a condensed version of an otherwise monumental work. However, it still contains a great variety of recipes, from basic staples, such as pasta and pizza, to the most sophisticated dishes with meat, fish and vegetables. The academic spice is provided in this edition by Pei's introduction, which surveys Italy's gastronomic heritage, with observations on its linguistic aspects.

875   **La grande cucina italiana e le sue salse.** (Great Italian cuisine and its sauces.)
Vincenzo Buonassisi.   Milan: Vallardi, 1983. 253 recipes.

An unassuming but important guide to some elusive Italian sauces. The author not only describes the classic Bolognese and Neapolitan sauces, along with many others, but he places them in their context. In addition, many of the ancient and regional sauces are produced, such as those made with garlic (*agliata*) or the green sauce made with tarragon which is used near Siena to accompany a boiled hen. They are ordered according to their main ingredient, such as vegetable, milk, cream and cheese, eggs, fish and meat. Most sauces are accompanied by further recipes for the dishes they traditionally accompany.

876   **The fruit, herbs and vegetables of Italy.**
Giacomo Castelvetro, translated by Gillian Riley.   Harmondsworth,
England: Viking/British Museum, Natural History, 1989. 176p.

Riley offers a welcome translation of a neglected little treatise written in England in 1614 by the Italian Giacomo Castelvetro (1546-1616) on the benefits of eating more fruit and vegetables. It has a foreword by Jane Grigson. An excellent introduction and splendid illustrations complement the volume.

877 **Italian food.**

Elizabeth David.   New York; Cambridge, England; Philadelphia; San Francisco; London, Mexico City; Sao Paulo, Brazil; Singapore; Sydney: Harper & Row, 1987. 240p. bibliog.

This book, almost as classic as its subject-matter, is the third updated edition in a larger format of that which first appeared in 1954. It was revised in 1963 and has been reprinted many times since then. The 1963 Penguin edition was illustrated with Renato Guttuso's pictures and drawings. The present edition is lavishly decorated with a vast assortment of plates, reproducing anything from Roman mosaics to canvasses by Great Masters and current commercial labels. The wealth of recipes are introduced, chapter by chapter, by annotations on regional characteristics and lively historical and autobiographical anecdotes. The book is completed by a series of surveys on wines, a bibliography on Italian cookery and guides to food and drink in Italy, as well as a fine section on the food dimension in some famous travellers' books on Italy.

878 **Gastronomy of Italy.**

Anna Del Conte.   London; New York; Toronto; Sydney; Auckland: Bantam Press, 1987. 384p. 1 map. bibliog.

This is a well-illustrated dictionary of Italian cookery, with the main contents arranged in alphabetical order. Each item is set in its regional and historical context and recipes are scattered throughout the text, whenever popular dishes are encountered. A variety of illustrations complement the book, with photographs of different sizes (some of which are details of classic paintings), drawings, and maps. The annotations are rich with interesting historical references, with *polenta* (maize porridge) for instance introduced as follows: 'The Romans puls or pulmentum was made with farro, [. . .] it was the staple of the Roman plebs [. . .]. In the Middle Ages and in the Renaissance, *polenta* was made with spelt, chestnut flour, millet and even ground acorns [. . .]. The *Friulani* [the people of] north-east Italy were the first to make *polenta* with the maize from the New World that was unloaded at Rialto in Venice'.

879 **The Renaissance of Italian cooking.**

Lorenza De' Medici, photographs by John Ferro Sims.   London: Pavilion, Michael Joseph, 1989. 192p.

A beautifully illustrated book, in which carefully prepared dishes are displayed against the sumptuous background of various forms of Italian art and glorious landscapes. The contents are presented on a regional basis, beginning in Piedmont and ending with Sicily, with all the main regions included. All but one chapter start with the description of a fabulous local castle, manor house or palace, belonging to some of the author's friends. Indeed, when it comes to Tuscany, De' Medici introduces the readers to her own ravishing home in Chianti: a renovated 11th-century abbey. The narrative introduction to each section is followed by a series of relevant recipes. Inevitably, this is a small selection with more than a hint at sophisticated eating habits.

880 **Italian vegetarian cookery.**
Paola Gavin. London: Optima, 1991. 2nd ed. 250p. 1 map.
Italian cookery books are full of dishes containing meat, fish and poultry. Yet, Gavin abundantly shows that the peninsula is truly a paradise for vegetarians, since each of the twenty regions has a distinct culinary style, never without strong vegetarian traditions. After a broad introduction to the Italian regions and their specialities, the chapters of the book focus, respectively, on sauces, soups, grains (including bread, pizza, pasta, rice, polenta and gnocchi), main courses (ranging from pies and tarts to casseroles, fritters, and stuffed vegetables), eggs, cheese, vegetables and desserts. Each section contains a brief presentation, a landscape or townscape drawing, and various relevant recipes.

881 **Edible Italy.**
Valentina Harris. London: Ebury Press, 1988. 176p.
A useful, no-nonsense paperback which contains accurate information about real regional and local dishes, and tips about restaurants (without any reference to price) in the main cities. It is extremely well informed about traditional dishes that can only be found in specific places, such as Ferrara with its *salama da sugo*, a succulent mixture of pork, spices and red wine, preserved for up to six months and slowly cooked. The author also supplies a recipe for the real *ragù* from Bologna, which has nothing to do with foreign 'Bolognese sauces'.

882 **The essentials of classic Italian cooking.**
Marcella Hazan. London: Macmillan, 1992. 722p.
The basic ingredients of this true encyclopaedia of Italian cooking are Hazan's two previous books on this subject, *The classic Italian cookbook* and *The second classic Italian cookbook*. The modernization did not go so far, however, as to include the use of the microwave oven, which 'does not produce the satisfying textures and vigorous, well-integrated flavours [of] Italian cooking'. The innovation is instead a chapter on 'Fundamentals', which emphasizes the central role of flavour in Italian dishes and considers the means by which good results can be achieved. Then follows a comprehensive guide 'to the products, the techniques, the dishes that constitute timeless Italian cooking': from appetizers to desserts, through many first courses (pasta, risotto, etc.), second courses (fish, game, poultry and meat), side dishes (vegetables, salads, etc.) and various doughs (bread, pizza, etc.). Finally, there are suggestions for composing an Italian menu. The book contains fine drawings.

883 **Italy: travellers wine guide.**
Stephen Hobley, photographs by Francesco Venturi. London: Waymark, 1990. 144p. 28 maps.
This is an informative and entertaining book, full of illustrations (pictures of monuments, views of people and cellars, maps and wine labels) and practical advice. After a sober introduction on the classification of wines, travelling in the peninsula and visiting a winery, the journey begins in north-west Italy, with the prestigious Piedmontese areas around Alba, Asti and Monferrato. All regions are accurately explored and their wines described, with useful added information on local food and festivals. Famous wine-growing areas are highlighted, such as the province of Verona, Tuscany and the Orvieto area. The Mediterranean coast and the islands complete the tour. A reference section concludes the book, with an annotated list of

important wines, a glossary of wine terms, and final recommendations as to how wines should be chosen.

884 Italy: a culinary journey.
Edited by Antony Luciano. London: Merehurst, 1991. 272p.

This is a beautifully illustrated, large-size book, with concise chapters on all Italian regions. An outline of their physical features, culinary characteristics and wines is followed by recipes and notes on some of their delicacies. For instance, sweets are mentioned as 'one of the main glories of Piedmontese cooking'; their best-known dessert is 'the golden, creamy *zabaione*'. One of the highlighted specialities of Veneto is Treviso's *radicchio rosso*; Emilia-Romagna has sections on Parma ham and Parmesan cheese; Leghorn's rich fish stew (*caciucco*) is mentioned in the chapter on Tuscany; and a note on *mozzarella* cheese can be found under Campania. A selected glossary is added at the end. This is not a very comprehensive book on Italian regional dishes, as this would probably be an impossible task, but its shortcoming is compensated for by the stunning photographs of places, monuments and landscapes, as well as of actual dishes, it contains.

885 Italian regional cooking.
Simonetta Lupi Vada, with an introduction by Linda Sonntag.
London: Ward Lock, 1987. 224p.

The photographs of dishes against the background of urban or countryside landscapes are an attractive feature of this book; recipes are indicated in adjoining pages. The first two chapters cover the main wines of all regions, and the essential tools and ingredients to be found in a well-supplied Italian kitchen. The rest of the volume is devoted to various types of food: *antipasti*; soups; pasta; rice; vegetables; fish; poultry and game; meat; and desserts. Within each chapter, regional variations are offered and in the brief introduction, on the origins of Italian cooking, Sonntag argues that 'while French cuisine tends to be elaborate and subtle, that of Italy is bold, simple and direct'.

886 The wine roads of Italy.
Marc Millon, Kim Millon, photographs by Kim Millon. London: HarperCollins, 1991. 529p. 53 maps. bibliog.

Italy, it is noted, identifies so much with wine that 'even criminals in State prisons are given a daily ration'. Such observations on the wine-drinking habits of Italians are frequently made by the authors throughout the text. The oenological journey follows the usual itinerary, starting with Piedmont and the other northern regions, then proceeding to the centre, the south (which strangely includes Latium, which belongs in the centre of the peninsula), and the islands of Sicily and Sardinia. For each region the description of wine roads and the listing of wines are accompanied by information on local gastronomy, festivals and useful addresses (on wineries, restaurants and agrotourism). Special features are also included, for instance on Piedmontese vermouth, Tuscan and Umbrian *mezzadria*, and olive oil in Gallipoli (Apulia). Local and regional maps, photographs and a glossary enrich the volume.

887 Dizionario dei vini italiani. (A dictionary of Italian wines.)
Antonio Piccinardi. Milan: Rizzoli, 1991. 634p. maps.

This paperback dictionary provides a history of wine in Italy and detailed information about the types of vine used. Addresses of wine shops in different regions are provided, along with a dictionary of terms referring to wine and wine-making, which precedes the detailed alphabetical list of all Italian wines. A table at the end of the volume offers vintage ratings for thirty-one Italian wines from Aglianico del Vulture to Vino Nobile di Montepulciano from 1945 to 1988.

888 The food of Italy.
Claudia Roden. London: Chatto & Windus, 1989. 218p.

A collection of distinctive recipes arranged according to the Italian region where they come from. Each section is preceded by an informative introduction on the history of gastronomy in the region and present-day culinary practice.

889 The Tuscan year.
Elizabeth Romer. London: Weidenfeld & Nicolson, 1984. 182p.

This is an unconventional cookery book, in that the author offers recipes of dishes which were actually prepared, throughout the year, by a farming family living 'in a green and secret valley joining Umbria and Tuscany'. The culinary information is interspersed with observations on the everyday life and culture of the region. The real protagonist, and a friend of the author, is Silvana Cerotti, the woman at the centre of the family concerned. For each month of the year, recipes are mentioned and introduced with annotations on the main activities in which the family was engaged. The book is informative, original, well written and elegantly produced.

890 Italian Jewish cooking.
Mira Sacerdoti, edited by Rita Erlich. London: Robert Hale, 1993. 262p.

Erlich points out in her foreword that 'Jewish cooking is pre-eminently family cooking' and that Sacerdoti's collection of recipes represents her own personal history, partly identified with the history of Jews in Italy. Ancient cooking rules directed by religious observance combine here with a great variety of regional cooking traditions in the Italian peninsula. They result in 'unmistakably Italian food and distinctively Jewish food'. Throughout the book Sacerdoti combines interesting information on this fascinating heritage with autobiographical anecdotes, oscillating between Venetian and Neapolitan cultures, and the role of women in her family. The contents are divided into six sections: first courses (including the intriguing 'Sabbath Beshalach noodles'); intermediate courses and eggs; fish (including 'Moses' red mullet'); meat and poultry; vegetables (a substantial chapter and a feast for vegetarians); sauces; and sweets and cakes (with many regional variations of charosset, one of the symbolic foods eaten during Passover).

891 Sicilian food.
Mary Taylor Simeti. London: Random Century, 1989. 340p. bibliog.

First published as *Pomp and sustenance*, this is a well-researched and authoritative book on the gastronomic tradition of Sicily. The author has collected an impressive documentation, from literary, historical, gastronomic and anecdotal sources, on ancient types of food, ingredients and recipes. Therefore almost every recipe is discussed in the context of its historical background, with specific reference to its Greek, Arab or Spanish origin. This is a book for the library as well as for the kitchen.

892   **Pâtisserie of Italy.**
      Jeni Wright.   London: Macdonald, 1988. 128p.
This is a sound introduction to cakes, tarts, biscuits and sweetmeats, regional specialities and basic recipes. Each recipe is put into context with reference to variants or other regional similarities by a short introduction.

Italian first! From A to Z.
See item no. 1.

The Italians: how they live and work.
See item no. 3.

The magic harvest.
See item no. 293.

L'arte della cucina in Italia. (The art of cookery in Italy.)
See item no. 294.

Fashion, Design and Interiors

893   **Italian fashion designing, 1945-1980: disegno della moda italiana, 1945-1980.**
Gloria Bianchino, with a text by Bonizza Giordani Aragno, translations by Kathryn D. Marocchino.   Parma: CSAC, 1987. 150p. bibliog.

This is a collection of 164 drawings (twenty-four in colour) of female Italian fashion, belonging to the CSAC, the Centre of Communication Studies and Archives at the University of Parma. A bilingual essay by Bianchino outlines the origins of Italian high fashion which date from 1945. The influence of Christian Dior, in particular, was in evidence. It was during the 1960s that the foundations were laid for what was to become known as the 'made in Italy' label. However, special attention is paid to the 1950s, with its fashion design as a 'genre', and to the 'revolution' of the 1970s, which brought about the 'ready-to-wear' clothes. Frequent references are made to the ateliers of Giorgio Armani and Krizia. The Benetton 'product of average class' is also mentioned. A shorter essay by Giordani Aragno, also in Italian and English, follows with: 'Notes on Italian fashion up until the Second World War'.

894   **The hot house: Italian new wave design.**
Andrea Branzi, foreword by Arata Isozaki.   London: Thames & Hudson, 1984. 156p.

This is presented as 'in part a manifesto and in part a spectacularly illustrated history of the most progressive and heretical experiments in the applied arts and design'. It discusses the roles of leading Italian design magazines and artists. This large-format book contains 400 illustrations (many in colour), divided into eighteen chapters with titles such as 'The Futurist metropolis', 'Italian design in the Fifties', 'Mass creativity', 'Dress design' (including Cinzia Ruggeri's 'Statute of Liberty' garment to which micro-ventilators could be applied 'so that the sleeves puff out'), 'Decorative design' and 'New Design'. A section on biographies of individuals and groups completes the book.

895   **Joe Colombo and Italian design of the sixties.**
Ignazia Favata.   London: Thames & Hudson, 1988. 126p. bibliog.
This is the text and catalogue of an exhibition. Joe Colombo (Milan, 30 July 1930-30 July 1971), who was an avant-garde painter before turning to interior design, stated in 1970 that 'All the objects needed in a house should be integrated with the usable spaces; hence they no longer ought to be called furnishings but "equipment" '. The book illustrates much of Joe Colombo's influential work, especially his chairs and lamps. It includes an introduction by Vittorio Fagone and a portrait of Joe Colombo.

896   **Visual design: 50 anni di produzione in Italia.** (Visual design: 50 years of production in Italy.)
Giancarlo Iliprandi, Alberto Marangoni, Franco Origoni, Anty Pansera.   Milan: Idealibri, 1984. 319p.
An introduction to Italian design covers the first thirty pages of this book. The remainder reproduces posters, book and magazine covers, images and icons dating from the 1930s to the 1980s, with notes on producers and artists toward the end of the book.

897   **The sympathy of things: objects and furnishings designed by Paolo Portoghesi.**
Giancarlo Priori.   Rome: Stoà, 1982. 165p.
A bilingual edition with a great number of illustrations from house interiors and especially of imaginative drawings and objects by the great Italian architect and art historian Paolo Portoghesi.

898   **Memphis: research, experiences, results, failures and successes of new design.**
Barbara Radice, translated by Paul Blanchard.   London: Thames & Hudson, 1985. 207p.
'Memphis was born in the winter of 1980-81 when a group of Milanese architects and designers felt an urgent need to reinvent an approach to design, to plan other spaces, to foresee other environments, to imagine other lives'. Ettore Sottsass, one of the main inspirers of the group, which came to be called Memphis, provides a humorous but deeply-felt introduction to this volume. Radice then examines the group's approach; she explains that their design is ironic, and uses geometric or occasionally fractal patterns for HPL Print Laminate. It is colourful, childish, dreamy, and occasionally recalls the shapes of the 1930s and 1940s (their Plaza dressing table, for example). Some innovative bookcases, with imaginative use of material, also feature among their designs, which, generally speaking, tend towards an emotional relationship with objects. Memphis, as a group, has no manifesto because it is anti-ideological, but some of their results look strangely like a kind of neo-futurism with a touch of pop-art and kitsch.

899 **Italian living design.**
Giuseppe Raimondi, interiors photographed by Carla De Benedetti.
London: Tauris Parke, 1990. 288p. bibliog.
This is an illustrated story of three decades of wealthy Italian life styles, through the
portrayal of interiors. The book is consequently divided into 'The sixties', 'The
seventies' and 'The eighties'. Each part consists of two sections: an introductory
commentary on the context, with reference to such topics as fashion, the media,
industry, furniture and exhibitions; and interiors by famous architects, 'in dialogue
with a clientele belonging to the Italian upper class'. A more interesting remark
points out that the very approach to photographing interiors has changed over the
years, mainly with the abandonment of artificial lighting so that, with natural light,
the photographer allows 'the exterior and interior to interact'.

900 **Italian style.**
Catherine Sabino, Angelo Tondini, photographs by Guy Bouchet.
London: Thames & Hudson, 1985. 300p.
The authors are very aware of the difficulties of defining 'Italian style', which 'is very
complex and difficult to pigeonhole from an aesthetic point of view'. They find that
'there is no one typical Italian interior, just as there really is no one representative
Italian city or one characteristic Italian dish'. Most Italians would agree. The book
illustrates mainly interior designs found in the homes of fashion designers, artists, and
film directors. The houses range from a 12th-century castle in the Roman countryside
owned and restored by Laura Biagiotti, to a house in Venice, apartments in Milan, a
Palladian villa and many others owned, furnished and occasionally designed by
people such as Barbi, Ferragamo, Armani, and Lina Wertmüller. A directory of
sources is also provided.

901 **Italian re-evolution: design in Italian society in the eighties.**
Conceived by Piero Sartogo. La Jolla, California: La Jolla Museum
of Contemporary Art, 1982. 205p.
This is a bilingual, large-size exhibition catalogue. It contains interesting essays on
Italian design, written by Giulio Carlo Argan (with an art historical view), Bruno Zevi
(on design and architecture), Sergio Pininfarina (on design and industry), and
Umberto Eco (on the meaning of 'articraft'). The ways in which everyday life is
immersed in aptly designed objects is shown by the large series of photographs
assembled here. They are accompanied by extracts from literary works, useful
statistical information on Italian society and a series of stills from significant films.
This is a unique, multifarious document of Italian society in the past decade.

902 **Italian design: 1870 to the present.**
Penny Sparke. London: Thames & Hudson, 1988. 240p.
In this interesting work Sparke traces the history of design after the unification of
Italy and shows how far its development was connected with the country's rapid
industrialization from a largely rural economy. Sparke discusses the important role
that firms such as Olivetti had in promoting new and original styles, and in creating
an atmosphere for the reception of bold innovations. The book contains six chapters,
covering the following: the period 1870 to 1914; the influence of Futurism on interior
design; the 1930s, the beginning of mass culture and the resulting tension between

tradition and modernity; the period of reconstruction after the Second World War, and the impulse given to the development of 'utility' design applied to the most ordinary of household objects; the 'economic miracle' of the 1960s and related designs for mass-produced objects, as well as the questioning of consumerism in the late 1960s and mid-70s; and finally, the new trends in design, to include fashion.

903   The Italian Renaissance interior, 1400-1600.

Peter Thornton.   London: Weidenfeld & Nicolson, 1991. 407p.

Profusely illustrated, this is a scholarly book on the decorating and furnishing of private dwellings of wealthy people in Renaissance Italy. In the first part Thornton surveys the 'architectural shell' (ceilings, walls, floors, and the chimney pieces) and shows the great variety of decorative forms that exist. The second part is devoted to furnishings, with particularly interesting sections on the development of beds and canopies, writing-desks, dining-tables and chest-of-drawers. Architectural planning is considered in the third part, covering such topics as the distribution of rooms, the early development of the apartment, and the role of symmetry. Finally, a section sets the Renaissance interior in its social context, and focuses on costs, fashion, patrons and clients, architects and designers, and the influence of women. At the end of the volume a series of drawings emphasizes aspects of various pieces of furniture.

904   Styles of living: the best of Casa Vogue.

Isa Vercelloni.   London: Thames & Hudson, 1985. 224p.

Over 300 illustrations with informative commentary are gathered here, depicting glamorous houses, mostly located in Italy. They are divided into nine chapters and categorizations. For instance, in the chapter 'Living today in an old house', the apartment of an 18th-century villa near Milan is visited to show how the old and the new blend harmoniously. Under 'Restoration', the breath-taking rooms of *Villa Foscari* (also known as 'La Malcontenta') are revealed. The building is one of the best examples of Palladian villas on the Brenta river, near Venice. At this magnificent level, other remarkable entries are the restored 14th-century castle near Milan (which once belonged to the Visconti), and the house on the Arno river in the countryside near Florence, from the 13th century.

Italian first! From A to Z.
See item no. 1.

Italia ventesimo secolo.
See item no. 8.

Italian country living.
See item no. 24.

The houses of Roman Italy, 100 B.C.-A.D. 250.
See item no. 137.

The Arts

General

905 **La maiolica italiana dalle origini alla fine del Cinquecento.** (Italian maiolica from its origins to the end of the 16th century.)
Gaetano Ballardini.   Faenza, Italy: Faenza Editrice, 1975. 207p.

Originally published in 1938 (Florence: NEMI [Nuova Enciclopedia Monografica Illustrata]), this edition has a preface by the well-known art critic, Carlo L. Ragghianti. The first chapter is devoted to the primitive ceramics which appeared in Italy in the early Middle Ages and which were later to involve (in the 14th century), the use of lead and tin calcinated together. The second chapter concerns the so-called *bacini* and the importation of pots from Majorca (in Italian *Maiorica* and then *Maiolica*). There is then a chapter dedicated to the Della Robbias in which the author refutes that Luca (1399-1482) was the inventor of tin-plated enamel. Other short chapters deal with graffito ceramics, with the *stile severo* and the transition to the *stile bello* or 'beautiful style'. Sixty-four illustrations arranged chronologically from the 8th-9th century through to the end of the 16th century and connected with the various styles mentioned in the text complete the volume.

906 **Manuale di numismatica: contiene i valori e le rarità di tutte le monete decimali italiane dal 1800 ad oggi.** (A handbook of numismatics: it contains values and rarity of all Italian decimal coins from 1800 to today.)
Remo Cappelli.   Milan: Mursia, 1987. 353p.

A handbook aimed mainly at beginners but with a considerable amount of information on Italian coins and Roman coins. Photographic reproductions of individual coins occupy 105 pages of the volume.

907   **Tin-glazed earthenware: from maiolica, faience and delftware to the contemporary.**
Daphne Carnegy.   London: A & C Black, 1993. 176p. 1 map. bibliog.
The book is divided into three sections. In section one there is a survey dealing with early tin glaze, with a chapter devoted to Italian maiolica. Section two covers materials and techniques, and section three contemporary perspectives. The techniques for the preparation of the glaze and aspects of workshop and factory production are also discussed.

908   **Saggio di bibliografia numismatica medioevale italiana.** (Mediaeval Italian numismatic bibliography.)
Raffaele Ciferri.   Pavia: Associazione Pavese di Numismatica e Medaglistica, 1961. 498p.
This bibliography is arranged alphabetically by author and lists material which is of historical and economic interest, but which has been largely ignored by those concerned with strictly numismatic bibliographies. One such example is by Francesco and Ercole Gnecchi, *Saggio di bibliografia numismatica delle zecche italiane medioevali e moderne* (Numismatic bibliography of Italian mints, mediaeval and modern), Milan: Cogliati 1889, in which entries are arranged according to the minting place.

909   **La moneta a Milano nel Quattrocento: monetazione argentea e svalutazione secolare.** (Coins in 15th-century Milan: silver coinage and secular devaluation.)
Carlo M. Cipolla.   Rome: Istituto Italiano di Numismatica, 1988. 68p.
Cipolla presents a study of the value of minted coins in 15th-century Milan, based on the 'minting orders' and contracts which have survived history. Silver circulation and monetary devaluation are also discussed. Some documents are transcribed in the appendices and eight tables with coin photographs complete the volume.

910   **"Ai confini della maiolica ed oltre . . ." il collezionista, l'antiquario, il restauratore, lo studioso, il museologo, la scuola, l'editoria specializzata.** ('At the borders of maiolica and beyond . . .' the antiques dealer, the restorer, the scholar, the museum expert, the school, the specialist publishers.)
Comune di Faenza.   Faenza: Comune di Faenza, 1988. 180p.
This is the catalogue of an exhibition held in September-October 1988 at Faenza. It deals with the images, emblems and characters used in ceramics from chivalric epic to modern times. The actual catalogue is followed by an illustration of ceramics which were for sale at various stands at the exhibition.

911   **Le medaglie di Maria Luigia Duchessa di Parma.** (The medals of Maria Luigia, the Duchess of Parma.)
Massimo Federico.   Parma: La Pilotta, 1981. 145p. bibliog.
This slim volume is devoted to a number of medals coined in the early 19th century in Parma and Piacenza to celebrate a variety of public events, such as the election of

Maria Luigia as Duchess of Parma in 1815, and the construction of two bridges, one on the river Taro, and the other on the Trebbia. Other medals were coined as prizes or to celebrate the visit of the Duchess and her consort to establishments of various kinds or the building of important new slaughterhouses (*beccherie*) in Parma.

912 **Il museo internazionale delle ceramiche a Faenza.** (The international museum of ceramics at Faenza.)
Giuseppe Liverani. Rome: Istituto Poligrafico dello Stato, 1956. 72p.

A succinct guide to the museum which was previously known as 'Il museo delle ceramiche a Faenza', with a ground-plan of the museum and 103 black-and-white photographs. This guide book is part of a series, with an English-language version, 'Guide books to museums and monuments in Italy', published by the Italian Ministry of Education (Ministero della Pubblica Istruzione, Direzione Generale delle Antichità e Belle Arti).

913 **Lenci dolls in full colours: toys for the rich and famous, 1920-1940.**
Helen Nolan. New York: Dover Publications, 1986. 32p.

The Lenci Company was established in Turin shortly after the end of the First World War. Several artists were involved in the production of dolls with an extraordinary range of faces and subjects. The material used was basically felt, both for the dolls and for the clothes, although organdie was also used for the latter. Some basic materials of wood and ceramic were also used. Over forty illustrations are included here, divided into five types of dolls: the Children; the Orientals; the Googlies (with wide-open eyes and hyper-astonished expressions); the Luscious Ladies; and the Good Sports. The book will interest fashion connoisseurs, social historians and anybody curious to know how the little daughters of the wealthy passed their time.

914 **Masterpieces of Italian violin making, 1620-1850.**
David Rattray, photographs by Clarissa Bruce. London: Royal Academy of Music, 1991. 72p. 1 map. bibliog.

A beautiful gallery of valuable musical rarities, consisting of twenty-six important stringed instruments from the collection belonging to the Royal Academy of Music. They were left to the London Academy by a number of generous patrons of music over the centuries, and are renowned for 'the range of tone colour, the extra resonance, the speedy response to the bow, the depth and carrying power'. The first instrument shown is a viola, made by Antonio and Girolamo Amati (Cremona, 1620); the last is a violin made by Joannes Francesco Pressenda (Turin, 1847). In between there are more instruments by Amati and also by Stradivari, Guadagnini and Gagliano. A discography and a glossary of violin-making terms conclude the book.

Visual arts

915 **Materialmente: scultori degli anni ottanta.** (Materially: sculpture of the eighties.)
Edited by Dede Auregli, Cristina Marabini. Ravenna: Essegi, 1989. 62p.

This is the catalogue of an exhibition held in Bologna in February and March 1989. In her introduction Dede Auregli outlines the main trends in the sculptures of the 1980s, from 'art pauvre' to an interest in personal, individual mythology, and in 1983 to a new futurism. Sculptors in the eighties also use a variety of materials, from noble sources, such as marble, natural sources, such as soil, water, leaves, and stones, to those produced by new technologies, such as vinyl and polyurethane. The book contains some interviews with artists and critics, and reproduces approximately fifty sculptures. The catalogue is completed by bio-bibliographies of the artists. The pages are not numbered.

916 **Giotto and the language of gesture.**
Moshe Barasch. Cambridge, England: Cambridge University Press, 1987. 196p. bibliog.

A study dealing with 'speaking hands' in the work of Giotto and in the preceding pictorial tradition. The position of hands may indicate a number of things, including: prayers; gesture of incapacity; covered hands; expulsion; and *noli me tangere*. Other uses of symbolism, for instance, that of colours, are also discussed.

917 **Giotto and the orators: humanist observers of painting in Italy and the discovery of pictorial composition 1350-1450.**
Michael Baxandall. Oxford: Clarendon Press, 1971. 185p.

In the first part of this work the author tries to show 'that the grammar and rhetoric of a language may substantially affect our manner of describing and, then, of attending to pictures and some other visual experiences and to see to what extent rhetorical and linguistic conditions of Latin constrained the description of paintings by humanists'. The second problem deals with how the concept of pictorial 'composition' came to Alberti in 1435.

918 **Fifteenth-century central Italian sculpture: an annotated bibliography.**
Sarah Blake Wilk. Boston, Massachusetts: Hall, 1986. 401p.
(Reference in Art History).

'Central Italian' refers to sculpture executed by artists born in the provinces of Tuscany, Lazio, Umbria and the Marches. The bibliography includes materials available before 1985 and contains 2,000 numbered entries. The book is divided into sections dealing with general entries, major cities (Florence, Siena, the rest of Tuscany, and Rome), specific materials (bronze, terracotta, wax, and wood), special topics and individual artists.

919 **Italian art in the 20th century.**
Edited by Emily Braun.   London: Royal Academy of Arts; Munich:
Prestel-Verlag, 1989. 465p. bibliog.

One of the most extensive works on Italian painting and sculpture from 1900 to 1988,
this was published on the occasion of the Royal Academy exhibition held in London
between 14 January and 9 April 1989. The book is divided into four main sections
(1900-19; 1919-45; 1945-68; and 1968-88), each one of which is preceded by an
essay written by an historian, and then followed by more specific essays on artistic
movements and individual artists. At the end of the book individual biographies and
photographs of the artists, are provided. Among these are: Umberto Boccioni;
Massimo Campigli; Carlo Carrà; Felice Casorati; Giorgio de Chirico; Filippo de Pisis;
Lucio Fontana; Renato Guttuso; Piero Manzoni; Arturo Martini; Amedeo Modigliani;
Giorgio Morandi; Alberto Savinio; and Emilio Vedova.

920 **The employment of sculptors and stonemasons in Venice in the
fifteenth century.**
Susan Connell.   New York; London: Garland, 1988. 308p. maps.
bibliog. (Outstanding Theses in the Fine Arts from British
Universities).

Based on a thesis which was originally submitted in 1976, with a new preface to bring
the bibliography up to date. Connell describes the working life and conditions of
stonemasons in Venice between circa 1380 and 1480. The study is largely based on
Venetian archive material, and includes biographies of a few stonemasons, only some
of whom were also sculptors.

921 **Rome: the biography of its architecture from Bernini to
Thorvaldsen.**
Christian Elling.   Tübingen, Germany: Ernst Wasmuth, 1975. 586p.
8 maps. bibliog.

First published in 1950 in Danish by Gyldendal (Copenhagen), this book deals with
the city of Rome between 1680 and 1797 and represents a personal view of its
architecture. Its main interest lies in the large number of impressive photographs
taken around 1947-50. The volume is illustrated with 212 plates.

922 **Venetian narrative painting in the age of Carpaccio.**
Patricia Fortini Brown.   New Haven, Connecticut; London: Yale
University Press, 1988. 310p. bibliog.

Based on research carried out for a doctorate at California University, the work is an
attempt to capture the meaning that some paintings by Vittore Carpaccio, Gentile
Bellini, Lazzaro Bastiani, and other Venetian artists between approximately 1470 and
1530, may have had for late 15th-century viewers. Most of the works discussed
belong to the 'stories' (that is, narratives) genre as defined by L. B. Alberti in his
book on painting. These artists are nevertheless said to belong to an 'eyewitness
style'. The book is very well structured, reads coherently and includes a detailed
bibliography, as well as a glossary and an index.

923 **Florentine Gothic painters: from Giotto to Masaccio: a guide to painting in and near Florence 1300 to 1450.**
Richard Fremantle. London: Secker & Warburg, 1975. 665p. maps. bibliog.

As the author states, 'The purpose of this work is to provide a handbook of the painters active in Florence during the fourteenth and first half of the fifteenth century'. It provides valuable information and illustrations on the works of lesser-known figures such as the Gaddi or the Cioni, and each painter's section is arranged with biographical quotations, a bibliography, a list of signed and dated works by the artist, and reproductions of each artist's work.

924 **Spirituality in conflict: Saint Francis and Giotto's Bardi Chapel.**
Rona Goffin. University Park, Pennsylvania; London: Pennsylvania State University Press, 1988. 142p. bibliog.

A discussion of Franciscan spirituality in connection with Giotto's paintings, and in particular with those depicting St. Francis's life in the Bardi chapel at Santa Croce in Florence. Goffin also discusses the 'Bardi Saint Francis Master Dossal', which was painted at a time when some of those who had known Francis were still living, and its influence on Giotto. The volume is completed by seventy plates and a detailed index.

925 **Caravaggio.**
Howard Hibbard. London: Thames & Hudson, 1988. 2nd ed. 404p. maps. bibliog.

After a largely biographical introduction which is well-written, enjoyable and informative, the text is divided into three sections dealing, chronologically, with Caravaggio's painting career. This ranges from early secular paintings to the early religious and to his mature activity in Rome. This book is an excellent starting point for the study of this painter. It includes appendices on 'Other paintings attributed to Caravaggio' and 'Old reports about Caravaggio, in the original and in translation'.

926 **Post-Impressionism.**
Edited by John House, Mary Anne Stevens. London: Royal Academy of Arts, Weidenfeld & Nicolson, 1979. 302p. bibliog.

Published on the occasion of the exhibition at the Royal Academy of Arts in London (17 November 1979-16 March 1980), this catalogue contains a substantial section on Italian post-impressionist painters, together with France, Germany, Norway, Switzerland, Great Britain, Ireland, and The Netherlands. The entries are arranged alphabetically and there is an essay on the origins of divisionism and its relationship to French post-impressionism.

927 **S. Andrea in Mantua: the building history.**
Eugene J. Johnson. University Park, Pennsylvania; London: Pennsylvania State University Press, 1975. 127p. bibliog.

The text of this detailed study which purports to answer the question 'Does the present church faithfully reflect Alberti's original design of the 1470s?' occupies the first sixty pages of the book. This is then followed by seven appendices containing annotated archival and other documents in the original Italian and Latin. Detailed endnotes, ninety-nine plates and fourteen ground-plans conclude the volume.

928   **Leonardo da Vinci: the marvellous works of nature and man.**
       Martin Kemp.   London; Melbourne; Toronto: J. M. Dent & Sons,
       1981. 384p. bibliog.

'This is intended to be a book about Leonardo as a whole', and indeed it is. Kemp draws extensively on Leonardo's own writings and drawings to illustrate his career, but rather than arranging the material in a chronological order it is centred more on Leonardo's interests and themes. The work is divided into five long chapters, the first of which is 'Leonardo da Firenze', referring to the years spent in that city from the apprenticeship with Andrea del Verrocchio to the experience that provided him with a vision of art as a rational pursuit. The following chapters deal with the microcosm, the exercise of fantasia, reference to grotesque styles, and the republic: new battles and old problems and the prime mover.

929   **Giuseppe Arcimboldo.**
       Werner Kriegeskorte, translated by Hugh Beyer.   Cologne, Germany:
       Benedikt Taschen Verlag, 1991. 79p. bibliog.

A basic introduction to the life and works of one of the most famous painters of visual metaphors. Giuseppe Arcimboldo was a Lombard painter who was probably born in Milan in 1527 and died in 1593. His main works (Spring, Summer, Autumn, Winter, air, fire, earth, and water) are accurately described with reference to their location and their symbolism and meaning. A few drawings by Arcimboldo complete the volume.

930   **Andrea Mantegna.**
       Edited by Jane Martineau.   London: Royal Academy of Arts; New
       York: Metropolitan Museum of Art, Olivetti-Electa, 1992. 500p.
       bibliog.

This volume was published to coincide with the exhibition, *Andrea Mantegna* at the Royal Academy of Arts in London (17 January-5 April 1992) and at the Metropolitan Museum of Art in New York (9 May-12 July 1992). The actual catalogue, with its entries prepared by various specialists on Renaissance arts and on Mantegna, is preceded by essays on 'Mantegna and the men of letters', 'The art of Andrea Mantegna', 'Mantegna as printmaker' and 'Mantegna and his printmakers', 'Some observations on Mantegna's painting technique' and 'Mantegna's paintings in distemper'. Each section of the catalogue is preceded by a scholarly introduction and there are 154 entries.

931   **The architecture of the monastic library in Italy: 1300-1600.**
       James F. O'Gorman.   New York: New York University Press, 1972.
       85p.

A catalogue of fifty-four Italian monastic libraries, preceded by a full introductory essay on their architecture, planning and layout. The catalogue also refers to libraries which are no longer in existence and includes a series of black-and-white photographs and drawings of plans and orientation of libraries in Bologna, Cesena, Florence, Milan, Modena, Padua, Parma, Perugia, Piacenza, Rome, Siena and Venice among others. The volume includes sixty illustrations.

932   **The art of Paolo Veronese 1528-1588.**
      William R. Rearick.   Washington, DC: National Gallery of Art;
      Cambridge University Press, 1988. 212p. bibliog.
This is a catalogue of the exhibition held between 13th November 1988 and 20
February 1989 to celebrate the four hundredth anniversary of the death of Veronese.
The introduction is written by Terisio Pignatti and paintings are arranged in
chronological order from 1545 to 1588.

933   **The province of painting: theories of Italian Renaissance art.**
      Jeroen Stumpel, translated from the Dutch (Het Domein Van De
      Schilderkunst).   Utrecht, Netherlands: [Jeroen Stumpel], 1990. 299p.
This is a collection of essays divided into three sections: Raphael by Raphael: the
story of the Madonna of the fish; The tiger and the dream: the aesthetic theory of the
birth of tragedy explained in pictures; and Speaking of manner: Maniera and its
meanings.

934   **The Palazzo del Te in Mantua: images of love and politics.**
      Egon Verheyen.   Baltimore, Maryland; London: Johns Hopkins
      University Press, 1977. 156p. bibliog.
Completed by the middle of the 1530s, the Palazzo del Te was commissioned by the
Duke of Mantua, Federigo II Gonzaga, to Giulio da Romano, as a suburban retreat.
The author offers not only an excellent concise study of the building and of its
decoration carried out by Romano, but first and foremost a study in art patronage
which shows that 'there is a direct relation between Federigo's political ambitions and
his decision to transform a modest retreat into a stately palace'. Part two is a
catalogue raisonné of the decoration whilst part three concerns the documentation.

The theatre

935   **The comedies of Ariosto.**
      Translated and edited by Edmond M. Beame, Leonard G. Sbrocchi.
      Chicago; London: University of Chicago Press, 1975. 322p.
A clear introduction provides the background to Italian comic theatre before Ariosto,
with reference to the poet's love for the theatre and his ability to adapt classical plays
to Renaissance themes. A brief note on the translation completes the introduction.
The translations of seven comedies then follow: *La Cassaria* (The coffer); *I Suppositi*
(The pretenders); *Il Negromante* (The Necromancier); *La Lena* (Lena); a second
version of *La Cassaria*; *Gli Studenti* (the students); and *La scolastica* (the
scholastics), which is a continuation of the previous work.

936   **Baroque theatre construction: a study of the earliest treatise on
       the structure of theatres by Fabrizio Carini Motta, architect and
       scene designer at the court of Mantua 1676.**
       Edward Craig.   [London]: Bedlow Press, 1982. 70p. (Plus facsimile
       of 1676 treatise). bibliog.
Little is known about F. Carini Motta from Mantua and this work of his is extremely
rare. The book has a sound introduction in English to the facsimile of the Italian text
which was published in 1972 in Milan. Interesting drawings from the 17th-century
edition complete the volume.

937   **A companion to Pirandello studies.**
       Edited by John Louis Di Gaetani.   New York; Westport, Connecticut;
       London: Greenwood Press, 1991. 443p. bibliog.
This book could justifiably be called: 'All you want to know about Pirandello'. An
introductory chapter covering his life and work is followed by a chronology from his
birth in Agrigento, Sicily in 1867 to his death in Rome in 1936 and the performance
of his last play, *The mountain giants*, in 1937. The contents are then structured into
six parts covering Pirandello's world, his relationship with other playwrights and with
European literary movements, his plays, his influence, and his attitude to women.
Four appendices complete the volume; they contain three poems by Pirandello with
an English translation, a production history of *Six characters in search of an author*
and *Henry IV*, a list of Pirandello's publications, and a detailed Pirandello
bibliography.

938   **Commedia dell'arte: a guide to the primary and secondary
       literature.**
       Thomas F. Heck.   New York; London: 1988. 450p.
Contains a wealth of scholarly information on Italian Renaissance comedy. Entries in
various languages are full and very competently annotated and the sections into which
the book is divided will offer an idea of its range and scope. After a general
introduction to the Commedia dell'Arte (CdA) there is a treatment of its sources and
its scenery. This is followed by a historical study of the Italian CdA and a discussion
of its diffusion outside Italy. Sections five to eight deal with: the actors of the CdA
and their legacy; the masques (stock characters); improvising and the mask; and
dance and music. Section nine considers the revival of the genre in the 19th and 20th
centuries and is followed by sections on the iconography of the CdA and literature
and the CdA. There is also an appendix of titles of *scenari* and a final bibliography
arranged in alphabetical order.

939   **Italian plays, 1500-1700 in the University of Illinois library.**
       Compiled by Marvin T. Herrick.   Urbana, Illinois; London:
       University of Illinois Press, 1966. 92p.
This collection consists mainly of Italian plays by 16th-century authors. It is a useful
checklist arranged in alphabetical order by author and with entries in short-title
catalogue format.

940 **Dario Fo and Franca Rame.**
David L. Hirst. Basingstoke, England; London: Macmillan, 1989.
218p. bibliog. (Modern Dramatists).

Dario Fo is admired as a leading clown, and both he and his wife Franca Rame have worked together as performers and created their own scripts. Hirst's study examines the significance of their theatre which has always been seen as a form of political drama, even when it works best as a farce. Fo's monologues, the most famous of which is *Mistero buffo*, and most of his plays are discussed in this book. There are twelve photographs illustrating most of the performances of Dario Fo and Franca Rame.

941 **Luigi Pirandello: an approach to his theatre.**
Olga Ragusa. Edinburgh: University Press, 1980. 198p. bibliog.

Ragusa provides a sound introduction to Pirandello's work. The work opens with a biographical sketch and analysis of Pirandello's early narrative and drama, with special reference to his grotesque theatre. A whole chapter ('A history and an analysis') is devoted to *Six characters in search of an author* and chapter five is concerned with the later Pirandello.

942 **The commedia dell'arte: a documentary history.**
Kenneth Richards, Laura Richards. Oxford: Blackwell, 1990. 346p.
bibliog.

This book is a substantial contribution to our knowledge and understanding of the *Commedia dell'Arte*, although in the preface the authors claim that it is 'neither a history nor a comprehensive survey of all aspects of the Italian professional theatre between the mid-sixteenth and mid-eighteenth centuries'. The volume opens with a chronology beginning in 1545, the first record of the formation of an Italian professional acting troupe in Padua, and ending in 1762 when Goldoni left Venice to work with the Comédie Italienne in Paris. Problems connected with an interpretation of the *commedia* as popular or improvised theatre are discussed in the introduction. After a chapter in which possible antecedents from Greek and Roman comedies are discussed, the book then deals with professional companies, masks and *scenarii*, improvisation and performance. Each chapter contains numerous documents from 16th- and 17th-century sources translated into English.

943 **Carlo Goldoni: life, works, and times.**
Eugene Steele. Ravenna, Italy: Longo, 1981. 185p. bibliog.

An investigation of Goldoni's life in Venice and in Paris and of a selection of his numerous plays, as well as of some of his lesser-known work like the intermezzos. Goldoni's international reputation was based, in his lifetime, on musical settings and librettos for musical dramas and farces. The last two chapters deal with Goldoni's reception and performance in various countries. Each chapter is subdivided into short sections, each dealing with one play or with one single subject, which makes it easy to consult the book. A chronology is provided at the beginning.

Music, opera and dance

944   The Italian 'trio' sonata: from its origins until Corelli.
Peter Allsop.   Oxford: Clarendon Press, 1992. 334p. 2 maps. bibliog.

A study devoted to lengthy free compositions (that is, not dances, sets of variations, or short introductory sinfonias) 'scored for instrumental combinations of two trebles, or two trebles and one melodic bas instrument and continuo which today frequently masquerade under the misnomer of 'trio' sonatas'. Part one deals with general problems of instruments, genre and function, and with the role of the composer in society. Part two considers 'regional developments' in the ducal courts (Mantua, with Salomon Rossi, Giovan Battista Buonamente, and Giuseppe Scarani, Modena, and Naples). Other locations include Emilia-Romagna, Rome and the northern regions. The book concludes with a study of the Corellian sonata. Numerous musical examples are provided.

945   Monteverdi.
Denis Arnold.   London: Dent, 1975. 212p. bibliog.

This is the standard biography of Monteverdi, with chapters on the earlier madrigals, madrigals with basso continuo, dramatic music, and church music. The book is completed by useful appendices including: a chronology, a catalogue of Monteverdi's works, and personalia.

946   The oratorio in Venice.
Denis and Elsie Arnold.   London: Royal Musical Association, 1986. 117p.

'Venice, in music, as in politics, was rarely in the forefront of development', therefore the oratorio arrived late in the lagoon. Although invented by the order of St. Philip Neri, the Oratorians, around 1550, the genre arrived in Venice only around 1660. The authors deal with this form of sacred music from the 17th century through 'the time of plenty: 1740-1777', to the last years of the 'most serene republic'. A list of oratorios performed in Venice 1662-1809 and an index of singers and one of oratorios are included in the appendix.

947   Donizetti and his operas.
William Ashbrook.   Cambridge, England: Cambridge University Press, 1982. 744p. bibliog.

Donizetti, more than other composers, is seen as the natural step towards the work of Verdi and later operatic drama. This book is divided into two parts, part one of which introduces the composer's career in terms of his operas; Donizetti's sacred or instrumental music is not included in Ashbrook's study. Part two studies the operas one by one and there are additional chapters on Donizetti's operatic world and his use of operatic conventions. The book is enriched by numerous appendices.

948   **Women musicians of Venice: musical foundations 1525-1855.**
      Jane L. Baldauf-Berdes.   Oxford: Clarendon Press, 1993. 305p.
      bibliog.

The first two chapters are devoted to an outline of the organization of Venetian
society. The third deals with music and its organization from the 14th to the 18th
centuries. Part two is concerned with the *ospedali*, which were early social welfare
institutions around which choirs and music were organized. Chapter six is one of the
most substantial chapters in this section of the book; it is devoted to 'the *cori* of the
ospedali' and studies the various meanings of *coro*, and of its composition. Part three
is dedicated to 'musicians at the *ospedali grandi*'. Female musicians were active
within such institutions and chapter eight deals with 'Internal musicians: *figlie del*
coro'. The final chapter focuses on women's status in Venice 'in the last three
centuries of the history of the republic'.

949   **Puccini: a critical biography.**
      Mosco Carner.   London: Duckworth, 1992. 3rd ed. 576p. bibliog.

A monumental work which deals with the life of Puccini in the first half of the book
and then concentrates on his individual operas, especially *Tosca, Madame Butterfly*,
La fanciulla del West, La Rondine, Il trittico, and *Turandot*. Appendix A provides a
genealogical table of the Puccini family, commencing with the 18th century and
Giacomo who was also a musician. Appendix B provides detailed opera plots.

950   **A catalog of Verdi's operas.**
      Martin Chusid.   Hackensack, New Jersey: Joseph Boonin, 1974.
      201p. (Music Indexes and Bibliographies, no. 5).

Consists of a listing of operas by the date of their first performance from *Oberto*,
Conte di San Bonifacio (17 November 1839) to *Falstaff* (9 February 1893).

951   **The oratorio in Modena.**
      Victor Crowther.   Oxford: Clarendon Press, 1992. 215p. bibliog.

This is a model study, devoted to one city in northern Italy in the duchy of Ferrara to
counterbalance the bulk of works devoted to Rome, the birthplace of the oratorio. In
the late 17th century circumstances peculiar to Modena sustained a thriving oratorio
tradition. Oratorios by Benedetto Ferrari, Alessandro Stradella, Vincenzo de Grandis
and Giovanni Battista Vitali, Alessandro Scarlatti, Giovanni Paolo Colonna, Antonio
Gianettini, Palermino, Francesco Antonio Pistocchi, and Benedetto Vinacesi are
discussed in detail.

952   **In cantu et in sermone: for Nino Pirrotta on his 80th birthday.**
      Edited by Fabrizio Della Seta, Franco Piperno.   Florence: L. Olschki,
      University of Western Australia Press, 1989. 400p.

This is an influential collection of essays in English and Italian ranging from early
polyphony to images connected with 'hearing' in Dante, the songs of 14th-century
Don Paolo Tenorista in Florence, 'Preliminary thoughts on the relations of music and
magic', Jewish musical thought of the Renaissance, the relationship between
paintings and music, Monteverdi's model for a multimodal madrigal and other essays
on early Italian music.

953   **Music and patronage in sixteenth-century Mantua.**
Iain Fenlon.   Cambridge, England: Cambridge University Press,
1980. 2 vols. maps. bibliog.

The marriage of Isabella d'Este, daughter of the Duke of Ferrara, to Francesco II
Gonzaga took place in 1490 and Mantua became the centre of a much more lavish
style of patronage which encompassed the letters, art and music. The period covered
by the book deals with the patronage by the ruling Gonzagas, of music in Mantua. A
first chapter 'The origins of Mantuan Renaissance culture' forms a very good concise
synthesis of a complex but absorbing period in Northern Italian arts and patronage.
Volume two is an anthology of Mantuan music by Jacquet of Mantua (Jacques
Colebault), Hoste da Reggio, Giaches de Weryt, Duke Guglielmo Gonzaga, Paolo
Cantino, Ippolito Baccusi, Giovanni Giacomo Gastoldi, Benedetto Pallavicino,
Alessandro Striggio, Annibale Coma, Francesco Rovigo, Claudio Monteverdi,
Luca Marenzio, and Salomon Rossi. Original texts with translations are provided.

954   **Masters of Italian opera: Rossini, Donizetti, Bellini, Verdi,
Puccini.**
Philip Gossett, William Ashbrook, Julian Budden, et al.   London:
Macmillan, 1983. 353p. bibliog. (The New Grove).

First published in the New Grove Dictionary of Music and Musicians in 1980, this
volume brings together the entries on great Italian composers, each arranged by life,
works, subject, work-list, and bibliography. It serves as a standard introduction to any
further study of the masters of Italian opera.

955   **Essays on Italian poetry and music in the Renaissance 1350-1600.**
James Haar.   Berkeley, California; London: University of California
Press, 1986. 245p.

A series of lectures dealing 'with poetry in musical settings, with emphasis on
declamatory and rhetorical aspects of those settings'. The examination of the
relationship between texts and music is carried out following a chronological
criterion.

956   **Girolamo Frescobaldi.**
Frederick Hammond.   Cambridge, Massachusetts; London: Harvard
University Press, 1983. 408p. bibliog.

Girolamo Frescobaldi's life is carefully reconstructed, from his early period in
Ferrara to Rome and Flanders (1607-08) and then Rome, Mantua, Florence and Rome
again where the composer died in 1643. Frescobaldi was an exceptional performer on
the organ and the harpsichord and chapter eight of this book is devoted to his
instruments. Part two deals with Frescobaldi's music with one chapter devoted
specifically to the performance of his keyboard music. The book is completed by a
catalogue of works, a detailed bibliography and an index.

957   **Girolamo Frescobaldi: a guide to research.**
      Frederick Hammond.   New York; London: Garland, 1988. 412p.
      bibliog.

In this volume Hammond refers to his own monograph on Frescobaldi (q.v.) and
corrects its misprints and mistakes. Then Frescobaldi's documentary biography is
introduced, followed by a list of 'places' concerning the composer, and one chapter
entitled 'useful knowledge' (after Gertrude Stein) in which information on Roman
government, pontifical household, liturgy and music, money, copying, printing and
distribution of music, as well as 'mail and the postal system' is provided. It is stated
that 'in the sixteenth and seventeenth centuries papal Rome . . . had the best postal
facilities in Europe'. Further information about 'persons' and 'performances' precedes
the annotated bibliography, in which special abbreviations are used as headings (for
example, BLUNG = *Guide to Baroque Rome*, New York, Harper & Row, 1982).

958   **A preliminary checklist of research on the classic symphony and
      concerto to the time of Beethoven (excluding Haydn and Mozart).**
      George R. Hill.   Hackensack, New Jersey: Joseph Boonin, 1970. 58p.
      (Music Indexes and Bibliographies, no. 2).

The section on Italy's symphony and concerto is accompanied by an alphabetical list
of composers. The bibliography is arranged alphabetically by author and contains
various items in English, French and German.

959   **Italian opera.**
      David Kimbell.   Cambridge, England: Cambridge University Press,
      1994. 2nd ed. 684p. 1 map. bibliog.

Italian opera was an international art-form and since it was performed in many
European capitals, some authors question the existence of 'the Italian operatic
tradition'. Kimbell provides the reader with an authoritative history ranging from the
earliest beginnings of opera in the Renaissance with specific reference to
Monteverdi's *Orfeo* to opera after Verdi. After an introduction on 'the Italianness of
Italian opera', part one deals with the origins of the genre, part two with the Venetian
hegemony, part three with *opera seria* with reference to Metastasio and post-
Metastasian works, and part four with comic opera, from the *commedia dell'arte* to
Rossini's *Barber of Seville*. Part five goes on to consider Romantic opera, including
Rossini, the young Verdi and Bellini's *Norma*. In Part six there is a discussion of
Italian grand opera, including the later works by Verdi, Puccini, Boito and Mascagni.
A detailed bibliography and a list of Personalia with reference to individuals
mentioned in the book complete the volume.

960   **Music in Renaissance Ferrara 1400-1505: the creation of a musical
      centre in the fifteenth century.**
      Lewis Lockwood.   Oxford: Clarendon Press, 1984. 355p. bibliog.

A fundamental study, largely based on documentary sources, of 15th-century music
and of the ways in which it developed under the patronage of the Este rulers of
Ferrara (Niccolò III, Leonello, Borso, Ercole I). Part three is devoted to Ferrarese
musical repertoires and styles in the late 15th century. Useful appendices complete
the volume, especially appendix five, which is 'A chronological list of musicians
active at Ferrara, 1377-1505'.

961   **Vincenzo Bellini and the aesthetics of early nineteenth-century Italian opera.**
       Simon Maguire.   New York; London: Garland, 1989. 204p. bibliog.
       (Outstanding Dissertations in Music from British Universities).
This was originally produced as a PhD thesis presented at Worcester College, Oxford in 1984. It is a serious attempt to study the Italian attitudes to opera, current while Bellini (1801-35) was studying and composing. The belief that ancient Greeks sang their dramas was still prevalent at the time and *bel canto* was regarded 'more as a poetic art than a musical one, since music itself was held to have little or no expressive power'.

962   **A thematic index to the works of Salomon Rossi.**
       Joel Newman, Fritz Rikko.   Hackensack, New Jersey: Joseph Boonin, 1972. 143p. (Music Indexes and Bibliographies, no. 6).
An index to the work of the 17th-century composer Shlomo Me-ha-Adumin, or Salomon de' Rossi, from Mantua (c. 1570-c. 1630), who wrote some of the earliest polyphonic synagogue music, as well as numerous madrigals, many dedicated to members of the reigning family of the Gonzagas. Title and first-line indexes are provided.

963   **Rossini.**
       Richard Osborne.   London; Melbourne: Dent & Sons, 1987. 2nd ed. 330p. bibliog. (The Master Musicians).
Rossini's career from his early years in Pesaro and Bologna through the periods in Venice, Milan, Naples and later in Paris is traced in a highly competent and confident manner in this well-researched and authoritative study.

964   **Berio.**
       David Osmond-Smith.   Oxford: Oxford University Press, 1991. 158p. bibliog. (Oxford Studies of Composers, no. 20).
Luciano Berio, the composer influenced by the Ligurian sea, near which he spent much of his life, produced innovative music from the start of his career in the 1930s, but only became known in the 1950s and later. His composition is analysed and numerous musical examples are provided. The book includes a 'work list' of Berio's music including works written for the theatre between 1937 and 1989.

965   **Guglielmo Ebreo da Pesaro e la danza nelle corti italiane del XV secolo.** (Guglielmo Ebreo from Pesaro and dancing in Italian 15th-century courts.)
       Edited by Maurizio Padovan.   Pisa: Pacini, 1990. 343p. bibliog.
These are the proceedings of an international conference held at Pesaro between 16 and 18 July 1987. The work contains a number of interesting papers on various aspects of 15th-century dancing, written in English and in Italian. Some investigate the position of Jewish dancing masters in the Italian Renaissance, whilst others, like Ingrid Brainard's 'Pattern, imagery and drama in the choreographic work of Domenico da Piacenza', are more technical. Others, such as Françoise Syson Carter's 'Dance as a moral exercise', investigate humanists' attitudes to dancing with special reference to Thomas Elyot.

327

966 **Music and culture in Italy from the middle ages to the baroque.**
Nino Pirrotta.   Cambridge, Massachusetts; London: Harvard
University Press, 1984. 485p.

This is a collection of essays written by one of the masters of Italian musicology.
They were originally published in journals and elsewhere and are generally
recognized as essential to the history of Western music. The best-known include
essays on oral and written tradition, and music and cultural tendencies in fifteenth-
century Italy.

967 **Courtly pastimes: the frottole of Marchetto Cara.**
William F. Prizer.   Ann Arbor, Michigan: University Microfilms
International, 1980. 607p. 1 map. bibliog. (Studies in Musicology,
no. 33).

Originally a doctoral dissertation at the University of North Carolina, Chapel Hill
(1972-73), this book contains a detailed chapter on music in Mantua, 1490-1530. It
also includes clarifications on Cara's life and Cara and music at Mantua, as well as
information on his contact with another famous 16th-century musician, Bartolomeo
Tromboncino. There is a full discussion of the *frottola*, a type of light-hearted verse,
frequently used by improvisers. The book contains five appendices: documents; the
sources; an alphabetical list of works; poetic classification of Cara's frottole; and
transcriptions from printed and manuscript music 'not presently available in modern
editions'.

968 **High Renaissance masters: Josquin, Palestrina, Lassus, Byrd,
Victoria.**
Gustave Reese, Jeremy Noble, Lewis Lockwood, et al.   London:
Macmillan, 1984. 330p. bibliog. (The New Grove).

The entry on Giovanni Pierluigi da Palestrina (1525/6-94) by Lewis Lockwood and
Jessie Ann Owens is devoted to his life, his relationship to the Counter-Reformation
and to his works (masses, offertories, hymns and lamentations as well as more than
140 madrigals), and to Palestrina's pupils, contemporaries and reputation. Palestrina,
the leader of the so-called Roman school, was considered by some of his
contemporaries as the 'very first musician in the world'.

969 **North Italian church music in the age of Monteverdi.**
Jerome Roche.   Oxford: Clarendon Press, 1984. 178p.

Much of the original information contained in this book, which is a thorough revision
of the author's doctoral dissertation, came from working on entries for the *New Grove
dictionary of music and musicians* (20 vols., London, 1980). Roche first considers the
climate of thought affecting church music, the social and geographical context, and
the liturgical context. The discussion of church music is then divided into two
sections: one on small-scale church music, and the other on large-scale church music
in the 17th century.

970 **The opera industry in Italy from Cimarosa to Verdi.**
     John Rosselli.   Cambridge, England: Cambridge University Press,
     1984. 214p. bibliog.

Based on original research, in which the author used the numerous letters of
impresari that have survived in all kinds of archives in Italy, this book uncovers what
lies behind the stage and what goes on in the preparation of opera performance. This
includes negotiations, contracts, and the relationship with the authorities from the
1780s to the end of the 19th century. This was a crucial period in Italian history
because of the change from despotism to democracy and unification. As shown in the
book the authorities also used opera houses as a means to control the behaviour of the
educated classes' during the hours of darkness. Part of the book's fascination lies in
its abundance of details of the everyday life of an impresario and in its portrayal of a
very realistic, and sometimes unpleasant, picture of Italian theatres in various parts of
the country, in particular in Milan, Parma, Rome and Naples. The role of agents and
the relationship between the impresario and the public are also investigated.

971 **Music in fascist Italy.**
     Harvey Sachs.   London: Weidenfeld & Nicolson, 1987. 271p.
     bibliog.

Sachs does not claim to have made a study of music throughout the fascist period.
Rather, he attempts to understand the relationship between the regime and some
musicians, the best-known of whom was certainly Arturo Toscanini. He managed to
have his passport returned by Mussolini and left for New York in 1939, only to return
in 1945 to a rapturous reception at La Scala in Milan. For a more scholarly treatment
of the subject, reference is made to Fiamma Nicolodi, *Musica e musicisti nel
ventennio fascista* (Music and musicians of the fascist period) (Fiesole, 1984).

972 **Frescobaldi studies.**
     Alexander Silbiger.   Durham, North Carolina: Duke University Press,
     1987. 389p. bibliog.

Girolamo Frescobaldi (1583-1643) is a relatively recent discovery in the musical
world and this book is a collection of papers delivered at a conference at Madison,
Wisconsin in 1983 to celebrate the quatercentenary of the Ferrarese composer's birth.
Three essays are devoted to 'Frescobaldi and his patrons', with further details in his
biography by F. Hammond. Six chapters cover 'predecessors, contemporaries and
followers', and a further three consider 'Frescobaldi's instrumental music:
compositional procedures and rhetoric'. The last three are on 'performance practices
and original performance conditions'.

973 **A checklist of writings on 18th century French and Italian opera
     (excluding Mozart).**
     Elvidio Surian.   Hackensack, New Jersey: Joseph Boonin, 1970.
     121p. (Music Indexes and Bibliographies, no. 3).

The bibliography, which has an introduction of fourteen pages, is divided into various
sections: general; 18th-century writings on opera; travel reports and memoirs;
librettos and librettists; singing and singers; theatrical production; and studies on
individual composers.

974 **Vivaldi.**
Michael Talbot. London: Dent, 1984. 275p. bibliog.

In the preface the author points out quite rightly that 'the admission of Vivaldi to the select company of the "Master Musicians" is a sign of the growing esteem in which he has been held in recent decades'. One should add that such esteem has also been augmented by the scholarly work of the author who offers a detailed biography of the 'red priest' in Venice and a critical account of his instrumental and vocal music. The appendices include a chronology, a catalogue of works and personalia.

975 **Antonio Vivaldi: a guide to research.**
Michael Talbot. New York; London: Garland, 1988. 197p. bibliog.

Commencing with a concise biography of the Venetian composer (Talbot is also co-author of the entry on this musician in the *New Grove Dictionary of Music and Musicians*), the bibliography deals with manuscript sources such as letters, and printed sources, chronologically arranged. Section two concerns the sources of Vivaldi's music with a useful guide to the four major cataloguing systems used for his music. The other sections cover iconography and Vivaldi research today (with useful hints for beginners) and reference is made to an invaluable research tool: Rita Benton, *Directory of Music Research Libraries*, University of Iowa, 1967-72, 3 vols. Volume three lists libraries in Italy, France and the Iberian peninsula.

976 **Tomaso Albinoni: the Venetian composer and his world.**
Michael Talbot. Oxford: Clarendon Press, 1994. 308p. bibliog.

Albinoni (1671-1751) is probably best known for an Adagio in G minor for strings and organ, which he never actually composed. A fragment of the music was allegedly found by Remo Giazotto, an Italian musicologist, in the late 1950s. Its style is certainly quite different from Albinoni's own, and the latter is better studied for his sonatas and concertos. This work is devoted to the life and career of this Venetian composer whose instrumental music has frequently been performed and recorded while his vocal music has been neglected. The book contains a complete catalogue of Albinoni's works and guide to modern editions.

977 **Puccini.**
William Weaver. London: Hutchinson, 1978. 150p.

A popular book on Giacomo Puccini's musical success, life and works, with a large number of good-quality photographs of singers, musicians, librettists and settings. It is a delightful work, written in a flowing but careful style. At the end there is a list of the world premieres of Giacomo Puccini's operas.

978 **The golden century of Italian opera from Rossini to Puccini.**
William Weaver. London: Thames & Hudson, 1980. 250p. 1 map. bibliog.

Full of anecdotes based on reliable sources, the book recreates the interest in opera which preoccupied much of European society from approximately 1815 to Verdi's death in January 1901. Illustrations include: contemporary cartoons; portraits of musicians, singers and their associates; theatrical settings; opera houses; city views; letters; and many other images that contribute to a vivid impression of an era.

979 **Venetian opera in the seventeenth century.**
Simon Towneley Worsthorne. New York: Da Capo, 1984. 194p.
bibliog.

This book, which was first published in 1954, follows the development of opera houses in the Veneto and in Venice from the earliest examples of the Teatro Olimpico in Vicenza to later theatres which sprang up in the following century. The Teatro Olimpico was the first building designed with a permanent set, planned originally by Palladio and finished by Scamozzi, and opened in 1585. Careful attention is paid to stage design and to the machinery that was used to produce special effects, such as the flying of Mercury, and some plates are devoted to such undecorated and decorated machinery. Apart from dealing with the 'spectacle', the book is also concerned with the performance of operas from a musical point of view, and discusses the aria, the chorus and the orchestra with numerous examples from musical scores.

Folklore and popular music

980 **Storia della canzone italiana.** (A history of Italian songs.)
Gianni Borgna. Rome-Bari: Laterza, 1985. 340p. bibliog.

The book opens with a preface by Tullio De Mauro who reflects on the language or rather the 'plurilingualism' of Italian songs. The first song to be included is 'Santa Lucia' by Enrico Cossovich and Teodoro Cottrau, and is dated 1848. The text is written in standard, literary Italian unlike many popular 19th-century songs, which were written in dialect. In fact, even the oldest popular song quoted in the book, which was a song of the washers from Vomero, dated around 1200, is in Neapolitan dialect. Borgna traces the history of Italian songs, which are frequently seen as witnesses of the evolution of Italian society, from the 19th century to the early 1980s. Reference is made to the most important authors and singers, such as Modugno, Claudio Villa, and Nilla Pizzi in the 1960s, and Jannacci, Dalla, and Conte more recently. Numerous texts are provided in the book and in a special anthology at the end of it where songs are listed in alphabetical order. A useful chronological list of the songs quoted in the book is given on p. 283-315.

981 **Folk tales of Italy.**
Jagmohan Chopra. New Delhi; Bangalore, India; Jalandhar, India:
Sterling Publishers, 1985. 110p.

Part of the publishers' series, 'Folk Tales of the World', in this collection Chopra selects twenty-seven Italian stories, including 'The magic donkey', 'The crab prince', 'The three castles', and 'Woman turned siren'. Unfortunately there is no explanation as to the criteria adopted for this selection, nor is there information on the sources used. The author simply informs the reader that the book was compiled 'after studying various books on the subject'. The tales are written in simple language and represent a good introduction to this rich oral tradition.

982 **Customs and habits of the Sicilian peasants.**
Salvatore Salomone-Martino, first edited by Aurelio Rigoli in 1968,
English version edited and translated by Rosalie N. Norris.   London;
Toronto: Associated University Presses, 1981. 256p. bibliog.

This is not a major classic work on Sicilian folklore, but it is highly interesting
nonetheless. Written originally at the turn of the century (1897), it was set by Rigoli
in the context of the debate on the 'social question' (that is, the problem of southern
underdevelopment and archaic ways of life). Aspects of the peasants' family life,
work and rituals are carefully observed and described. The chapter titles show the
distinct comprehensive topics: 'The peasant's family'; 'The peasant's home';
'Reapers and gleaners'; 'Sowing'; 'The olive harvest'; 'Sunday'; 'Carnival'; 'Easter';
'Marriage'; 'Calamities'; 'Domestic animals'; and 'The clothing of the peasant'.
There are refined illustrations of peasants.

Italian first! From A to Z.
See item no. 1.

Stato dell'Italia. (The state of Italy.)
See item no. 7.

Italia ventesimo secolo. (Italy in the 20th century.)
See item no. 8.

How to find out about Italy.
See item no. 25.

The magic harvest.
See item no. 293.

Italian folklore: an annotated bibliography.
See item no. 1053.

Sport and Recreation

983   **Storia critica del calcio italiano: con le calciostatistiche a cura di Giorgio Sali.** (A critical history of Italian football: with football statistics by G. Sali.)
Gianni Brera.   Milan: Bompiani, 1975. 580p.
Written by the most famous football journalist in Italy, in his own flamboyant and idiosyncratic style, this is a classic history of Italian football from the foundation of the Genoa Cricket and Athletic Club in 1887 and the International Football Club of 1891 to 1975. Teams and matches and a list of important football events are provided in chronological order.

984   **Storia fotografica del calcio italiano: dalle origini al Campionato del Mondo 1982.** (A photographic history of Italian football: from its origins to the 1982 World Cup.)
Lino Cascioli.   Rome: Newton Compton, 1982. 558p.
The introduction outlines the history of Italian football from its origins to the 1980s, attempting to trace the reasons for the popularity of the sport in Italy. The rest of the book is then devoted to one of the richest collections of pictures of Italian teams, individual footballers, trainers, spectacular goals and incidents, accompanied by a clear commentary.

985   **Enzo Ferrari: 50 years of greatness.**
Piero Casucci.   Sparkford, England: Haynes, 1982. 167p. bibliog.
The first part of this richly-illustrated book is dedicated to Enzo Ferrari and his life and work, his views of his drivers, the drivers' opinions of Ferrari, an interview with the old man, and an outline of the birth of his automobile factory. The second part constitutes a survey of the Ferrari drivers, racing managers, and technicians. Part three is concerned with 'Formula 2 Ferraris' and the body designers, with a photographic section on all of Pininfarina's and Bertone's models. More specific technical details are included in two special sections on 'Formula 1' and 'Sport cars'.

986　**The world's great marques.**
Edited by Chris Marshall.　Hong Kong: Aerospace Publishing, 1992.
161p.

An entire section of this lavishly illustrated book is devoted to Italian sports cars.
These include: Ferrari F40, Lamborghini Countach, Lamborghini diablo, and
Maserati Bora. Included for each case is a concise history, in-depth analysis, design
information, performance and specification data including comparisons with other
supercars.

987　**Viva! Alfa Romeo.**
David Owen.　Yeovil, England: Haynes, 1976. 267p.

A narrative and pictorial history of the famous Milanese car which, however, had its
origins in Naples. It was first made there by a Frenchman and appeared with the
uninspiring name of SAID (*Società Anonima Italiana Darracy*, from the name of the
motor-pioneering Frenchman). The company moved to Milan in 1906 and four years
later was renamed ALFA (*[Società] Anonima Lombarda Fabbrica Automobili*). The
rest of the much more complicated and fascinating story is told with many details and
overt affection. The long series of race successes and the various models are
meticulously examined by a self-confessed Alfa fanatic. There are many illustrations
and a final section on model specifications for the whole period, 1910-76.

988　**Italian motorcycles: classic sport bikes.**
Tim Parker.　London: Osprey, 1984. 128p.

The demise of the mainstream British motorcycle industry and its near-domination by
the Japanese models is partly responsible for the charisma attached to the Italian sport
bikes. This book is a colourful visual feast for motorcycle connoisseurs, with sections
on eight famous manufacturers: Benelli; Bimota; Cagiva; Ducati; Guzzi; Laverda;
Morini; and MV Agusta. Only one big name appears to be missing and that is Gilera,
although a large photograph of the Gilera Saturno 500 Special somehow found its
way to the end of the book. Background information on the makers, race prizes, and
technical details are provided throughout.

989　**La storia dello sci in Italia (1896-1975).** (A history of skiing in Italy
[1896-1975].)
Francesco Viola.　Milan: Sole Editrice, 1976. 354p.

The existence of skis was revealed by a Swedish historian, Olaus Magnus (1490-
1557), who spent a long period of his life in Italy, during which time he printed a
woodcut showing three hunters, a woman and two men on skis. Nevertheless, it was
not until 1896 that skiing became a relatively 'popular' activity, and in the First
World War it was an important aspect of war activities. Viola considers the
development of skiing in Italy and provides a list of Italian skiers in an appendix.

990　**Italian motorcycles.**
Mick Walker.　Bourne End, England: Aston, 1991. 247p.

This is a true encyclopaedia of Italian motorcycles, combining a wealth of
photographs (some in colour) and effective drawings, with technical descriptions and
historical profiles of some twenty major marques. These range from the famous
Benelli, Ducati, Gilera, Laverda, Moto Guzzi and MV Agusta, to the less known

Aprilia, Bimota, Capriolo, Motobi and Rumi. A chapter is devoted to each of such marques. The final section of the book provides concise references to almost 200 minor marques, some of which had only an ephemeral existence. The gallery begins with Adrictina (1979-80) and concludes with Zeta (1948-54), and also includes famous scooters, such as Lambretta and Vespa. In a more selective book on the same subject, *Classic Italian racing motorcycles* (London: Osprey, 1991. 192p.), Walker points out that the two ingredients of the success of Italian racing motorcycles in the 'golden' 1950s, were innovation and courageous riders.

991   **Classic Italian marques.**
Jonathan Wood, foreword by Giovanni Agnelli.   Twickenham, England: Hamlyn, 1987. 208p.

A handsomely illustrated survey of the Italian motor car industry and its products. Six leading marques are presented in as many chapters and these are: Alfa Romeo; Ferrari; Fiat; Lamborghini; Lancia; and Maserati. In characteristically laconic and nonchalant style, the chairman of Fiat writes in his foreword that 'through our ownership of Lancia, Ferrari and now Alfa Romeo, Fiat offers a broad range of vehicles'. In fact, the acquisition of Alfa Romeo in 1987 gave Fiat effective control of the entire Italian motor industry. The politics behind it and its wider implications, however, are not the subject of this large-size book, which tells the story of a post-war success and the establishment of a myth about engineering and aesthetics attaining near perfection. There is plenty of information on motor-racing achievements and technical details.

Italian first! From A to Z.
See item no. 1.

Stato dell'Italia. (The state of Italy.)
See item no. 7.

Italia ventesimo secolo. (Italy in the 20th century.)
See item no. 8.

How to find out about Italy.
See item no. 25.

La Gazzetta dello Sport. (The sport news.)
See item no. 1006.

Mass Media

992 **Bibliografia del giornalismo italiano.** (A bibliography of Italian
     journalism.)
     Ugo Bellocchi.   Rome: Centro di Documentazione Giornalistica,
     1991. 561p.

The bibliography opens with a well-documented introduction to the problems of
producing a work of this kind, which is also an outline of a history of Italian
journalism. There are 9,619 entries, alphabetically arranged, usually by the name of
the author of a particular item or by the institution to which it refers. This is the
largest bibliography on all aspects of journalism, including television and radio
journalism, and it is completed by a useful subject index.

993 **La stampa italiana nell'età della TV, 1975-1994.** (The Italian press
     in the age of TV, 1975-1994.)
     Edited by Valerio Castronovo, Nicola Tranfaglia.   Rome-Bari:
     Laterza, 1994. 633p.

This is the seventh and final volume in a series of studies on the history of the Italian
daily and periodical newspapers, extended here to include radio and television. Its
publication has been particularly timely, after the national election of 1994, in which
the role of commercial television has been considered paramount for Berlusconi's
success. This is the context of P. Ortoleva's post-script to his essay on Italian
television. Other interesting contributions include: the introductory piece, on the
vicissitudes of the main dailies in the last twenty years (P. Murialdi and N.
Tranfaglia); language and advertising in the media (M. Dardano and A. Pilati,
respectively); women's magazines (L. Lilli); and the satirical press (A. Chiesa). A
useful, concluding section provides informative profiles of all the dailies, periodicals
and television channels, with details on ownership changes.

994 **Communication and citizenship: journalism and the public sphere in the new media age.**
Edited by Peter Dahlgren, Colin Sparks.   London; New York: Routledge, 1991. 266p. bibliog.

Paolo Mancini makes a contribution to the second part of this book (on 'Politics and journalism') with a concise essay on the awkward relationship between the media and politics in Italy. He focuses on some important recent changes, notably the use of news in a system based on coalition government, and the consequent negotiable use of political communication. He also touches upon such aspects as the personalization and dramatization of politics and political information.

995 **The press in post-war Italy.**
Audrey Parnell.   In: *European insights: post-war politics, society, culture.*   Edited by Audrey M. Brassloff, Wolfgang Brassloff.
Amsterdam; New York; Oxford; Tokyo: Elsevier Science Publishers, 1991, p. 197-213. bibliog.

In this condensed and informative essay, Parnell surveys the Italian newspapers and magazines, examining the structure and organization of the press industry and showing that no clear-cut divide exists between 'quality' and 'popular' titles. She also underlines the volatile pattern of ownership, the regional character and the financial problems facing the independent press. There is an interesting reference to the fringe press in the 1970s and to the remarkable success of the daily, *La Repubblica*, which was established in 1976. The author's final words concern the dangers to editorial liberty and pluralistic information posed by an increasingly concentrated ownership.

996 **The Italian journalist.**
William E. Porter.   Ann Arbor, Michigan: The University of Michigan Press, 1983. 234p. bibliog.

In this study Porter provides a full picture of the professional journalist in Italy during the 1970s, with an emphasis on the reform movement that peaked at the beginning of the decade. This movement attempted to introduce reforms both within the profession and within the mass media in general. It grew out of the initiative of journalists who were also militant trade unionists in their professional organization. Porter points out that by the end of the decade the activist spirit had virtually disappeared, but that important and permanent results had been achieved in terms of professionalism. Much information contained in the book was gathered by interviews with Italian journalists. A final, short section looks into the 1980s; the author expects 'more professionalization, less politicization, and therefore less factionalism in the Italian newspaper press'. One notes, in passing, that Porter's language may have been influenced by the Italian style, with long, complicated words.

Italy today: social picture and trends, 1984- .
See item no. 5.

Stato dell'Italia. (The state of Italy.)
See item no. 7.

Books and Publishing

997 **Bibliography: history of a tradition.**
Luigi Balsamo, translated from the Italian by William A. Pettas.
Berkeley, California: Bernard M. Rosenthal, 1990. 209p. bibliog.

The ways in which books are classified and catalogued have obviously changed over the centuries. This book deals briefly with information about books and book distribution in the Middle Ages and with the bibliographical canon of the 15th century and the introduction of printing. The bulk of the book is concerned with developments since Tritheim's bibliography (1494) to the end of the 18th century, and also deals with bibliographical censorship, the Catholic Church's *Index* of prohibited books, and the *Bibliotheca selecta* by Antonio Possevino.

998 **Printing and publishing in fifteenth-century Venice.**
Leonardas Vytautas Gerulaitis. Chicago; London: American Library Association, 1976. 190p. bibliog.

An authoritative and well-researched account of early printing, with reference to technique, partnership, privileges and censorship. The second part of the book contains much information on contents analysis of books printed in Venice, as well as Bologna and Nuremberg, with numerous tables.

999 **Book production and letters in the Western European Renaissance: essays in honour of Conor Fahy.**
Edited by Anna Lepschy, John Took, Dennis E. Rhodes. London: The Modern Humanities Association, 1986. 300p.

This collection of essays considers the problems of textual bibliography and early printing. Some essays are in Italian and one in French. Among the ones in English are: Giovanni Aquilecchia, on the problems of textual criticism; C. P. Brand, on editions of the *Orlando Furioso*; D. W. Cruikshank, on Italian type in Spain and the Spanish Empire; Lotte Hellinga, on two early editions of Poggio Bracciolini's *Facetiae*; Anna Laura Lepschy, on the incunables of John Mandeville's travels;

Dennis E. Rhodes, on the early editions of Baptista Fiera; and David J. Shaw, on setting in formes in some early Parisian Greek books.

1000 The world of Aldus Manutius: business and scholarship in Renaissance Venice.

Martin Lowry.   Oxford: Basil Blackwell, 1979. 350p. bibliog.

Lowry states that Aldus, the scholar-turned-printer, 'was freeing literature from the study and the lecture-room. But was he also putting literature into the hands of men who would not previously have been able to afford such a luxury? Most modern writers would say "yes" . . . Unfortunately, this chain of reasoning rests on no contemporary evidence'. This is a characteristic example of the way in which the book relies on first-hand evidence, on primary sources and on critical reading. It is an important and well-written analysis of a leading figure in Renaissance Venetian culture, with a witty and enthusiastic approach which does not detract in the least from its scholarly attitude.

1001 Nicholas Jenson and the rise of Venetian publishing in Renaissance Europe.

Martin Lowry.   Oxford: Basil Blackwell, 1991. 286p. bibliog.

A scholarly study of the culture that surrounded one of the prominent printers in Venice in the 1470s, the Frenchman Nicholas Jenson, who may have learned printing from Gutenberg. It deals admirably with the complex relationships which existed in Venice among scholars, noblemen, and patrons and also throws light on the organization of the market for an early typographer. Jenson's company had distribution centres in the principal university towns of Italy, and took paper supplies from one of the most important mills in the centre of the peninsula, Fabriano. Detailed references to editions printed by Jenson are also made in the book.

1002 The Italian book 1465-1800.

Edited by Denis V. Reidy.   London: The British Library, 1993. 401p. bibliog.

A collection of essays to celebrate the seventieth birthday of the great bibliographer Dennis E. Rhodes. It contains the results of recent discoveries and research in the field of incunabula, especially from Northern Italy and Tuscany. It also covers: 16th-century collections of portraits; 17th-century books of military interest; a Ptolemy of 1548; a study of printing houses in Romagna in the 17th century; and other essays on book collectors such as Consul Smith (18th century) and Marquis G. B. Costabili. A bibliography (438 items) of D. E. Rhodes's works completes the volume.

1003 Cartolai, illuminators and printers in fifteenth-century Italy.

M. A. Rouse, R. H. Rouse.   Los Angeles: UCLA Research Library, Department of Special Collections, 1988. 127p. bibliog. (Occasional Papers, no. 1).

A lively and valuable discussion of the role of *cartolai* (stationers, originally sellers of *carta* [parchment paper]) in the early period of printed books. This is followed by a catalogue of an exhibition of illumination and decoration in early printed books in the libraries of the University of California, Los Angeles (forty books). Indexes of names, books, manuscripts, plus twenty-five plates complete the volume.

Newspapers, Magazines and Periodicals

Newspapers

1004 Il Messaggero. (The messenger.)
Rome, 1878- . daily.

One of the few dailies with a gothic script title, *Il Messaggero* is an independent newspaper with a good circulation in Rome and central Italy of approximately 390,000.

1005 Giornale di Sicilia. (Sicily's newspaper.)
Palermo, 1860- . daily.

This is one of the major Sicilian newspapers, together with *L'Ora* (The hour), which is perhaps more left of centre.

1006 La Gazzetta dello Sport. (The sport news.)
Milan, 1896- . daily.

Daily newspapers totally dedicated to sport and to the analysis of football matches are a typically Italian feature; the *Gazzetta* is the oldest and is still printed on pink paper. It has a circulation of approximately 830,000. In Rome another similar newspaper, the *Corriere dello Sport* (The sport messenger), is printed with a circulation of some 622,000. *Tuttosport* (Allsport) in Turin has a circulation of around 195,000.

1007 Il Popolo. (The people.)
Rome, 1944- . daily.

With a circulation of around 43,800 this is the organ of the PPI or *Partito Popolare Italiano*, which succeeded the *Democrazia Cristiana* (Christian Democratic Party).

1008   **Il Secolo d'Italia.** (The century of Italy.)
       Rome, 1951- . daily.
This is the organ of the *Alleanza Nazionale* (National Alliance Party), which was formed as a coalition of the former neo-fascist party and other right-wing groups. It has a circulation of 32,500.

1009   **La Notte.** (The night.)
       Milan, 1952- . daily.
A Milan evening newspaper, with a penchant for scandal headlines. It has a circulation of approximately 98,000.

1010   **Il Sole/24 Ore.** (The sun/24 hours.)
       Milan, 1865- . daily.
This is mainly a financial newspaper but it has political and economic sections and also produces a very good cultural section, especially on Sundays. It has a circulation of approximately 353,000.

1011   **L'Unità.** (Unity.)
       Rome, 1924- . daily.
This was the official paper of the Italian Communist Party, now PDS or *Partito Democratico della Sinistra* (Democratic Party of the Left). However, it also has a good circulation among non-party members and a good distribution across Italy, with special regional issues. The circulation of around 257,000 on weekdays rises to 800,000 on Sundays.

1012   **La Stampa.** (The press.)
       Turin, 1868- . daily.
An independent newspaper with a good circulation in Northern Italy and abroad of approximately 403,000. Once a week it includes *Tuttolibri* (All books) which contains book reviews and cultural events. It also publishes an evening edition *Stampa Sera* (Evening press) with a more limited circulation.

1013   **Corriere della Sera.** (The evening messenger.)
       Milan, 1876- . daily.
One of the oldest independent newspapers in Italy, with a circulation of 660,000. It has always given wide coverage to both national and international news as well as to cultural and scientific issues, sports and local events.

1014   **La Nuova Sardegna.** (New Sardinia.)
       Sassari, 1891- . daily.
One of the two newspapers published in Sardinia (the other being *L'Unione Sarda* [The Sardinian Union]) this has a circulation of approximately 101,000. Most of its space is devoted to local news.

341

1015 **Il Mattino.** (The morning.)
      Naples, 1892- . daily. (reformed 1950).
This independent newspaper has a good circulation in Naples and in Southern Italy of around 227,000.

1016 **Il Manifesto.** (The poster.)
      Rome, 1971- . daily.
An austere newspaper with a less flowery style than most. Apart from comments on national and international politics, largely from a splinter communist point of view, the newspaper devotes space to cultural events and interpretations. It has a circulation of approximately 89,000.

1017 **La Repubblica.** (The republic.)
      Rome: Editoriale L'Espresso, 1976- . daily.
La Repubblica was founded with the participation of independent groups and individuals in an attempt to escape from press monopolies. At its outset it claimed to follow the best principles of 'anglo-saxon' journalism and keep news separate from commentaries. It is a moderate left-wing/liberal newspaper which appears with regional pages or inserts. The circulation is approximately 726,000.

Magazines

1018 **Intimità.** (Intimacy.)
      Milan: Cino Del Duca. weekly.
A popular magazine of general interest with serialized fiction, sometimes illustrated by photographs used as cartoons.

1019 **L'automobile.** (The car.)
      Rome, 1945- . monthly.
A monthly magazine devoted to motor mechanics and tourism. It has a wide circulation of approximately 1,500,000.

1020 **Quattroruote.** (Four wheels.)
      Milan, 1956- . monthly.
One of the most popular magazines covering motoring, this includes discussion of new and old cars, and has a circulation of some 700,000.

1021 **Gente.** (People.)
      Milan, 1957- . weekly.
This is a very popular illustrated magazine, with most articles covering such topics as the private lives of celebrities, and strange events, as well as general political and current affairs. It has a circulation of 901,000.

1022   **Oggi.** (Today.)
　　　　Milan: Gruppo Rizzoli, 1945- . weekly.

A popular, illustrated, topical magazine which devotes much space to the private lives of television celebrities, aristocrats, and VIPs, as well as to special columns of advice from experts (legal and medical, for example). It has a circulation of 696,000.

1023   **Panorama.**
　　　　Milan: Arnoldo Mondadori Editore, 1962- . weekly.

Similar in contents and outlook to *L'Espresso* (q.v.), this publication covers current affairs, politics and economics as well as cultural topics. It has a circulation of approximately 504,000.

1024   **A Tavola.** (At table.)
　　　　Milan: De Agostini-Rizzoli Periodici, 1986- . monthly.

An influential illustrated magazine which covers innovative international, as well as regional and traditional, cuisine. It also concerns nutritional problems, food and wine production, and regional Italian restaurants.

1025   **Amica.** (Lady friend.)
　　　　Milan, 1962- . weekly.

An illustrated weekly magazine with a variety of features ranging from fashion, beauty and romance, to careers, domestic and personal problems. It has a circulation of some 211,000.

1026   **La Cucina Italiana.** (Italian cuisine.)
　　　　Milan, 1929- . monthly.

This is a fully illustrated magazine which explains techniques for food preparation, and divides its recipes according to different courses. Some articles are devoted to nutritional and health problems.

1027   **Epoca.** (Era.)
　　　　Milan: Arnoldo Mondadori Editore, 1950- . weekly.

An illustrated topical magazine with a tradition of high quality journalism and very good photography. Its circulation is approximately 192,000 copies.

1028   **La Civiltà Cattolica.** (Catholic civilization.)
　　　　Rome, 1850- . fortnightly.

Traditionally the magazine 'of the Jesuit order', this devotes articles to high-level analysis and discussion of political and cultural events, and publishes numerous book reviews.

1029   **L'Espresso.** (The express.)
　　　　Rome, [1952]. weekly.

An illustrated magazine covering political, current and international affairs. Considered by some as an 'independent left' magazine, it has a circulation of around 373,900.

1030   **Grazia.** (Grace.)
       Milan: Arnoldo Mondadori Editore, 1938- . weekly.
One of the oldest illustrated weekly magazines, this is devoted to current affairs, personal health and beauty, fashion and careers for women, and contains film and book reviews. It has a circulation of 360,000.

1031   **Famiglia Cristiana.** (A Christian family.)
       Milan, 1931- . weekly.
An illustrated magazine for Roman Catholic families, as well as for members of the clergy or monastic orders. It deals with current affairs, general advice and pastoral care and is distributed through parishes and Catholic churches, reaching 1,070,824 people.

English-language periodicals

1032   **Economic Notes.**
       Monte dei Paschi.   Siena: Monte dei Paschi di Siena, 1971-
       tri-annual.
Published three times a year by the Monte dei Paschi Bank in Siena, this journal contains articles on various aspects of banking and economics, as well as book reviews. All the articles and reviews are in English.

1033   **Forum Italicum.**
       Buffalo: State University of New York, 1967- . biannual.
An American journal of Italian studies, this publishes articles in English and Italian on the literature, language and culture of Italy. It is published twice a year and every issue contains articles, poetry, prose, book reviews and news.

1034   **Il Nuovo Cimento: Della Società Italiana di Fisica.**
       Edited by Renato Angelo Ricci.   Bologna: Editrice Compositori,
       1855- . monthly.
This international journal of physics was founded in Pisa in 1855, and it has been the official journal of the Italian Society of Physics since 1897. It is edited by Renato Angelo Ricci and sponsored by the Italian Research Council, and is recognized by the European Physical Society. Specialized articles are published in the journal as well as short notices in English. It is published in two different formats, distinguished by different coloured covers: A is green and B is yellow. A is devoted to nuclei, particles and fields, and B to general physics, relativity, astronomy and mathematical physics and methods.

1035 **The Italianist.**
Reading, England: University of Reading, Department of Italian
Studies, 1981- .
This journal publishes articles mainly in English on all aspects of Italian culture.
Recent issues have included critical articles on 16th-century and modern and
contemporary authors, analyses of the political situation in Italy and of immigration,
and articles on the Italian language and linguistics.

1036 **Italian Studies.**
Leeds, England: Society for Italian Studies, 1945- . annual.
This journal is published annually and it contains articles on all aspects of Italian
literature and culture, as well as numerous reviews and review articles.

1037 **Italica, Journal of the American Association of Teachers of
Italian.**
American Association of Teachers of Italian. Columbus, Ohio:
Ohio State University, 1923- . quarterly.
One of the oldest journals of Italian studies in America, it is published four times a
year. The journal contains articles on language, literature and culture, and
occasionally information about the activities and the membership of its sponsoring
association. A very recent periodical produced by American scholars and published
by Routledge is the *Journal of Modern Italian Studies* (vol. 1, 1995/96). It will
appear three times a year and will devote articles to historical, sociological and
anthropological topics.

How to find out about Italy.
See item no. 25.

Reference Works

1038   **Grande dizionario enciclopedico.** (A comprehensive encyclopaedic dictionary.)

Founded by Pietro Fedele.   Turin: UTET, 1986-93. 20 vols. + index + 1 atlas: *Grande Atlante Geografico e Storico* (Comprehensive Geographical and Historical Atlas).

This is one of the best compact encyclopaedias available in Italian. It is a completely new edition of an encyclopaedic dictionary originally begun in 1954, and which has been used for a long time as the standard on which to base the spelling of difficult terms or of foreign languages and nations. It is one of the most reliable monolingual dictionaries which, apart from providing accurate linguistic information on individual words, including their pronunciation, also provides concise information of an encyclopaedic nature.

1039   **Enciclopedia.**

Turin: Giulio Einaudi, 1977-84. 16 vols.

Better known as the *Enciclopedia Einaudi*, this reference work consists of full-length articles on selected items of knowledge, from Abaco and Abbigliamento to Zero. In the first fourteen volumes there were over 556 entries by 239 authors, filling a total of 16,302 pages. Volumes fifteen and sixteen contain a 'systematic outline' and detailed indexes.

1040   **Enciclopedia italiana di scienze, lettere ed arti.** (Italian encyclopaedia of sciences, letters and art.)

Rome: Istituto della Enciclopedia Italiana, 1949. 35 vols. + 4.

This monumental work was originally published between 1929 and 1936 in thirty-five volumes. This is a reprint of the fundamental encyclopaedia, popularly known as the *Treccani*, taken from the name of the founder of its publishing institute. It is still an important tool for basic research especially in the humanities. There are three volumes of appendices and one of indexes.

1041 **The world of learning 1994.**
London: Europa. 44th ed. 2,094p. annual.

The institutions of Italy are listed on p. 798-840. Academies, learned societies, research institutes, libraries and archives, museums and art galleries and universities are covered, with addresses, telephone numbers and some information about membership, as well as library holdings.

How to find out about Italy.
See item no. 25.

Agricultural encyclopedia.
See item no. 112.

Dizionario biografico degli italiani. (Biographical dictionary of the Italians.)
See item no. 332.

World directory of minorities.
See item no. 360.

The mafia encyclopedia.
See item no. 507.

Women's movements in the world.
See item no. 537.

The radical right: a world directory.
See item no. 612.

Trade unions of the world, 1992-1993.
See item no. 762.

Dizionario dei vini italiani. (Dictionary of Italian wines.)
See item no. 887.

Bibliographies

1042 **Italy.**
Vilma Alberani. In: *Official publications of Western Europe*, Vol.
1. Edited by Eve Johansson. London: Mansell, 1984, p. 107-49.
bibliog.

Following an introduction which outlines the structure of central and local government, this full bibliographical guide is divided into six sections. The first, and largest, surveys all the main official publications of central government, from the *Official Gazette of the Italian Republic* to the publications of all government departments and agencies. Works published by government-sponsored and non-governmental institutions are also included here. The following two sections deal with the manner of publication and bibliographical control, respectively. Useful information is then provided on publications concerning library collections, and regional and local governments. The last section concerns the very bibliographical sources used to compile the entire chapter. Information on periodicals issued by regional governments is included in the appendix.

1043 **An annotated bibliography of Moravia criticism in Italy and the English-speaking world (1929-1975).**
Ferdinando Alfonsi, Sandra Alfonsi. New York; London: Garland,
1976. 261p.

The 3,612 entries which constitute this bibliography are listed in chronological order. Even reviews of Moravia's books are included. Many entries refer to articles or reviews which are no longer than one page. Not many items, however, are annotated and some annotations are somewhat cursory.

1044   **Lingua e dialetti italiani: contributo alla bibliografia della lingua e dei dialetti italiani per gli anni 1967-1971.** (Italian language and dialects: a contribution to the bibliography of Italian language and dialect covering the period 1967-1971.)
Anna Maria Arnuzzo, Gianna Marcato.   Pisa: Pacini, 1976. 407p.

This bibliography purports to continue the work initiated by R. A. Hall, Jr. in his *Bibliografia della linguistica italiana*, which covered the years up to 1966. It follows a similar arrangement, dividing the sections into: History of the Italian language; Description of Italian; Dialect studies; and History of Italian linguistics. It is complemented by useful indices of author, place-names and words which appear in the titles of individual entries. Pages 38-47 deal with the influence of Italian on other languages and of foreign words in Italian.

1045   **Romanzo storico, d'appendice, di consumo: guida bibliografica 1960-1980.** (Historical, serialized, pulp novels: a bibliographical guide 1960-1980.)
Antonia Arslan, Patrizia Zambon.   Milan: Unicopli, for the Università degli Studi di Padova, Quaderni dell'Istituto di Filologia e Letteratura Italiana 2, 1983. 71p.

Italian popular novels have not received much critical attention but this is a list of critical literature on the mainly 19th-century authors of such novels, published between 1960 and 1980. The novels are divided into three main sections: historical novels; popular and serialized novels; and pulp novels. They range from imitators of D'Annunzio to science-fiction. This booklet has only a table of contents at the end and lacks an analytical index.

1046   **Catalogo dei libri in commercio 1993.** (Books in print 1993.)
Associazione Italiana Editori.   Milan: Editrice Bibliografica, 1993. 3 vols.

These three volumes list all the books available in Italy. Volume one is arranged alphabetically according to authors and in its initial pages it contains, as do the others, a full list of the publishers' addresses, and their ISBN, as well as an index of the available series. Volume two is arranged by titles, and volume three by subject. The volumes are updated every year. Each book entry is listed in full with its year of publication, format, current price, series if relevant and ISBN.

1047   **Teaching materials for Italian: a teaching materials list.**
T. D. Baldwin.   [London]: Centre for Information on Language Teaching and Research, 1983. 132p.

An annotated bibliography of 189 publications which includes major reviews of some of the works cited. In the case of miscellaneous volumes, a detailed list of contents is given. This bibliography does not include reference grammars and dictionaries, but the level at which language courses are aimed is indicated. The entries are arranged alphabetically and annotations are sometimes quite comprehensive.

1048   **Bibliografia machiavelliana.** (A Machiavellian bibliography.)
Sergio Bertelli, Piero Innocenti.   Verona: Valdonega, 1979. 433p.

Over 270 pages of introduction outline the early editions and the editorial *fortuna* of Machiavelli's works. They are followed by a detailed bibliography, with full entries, of Machiavelli's works, with reference to relevant bibliography and to the location of individual copies. Printed works by Machiavelli are arranged chronologically by century, from the 16th to the 19th. Indexes of publishers, editors, translators, annotators of illustrated editions and of provenance complete this elegant volume.

1049   **Illuminated manuscripts of the Divine Comedy.**
Pieter Brieger, Millard Meiss, Charles S. Singleton.   London: Routledge & Kegan Paul, 1969. 2 vols.

The first volume opens with an essay by Charles S. Singleton, 'The irreducible vision', which discusses the relationship between 'words and pictures'. This is followed by Millard Meiss, 'The smiling pages' which is more specifically on illuminations. Peter Brieger, in 'Pictorial commentaries on the *Commedia*', examines the pictorial cycles illustrating Dante's poem. Brieger also contributes 'Analysis of the illustrations by canto' which refers to the plates contained in volume two, some of them in colour. The subject matter for the catalogue was compiled by Brieger and the styles and dates by Meiss. Comparative illustrations are provided (130 in all) and a general bibliography, an iconographic and a general index complete the volume.

1050   **Italian Renaissance poetry: a first-line index to Petrarch, Ariosto, Tasso and others.**
Maureen E. Buja.   New York; London: Garland, 1987. 204p.

This is an interesting and potentially useful list for tracing anonymous poems which could be found in manuscript or other sources. Apart from Petrarch, Ariosto and Tasso, first-lines are provided for P. Bembo's *Rime*, Giovanbattista Strozzi the Elder's *Madrigali*, Luigi Cassola's *Madrigali* and Giovanni Della Casa's *Rime*. There are, however, unfortunate misprints in the introduction.

1051   **Italian foreign policy, 1918-1945: a guide to research and research materials.**
Compiled and edited by Alan Cassels.   Wilmington, Delaware: Scholarly Resources, 1991. Rev. ed. 261p.

First published in 1981 and part of a series of research guides on European diplomatic history intended for scholars, this book also offers a chapter of wider interest, describing how Italian foreign policy was made throughout the period considered. Appendices to this chapter supply the names of leading Italian diplomats and foreign diplomats in Italy. A subsequent chapter deals with the relevant public and private archives, libraries, research institutes and newspaper collections. The final, longest chapter constitutes the bibliography and consists of four parts: general; documentary and official publications; diaries and memoirs; and secondary literature. Each part is subdivided into various categories. Most items are in English and Italian. A comprehensive index contributes to the usefulness of the volume, which is of great value, incidentally, for the study of general aspects of fascist Italy, as well as for that of Mussolini's foreign policy.

1052 **Modern Italian history: an annotated bibliography.**
Compiled by Frank J. Coppa, William Roberts. Westport,
Connecticut: Greenwood Press, 1990. 288p.

This is an indispensable, if selective, bibliographical survey of works on Italian
modern and contemporary history, focusing on the last three centuries. It is a
companion volume to the *Dictionary of modern Italian history*, edited by Coppa
(q.v.), and follows the same periodization, with reference to works on 18th-century
Italy, the *Risorgimento*, liberal Italy, fascist Italy, and the Italian republic. These are
preceded by two general sections of reference works and monographic studies
encompassing more than one such period. Altogether, nearly 900 works are listed and
concisely annotated. The overwhelming majority refer to items published in the
United States and Italy and only in a few instances are works which appeared before
1970 mentioned. Books, journal articles, and some interesting dissertations are cited.

1053 **Italian folklore: an annotated bibliography.**
Alessandro Falassi.   New York; London: Garland, 1985. 438p.

With exactly 3,000 bibliographical items, this extensive reference work is of
fundamental importance for those interested in any aspect of Italian folklore. The
introduction provides a historical perspective of folklore studies in Italy. A large
number of titles originate from the 19th century; some from previous centuries. With
regard to the present century, Falassi points out that he tried 'to adequately represent
all trends in contemporary Italian folklore scholarship including the traditional
philological, historic-geographical approaches, and also the ideology of a Marxist
matrix, and the methodology related to structural and semiotic approaches'. Italian-
American folklore is not included, but there are hints to bibliographical sources in
that direction. Annotations are brisk and often indicate the contents of items by
translating their original Italian title.

1054 **Fondo manoscritti di autori contemporanei.** (The manuscript
collection of contemporary authors.)
Edited by Giampiero Ferretti, Maria Antonietta Grignani, Maria Pia
Musatti (Università degli Studi, Pavia), with a foreword by Maria
Corti.   Turin: Einaudi, 1982. 336p.

This is a catalogue of literary manuscripts donated to Pavia University, in Northern
Italy, or bought by them between December 1969 and December 1979. The catalogue
describes the manuscripts of numerous modern and contemporary authors. The
descriptions are detailed and accurate, some passages of particular importance are
quoted in a transcription, and a number of letters, poems and postcards are
reproduced in black-and-white. The manuscripts can be consulted at the Centro di
Ricerca Sulla Tradizione Manoscritta di Autori Contemporanei (Centre for the
research on contemporary authors' manuscripts) at the Faculty of Letters of the
University of Pavia. Other volumes will follow, since manuscripts acquired between
1979 and the publication date of this volume are mentioned in a footnote. The
arrangement of the entries is alphabetical, by author.

1055   **Dante in America: bibliografia 1965-1980.** (Dante in America: a
        bibliography 1965-1980.)
        Luciana Giovannetti.   Ravenna, Italy: Longo, 1987. 197p.

This bibliography contains over 1,500 entries, consecutively numbered, but divide
into: concordances; dictionaries; bibliographies; general introductions; miscellanie,
life and times of Dante; Dante's culture and sources; Dante's ideology; allegor;
structure, art and technique; *Lecturae Dantis*; periods in Dante's *fortuna*; and Dant
in comparative literature, editions and translations.

1056   **Modern Italian language and literature: a bibliography of
        homage studies.**
        Herbert H. Golden, Seymour O. Simches.   Cambridge,
        Massachusetts: Harvard University Press, 1959. Reprinted, New
        York: Kraus Reprint, 1971. 207p.

The purpose of the volume, which has parallel French and Iberian versions, is '
bring together those elusive and widely scattered studies which have appeared i
Festschriften'. Not only are individual volumes 'in honour of . . .' listed in full, bu
the articles contained in them appear also as individual items, with clear cross
referencing. The index (p. 181-207) is clear and useful. It lists the names of author;
subjects and libraries but not the dialect terms or other individual words appearing i
the titles of individual entries.

1057   **Bibliografia nazionale italiana: nuova serie del bollettino delle
        pubblicazioni italiane ricevute per diritto di stampa.** (Italian
        national bibliography: new series of the bulletin of Italian
        publications received by copyright law.)
        Edited by Carla Guiducci Bonanni.   Rome: Istituto per il Catalogo
        Unico delle Biblioteche Italiane; Milan: Editrice Bibliografica,
        1958- . monthly.

This monthly bulletin lists all the publications received by law. Entries are compile;
according to the international standard bibliographical description, with a heading an
Dewey classification in the left-hand corner. Two indexes by author and title and b
subject complete each issue of the BNI Bulletin.

1058   **Bibliografia della linguistica italiana.** (A bibliography of Italian
        linguistics.)
        Robert A. Hall, Jr.   Florence: Sansoni, 1958. 2nd ed. 3 vols.

Containing 6,898 entries, this bibliography lists the most important works on th
history of Italian, dialect studies, and the history of Italian linguistics, which hav
appeared since approximately 1860. It is therefore one of the most comprehensiv
tools for Italian linguistics and philology. The list of individual words, especiall;
those under etymological investigation, is provided at the end of volume three. This i
one of the lists which are essential to any preliminary study of individual, usuall;
difficult, words in the Italian language and in some of its dialects.

1059 **Bibliografia della linguistica italiana: primo supplemento decennale (1956-1966).** (A bibliography of Italian linguistics: first ten-year supplement 1956-1966.)
Robert A. Hall, Jr. Florence: Sansoni, 1969.
The entries included in this supplement are additions to previous volumes and new entries up to number 9,394. The same format is followed as in the main volumes with a list of words and an index provided.

1060 **Nineteenth-century European catholicism: an annotated bibliography of secondary works in English.**
Eric C. Hansen. New York: Garland, 1989. 558p.
In the chapter concerned with individual countries, books referring to Italy are divided into six sections entitled: general works; the hierarchy; the press; piety and devotion; social catholicism; and special challenges. The last section, in particular, contains the largest number of entries and is itself subdivided into the following: Church and State; Catholic political activity; anti-clericalism and anti-catholicism; and liberal catholicism. There are many references to articles from a wide range of journals.

1061 **Printed Italian vernacular religious books: 1465-1550: a finding list.**
Anne Jacobson Schutte. Geneva: Droz, 1983. 470p.
This is a thorough bibliography, alphabetically arranged, of books of interest to the religious historian, from the beginning of printing in the 1460s to the middle of the following century.

1062 **Renaissance humanism 1300-1550: a bibliography of materials in English.**
Benjamin G. Kohl. New York; London: Garland, 1985. 354p.
Prefaced by a succinct definition of Renaissance humanism, this useful checklist has been prepared with 'the needs of the undergraduate student in mind'. It contains 3,051 entries arranged by 'areas'; section fourteen, for example, covers humanism in Tuscany, Rome and Naples, 1440-1550.

1063 **Iter italicum: a finding list of uncatalogued or incompletely catalogued humanistic manuscripts of the Renaissance in Italian and other libraries.**
Paul Oskar Kristeller. London: Warburg Institute; Leiden: E. J. Brill, 1965-92. 6 vols.
An indispensable guide for finding manuscripts which deal with humanism, the history of ideas, and literature, especially of the 15th and 16th centuries. Volumes one and two are devoted to the holdings of Italian libraries, most of which were visited personally by the author. For each manuscript the shelf-mark, approximate date, and a succinct summary of contents are provided, with notes on special collections existing in libraries and archives. In volumes five and six there are additions and supplements referring to Italy and Italian libraries, arranged alphabetically by location, city, town or village.

1064 **Studies on Italy, 1943-1975: select bibliography of American and British materials in political science, economics, sociology and anthropology.**
Peter Lange, with the assistance of Robert Samuels.   Turin: Fondazione Giovanni Agnelli, 1977. 184p.

This is an indispensable guide to bibliographical sources on the subjects and dates indicated in the title. The volume includes mainly references to book, journal articles and doctoral theses, which are exclusively, principally, or even partially on Italy. Consisting of three parts, these are divided into sections which, in turn, are broken down into more specific topics. Part one covers political items, both on domestic politics (including: clientelism, local government, and trade unionism) and on foreign relations and policy (including: defence, NATO, the United Nations, and former colonies). Part two is devoted to sociology and cultural anthropology and includes: the family; women; urban sociology; and religion. Finally, part three covers economics and examines: periods of development; economic structure; labour conditions; and international relations.

1065 **Bibliografia della massoneria italiana e di Cagliostro.** (A bibliography of Italian freemasonry and of Cagliostro.)
Agostino Lattanzi.   Florence: Olschki, 1974. 457p.

Over 500 works are listed in this specialized bibliography, including histories of general interest which contain a reference to freemasons. This is a major, annotated bibliography and it also mentions the libraries in which some of the works can be found.

1066 **Bibliografia generale della lingua e della letteratura italiana (BiGLLI).** (A general bibliography of Italian language and literature.)
Edited by Enrico Malato.   Rome: Salerno, 1993- .

The first volume deals with works published in 1991. Entries are annotated and listed in the general section under specialized headings (such as, bibliography, philology, reference, linguistics, and rhetoric) and then chronologically by century. Cross-references are provided all through and this should become one of the standard bibliographies for Italian language and literature studies.

1067 **Libri e Riviste d'Italia.**
Rome: Ministero per i Beni Culturali e Ambientali, 1966- .

This periodical produced by the Italian Ministry for Culture and the Environment contains selected book reviews, divided into groups such as: literature; philosophy; history; biography; politics; economy; law; public administration; music; theatre; cinema; radio and television; archaeology; town planning; and science and technology. It also provides indexes and a few summaries of articles, of numerous Italian journals dealing with the categories indicated for books.

1068   **Itinerari archivistici italiani: Emilia Romagna.** (Italian archive itineraries: Emilia-Romagna.)
Rome: Ministero per i Beni Culturali e Ambientali, Ufficio Centrale per i Beni Archivistici, 1991. 59p.

This is one in a series of short introductions to the Italian archives, organized by region. They contain such information as the opening times and clear indications of the collections, strengths and weaknesses of the archives of each city in a given region. In the case of Emilia-Romagna, for instance, information is provided on the Archivio di Stato of Bologna, Ferrara, Forlì, Modena, Parma, Piacenza, and Ravenna and on smaller 'sections' in Cesena, Faenza, Imola and Rimini. Each booklet is illustrated with colour and black-and-white photographs. Reference is also made to the more extensive *Guida agli archivi di stato*, which contains more detailed information about the holdings of each of the 'State Archives'.

1069   **The year's work in modern language studies.**
Edited for the Modern Humanities Research Association.
Cambridge, England: Cambridge University Press, 1930- . annual.

This annual bibliography includes a section on Italian studies, which is usually divided into language and literature, and arranged by century.

1070   **Prime edizioni italiane.** (First Italian editions.)
Marino Parenti.   Florence: Sansoni, 1951. new ed. 526p.

Parenti's bibliography, which is arranged alphabetically, is still a useful checklist of first editions of Italian authors. It ranges from incunables to 19th-century editions and although somewhat dated, still provides useful information to book collectors, traders and librarians.

1071   **Nuptialia: saggio di bibliografia di scritti italiani pubblicati per nozze dal 1484 al 1799.** (Nuptialia: bibliography of Italian works published for weddings from 1484 to 1799.)
Olga Pinto.   Florence: Olschki, 1971. 451p.

Ephemeral publications produced on the occasion of weddings are notoriously difficult to trace. However, they are listed here with a full bibliographical entry and a detailed index to authors, translators, and collectors, as well as an index of the married couples for whom the homage was originally written. Each entry indicates the library in which the book or leaflet was consulted.

1072   **I vocabolari delle parlate italiane.** (Dictionaries of Italian dialects.)
Angelico Prati.   Bologna: Forni, 1965. 66p.

By using the dialect index in this volume it is possible to find the relevant dictionary as a main entry. Specialized dialect dictionaries by subject are also indexed (*Indice per argomenti*), and it is therefore possible to trace glossaries of special terms (for example, marine or geographical). Though obviously dated (it was first published in 1931) this is still a useful publication since many dictionaries of this kind date back to the 19th century.

1073 **Manuale critico-bibliografico per lo studio della letteratura italiana.** (A critical bibliographical handbook for the study of Italian literature.)
Mario Puppo. Turin: Società Editrice Internazionale, 1987. 8th ed. 462p.

Students of Italian literature will find this a very useful reference work, covering both the general areas of histories of literature, encyclopaedias and dictionaries as well as devoting sections to specific methodology in literary criticism. General periods and themes are dealt with in section four, while section five contains introductions and bibliographies on over twenty individual authors. A concise dictionary of technical terms is included as an appendix.

1074 **Gender and sexuality in Renaissance and Baroque Italy: a working bibliography.**
Patricia Simons. Sydney: University of Sydney, Power Institute of Fine Arts, 1988. 70p. (Occasional Paper, no. 7).

The bibliography is not annotated, and is divided into eight sections: methodology, bibliographies, primary sources, women, especially in social history, sexuality, women and religion, women as producers, representation, especially in visual arts and literature.

1075 **Italian-Americans and religion: an annotated bibliography.**
Silvano M. Tomasi, Edward C. Stibili. New York: Center for Migration Studies, 1992. 2nd ed. 365p.

Some 1,800 items are included in this extensive bibliography of the religious experience in the history of Italian-Americans. Although the emphasis is obviously on Roman Catholicism, works referring to any other religious groups are also considered. The entries are divided into two major sections: primary and secondary materials. The former contains items on repository and archival works and has been substantially enlarged in the present new edition. The latter lists bibliographies, serials, theses and dissertations, parish histories, books and articles. Both American and Italian sources are surveyed.

1076 **Mafia: a select annotated bibliography.**
Compiled by Lloyd Trott, with contributions by Dwight C. Smith, Jr. Cambridge, England: University of Cambridge, The Institute of Criminology, 1977. 141p.

This repertory includes most books and articles on the mafia, which had appeared by 1974. They are mainly in English, but there are also references to several Italian works, as well as a few in French and German. Annotations emphasize the hypotheses on the nature of the phenomenon, and the entries are consequently arranged in appropriate sections. The most important are: section B, which contains works stressing the mafia's controlling power over organized crime in the United States; section C, on sources focusing upon the link between Italian immigrants and the mafia in the United States; section D, with material which views the mafia mainly as a United States criminal formation; and section E, on entries concerning the mafia as a basically Sicilian reality.

Indexes

There follow three indexes: authors; titles; and subjects. Title entries are italicized and refer either to the main titles, or to other works cited in the annotations. The numbers refer to bibliographical entries and not to pages.

Index of Authors

369

Wright, V. 653
Wynn, M. 700

Y

Yans-McLaughlin, V. 378
Young, H. B. 379
Young, M. 506

Z

Zamagni, V. 273, 289
Zambon, P. 1045
Zampolli, A. 422
Zangheri, P. 125
Zanichelli 453
Zariski, R. 583-84
Zevi, A. 750

Zevi, B. 901
Zevi, T. 346
Zingarelli, N. 441
Zolli, P. 425
Zucchi, J. E. 391, 558
Zuccotti, S. 355
Zuckerman, A. S. 609

Index of Titles

C

383

L

Labor divided: austerity and working-class politics in contemporary Italy 754

Labour relations and economic performance 753

Land and economy in Baroque Italy: Valpolicella, 1630-1797 285

Land and family in Pisticci 477

Land and power in late medieval Ferrara: the rule of the Este, 1350-1450 310

Land of the Etruscans from prehistory to the Middle Ages 153

Landscape and society: prehistoric central Italy 134

Languages of Italy 404

Last days of Mussolini 266

Last Italian: portrait of a people 18

Law and practices relating to pollution control in Italy 775

Law, family and women: toward a legal anthropology of Renaissance Italy 167

La Lena 935

Lenci dolls in full colours: toys for the rich and famous, 1920-1940 913

Leonardo da Vinci: the marvellous works of nature and man 928

Leopardi reader 836

Lessico di frequenza dell' italiano parlato 428

Lessico di frequenza della lingua italiana contemporanea 422

Let's go Italy: 1995 63

Letteratura italiana: storia e geografia 803

Liberazione della donna; feminism in Italy 526

Liberty and order: the theory and practice of Italian public security policy, 1848 to the crisis of the 1890s 178

Libri e Riviste d'Italia 1067

Life and politics in a Venetian community 479

Life in Italy at the time of the Medici 161

Lime, lemon & sarsaparilla: the Italian community in south Wales, 1881-1945 383

Linee di una storia della critica al Decameron 814

Lingua e dialetti italiani: contributo alla bibliografia della lingua e dei dialetti italiani per gli anni 1967-1971 1044

Linguistic history of Italian 408

Lion by the tail: the story of the Italian-Ethiopian war 300

Little girls: social conditioning and its effects on the stereotyped role of women during infancy 522

Live and work in Italy 21

Living in Italy: the essential guide for property purchasers and residents 16

Lombardy: the Italian lakes 46

Lonely mirror: Italian perspectives on feminist theory 535

Long live the strong: a history of rural society in the Apennine mountains 488

Ludovico Ariosto: an annotated bibliography of criticism 1956-1980 851

Luigi Pirandello: an approach to his theatre 941

M

Macmillan dictionary of Italian literature 805

Made in Italy: small-scale industrialization and its consequences 724

Madonnas that maim: popular Catholicism in Italy since the fifteenth century 462

Madrigali 1050

Mafia and clientelism: roads to Rome in post-war Calabria 582

Mafia and mafiosi: the structure of power 503

Mafia and politics 505

Mafia business: the mafia and the spirit of capitalism 496

Mafia encyclopedia 507

Mafia: the long reach of the international Sicilian mafia 508

Mafia of a Sicilian village, 1860-1960 497

Mafia wars: the confessions of Tommaso Buscetta 506

Mafia, peasants and great estates: society in traditional Calabria 495

Mafia: a select annotated bibliography 1076

Magic harvest: food, folklore and society 293

La maiolica italiana dalle origini alla fine del Cinquecento 905

Major languages of Western Europe 394

Making democracy work: civic traditions in modern Italy 658

Making of Italy: 1796-1866 182

Malafemmina: la donna nel cinema italiano 861

Mammals of Britain and Europe 117

Il Manifesto 1016

Manuale critico-bibliografico per lo studio della letteratura italiana 1073

Manuale di numismatica: contiene i valori e le rarità di tutte le monete decimali italiane dal 1800 ad oggi 906

Masterpieces of Italian violin making, 1620-1850 914

Masters of Italian opera: Rossini, Donizetti, Bellini, Verdi, Puccini 954

Materialmente: scultori degli anni ottanta 915

Mattei: oil and power politics 333

Il Mattino 1015

Mazzini 339

McGraw-Hill, dizionario enciclopedico scientifico e tecnico inglese / italiano, italiano / inglese 453

Le medaglie di Maria Luigia Duchessa di Parma 911

Medieval Italian commune: Siena under the Nine, 1287-1355 308

Mediterranean family structures 512

Mediterranean wild flowers 105

Memoirs of a fortunate Jew: an Italian story 350

Memphis: research, experiences, results, failures and successes of new design 898

Men of honour: the truth about the mafia 500

Men of respect: a social history of the Sicilian mafia 498

Merchants, monopolists and contractors: a study of economic activity and society in Bourbon Naples, 1815-1860 281

Merton tradition and kinematics in late sixteenth and early seventeenth century Italy 297

Il Messaggero 1004

Michelangelo architect 792

Michelin Italy 85

Midday in Italian literature: variations on an archetypal theme 850

Migrants or mates: Italian life in Australia 386

Militants and migrants: rural Sicilians become American workers 371

Le minoranze linguistiche: stato attuale e proposte di tutela 356

Mitchell Beazley pocket guide to Italian wines 871

Modern Italian history: an annotated bibliography 1052

Modern Italian language and literature: a bibliography of homage studies 1056

Modern Italian social theory: ideology and politics from Pareto to the present 616

Modern Italy, 1871-1982 196

Modern Italy: images and history of a national identity 195

Modern Italy: representation and reform 574

Modern Italy: a topical history since 1861 208

La moneta a Milano nel Quattrocento: monetazione argentea e svalutazione secolare 909

Monetary approach to external adjustment: a case-study of Italy 721

Monetary policy, fiscal policy and economic activity: the Italian experience 691

Moneychangers 631

Monte Carmelo: an Italian-American community in the Bronx 374

Montevarese: a study of peasant society and culture in southern Italy 473

Monteverdi 945

Moral basis of a backward society 471

Moro affair and the mystery of Majorana 640

Moro morality play: terrorism as social drama 641

Moscow and the Italian Communist Party: from Togliatti to Berlinguer 589

Mountain giants 937

Mr Palomar 833

Il museo internazionale delle ceramiche a Faenza 912

Mushrooms and other fungi of Great Britain and Europe 119

Music and culture in Italy from the Middle Ages to the Baroque 966

Music and patronage in sixteenth-century Mantua 953

Music in fascist Italy 971

Music in Renaissance Ferrara 1400-1505: the creation of a musical centre in the fifteenth century 960

391

Index of Subjects

Catholicism *contd.*
power 482
See also Christianity;
Church-State
relations; Politics
(Catholicism);
Religion
Cattaneo, Carlo 175
Cavani, Liliana 859, 870
Cavour 169, 177, 180,
183, 186-87, 337
Cefalù 155
Celts
language 404
See also History
(Celts)
Censorship 998
Central Italy 6, 37-38, 61,
63, 71, 89
See also History
(central Italy)
Ceramics *see* Pottery
CGIL 558, 754, 759, 763
Character 1-2, 10, 14,
17-20, 23, 26, 28, 97
regional 44
Charts 50
Chemicals 728, 765
explosion 777
state company 333
Chemists *see* Pharmacies
Chianti 74
history 312
Chiarini, Marco 78
Childhood 26
Children 385
Chioggia 315
Chiusi 153
Christian Democrats *see*
Politics (Christian
democracy)
Christians for Socialism
550
Christianity 139, 150, 154
See also Catholicism;
Religion
Church 10, 23, 78, 83, 96,
161, 166, 413, 461
plans 67, 73, 77-78
style 99, 796, 798, 927
See also Catholicism;
Church-State
relations; Religion

Church-State relations
213, 216, 218, 317,
565-66, 608, 624-27,
672
See also Catholicism
(political role)
Ciampi, Carlo Azeglio 560
Cicadas 109
Cinema 61, 65, 85, 200,
238, 543, 859-70
commedia all'italiana
859
fascism 864, 867
history 862
neo-realism 859, 865,
868
women 520, 536
See also names of
individual directors,
i.e. Fellini
Cines studio 867
CISL 754, 759, 763
Cities 26
guides 62, 68, 80
history 307-10, 313-30
Romans 150
See also History
(city-states); travel
(guides); urbanization
City-states *see* History
(city-states)
Civil Code 649-50
Civil Service 196, 656
Class structure 162, 172,
188, 257, 493-94,
734-35
cinema 860
Class struggle 238, 251
Classicism *see* History
(classicism)
Claudius 145
Clergy 158
Clientelism 509, 562, 571,
582, 609, 659
Climate 40
See also Rain
Clothes 704, 728
See also Fashion
Coast 24, 33
architecture 793
siltation 39
See also Riviera
Codussi, Mauro 798

Coins 906, 908-09
Cold War 273, 594, 621,
668, 673
Collison-Morley, L. 100
Colombo, Joe 895
Colonialism 198, 220-21,
224, 243, 247, 258,
300-05
See also History
(Greeks); Libya;
Turkey
Colonna family 4
Colosseum 32, 84
Comédie Italienne 942
Comedy 864
See also Commedia
dell'arte
Comencini, Luigi 868
Commedia all'italiana *see*
Cinema (commedia
all'italiana)
Commedia dell'arte *see*
Literature (commedia
dell'arte)
Commerce 13, 21, 26-27,
553, 564, 682, 688,
694, 704, 719, 746-50
dictionaries 456-57, 460
law 645-46, 648-50
mafia 498
See also Economy;
Industry; Trade
Common Market 680, 693,
715, 734
See also European
Community
Communes *see* History
(communes)
Communications 1, 16,
195, 200, 683
Communist Party 132,
200, 210, 273, 539,
549, 552-57
foreign policy 605
relations with church
550, 566
relations with unions
754
See also Democratic
Party of the Left;
Politics (communism)
Como (town) 279
Como, Lake 45-46, 88

Migration 188, 481
  birds 110
  labour 473
  See also Economy
    (return migration);
    Emigration;
    Immigration
Milan 4, 45-46, 513
  architecture 799, 801
  coins 909
  immigration 358
  Jews 352
  literature 17
  photographs 32
  women 534
  See also History
    (Milan)
Military 541, 660-65,
  673
  See also Army; History
    (military); Mussolini
    (military concerns);
    Soldiers (Roman)
Military service 553
Milton, John 95
Mining 729
Minority groups *see*
  Population
    (minorities)
Modena 951
Modena, Rabbi Leon 348
Moderatism *see* Politics
  (moderatism)
Molise 63, 66, 76, 92
  dialect 392
  emigration 478
Monarchy 204
  coup of 1943 266
  See also Kings
Money *see* Currency
Monk Seal 124
Monreale 80
Montale, Eugenio 832,
  835
Montecassino 155
Montecchio 20
Monteverdi, Claudio 945,
  952, 959, 969
Monuments 32, 34, 67, 75,
  77, 90, 97
  See also Architecture
Moors 99
Morality 2, 100, 160

Moravia, Alberto 834
Moretti, Nanni 870
Morgan, Lady 100
Mori, Cesare 237
Moro, Aldo 602, 634-37,
  640-41, 643
Morphology 394, 396-97,
  405-06, 412
Mortality 343
Mosaics 137, 140
Mosca, Gaetano 205,
  616
Moscato, Judith 348
Motherhood 520, 531
Moths 108
Motorcycles 722, 988,
  990
Mountains 24, 33, 47, 81,
  86
  fauna 107, 124
  flora 113-15
  See also names of
    individual
    mountains,e.g.
    Dolomites
Movimento Sociale
  Italiano 610, 612
Muflone (goat) 107
Mugello 81
Multinationals 729
Murano 315
Museums 75, 78, 83, 731,
  912
Mushrooms 119, 122
Music 65, 98, 161, 166,
  227
  classical 803, 944-79
  fascism 971
  popular 980
Musical instruments 914
Muslims 155
Mussolini, Benito 2, 197,
  201, 206, 213,
  224-57, 335, 338,
  347, 619
  domestic policy 224
  fall 265-66
  foreign policy 224-25,
  247
  military concerns
    225-26, 239, 256,
    269, 300
  subversion 250

  See also Cinema
    (fascism); History
    (Fascism); History
    (foreign relations);
    History (Second
    World War)
Mythology 151

N

Nabobs 145
Naples 22, 86-87, 93, 100,
  472
  architecture 799
  cinema 860
  literature 17-18
  politics 542
  society 472, 481, 542
  See also History
    (Naples)
Napoleon *see* Bonaparte,
  Napoleon
National identity 127, 185,
  195, 391
Nationalism 176, 186,
  221, 233, 241, 251,
  254, 362
  See also History
    (Risorgimento);
    History (unification)
NATO 554-55, 668, 673
Natural science 25
Navigation 50
Navy 554, 663
Nazism 226, 245, 257,
  269, 283, 611
  See also Germany
'Ndrangheta 65, 502,
  582
Negri, Toni 634
Nelson, Horatio 99
Nenni, Pietro 594
Neoclassism 52
Neo-fascism 555, 610-13
Neo-realism *see* Cinema
  (neo-realism)
Nero 145
Nesting 110, 117
New Orleans lynchings
  377
New Yorker, The 17

Population *contd.*
  See also Emigration;
    History (population);
    Immigration;
    Minority groups
Populism 238
Portoghesi, Paolo 897
Portoscuso 485
Ports 147
Portugal 549, 700
Post-Impressionism 926
Post-war *see* History
  (post-war)
Potenza 10
Potere Operaio 620, 623,
  634
Pottery 133-34, 153, 905,
  907, 910, 912
Poverty 168, 172, 472,
  481, 571
Prato 74
Prehistory 128, 130,
  133-34, 141, 145,
  149, 153
  See also Archaeology
Presidents 126, 644
Press *see* Journalism;
  Media
Prima Linea 595, 620, 632
Prime ministers 126, 203
Printing 997-1003
Prisoners of war 269, 390
Private protection 501
Privatization 558, 689
Propaganda 244, 255-56
Propaganda Due 620, 628,
  630-31, 643
Property 645, 648
Property ownership 15-16,
  21, 92, 477, 510
Prostitution 11, 296
  See also Courtesans
Protest *see* Political
  movements
Proverbs 437
PSI *see* Politics
  (socialism)
Psychiatry *see* Health
  (mental)
Public enterprise 709, 713,
  723
Public life 140
Publishing 200

history 997-1003
Puccini, Giacomo 949,
  954, 977
Puglia *see* Apulia
Punctuation 395

R

Racism 26
Radicalism *see* Politics
  (radicalism)
Radio 993
Railways 731
  construction 282
Rain 22
Rame, Franca 940
Rape 537
Ravenna 726, 799
Recipes *see* Cookery
Reconstruction 195
Red Brigades 595, 620,
  622, 632, 634-43
Red week 217
Referendums 552-58, 560
Reggio Emilia 534
Regionalism 6-7, 19, 23,
  26, 37-38, 61-62, 564,
  576, 728
  cooking 872-73, 875,
    879-81, 884-85,
    888-92
  development 13
  economy 694-707
  family 510
  literature 803
  music 944
  planning 708-16
  politics 38, 576, 578,
    584, 657, 705
  religion 462
  See also Government
    (local); History
    (regionalism);
    Language (dialects);
    North-South divide
Relations 26
Religion 7, 11, 25-26, 71,
  154, 157, 160, 208,
  461-70, 624
  change 468
  cinema 860
  immigrants 372, 387

politics 543, 584, 624-27
  practices 476, 482, 486
  See also Catholicism;
    Christianity; Church;
    Women
Renaissance 930, 933
  gardens 52
  Florence 78
  interiors 903
  music 952, 955, 959-60,
    968
  See also Art; History
    (Renaissance);
    Literature
Rental (property) 21
Reptiles 104, 106
Republic 126-27, 198,
  276-77, 541, 644
Republican Constitution 9,
  197, 277, 549,
  624-25, 644, 646
Research institutes 789,
  1041
Resistance (Italian)
  267-69, 271-72, 277,
  540, 594, 604
  See also History
    (anti-fascism)
Restaurants 24, 62, 73, 78,
  80, 83, 682, 881, 886
Restoration *see*
  Conservation
  (buildings)
Return migration *see*
  Economy (return
  migration)
Revolution 23
Rhaeto-Romance 397
  See also Ladins
Rhineland 258
Rialto 98
Rimini 4
Riots 178
Risorgimento *see* History
  (Risorgimento)
Ritual 87
  mafia 501
Riva (degli Schiavoni) 98
Rivers 40
Riviera 76
  See also Coast
Roads 76
  See also Romans
    (roads)
Rocco, Alfredo 241

408

Map of Italy

This map shows the more important towns and other features.

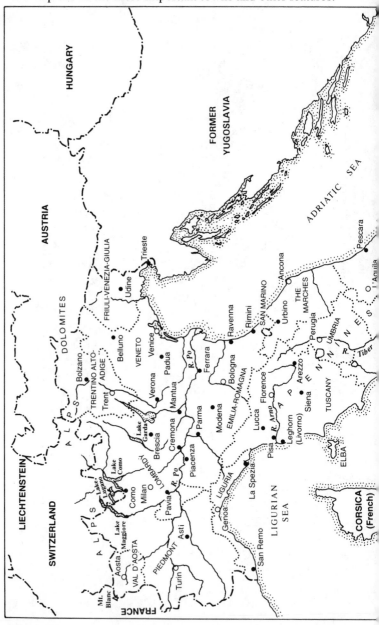

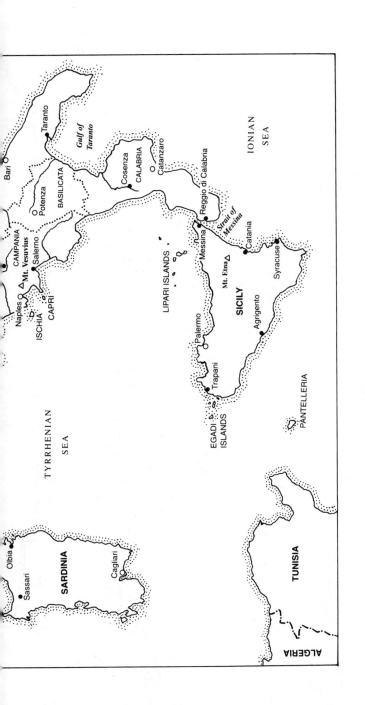

ALSO FROM CLIO PRESS

INTERNATIONAL ORGANIZATIONS SERIES

Each volume in the International Organizations Series is either devoted to one specific organization, or to a number of different organizations operating in a particular region, or engaged in a specific field of activity. The scope of the series is wide-ranging and includes intergovernmental organizations, international non-governmental organizations, and national bodies dealing with international issues. The series is aimed mainly at the English-speaker and each volume provides a selective, annotated, critical bibliography of the organization, or organizations, concerned. The bibliographies cover books, articles, pamphlets, directories, databases and theses and, wherever possible, attention is focused on material about the organizations rather than on the organizations' own publications. Notwithstanding this, the most important official publications, and guides to those publications, will be included. The views expressed in individual volumes, however, are not necessarily those of the publishers.

VOLUMES IN THE SERIES

1 *European Communities*, John Paxton
2 *Arab Regional Organizations*, Frank A. Clements
3 *Comecon: The Rise and Fall of an International Socialist Organization*, Jenny Brine
4 *International Monetary Fund*, Anne C. M. Salda
5 *The Commonwealth*, Patricia M. Larby and Harry Hannam

6 *The French Secret Services*, Martyn Cornick and Peter Morris
7 *Organization of African Unity*, Gordon Harris
8 *North Atlantic Treaty Organization*, Phil Williams
9 *World Bank*, Anne C. M. Salda
10 *United Nations System*, Joseph P. Baratta

TITLES IN PREPARATION

British Secret Services, Philip H. J. Davies
Israeli Secret Services, Frank A. Clements

Organization of American States, David Sheinin